D1287325

A Revolution in Commerce

AMALIA D. KESSLER

A Revolution in Commerce

THE PARISIAN MERCHANT COURT AND THE RISE OF COMMERCIAL SOCIETY IN EIGHTEENTH-CENTURY FRANCE

Yale University Press
New Haven &
London

Published with assistance from the Mary Cady Tew Memorial Fund.

Set in Sabon type by Keystone Typesetting, Inc.
Printed in the United States of America by Sheridan Books, Ann Arbor, Michigan.

Library of Congress Cataloging-in-Publication Data
Kessler, Amalia D.
A revolution in commerce : the Parisian merchant court and the rise of commercial society in eighteenth-century France / Amalia D. Kessler.
p. cm.
Includes bibliographical references and index.
ISBN 978-0-300-11397-6 (cloth : alk. paper)
1. Paris (France). Juge et consuls des marchands — History. 2. Commercial courts — France — Paris — History. 3. Paris (France) — History — 1789–1799.
I. Title.
KJV2221.P38K47 2007
346.44070269 — dc22

2007013814

A catalogue record for this book is available from the British Library.

The paper in this book meets the guidelines for permanence and durability of the Committee on Production Guidelines for Book Longevity of the Council on Library Resources.

10 9 8 7 6 5 4 3 2 1

For my parents

Le Commerce est sans contredit le plus solide fondement de la Société civile, et le lien nécessaire pour unir entr'eux tous les hommes, de quelques pays, et de quelques conditions qu'ils soient; par son moyen le monde entier semble ne former qu'une seule Ville, ou plutôt qu'une seule famille.

[Commerce is without question the most solid foundation of civil society, and the tie necessary to unite amongst themselves all men, from whatever country and whatever conditions they might hail; by means of it, the entire world seems to form but a single town, or rather a single family.]

—Jean-Baptiste-Thomas Bléville, *Le banquier et négociant universel; ou, Traité général des changes étrangers et des arbitrages, ou viremens de place en place*

Contents

Acknowledgments

I have accrued a great many debts in the process of researching and writing this book. My heartfelt gratitude goes to Keith Baker and James Whitman, who generously provided me with invaluable criticism, challenging questions, and moral support throughout the various stages of the manuscript's preparation. As teachers and scholars, they set a model of rigor and creativity that has long inspired me and continues to do so. I also owe particular thanks to Thomas Green, for his selfless expenditure of time and energy in advising me on the manuscript at a crucial stage in its development. And I am deeply indebted to Gail Bossenga and Clare Haru Crowston for their very helpful readings of my work.

Along the way, many others offered comments, questions, or support from which I benefited greatly. With apologies for any inadvertent omissions, I am especially grateful to Richard Craswell, Charles Donahue, Lawrence Friedman, Robert Gordon, Paul Robinson, and John Witt. I would also like to acknowledge Gregory Alexander, Stuart Banner, Raymond Birn, Henry Clark, Kevin Clermont, Vivian Curran, Ariela Dubler, Avner Greif, Sarah Hanley, Tamar Herzog, Martha Howell, Daniel Hulsebosch, Thomas Kaiser, Emmanuel Lazega, Bernadette Meyler, Susan Rose-Ackerman, Jean-Laurent Rosenthal, Richard Ross, Emma Rothschild, Mary Salzman, John Simon, David Kammerling Smith, Christopher Tomlins, Dalia Tsuk, John Wallis, and Gavin

Wright. Many thanks as well to Michael O'Malley, my editor at the Yale University Press, to Marie Blanchard for her excellent copyediting, and to the participants of conferences and workshops at which I presented portions of the text. Included among these were the Society for French Historical Studies, the American Society for Legal History, the Gimon Conference on French Political Economy, the Law and Society Association, the Research Committee on the Sociology of Law, the Columbia Legal History Series, the Cornell Law and Humanities Colloquium, the NYU Legal History Colloquium, the UCLA Legal History Workshop, the Stanford Social Science History Workshop, and the Stanford Law School Faculty Workshop.

I greatly appreciate the research assistance provided by Kyle Lakin and Mary Campbell and the support that I received from the staff of Stanford's Green Library (including especially John Keith, John Mustain, and Sarah Sussman) and the Robert Crown Law Library (including especially Paul Lomio, Sonia Moss, Richard Porter, and George Wilson). Tremendous thanks as well are due to my colleagues at Stanford Law School for providing an ideally supportive and engaging environment in which to begin an academic career and to complete this manuscript. I am also grateful to the publishers of *Law and History Review*, the *Journal of Legal Studies*, and *A Vast and Useful Art* for permitting me to use portions of material published previously in a different form. And I would like to acknowledge the research support that I received from Yale Law School's John M. Olin Center for Law, Economics, and Public Policy.

My final and deepest thanks go to my immediate family. My husband, Adam Talcott, has given me more love and support than I could ever have hoped for from a life partner. For this, as well as for his sharp insight, good humor, and endless enthusiasm about both me and my work, I am deeply grateful. This book is dedicated to my parents, Laure Aurelian and Irving I. Kessler, who set an example of scholarly commitment and deep humanity that I continue to find unparalleled. Their unswerving love and devotion have sustained me in more ways than I could begin to enumerate.

Introduction

In the spring and summer of 1790, the Constituent Assembly of revolutionary France set about the massive task of restructuring the judiciary—that set of institutions that for many revolutionaries most fully embodied the evils of the Old Regime. The end results of its endeavors are well known. After abolishing the organized bar, the Assembly made permanent the ouster of the dreaded *parlements* and the lower royal courts (including *bailliages, sénéchaussées,* and *présidiaux*). In their place, it created an entirely new set of courts to be headed by salaried bureaucrats, rather than venal officeholders, whose powers were to be strictly confined to the judicial rather than legislative sphere. At the same time, the Assembly instituted a panoply of more informal and democratic dispute-resolution mechanisms, including criminal juries and justices of the peace. As the Revolution became progressively more radical, the Assembly sought to wrest dispute resolution from professionally trained judges and lawyers. Accordingly, it created arbitral institutions, such as family courts staffed by the litigants' relatives and friends, and later declared (though never implemented) its intent to replace the entire court system with annually elected "public arbiters" (*arbitres publics*). With the passing of the Terror, revolutionary distaste for legal formality and professionalism receded, as did the more radical attempts to remake the judicial system. Lawyers returned and arbitration largely disappeared, but the new bureaucratic court system instituted by the revolutionaries in 1790 remained.[1]

While this broad-brushed narrative of the revolutionaries' efforts to remake the judicial system is familiar, there is at least one aspect of the story that has received short shrift.[2] On May 27, 1790, just a few months before the National Assembly passed the judiciary act that undertook the fundamental restructuring of the court system, its deputies agreed after very little debate that there was one judicial institution of the Old Regime that could and should remain essentially unchanged: the *juridictions consulaires,* or merchant courts. As one deputy explained, "We . . . have been for a long time unaware of the advantages [of commerce]; we have remained behind other peoples because of the brutal impact [*choc*] of royal authority and feudal power."[3] Accordingly, while the monarchy had the wisdom to establish merchant courts in the late sixteenth century, the ordinary courts of the Old Regime, including both the lower royal courts and the *parlements,* were "jealous of their jurisdiction, [and] tried to strip them of it."[4] With the Revolution, however, France had finally arrived "at a moment in which commerce [was] delivered from the shackles and prejudices that enchained it, . . . in which it will be a resource for all citizens."[5] At this moment of enlightenment, there was no question but that "the merchant courts . . . [be] preserved."[6] Thus, renamed and very modestly reconfigured, the Old Regime merchant courts survived the Revolution's overhaul of the judiciary—and then, remarkably, survived the Revolution as well. And while their existence has been challenged in recent years,[7] these extraordinarily long-lived institutions continue to operate in the twenty-first century.

This book is a history of the merchant courts of eighteenth-century France—and, in particular, of the *juridiction consulaire de Paris,* or Parisian Merchant Court, which was designated by the monarchy and its sister courts as the leading such institution. As such, it tackles two distinct but related tasks, each quite difficult. First, it undertakes the challenging technical business of reconstructing the actual, daily workings of this far-away court in a far-away society. As we shall see, this is a task at which legal historians have failed, to date. Yet there is far more to legal history than mere technical reconstruction. The law—even a corner of the law as seemingly limited as commercial law—belongs to a broader culture and society; and the legal historian must relate the technical law to a wealth of other aspects of history. Accordingly this is a book not just about commercial law but about commercial law in the context of eighteenth-century French neighborhoods, family relations, and religion. It is a book not only about early-modern partnerships but about early-modern partnerships as seen through the theological eyes of anxious moralists like the Jansenists. It is a book not only about commercial arbitration but about commercial arbitration in a world supervised by priests who pried into every corner of private life. It is a book, in short, about law and society.

In thus situating the Parisian Merchant Court within a broader social context, the book focuses on how the elite merchants responsible for the court's operation sought to navigate the complex changes in commercial practice and relations, and in royal administration, that accompanied the rise of commercial society. These changes engendered a set of problems—legal, social, political, and moral—that were, this book argues, profoundly difficult. And in their efforts to address these problems, merchants helped to transform legal doctrine, as well as broader social and political institutions, in ways that contributed to what I am calling a revolution in commerce.

By "revolution" I mean to refer to a complex set of interrelated phenomena, including fundamental transformations in commercial practice and conceptions of commerce, which ultimately fed into the vastly complex social and political revolution of 1789. As concerns commercial practice, the eighteenth century witnessed a remarkable expansion in the use of commercial paper, fueled by the emergence of the principle of negotiability and associated practices, which served greatly to increase holders' ability to enforce payment. The widespread use of negotiable paper dramatically increased access to short-term credit, which in turn played a key role in facilitating the significant growth in trade (both foreign and domestic) that occurred over the course of the century. Such paper, moreover, fueled a number of new and controversial market practices, ranging from the development of a volatile exchange, or *bourse,* to the emergence of a consumer-oriented economy (characterized by the mass advertising of, and increased access to, many goods, including those once reserved for a noble elite).

The merchants studied in this book, however, contributed not only to these changes in commercial practice but also to a fundamental reconceptualization of commerce, thus helping to provoke a profound reconfiguration of social relations, state regulation, and even political governance. Over the course of the eighteenth century, a traditional conception of commerce as a public hazard that had to be carefully regulated increasingly (though never entirely) gave way to a modern conception of commerce as free private exchange naturally redounding to the social good. While the merchants studied in this book were not themselves advocates of laissez-faire—and were, in fact, committed defenders (and leaders) of the guild system—they played a very important part in enabling and promoting this reconceptualization of commerce. And by deploying the new conception of commerce as part of the merchant courts' ongoing struggles with other corporate entities for status and jurisdiction, merchants achieved important, real-world, institutional changes—including notably, partially transforming the basis of merchant court jurisdiction from the merchant status of the litigants to the commercial nature of the litigation.

The reconceptualization of commerce to which merchants so greatly contributed thus served to undermine the assumptions underlying the corporatist order, and to help make possible the Revolution of 1789—including, in particular, the revolutionaries' decision to dismantle the corporatist system, and eventually the guilds. But precisely because the merchant courts had long sought to legitimate themselves by means of a modern (functionalist, rather than corporatist) conception of commerce, they, alone among judicial institutions of the Old Regime, managed to survive the revolutionary upheaval.

Moreover, as merchants came to view commerce as a necessary, natural, and socially beneficent force, so too they came to believe that those responsible for undertaking it—and thus for producing the wealth that sustains the social order—are entitled to a voice in governance. By organizing joint campaigns to petition the monarchy on behalf of common interests, eighteenth-century merchants increasingly institutionalized this claim to political participation—ultimately demanding representation in the Estates General in the fall of 1788. And while they were denied representation as a (national) *corps* of commerce, their insistence that those who engage in economically productive activity are entitled to representation was thereafter embraced by the Third Estate in its decision to declare itself the National Assembly.

To examine the revolution in commerce that occurred during the eighteenth century is to address a topic that has been of increasing interest to historians over the last several decades—namely, the rise of commercial society in Old Regime France. Such interest has been spurred by at least two historiographic developments. First, the revisionist turn in the 1970s away from social and economic determinism and toward the study of political culture[8] has had the somewhat ironic effect of refocusing scholarly attention on commercial questions. Having rejected the once reigning Marxist paradigm, revisionists closely examined contemporary discourse, in an effort to understand the ways in which revolutionary transformation became conceptually possible. And much of this discourse, they increasingly realized, addressed commercial and economic questions. Indeed, by the second half of the eighteenth century, concerns about such matters as the socially pernicious effects of luxury, the permissible bounds of royal taxation, the merits and demerits of selling privileges, and the virtues and vices of a free market pervaded contemporary plays, newspapers, political pamphlets, and books. Contemporaries, in short, understood themselves to be living in a new commercial age in which liquid capital was fast becoming as important as land in establishing the foundations of wealth and power, and in which even the mightiest of monarchs had to concern themselves with base commercial matters. For historians interested in exploring transformations in discourse, and the ways in which these both mirrored and shaped changing social norms, all this talk about commerce — particularly in the second half of the eighteenth century — suggested that something fundamentally important was afoot.[9]

The second historiographic development contributing to a new interest in the rise of commercial society is the paradigm shift in French economic history that began around the late 1970s. At about the same time that historians of the French Revolution turned toward political culture, economic historians rejected the once established view that the eighteenth-century French economy was characterized by stagnation. Disputing the longstanding view that eighteenth-century France lagged significantly behind contemporary England in almost all markers of commercial and industrial development, a new generation of economic historians suggested that the two countries diverged far less than had been assumed.[10] French agricultural production expanded greatly over the course of the century, sparing the population from the once pervasive horrors of widespread famine. Accordingly, the population grew from about 21.5 million people in 1700 to 26 million in 1781.[11] At the same time, an increase in the production of raw materials, as well as great improvements in such infrastructure as roads and canals, enabled significant industrial growth.[12] Such growth was also fueled by France's highly profitable exchange with its colonies, and in particular, with the sugar islands of the West Indies.[13] Thus, according to some economic historians, French agricultural and industrial growth actually outpaced that of eighteenth-century England. Moreover, such growth manifested itself in what a number of social and cultural historians have come to identify as a consumer revolution. Studies of consumer practices, particularly in Paris, have suggested that the market for such items as dresses, furniture, umbrellas, and watches expanded significantly over the course of the eighteenth century. Not only were more of these items purchased, but in addition, those purchasing them were from lower down the social scale. Items like the dress and the watch, which had once been staples of the nobility, became increasingly accessible to ordinary, non-noble Parisians.[14]

Recent historiographic work has thus, broadly speaking, traced two distinct developments — changes in discourse concerning commerce, on the one hand, and changes in commercial practice, on the other. In so doing, this work has highlighted the omnipresent and ever elusive question of how discourse and practice interrelated. Indeed, the question of how to study the relationship between discourse and practice (not solely as concerns commerce, but more generally) has been of great interest to a recent generation of historians struggling with the problem of what methodological paradigm should follow the revisionist (cultural) turn. Among the studies that have proven the most fruitful in addressing the relationship between discourse and practice are those that have focused on particular (broadly speaking, governmental) institutions—including, to name but a few, Gail Bossenga's analysis of corporate entities in Lille (such as the *Bureaux des Finances*), and Michael Kwass's exploration of royal efforts to transform key fiscal institutions.[15] By examining how and why particular institutions acted as they did, these and other historians have been able to trace—within particular institutional contexts—the complex dynamic linking together new ways of thinking and talking about society with actual, on-the-ground shifts in practice. Along similar lines, a study of the Parisian Merchant Court is well suited to shed light on the interrelationship between discourse and practice. Indeed, courts are arguably the ideal institutions through which to study the connection between cultural history or discourse analysis, on the one hand, and political and socioeconomic structures, on the other, since by their very nature they seek to deploy language for the purpose of acting on society.

Courts, moreover, are unique in the extent to which they provide the historian with access to voices from the past that would otherwise not be recorded. Legal documents, in other words, are a particularly rich source for exploring non-elite discourse. This book seeks to deploy documents filed by and with the Parisian Merchant Court (in addition to treatises and other writings by merchants) to examine how merchants themselves—the people whose lives were arguably most affected by changes in commercial discourse and practice—thought about these changes and the role they played in making them possible. This is a topic about which we still know remarkably little. Elite discourse concerning the rise of commercial society—including, though by no means limited to, that of the Physiocrats and their opponents—has been extensively studied. And work has been devoted in recent years to the commerce-related works produced by lesser-known authors engaged broadly with questions of political economy.[16] But the views of merchants themselves have received relatively little attention—in no small part because such ordinary individuals had little occasion to record their views in writing.

Merchant institutions—including, notably, guilds and the merchant courts—serve as an important exception to this generalization, in that they offered merchants many opportunities to commit their views to writing. Making use of this resource, a number of historians, including, among others, Stephen Kaplan, Claire Crowston, and Michael Sonenscher, have produced excellent studies of particular guilds and of the guild system as a whole. Much of this work has been motivated by an effort to rescue guilds from the historiographic oblivion into which they had fallen due to longstanding assumptions that they were archaic, outdated institutions whose elimination was required and indeed inevitable for the forward movement of history. These historians have rightly argued that such a teleological approach to the study of the guilds necessarily obscures our understanding of what functions these institutions actually served in their day and how contemporaries conceived of these. Accordingly, their writings seek to recover the lost history of the guilds as institutions that played an important role not only in the economic life of Old Regime France, but also in municipal politics.[17]

To focus exclusively on the guilds, however, as historians exploring eighteenth-century merchant discourse have largely done, is to ignore a key set of merchant institutions—including especially the merchant courts, but also chambers of commerce and the royal *Bureau du Commerce*—which operated in an institutional context that, while related to that of the guilds, was not perfectly coextensive with it. These other merchant institutions gave rise to important interests, practices, and discourses that were distinct from those associated with the guilds and that merit serious study in their own right. While some work has been done on individual chambers of commerce and on the *Bureau du Commerce,* little attention has been paid to the merchant courts. Moreover, most studies of chambers of commerce have focused on nineteenth-century developments, while those concerning the *Bureau du Commerce* have deployed it primarily as an entry point for exploring practices of royal administration and state-building, rather than merchant discourse.[18]

As concerns the guilds, recent efforts to examine these from the perspective of contemporaries have enriched our understanding of Old Regime society. But they have also tended to displace the question of how corporatism was ultimately undermined—or more precisely, the question of what role merchants and their guilds played in the ultimate demise of the corporatist system. A notable exception is the work of historians, like David Bien and Gail Bossenga, who have described how tensions implicit in the corporatist system—and, in particular, the disjunction between the monarchy's continued promotion of corporatism, on the one hand, and its reforming efforts, on the other—ultimately led it to self-destruct.[19] But by exploring corporatism as an entire system, these historians have situated guild members within a broader array of corporate officeholders, thus eschewing, to some extent, questions of merchant particularity.

It is a central contention of this book that guild merchants, serving as merchant court judges, played an important though unintended role in undermining the corporatist social order, by contributing to a significant reconceptualization of commerce that occurred over the course of the eighteenth century. This reconceptualization is neatly captured by comparing the entries for "commerce" in two versions of the *Dictionnaire de l'Académie française,* one issued in 1694 and the other in 1798. In the 1694 edition, the entry is simply "see merchant [*marchand*]."[20] In contrast, the 1798 edition defines commerce primarily as "traffic, trade of merchandise, of money" and only then notes that "commerce is sometimes taken to mean the corps of traders [*commerçants*] and wholesalers [*négociants*]."[21] In sum, over the course of the eighteenth century, the term "commerce" shifted from designating the function of those persons possessing the status of merchant to designating the function or activity itself.

Why would the guild leaders who headed the Parisian Merchant Court (as well as its sister courts across France) help to redefine commerce in this way? One might expect that, as guild leaders, these individuals would be committed to a traditional conception of commerce as the status function of those who were guild members—a conception that justified their guild monopolies and privileges. But while they were, in fact, deeply committed to this traditional conception, they also came—in their capacity as merchant court judges—to advance a modern conception of commerce as a necessary function of an interdependent social order, and thus implicitly open to all.

Merchants embraced this modern conception of commerce for a variety of reasons, only some of which were economic. Other, more important reasons had to do with their interests in status and privilege—interests that were fully consonant with traditional corporatist concerns. Accordingly, to argue that guild merchants played an important role in undermining the corporatist order is not to suggest, as historians once did, that merchants sought to destroy the guilds because these hindered economic progress and thus merchant self-interest. Recent historians have rightly rejected this argument, demonstrating that many successful Old Regime merchants found ways of deploying the guild system to promote their financial well-being. Thus, these powerful individuals had no interest in seeing the guilds abolished.[22] But if we take seriously recent research showing that the corporatist order was far from defunct and examine what functions guild leaders actually served in Old Regime society, it becomes clear that, as merchant court judges, they helped to undermine both the logic and institutional structure of corporatism—though this goal could not have been further from their minds.

The merchants who served as judges in the Parisian Merchant Court were among the most powerful merchants—indeed, arguably, among the most powerful individuals—of Old Regime France. They were the leading members of Paris's six leading guilds, the *six corps de Paris,* and as such, frequently engaged in extensive international trade and banking activity, which enabled them to accrue a great deal of wealth. In an age when the annual income of such skilled workers as cabinetmakers is estimated to have been on the order of 300 to 1,000 livres annually and that of noblemen anywhere from 40,000 to 100,000 livres,[23] these judges were able to pay from 40,000 to 300,000 livres to purchase their guild offices within the *six corps*.[24] Moreover, in their capacity as merchant court judges, they had tremendous power to shape the development of commercial doctrine and practice in an era of significant commercial transformation and growth. They also played a predominant role in electing merchant deputies to the royal *Bureau du Commerce,* a central administrative agency that significantly influenced French commercial policy. And once they recognized the possibility of petitioning the *Bureau* and its deputies to act on their behalf, these judges succeeded in utilizing the *Bureau* as a tool for galvanizing into common action merchant courts and chambers of commerce throughout France—thus mobilizing the opinion of the country's leading merchants. The judges of the French merchant courts, and in particular the Parisian Merchant Court, were, in short, very important figures in Old Regime society. Accordingly, if we are to understand how it is that France made the transition to commercial modernity, the way in which these particular individuals did so is surely a significant part of the story.

While merchants, and not just elite thinkers and royal reformers, played an important role in reconceptualizing commerce, they did not foresee, much less intend, the radical consequences that would follow from their reconceptualization. Indeed, it is precisely because merchant court judges did not view the modern conception of commerce that they helped to develop as being incompatible with corporatist guild structures that they were willing to embrace it. That merchants, even while adopting a modern conception of commerce, did not seek to undermine the corporatist order suggests the complexity of their interests and motivations. And this, in turn, sheds important light on the longstanding—though remarkably unsubstantiated—narrative of "the law merchant."

The standard narrative of the law merchant, which has been constructed more on the basis of speculation than research, begins around the twelfth century and continues well into the early-modern period. During these many centuries, so the narrative goes, merchants across Europe developed common customs of merchant practice designed to facilitate a supposedly predominant interest in market growth. These customs ran counter to the traditional substantive and procedural law applied in the ordinary, noncommercial courts. Accordingly, merchants eschewed these courts and developed their own merchant-run courts, in which to apply their merchant customs. Perhaps first and foremost among these customs were those allowing for that quintessential emblem of the law merchant: the negotiable bill of exchange.[25]

In recent years, a number of scholars—including James Steven Rogers, J. H. Baker, and Charles Donahue Jr.—have begun challenging the standard narrative of the law merchant.[26] These authors, however, have focused primarily on English developments, rather than on Continental ones. Moreover, precisely because the standard narrative spans so many centuries and borders and embraces so many different (and often only vaguely defined) aspects of commercial practice and legal doctrine, the task of tracing the law merchant as it existed in reality rather than myth is an enormous one. By closely examining the law and procedure applied by the eighteenth-century Parisian Merchant Court, I hope to contribute to this enormous task, and to do so in a way that sheds much-needed light on certain Continental developments.

While my study suggests that some aspects of the standard narrative are accurate, it also confirms many of the suspicions of scholars who have recently challenged it. Most importantly, it reveals that the nature of merchant interests was far more complex than the standard account would imply. Different merchants had different interests. Moreover, some merchant interests were distinct from (and cannot be reduced to) interests in promoting market expansion and other core values often associated with the rise of a liberal economic order. Thus, while merchant court judges contributed to the development of a modern conception of commerce as private exchange, they also sometimes resisted developments (like the rise of negotiability and associated practices) that would tend to facilitate the extension of credit and thus market growth.

In addition to works concerning the pan-European narrative of the law merchant, a number of books have been written specifically on the commercial law of Old Regime France.[27] These, however, tend to present legal doctrine as a set of self-contained rules bearing little, if any, relation to business practice, to broader political, social, and cultural trends, and to the law as applied in actual cases. This conception of the law as a science with its own internal logic enjoyed only a brief following in the United States (around the late nineteenth century). It has, however, long been an aspect of the Continental legal tradition, dating back to the initial efforts in the High Middle Ages to elaborate the hybrid of Roman and canon law utilized within the *ius commune,* or common law of Europe. But while this tendency to conceive of law as a self-contained, logical system is of longstanding origin, it was greatly strengthened in the years after 1789, when codification was embraced as a means of ensuring that judges would simply apply the law enacted by the legislature, rather than create it themselves. Only by conceiving of the law as an internally coherent logical system was it possible to imagine that a code might contain all law within itself, such that the judge's role as mere law-applier was feasible.[28]

Because the law-as-science approach was in no small part a product of the Revolutionary reaction to the Old Regime, it is particularly out of place in any attempt to understand the early-modern French legal system. Early-modern legal scholars continued a long tradition of elaborating the abstract doctrine of the *ius commune*—a tradition that bore fruit in the development of natural-law jurisprudence—but legal practitioners and ordinary observers were well aware that law on the ground often bore little resemblance to this law in the books. Law on the ground was implemented by a near dizzying array of overlapping jurisdictions, whose judges—constantly vying with one another for the right to adjudicate—were widely understood to have the power to make law through (among other methods) deciding particular cases. Moreover, the Parisian Merchant Court, in particular, prided itself on its equitable nature—on the fact that it readily overlooked the letter of the law in order more fairly and humanely to address the factual particulars of the case before it. Thus, while this book's focus on the individual cases that came before the court and the factual narratives underlying them will likely appear odd to many (though by no means all) present-day European legal scholars, it would seem entirely natural to the Old Regime merchants who served as the court's judges and disputants.

The time, moreover, is ripe for a study of the Parisian Merchant Court. The two monographs that have been written concerning the court during the Old Regime are now quite old. While these offer a very thorough and useful account of the internal workings of the court as an institution, they do not describe the law that it helped to develop or situate it in broader social context.[29] There are a few studies of Old Regime merchants—most notably Stephen Kaplan's work on those involved in the grain trade and Thomas Luckett's unpublished dissertation on credit in Old Regime society—that briefly touch on the Parisian Merchant Court.[30] These studies do not, however, examine the court in depth. And while Jacqueline-Lucienne Lafon has written a very insightful article on the arbiters who appeared before the Parisian Merchant Court and the law that they applied, her study is of limited scope, and, moreover, neglects broader questions of social context.[31]

The dates that frame this study are roughly 1673 through 1791. It was in 1673 that Colbert called upon Jacques Savary—a successful merchant, who had begun his career as a member of the haberdashers' guild (one of the *six corps de Paris*)—to draft a commercial ordinance. This ordinance not only codified certain elements of commercial law but also mandated uniformity among the merchant courts that were to apply it. Moreover, in the same year, the monarchy issued an edict seeking dramatically to expand the guild system, by requiring merchants outside of Paris proper, and indeed across the country, to establish themselves in guilds. The year 1673 thus represents a pivotal moment in the monarchy's growing efforts to rationalize and centralize the administration of commerce—efforts which, as described below, came to play an important role in shaping merchants' understandings of commercial society and their relation to it. At the other end of this study lies the year 1791, when the Constituent Assembly renamed—and very minimally restructured—the *juridiction consulaire,* transforming it into the *tribunal de commerce.* Although the *tribunal de commerce* was in most respects a continuation of its Old Regime predecessor, its establishment nonetheless marked the dawning of a new era, in which a conception of *le commerce* as a function of society triumphed over the traditional notion of *le commerce* as a particular subset of people within the corporatist social order.

I draw in this study on several different kinds of primary sources, including both archival materials and published works. The materials from the archives of the Parisian Merchant Court (located at the *Archives de Paris*) include: reports written by arbiters appointed by the judges of the Parisian Merchant Court to help resolve disputes; legal briefs (or *mémoires judiciaires*) filed by the parties; records of the judgments entered by the court; correspondence between the court and other institutions; records and receipts of the court's expenditures; and miscellaneous documents concerning policy matters of interest to the court (such as regulation of the guilds). In addition, I rely on records of the royal *Bureau du Commerce,* filed in the *Archives nationales*—in particular, its correspondence concerning merchant courts across the country, as well as matters of guild regulation. These archival materials are supplemented by a variety of contemporary published works, including statutory law, legal treatises, legal dictionaries, newspapers, plays, and merchant diaries.

While the book spans from 1673 to 1791, the extant archival materials on which it draws—and, in particular, the reports drafted by court-appointed arbiters—cluster primarily in the second half of the eighteenth century. Though a more complete record would, of course, be desirable, it is precisely in this period that many of the key developments associated with the rise of commercial society took place. It was during the latter half of the eighteenth century that, to name but a few examples, the Physiocrats succeeded in making their call for laissez-faire a matter of extensive public debate and government action, that the new theatrical form of the *drame bourgeois* replaced the hero of old with the figure of the virtuous merchant, and that the annuities market brokered by Parisian notaries began to soar.[32] Similarly, it was in this period that many of the transformations in Old Regime commercial culture explored in this book took root and flourished. These include a rise in new types of complex business association, the development of a widespread market in negotiable instruments, and the emergence of a unified, national front among previously distinct merchant courts and chambers of commerce.

As a final matter of introduction, a few words are in order about the structure of the book. Chapter 1 situates the Parisian Merchant Court within the broader institutional landscape of municipal governance and police regulation in Old Regime Paris. As part of its late- seventeenth-century program for rationalizing the administration of commerce, the monarchy developed a set of regulatory institutions, some of which—namely, guilds and police—were premised on a longstanding, religiously informed conception of commerce as a public hazard. Seeking to overcome the disdain of merchants implicit in this conception of commerce, the merchant court embraced a rhetoric of merchant virtue, through which it tried to demonstrate its commitment to promoting fraternal and charitable merchant relations. But for reasons having to do with institutional politics—and, in particular, a set of inter-guild battles for control of the merchant court and jurisdictional conflict with the municipal government—the court came in the second half of the eighteenth century to abandon this traditional rhetoric of merchant virtue. It began, instead, to appeal to a new conception of commerce as the credit-fueled private exchange necessary for society to survive and thrive.

As traced in Chapters 2 through 5, the shift in the rhetoric that the court employed as part of these institutional struggles was paralleled by a shift in the nature of its legal reasoning. Chapter 2 describes the procedures that the court used to resolve litigation, including appointing arbiters from the community, relying on witness testimony, and requiring litigants to take oaths. These procedures both followed from and reinforced the kinds of highly relational (long-term and repeat) contracting that typified much of commercial practice in the Old Regime—a form of contracting that was itself grounded in a deep-rooted network of communal institutions. By means of such devices, the court reinforced its carefully constructed image as a bastion of virtue, devoted to restoring severed ties of brotherly love and thereby making the community whole.

Chapter 3 provides an overview of the law applied by the merchant court and then focuses on the relational contract disputes that, through to the end of the Old Regime, constituted the majority of the cases that came before the court. These included suits regarding sales of goods and services, employment relations, and marriage contracts. In all these disputes, the court's decisions were based far less on the application of fixed legal rules than on its effort to achieve an equitable result in the particular case before it. As equitable determinations necessarily turned on the eye of the beholder, the court's rulings in such cases hinged in part on the identity of the arbiter. Thus, a particular arbiter's approach to achieving equity might vary somewhat depending on whether he was, for example, a parish priest or a guild leader. Significantly, however, and contrary to what the standard narrative of the law merchant would suggest, arbiters of all kinds understood their role in promoting equity to require first and foremost that they facilitate such merchant virtues as charity and brotherly love, rather than ex ante predictability and other conditions normally associated with market development. Thus, for example, arbiters weighed heavily such factors as the relative wealth of the litigants and, when they determined that debtors were too poor to pay and creditors could afford the loss, they willingly rewrote contract terms to forgive debt or granted extended moratoria.

Chapter 4 examines the court's resolution of disputes concerning business associations. The general partnership, it argues, was the prototypical business association, or *société commerciale,* of the Old Regime. Natural-law jurists identified the partnership as a quintessential institution of human sociability, which demonstrated that, contrary to the Hobbesian view, society was natural to humankind. Drawing on this highly influential school of legal thought, contemporary merchants embraced the partnership as epitomizing a distinctive sort of merchant sociability, characterized by the willingness to place community, family, and friendship above short-term self-interest. But over the course of the eighteenth century, the increased use of limited liability and the rise of early *sociétés de capitaux* (akin to the Anglo-American corporation) gave rise to a new view of the *société commerciale* as an abstract juridical person distinct from its individual members. This, in turn, served to undermine the traditional conception of the *société commerciale* as the embodiment of merchant sociability. For a number of reasons, however—including the fact that the institutional structure of *sociétés de capitaux* remained very much in flux in the final years of the Old Regime—the court was never forced before the Revolution to come to grips with the challenges posed by these developments.

As explored in Chapter 5, the court had no choice but to address another set of developments that challenged traditional commercial culture and its own much prized self-conception as a bastion of virtue—namely, the rise of negotiability and associated practices, which led to the emergence of a robust market in short-term commercial paper. Trade in negotiable bills of exchange and notes permitted merchants to circumvent more traditional credit networks grounded in personal, community-based relationships—precisely the relationships that undergirded merchants' belief in their own distinctive virtue. As a result, the rise of negotiable instruments raised fears that merchant virtue would be destroyed by a triple threat of anonymity, bad faith, and usury. While the court ultimately came to embrace negotiability and the practices associated with it, its path to doing so was far less direct—and far more fraught with doubt and resistance—than the standard narrative of the law merchant would suggest. Moreover, the court's eventual embrace of negotiability hinged on its ability to reconceive of its purpose. Negotiability became palatable, in other words, only to the extent that merchants succeeded in reconfiguring their understanding of virtue, and thereby persuading themselves that the court's key function was to facilitate commerce—now conceived as the credit-fueled private exchange necessary to sustain an interdependent social order.

In Chapter 6, the book returns to the question of the Parisian Merchant Court's place within a broader institutional landscape—a landscape now expanded to encompass not only Old Regime Paris but France as a whole. In particular, it examines the court's relationship with merchant courts and chambers of commerce throughout France, as well as with the royal *Bureau du Commerce*. While the monarchy's goal in establishing the *Bureau* was to augment the tax base and thereby empower itself, the ironic effect of its actions was to cause merchant courts and chambers of commerce that had previously viewed themselves as divided by corporate and geographic barriers to unite in defense of interests (in jurisdiction and status) that they came to view as common. On behalf of these interests, which were themselves fully consonant with the corporatist order, merchants appealed to a modern conception of commerce as a necessary social function—the same conception that the Parisian Merchant Court had had occasion to develop through both its own institutional battles and its adjudication of lawsuits concerning negotiable instruments. With the calling of the Estates General, this informal association of merchant institutions demanded representation by relying on a vision of *le commerce* that combined both the corporatist and functionalist conceptions of commerce. But with the abolition of corporatism in 1789, the mixed conception of commerce that Old Regime merchant courts had helped to develop (and to which they adhered) ceased to be tenable. As the revolutionaries nationalized merchant court property and abolished the guilds—results that merchants themselves had never intended—commerce as a legally enshrined marker of status gave way to commerce as a function of society.

I

Situating the Court: Institutional Structure, Jurisdictional Conflict, and the Rise of a New Conception of Commerce

Commerce has long groaned under the weight of an unjust prejudice concerning interest, honor, and even probity.

—*Journal de Commerce*

In 1776, shortly after the issuance of Turgot's ill-fated edict abolishing the guilds, the merchant court of Paris drafted a memorandum observing that its judge and consuls "were not able to learn of this . . . [abolition] with indifference," as they were "themselves members of the principal guilds [*corps*] included in . . . [Turgot's] proscription."[1] The court thereby joined the mounting opposition to the edict and reaffirmed its longstanding support of the guild system. But while the merchant court and its judges, in their capacity as guild leaders, fought to preserve guild privileges well into the Revolution, they also played a central role during the Old Regime in developing a new conception of commerce that would ultimately be deployed to justify abolishing the corporatist foundations of the social order. Pursuant to this new conception, commerce was a form of free, private exchange that naturally redounded to the public good and thus required no guild regulation. Although historians associate the rise of this conception of commerce with the Old Regime's intellectual and political elite—most especially with the Physiocrats and their allies in the reforming monarchy—a study of the Parisian Merchant Court reveals that, remarkably, this conception also emerged among ordinary, guild-based merchants.

To understand how the Parisian Merchant Court, while a staunch supporter of the guilds, nonetheless contributed to developing a theory of commerce that was ultimately used to justify their destruction, it is necessary to begin by exploring the guild system and the traditional conception of commerce on which it was premised. As traditionally understood, commerce was a potentially destructive force that, left to its own devices, would wreak havoc, and therefore had to be carefully regulated and contained. It was toward this end that the monarchy established the guilds, as well as the merchant court, which was viewed largely as an extension of the guild system. For a variety of reasons, however, the merchant court ultimately came to challenge this traditional conception of commerce—a conception to which it owed its very existence. Among these reasons were changes in commercial practice and in royal administration, described later in this book. Ironically, however, the merchant court judges' own guild-based interests—in gaining control of the court and in prevailing in jurisdictional conflict—also played a role. It was in an effort to advance these guild-based interests that the merchant court judges rejected the conception of commerce as a public hazard and argued instead that it was a form of credit-fueled, private exchange that naturally promoted the social good.

Guilds, Police, and the Traditional Conception of Commerce as a Public Hazard

It was a matter of longstanding belief in the Old Regime that commerce was a potentially destructive force that had to be carefully policed if its harmful effects were to be avoided. This traditional conception of commerce stemmed, in no small part, from a Christian worldview in which the pursuit of wealth was associated with sin. The virtuous Christian was someone who loved God and fellow man above all else. Accordingly, commercial pursuits—by focusing on the achievement of base, material ends—were thought to detract from virtue and thus to be harmful both to self and community.[2] Commercial self-interest was held to jeopardize not only spiritual salvation but also material welfare, since wealth-seeking merchants might seek to price gouge, produce shoddy merchandise, and otherwise profit at the expense of the public. As noted in a 1670 publication celebrating the life of a master cobbler praised for exemplifying the antithesis of the typical, self-interested merchant: "There is so little justice and fidelity among merchants and artisans that it appears that interest and the insatiable desire to acquire extinguishes in them all sentiments of religion and smothers all the respect that they owe to the laws that God Himself has imposed on them in the Holy Scriptures."[3]

That commerce was traditionally regarded with suspicion does not, however, mean that it was universally disdained. Seventeenth-century France, in fact, witnessed a notable valorization of commerce, as the burgeoning absolutist monarchy entered into what would prove to be a long and intense competition with its rivals to build a commercial empire. But crucially, as Henry Clark has shown, those who came to valorize commerce were drawn by the ways it served royal interests and not, as were some of their English and Dutch contemporaries, by a newfound respect for "the activities intrinsic to being a merchant."[4] The growing legitimacy of commerce thus derived from the fact that it operated directly under—and on behalf of—royal power, rather than as an autonomous sphere of private activity. Extensive government regulation and control were thought to be essential if rewards were to be reaped from a set of endeavors that continued to be viewed as "radically unstable, uncertain, and fluid."[5]

Such attitudes to commerce were embraced not only by elite mercantilist thinkers, focused on the intersection between statecraft and trade, but also by practicing merchants, who, as argued below, responded to the contempt with which merchants were generally regarded by embracing a rhetoric of merchant virtue. Even while insisting on the virtues of commerce and its practitioners, such merchants claimed that these virtues would not emerge unless commerce was subject to proper regulation. Commerce, in sum, was widely understood to be a public hazard, and as such it was appropriately the subject of public law—both administrative and criminal. The key institutions by means of which the monarchy traditionally sought to subject commerce to such administrative and criminal regulation were the police and the guilds.[6]

The close relationship between police and guilds—and the way that both were deployed as tools for regulating commerce—is evident from the monarchy's efforts to develop the two in tandem. Under the stewardship of Comptroller General Colbert, the monarchy launched a massive campaign to gain centralized control of Parisian commerce. In October 1666, it established the *Conseil de Police,* headed by Colbert himself, to devise a plan for reforming Paris's police[7]—a term that in the lexicon of the Old Regime broadly encompassed all forms of administration necessary to ensure a well-ordered society. The *Conseil* issued a decree on November 5 of the same year granting Paris's main royal trial court, the *Châtelet,* precedence in police matters over all other Parisian jurisdictions.[8] Within the *Châtelet,* however, it was unclear whether the *lieutenant civil* or the *lieutenant criminel* should be responsible for deciding police matters. The problem was that these police disputes—often concerning such commerce-related problems as the charging of scarcity prices for grain—might easily be categorized as either private, civil matters or public, criminal ones.[9] Accordingly, on March 15, 1667, the monarchy created within the *Châtelet* a *lieutenant général de police,* who was to be henceforth responsible for all police matters.[10]

While officially situated beneath the civil and criminal lieutenants, the lieutenant general of police was endowed with significant authority and quickly rose to far greater prominence than his nominal superiors.[11] Indeed, as Alan Williams has argued, the lieutenant general of police functioned in essence as a royal intendant for the city of Paris, exercising enormous powers—both executive and judicial, and often concerning commercial and economic matters.[12] The executive responsibilities of the lieutenant general and his staff included not only protecting against crime, fire, and flood, but also ensuring the provisioning of Paris with basic necessities (most importantly, bread) and enforcing guild regulations regarding price and quality. Likewise, in his capacity as a judicial officer, the lieutenant general adjudicated, among other matters, actions brought by the police for violation of guild ordinances and actions arising between and among guilds and non-guild merchants.[13]

In February 1674, the monarchy attempted to consolidate the power of the *Châtelet*—and, in particular, its newly fortified police power—by suppressing the nineteen seigneurial courts that continued to sit in Paris and its environs.[14] In so doing, the monarchy sought to ensure its primacy over manufacturing and trade [*arts et métiers*], and thus over matters of guild regulation—matters of great interest to its newly created police. Of particular concern to the monarchy was that these seigneurial courts regularly permitted non-guild merchants and artisans within their jurisdictions to practice trades that fell within the monopolies of the royal Parisian guilds. Accordingly, in 1675 and then again in 1678, the monarchy issued edicts that banned all communities of merchants and artisans operating within the jurisdictions of the recently suppressed seigneurial courts.[15] Henceforth, merchants and artisans who practiced in such "refuges of liberty" [*asiles de liberté*] or "privileged places" [*lieux privilégiés*] as the faubourg Saint-Antoine and the enclos du Temple[16] would be required to purchase masterships directly from the crown.

That the monarchy's goal in seeking to eliminate seigneurial courts was, in part, to bolster its own authority in matters of police regulation—particularly concerning the *arts et métiers*—is evident from the language of the 1678 edict itself. As the edict explained, the seigneurial courts—despite the effort to suppress them—continued to shelter a "variety of guilds . . . [since] each of the judges and officers of the *seigneurs* have given themselves the liberty of establishing [these] within the bounds of their jurisdiction."[17] So eager was the monarchy to eliminate all practice of commerce outside the royal guilds that when it soon caved in to pressure and reestablished the seigneurial courts,[18] it was careful to deny them the right to police the *arts et métiers*.[19]

As part of this process of developing the royal police and seeking to weaken the seigneurial courts, the monarchy also tried to ensure that all merchants and artisans would henceforth be organized in royally established guilds, known as *métiers jurés* or *jurandes* — a name derived from the fact that members were required to take an oath [*jurer*] upon joining. Governed by its own particular charter, each guild was a corporate entity, possessing a single, legal personality, such that it could undertake debt and pursue litigation in its own name and thereby bind the membership as a whole. Membership in the guild, in the form of a mastership, was established by the monarchy upon receipt of a substantial fee, and thus, like other royal *corps*, guilds were an important source of income for the crown.[20] In addition, however, the monarchy viewed the guilds as essential for regulating commerce and thereby ensuring that it did not become a public hazard.

Accordingly, in March 1673 the monarchy issued an edict providing that in all French cities or towns where royal guilds were established, merchants and artisans were required to join or form a guild in order to practice their trade.[21] Pursuant to this edict, the lieutenant general of police was responsible for ensuring that all merchant-artisans in Paris and its suburbs were established in guilds — a responsibility that in the rest of France was assigned to royal judges.[22] To facilitate these efforts, the monarchy declared in June 1673 that royal judges and prosecutors from around the country were to provide Colbert with the names of those individuals who practiced commerce without belonging to one of the formally established, royal guilds.[23] Through such means, the monarchy's policy of promoting guilds proved remarkably successful. While there were just 60 guilds in France prior to the March 1673 edict, there were as many as 129 in 1691.[24]

By means of this coordinated program to develop the police and the guilds, the monarchy sought to centralize its control over commerce — thereby ensuring that merchant self-interest would be properly contained. It was the police's responsibility to enforce the many rules and regulations that governed the internal workings of the guilds, required each to operate within the limits of its own monopoly, and prohibited improper competition from those merchant-artisans not associated with a guild. To exercise this enforcement authority effectively, the police determined that it was vital to make surprise visits to workshops and stores. This, in turn, required both manpower and information about potential violations. Given the vast scope of this undertaking, the police necessarily relied on the guilds themselves to provide much-needed aid. In general, the leaders of the guilds were only too happy to assist, since they in turn required police support to enforce those rules that maintained their power within the guilds, as well as their guilds' monopoly privileges.[25]

The symbiotic relationship between the police and the guilds is evident in a series of edicts issued by the monarchy between 1716 and 1734. In an edict of November 1716, the monarchy declared that, despite efforts to the contrary, numerous merchants and artisans continued to practice their trade outside the guild system and under the protection of the seigneurial courts.[26] As a result of this illicit practice of commerce, explained the edict, the *arts et métiers* were escaping police regulation—and, in particular, the surprise visits undertaken by police inspectors in conjunction with guild leaders.[27] To remedy this problem, the edict provided that all who claimed privileges of any kind—including "privileges concerning commerce, manufacturing and the arts"—were obligated to present documents establishing these.[28] The latter would be examined by a special commission consisting of, among others, members of the King's Council, who were to advise the king about which privileges were valid, and more generally, about "the best means for reestablishing or maintaining . . . the observation . . . of the statutes concerning the arts and manufacturing in the city of Paris."[29]

Compliance with the edict of November 1716 was evidently less than perfect, since the same legislation was reissued repeatedly thereafter, culminating in a final edict of March 1734.[30] Yet, however ineffectual they may have been, these edicts clearly reflect the monarchy's understanding that the police and the guilds were to work together to enforce police and guild regulations. Moreover, the response that the edicts elicited from guilds suggests that many merchants shared this understanding. Paris's leading guilds treated the edicts as a royal invitation to demand police support in pursuing those merchant-artisans who continued to practice their trade in violation of guild monopolies (and under the auspices of the seigneurial courts).

Consider, for example, a brief addressed by the *six corps de Paris* to the royal commission appointed to examine privileges. The *six corps* were the six elite guilds that specialized in luxury items and that, as discussed below, controlled the merchant court. They complained to the commission that the failure to enforce the royal edicts meant that "abuses . . . are perpetuated in the *lieux privilégiés*."[31] In particular, they explained, the seigneurial courts continued to permit merchant-artisans within their jurisdictions to violate the monopoly of the *six corps* and to obstruct the surprise visits undertaken by the police and guild leaders to detect such violations. According to the *six corps*, it was imperative that these abuses be corrected, since otherwise the public would suffer:

> Unfortunate experience has taught . . . that . . . an infinite number of individuals without experience, often suspect, take daily refuge there [within the jurisdiction of the seigneurial courts] in order to work and undertake the commerce of all the merchants and artisans of Paris; the public is ordinarily the victim of their greed, as a result of the poor quality of the merchandise and products that they sell there; no one inspects the commerce of these individ-

> uals; they believe themselves to be independent, and under the protection of their supposed privileges, they take away from the merchants and artisans of the city of Paris the fruit of their commerce and the retail of their merchandise; the difference between the one and the other is nonetheless quite significant; the merchant and artisan have acquired through their knowledge and experience certain qualities that serve as guarantees [of the quality of their work], while the individual claiming privilege has neither enlightenment nor capability, and in the hope of paying less in these sorts of privileged places, the public is almost always cheated there.[32]

In sum, the *six corps* insisted that without proper police and guild regulation, those engaged in commercial activity were prone to a greed-driven pursuit of wealth, whereby they would serve their own interests, at the expense of the community as a whole.

As suggested by the words of the *six corps,* guilds were thought to assist in the policing of commerce in a variety of ways. Guilds regulated the quantity and quality of goods produced by their members, thereby deterring merchants from any temptation to profit by flooding the market (and thus undermining their fellow merchants), or by producing cheap, poor-quality merchandise (and thus harming the public). To enforce these regulations, guild leaders—like the police—were empowered to make surprise visits to the workshops of guild members, imposing fines on those who produced nonconforming goods, and destroying the offensive merchandise (in order to prevent its use and the concomitant tainting of the guild's reputation).[33]

Because the failure to comply with guild and police regulations was deemed a moral failing—one that stemmed from laziness, self-interest, and greed—guilds were also expected to police commerce by shaping and regulating their members' moral character and conduct. They were to admit only those individuals who could prove that they had led upstanding lives. Indeed, formal guild rules barred those categories of people who, as a result of their own actions or those of their ancestors, were considered to have been defamed—those who, for example, had been imprisoned or were born out of wedlock, whose very bodies were thought to bear the mark of God's shame.[34] In addition, as to those individuals who passed this initial hurdle and were admitted to membership, guilds developed practices intended to inculcate appropriate values and conduct. Through service as an apprentice and then a journeyman—during which time the novice traditionally lived with the master and his family[35]—the young merchant-artisan worked closely with a master, whose job it was to teach the complex skills of the trade, as well as such quintessential merchant virtues as diligence, patience, and charity. Thus trained, it was thought, the merchant-artisan would be able to withstand the temptations of financial self-interest, placing communal well-being above his own.

In reality, especially as the eighteenth century progressed, actual practice often deviated significantly from this ideal type. Competition for scarce placements and increasing mobility within the workforce meant that the familial model of guild training and membership came under serious strain. As Michael Sonenscher has shown, many would-be masters never actually completed their apprenticeships, and even those who did faced serious, often insurmountable competition from migrant journeymen.[36] As a growing number of journeymen moved regularly from one job to the next, many stopped residing with their masters and lived, instead, with their own families or with other journeymen traveling in search of work.[37] Moreover, among those who succeeded in obtaining a much-coveted Parisian mastership, such success was often attributable to the journeyman's (easily displayed) familial connections and wealth, rather than to his (time-tested) moral stature.[38] And since many journeymen failed to attain a mastership, conflicts between masters and journeymen became common.[39]

Neither the prevalence of such strife nor the mobility of journeymen was conducive to the inculcation of shared moral values within the guilds. But however great the divide between practice and ideal, the fact is that the great majority of eighteenth-century Parisian artisans belonged to one or another royal guild in some capacity. According to one estimate, there were about 35,000 guild members in Paris in the 1720s, and at most a quarter as many artisans practicing outside the guild system in the various *lieux privilégiés*.[40] Furthermore, the guilds, which were so important to so many, continued to legitimate themselves—and their monopoly privileges—by claiming to police merchant morality and thereby protect the public. Even the journeymen's associations, or *compagnonnages*, that came to compete with the (masters') guilds—and were, accordingly, deemed illegal—mirrored guilds in their embrace of religious ritual and the moralizing mission that such ritual implied.[41]

Guilds employed religious ritual primarily through the confraternities with which they were usually associated. Although scholars dispute the exact nature of the relationship between the guild and the confraternity,[42] all agree that the confraternity was a kind of religious association and that it played a fundamental role in the life of the trades. Frequently, a confraternity and the guild it served would share the same patron saint, which each institution displayed on its ceremonial banner, and guild leaders (*jurés, syndics*, or *gardes*) were often elected from amongst former leaders of the confraternity (*syndics* or *bâtonniers*).[43] The main function of the confraternity was to attend to the spiritual life of guild members,[44] and thereby ensure that all would be good, upstanding Christians. Typically, the confraternity established and decorated a special chapel, often in the parish church or in a nearby monastery or convent, where members of the guild could attend Mass. In addition, the confraternity arranged the annual Mass and procession on the patron saint's day, during which members prayed for the souls of their deceased colleagues, made confession, and took communion. Likewise, the confraternity was responsible for ensuring attendance at the funeral Mass of members who had died and for providing financial assistance to members and their families who were in need because of age, sickness, widowhood, or other circumstances.[45]

By thus overseeing merchants' spiritual practices and providing a framework in which they could be charitable to their brothers and sisters in need, the confraternity — in association with the guild — was thought to play a key role in policing commerce. This does not mean, of course, that all Old Regime merchants were genuinely devout, God-fearing souls. Indeed, there is significant evidence to suggest that, at least among certain portions of the populace, including notably Parisians, religiosity was on the wane during the eighteenth century.[46] Nonetheless, it is clear that Christian practices remained important features of most merchants' daily lives.

Through their involvement in such practices — as mediated by guild, confraternity, and *compagnonnage* — merchants sought to disprove the pervasive perception that they lacked virtue. Thus, for example, in his remarkable autobiography Jacques-Louis Ménétra, a master in the glaziers' guild of eighteenth-century Paris,[47] proudly described his participation as a young man in a religious processional held by members of his journeymen's association to thank God for the king's recovery from an illness.[48] Throughout this same work, however, he repeatedly criticized priests as hypocritical and intolerant.[49] For Ménétra, as for many of his merchant contemporaries, there was no contradiction here. Ménétra had come to feel great antipathy toward Catholic officialdom, but this had no bearing on his eagerness to participate in religious processionals. Such communal religious practices remained essential for preserving and promoting the merchant's standing as virtuous and thus reliable.

While guilds did not always embody the ideals of Christian virtue that they espoused, these ideals remained essential to their self-conception. Indeed, it was the fact that guilds sought to shape the moral character of merchants and thereby suppress the self-interest so destructive to communal well-being that justified their entitlement to monopoly privileges — and to the assistance of the royal police in enforcing these. Until their abolition during the Revolution, guilds constantly struggled to preserve their privileges, and they did so by arguing that any infringement would unleash a torrent of greed detrimental to the public good.

Consider, for example, the way in which the grocers' guild — one of the elite *six corps* — challenged a proposed royal edict of 1761, which sought to encourage noblemen to undertake wholesale commerce.[50] The edict provided that noblemen could engage in such commercial activity without being admitted into a guild, and thus without suffering the taint to their honor that would follow from being marked as merchants. Not surprisingly, the grocers rejected the proposed edict because it permitted noblemen to infringe their guild monopoly. They did so, however, not by focusing on their own entitlement, but instead by painting a dire portrait of the hazards to public welfare that would ensue from any infringement of their monopoly privileges. Should such an infringement occur, they queried, were the following events not probable?

> It would then be in [the noblemen's] power to establish, contrary to the most definite and precise regulations of the police, as many secret warehouses as they judged appropriate? And the way then to visit the merchandise that is thus concealed, in order to judge whether it is of good or bad quality and save the public from the risk of being tricked? The way to prevent monopolies, plots . . . , false weights, false measures, frauds . . . which would become so easy, and all the other disorders of this type, which unfortunately greed is only too ingenious at multiplying? Will Monsieur the lieutenant general of police, whose duties are already so numerous, be obliged to resort to new expedients to shine light perpetually on the conduct of a multitude of new types of traders, who will occupy themselves exclusively with the task of concealing themselves from his vigilance? And the sole consideration of the trouble that . . . [this edict] would be capable of bringing to the admirable order that one sees reigning in the police of Paris, would it alone not suffice to make one reject it?[51]

Arguments tying guild privilege to the policing of merchant morality and thus to the public good appeared with renewed force in February 1776, upon Turgot's brief-lived abolition of the guilds.[52] Joining many other guilds, all demanding their restoration, the locksmiths suggested that:

> The arts and industry far from perfecting themselves through liberty . . . will slacken . . . to the contrary, whether because of the multiplicity of entrepreneurs who pressed by the need to live will be obliged to ignore [the virtues of] emulation, or because of the entry of foreigners who will soon bring with them their coarseness and their bad taste, or because of the ambition of almost all the workers who in order to carry on many trades do not undertake any with diligence, or finally because of a lack of studies in general, because knowing hardly the first elements of the art or trade to which they will be destined, apprentices will nonetheless believe themselves in a position to become masters and to establish themselves by profiting from this projected liberty.[53]

This insistence that the restoration of guild privileges was necessary to stem the potential hazards of commerce was obviously self-promoting. But whatever the extent to which those who made such arguments truly believed them, it is clear that guilds continued throughout the eighteenth century vigorously to defend their privileges and that they did so by appealing to a public-hazard conception of commerce (and concomitant view of their own policing role) that had long justified their existence.

The Limits of Virtue and the Merchant Court's Role as an Extension of the Guilds

Although the guilds were designed to promote fraternal harmony and thereby contain disorder, conflict among Old Regime merchants was nonetheless rampant. Indeed, it was precisely because conflicts were so common that merchant courts proved necessary—and since the Parisian Merchant Court entertained between 200 and 350 cases each of the days that it was in session, very necessary at that.[54] Given, however, the established wisdom that the guild system successfully promoted virtue and thus harmony, the court's very existence posed a conceptual challenge.

As several historians have recently argued, guilds' rhetoric of virtue and harmony belied a great deal of self-interest and conflict.[55] Guilds fell short of their own rhetoric for a number of reasons—not the least of which was that one of the main purposes of such exaggerated rhetoric was precisely to shield from view the disturbing reality of conflict. An additional problem was that, despite the monarchy's best efforts, a significant amount of trade and manufacturing actually took place outside of the guilds—and thus beyond the reach of their moral policing. For example, the merchant elite, known as *négociants,* often operated largely unconstrained by guild rules and regulations. These individuals were wholesale merchants who engaged in widespread, frequently international trade. They also served as bankers, making credit available to customers throughout France and abroad, in part through brokering trade in bills of exchange.[56] Most *négociants* began their careers within a high-ranking guild, such as one of the *six corps de Paris,*[57] but the scale of their endeavors was such that they tended to abide by guild constraints selectively at best.

Also operating beyond the control of the guilds and their moral policing were the many non-guild merchants and artisans who lived in the various *lieux privilégiés* (most notably the faubourg Saint-Antoine), where despite the monarchy's best efforts—and to the great chagrin of the Parisian guilds—they continued to practice their professions.[58] Similarly, the many *marchands forains*—who came to Paris to sell produce from the surrounding rural villages—did not belong to any formal trade corporation.[59] Even among those merchants and artisans who did operate within the guild system, however, conflict was frequent. Within individual guilds, artisans and journeymen regularly struggled with masters over the conditions of their employment, and many of these disputes found their way into litigation (often before the Parisian Merchant Court). Likewise, masters fought among themselves over questions of guild leadership, giving rise to what a number of historians have characterized as a democratic movement within the guilds over the course of the eighteenth century. Such conflict often concerned questions of guild management, pitting younger masters (*modernes* and *jeunes*) against an older elite (*anciens*), whom they charged with various kinds of corruption, including engaging in illegal cabals designed to facilitate their despotic control.[60]

Among the causes of such intra-guild strife was the fact that, as Sonenscher has argued, a significant amount of trade in the eighteenth century took the form of subcontracted work. Building a carriage, for example, required the input of, among others, saddlers, joiners, wheelwrights, and locksmiths. As a result, certain master saddlers, seeking to expand their capital base, began to distinguish themselves from others within their guild by contracting to produce the finished carriage, while subcontracting the work itself to other saddlers, as well as to members of other guilds with the necessary expertise.[61] Such subcontracting practices often violated guild rules, such as those prohibiting one master from hiring another from the same guild, or those prohibiting a master from one guild from hiring journeymen from another. Subcontracting nonetheless continued and was a source of much conflict between those masters who adhered to the guild rules and those who sought to expand their business opportunities by serving in essence as general contractors.[62]

To the extent that subcontracting of this kind occurred, it was a source of conflict not only within, but also between guilds. Guild elites, for example, were often less than pleased by the competition for labor—and thus pressure to pay higher wages—that followed from masters in another guild seeking to subcontract work to their journeymen, in flagrant violation of guild rules. Even aside from the practice of subcontracting, however, conflict between different guilds was quite common.[63] Guilds constantly struggled to extend their legalized monopolies, and in so doing, often infringed on the privileges (real or perceived) of their fellow guilds. Moreover, given the highly status-oriented nature of Old Regime society, the organization of trades into distinct corporate entities was rife with opportunities for status conflict. For example, the *six corps de Paris* struggled among themselves continuously to establish an order of precedence. Likewise, the *six corps* and the guilds just below them—in particular, the wine sellers' and the printers' guilds—regularly debated whether the latter should be admitted into the ranks of Paris's top guilds.[64]

And guilds of even lower status—including those devoted to selling items of basic necessity (often primary materials transported by means of water)—also challenged the power of their superiors.[65]

For the Parisian Merchant Court, such conflicts among and between guild and non-guild merchants—as well as the daily disputes that arose regarding sales and other commercial transactions—were both its raison d'être and an existential dilemma. As an institution whose purpose was to deal with lapses in merchant virtue and the consequent loss of social harmony, the merchant court was quite literally based on conflict. At the same time, the court's very existence served to demonstrate that, despite guilds' efforts and their proclamations to the contrary, lapses in merchant virtue were actually widespread. Merchants regularly failed to honor their obligations, and fraternal charity was often so lacking that there was no alternative to litigation. The Parisian Merchant Court responded to this existential dilemma by developing an ethos of virtue and harmony that was perhaps even more exaggerated than that of the guilds, from which it drew its membership and support.

This virtuous ethos is evident in the description of the court that appears in the *Tableau de Paris,* the famous guide to life in Paris published by Louis-Sébastien Mercier in the final years of the Old Regime. Though in no way associated with the Parisian Merchant Court, Mercier lavishly praised it as the embodiment of such virtues as simplicity, honesty, and good faith:

> This court disposes of more cases in a single day than the *Parlement* does in a month. The parties plead themselves. All vain subtleties are banished from this tribunal, as well as the lengthy formalities of the ordinary court. The judges, who are merchants, seek only to identify the good faith of one of the litigants and the bad faith of the other. They do not rely on meaningless words; they examine the particular facts and judge on the basis of their daily experience with the frauds committed in trade. . . . Without this court, whose utility is equal to its power, there would be neither order nor security in commerce, the other courts taking months to render a decision or decree, such that chicanery can postpone a definitive judgment for several years.[66]

At the core of this virtuous image that the court succeeded in perpetuating was the notion that merchant litigants, required to argue on their own behalf, would be forced to speak the simple truth, instead of relying on lawyers to couch their claims in complex legal fictions and technicalities. This, in turn, would save merchants a great deal of time and money, thus encouraging them to abide by the court's simple, honesty-promoting procedures. And to the extent that parties were nonetheless tempted to obscure the truth, merchant-judges, chosen by their peers, would have the practical experience (and knowledge of the litigants' reputations) necessary to assess moral character and thereby detect and deter bad-faith behavior.

As an institution designed to promote virtue and police bad faith, the Parisian Merchant Court was in many ways but an extension of the guild system. Indeed, the relationship between the court and the leading Parisian guilds was so close that institutional boundaries were necessarily blurred. The court's officers consisted of one judge and four consuls—hence the official name of the court, *la juridiction consulaire de Paris*. All five of these officials possessed ultimate decision-making power, such that any three could form a panel authorized to issue rulings.[67] Judge and consul differed only in that the former served as the court's chief judge, or administrative head. The judge and consuls were elected on an annual basis through a procedure that, although varying slightly over time, accorded the *six corps de Paris* and other leading guilds—in particular, the wine sellers' and printers' guilds—a predominant role.[68]

Because of the close relationship between the elite guilds and the court, the judge and consuls were commonly referred to as the *juge et consuls des marchands,* or the judges of the merchants[69]—and as the leading members of these guilds, this is precisely what they were. Perhaps nothing more clearly reveals the interdependence of court and guild than the fact that the lease to one of the first buildings in which the court sat was in the name of the *six corps*.[70] In fact, the November 1563 edict establishing the Parisian Merchant Court provided for a courthouse by authorizing the merchants of Paris to levy a tax on themselves for this purpose.[71] In this sense, the merchant court was a kind of subsidiary of the guilds—a specialized branch designated to resolve legal disputes—rather than an independent entity or arm of the state.

The court was, in fact, structured much like a guild. It was organized as a hierarchy, with a select group of officers, known as the *anciens,* holding the reins. The *anciens* formed their own organization, the *compagnie des anciens,* which was established early in the life of the court and which wielded a great deal of power. The *anciens* advised the court on important and undecided questions of law, on how to proceed in jurisdictional conflicts with other courts, on whether and how to petition the king or *parlement,* on matters concerning court property, and on issues related to the employment of staff. Moreover, whenever a current judge or consul was absent, it was one of the *anciens* who would replace him.[72]

There was one significant respect, however, in which the guilds' *anciens* differed from those of the court—one that highlights a key difference between the guilds and the merchant court. In the guilds, the *anciens* were an elite, who having previously served as guild leaders, continued to own their offices as masters. In contrast, merchant court judges were elected annually and thus did not own offices purchased from the crown. After their year of service was complete, the judge and consuls became *anciens* and ceased to possess formal offices within the court. That the judge and consuls did not own their offices meant that the merchant court, unlike a guild, was not a true royal *corps* in the formal legal sense of the term. But this was a point of great pride for the court, which insisted that one of the reasons that it could operate virtuously and avoid technicalities—thus offering the speedy, simple procedure that merchants craved—was that its judges worked for free. While officers in royal *corps,* such as guild masters, earned *gages* of various kinds as recompense for the property interest they had purchased from the crown, the judge and consuls served on a voluntary basis and were therefore, they claimed, purely disinterested.

But while the judge and consuls were not venal officeholders, the court was otherwise much like any other corporate entity, including the guilds, in that it had a single legal personality. The *compagnie des anciens,* which served as the court's decision-making body, had authority to act on its behalf, undertaking debt or pursuing litigation in the name of the court as a whole, and thereby obligating judges and consuls who had yet to serve. Moreover, like the guilds (and the confraternities with which these were associated), the court understood itself to be responsible for overseeing the spiritual lives of its officers, as well as the merchants whom it served. Accordingly, the court was at all times housed in a religious establishment. After it was created in 1563, and before it had collected the taxes levied for the purpose of establishing its own space, the merchant court sat in the Abbey of Saint-Magloire. When in 1570 the court finally obtained sufficient funds to purchase its own building, it selected one located in the cloister of Saint-Merry (fig. 1).[73]

In 1630, the court built its own chapel within the courthouse, and Mass was held there every Monday, Wednesday, and Friday morning—the days that the court sat to hear new cases.[74] Generally, the judge and consuls attended this Mass, but when time did not permit, they and all others in the main courtroom were still able to hear it, because the chapel was separated from the courtroom by only a grille. The court hired a priest from the parish of Saint-Merry to serve as chaplain, leading the Mass on these weekday mornings, and also holding the annual Mass of the Holy Spirit on the day that the new judge and consuls were elected. The chaplain also held Requiem Masses for the souls of any current or former judges and consuls who died during the year. In addition to celebrating religious events in their own chapel, the judge and consuls participated in some larger celebrations held outside the courthouse. For example, they sometimes joined in the procession held by the parish church on Corpus Christi, and they attended the Cloister of Saint-Merry for an annual service held to pray for the souls of their deceased colleagues.[75]

Fig. 1 The Parisian Merchant Court (Lithograph by A. Lemercier, based on drawing by T. Turpin de Crissé, *Tribunal des juges consuls*, 1833. Courtesy of Musée Carnavalet.)

The court sought to demonstrate its moral oversight, not only by undertaking religious ritual, but also in the manner that it resolved litigation. Most importantly, the court understood its main function to be mediation—a means of reconciling the parties to an agreed-upon compromise and thereby restoring severed bonds of friendship and trust—rather than adjudication, or the handing down of judgments from above. Accordingly, the court sent most litigants to arbiters, whom it charged with reconciling the parties and only if this failed, with proposing a judgment to be entered by the court.[76] Usually merchants but often also priests, the arbiters lacked a clear institutional identity, and perhaps for this reason, were largely ignored by Denière and Leclerc in their comprehensive accounts of the structure of the Parisian Merchant Court. But it is impossible to understand the court without recognizing the crucial role played by arbiters. Indeed, the arbiters were essential not only to the court's self-conception as a bastion of merchant virtue but also in enabling it to manage its massive docket. The judge and consuls, who heard between 200 to 350 cases per day during the three weekdays that the court was in session,[77] could not possibly have stayed afloat without the arbiters' help.

The court's commitment to mediation—which, in turn, stemmed from its efforts to portray itself as promoting merchant virtue—led to its (at least theoretical) rejection of lawyers. As indicated in Mercier's commentary, lawyers were forbidden in the merchant courts, because they were thought to promote chicanery and bad faith. So stated both the Edict of 1563, which established the Parisian Merchant Court, and the Civil Procedure Ordinance of 1667. According to the ordinance, the parties were to appear on their own behalf, and in case of illness or some other legitimate hindrance, they were to send a signed brief with one of their relatives, neighbors, or friends.[78]

Despite this clear prohibition, however, lawyers began to appear in the Parisian Merchant Court shortly after its creation. By the eighteenth century, they were not only tolerated but deemed an integral component of the court with significant powers and privileges. These commercial lawyers, known as *agréés,* were formally appointed by the judge and consuls to represent parties before the court—hence their name, meaning "approved." And while the judge and consuls were elected on an annual basis, the commercial lawyers came by the early eighteenth century to have life tenure, as well as the right to transmit their offices to their heirs.[79] In this sense, even though the *agréés* did not purchase their offices from the crown, and thus were not technically venal officeholders, they operated as such in certain key respects, thereby contravening a fundamental tenet by means of which the merchant court sought to establish its virtue. Nonetheless, arbiters' reports filed with the Parisian Merchant Court suggest that lawyers were regularly used.[80] Moreover, there is no doubt that their existence was common knowledge—and not only among merchants and commercial jurists. In their broad-ranging legal dictionaries, the civil-law jurists Denisart and Guyot acknowledged that, despite statutory law to the contrary, there were many lawyers active in the merchant courts.[81]

But while the existence of commercial lawyers was well established and broadly recognized,[82] it remained a defining feature of the Parisian Merchant Court's identity that parties were supposed to represent themselves—and thus, as late as 1782, Mercier continued to insist that they did. Shortly thereafter, in portions of his *Tableau* published in 1788, he acknowledged that the court sometimes permitted the use of lawyers, but he did so in a manner that served further to highlight the remarkable tenacity of the court's virtuous image. As Mercier depicted them, commercial lawyers appearing before the merchant court were not eager to engage in lengthy litigation as a means of augmenting their fees, but were instead quite simply advocates of virtue: "Agents or solicitors [*procureurs*], who are entitled lawyers [*avocats*], plead up to seventy-two cases a day, at the price of twenty-four sous per case; but their clients do not suffer for that. When the lawyer discovers that he has somehow obtained the writ of opposing counsel, he simply stretches out his arm and passes it to his colleague. The multiplicity of cases and the confusion arising from so many names means that sometimes lawyers find themselves charged with representing both the prosecution and the defense; but in a moment the confusion is clarified and another lawyer is found as is proper."[83]

This account of the lawyer as a self-sacrificing hero who tirelessly takes on vast numbers of cases for very little money, who freely hands over documents that belong to his opponent, and who is so lacking in a spirit of partisanship that he sometimes finds himself having to represent both the plaintiff and the defendant surely rang as false in the Old Regime as it does today. Eighteenth-century France was a notoriously litigious society, and the later years of the Old Regime were plagued by an overpopulation of lawyers, many of whom could not find work and were regarded with little sympathy.[84] As Jean Toubeau, a leading Old Regime commercial jurist, wrote in the late seventeenth century, "Doesn't one see that the majority [of lawyers] only seek to win the case, and not to serve justice; and that if some sell their words, the others sell their silence, which is no less dangerous."[85] Half a century later, the anonymous author of a treatise on commercial litigation repeated this criticism, observing—in language no doubt borrowed from Toubeau—that they "often . . . speak more for their own gain than for justice; some sell their words, others their silence."[86] Given this general conception of the lawyer as a self-interested mercenary, Mercier's completely contrasting account of the commercial lawyer as a paragon of virtue must be viewed more as myth than reality. But this was a myth of profound importance, as it, perhaps more than any other, highlighted the power and prominence of the merchant court's image as a realm of merchant virtue—a realm where brotherly ties forged through guild and confraternity, though thereafter weakened in conflict, would be reestablished and bolstered.

Electoral Disputes and the Merchant Court's Turn Away from the Traditional Rhetoric of Virtue

The Parisian Merchant Court's extensive efforts to portray itself as promoting virtue belied an underlying anxiety that it, like the guilds themselves, might be less than perfectly virtuous. Indeed, the life of the court, like that of the guilds, was far from harmonious, as it was punctuated regularly by extensive conflict among those guilds vying to control it. Such conflict, which surfaced primarily in the context of the annual elections of the judge and consuls, tested the court's espoused commitment to values of fraternal charity and harmony. In response to this challenge, merchants who were engaged in conflict at first sought to demonstrate their virtue by accusing opponents of generating strife and thus of lacking virtue themselves. In the 1750s, however, the court and its supporters in the *six corps de Paris* abandoned this rhetoric of virtue and the concomitant conception of the court as an extension of the guild system, designed to promote virtue by restoring fraternal harmony. The purpose of the court, they came to argue, was not to reinforce the guild system, but instead to facilitate commerce—now conceived as an activity distinct from those particular status groups (such as guilds) that happened to engage in it.[87]

The Edict of November 1563, which created the Parisian Merchant Court, established a standard procedure for electing the judge and consuls. This did not, however, obviate subsequent debate over the edict's intended meaning. According to the edict, the judge and consuls in office were to assemble sixty Parisian merchants to serve as electors.[88] The latter were to select thirty from their number, who along with the current judge and consuls, were to elect the new judicial officers. Not surprisingly, the electors invariably hailed from the merchant elite, most of whom belonged to the *six corps de Paris*—consisting in descending order of prominence, of drapers, grocers, haberdashers, furriers, hosiers, and goldsmiths.[89] Also among this group of elite merchants serving as electors were members of the wine sellers' and printers' guilds.

Even among these elite guilds, competition to place their members in the merchant court was fierce, and disputes frequently arose concerning which guilds were entitled to representation and how the electoral procedure should be structured. Such conflict dated at least as far back as the late seventeenth century and continued into the second half of the eighteenth. Over time, merchants engaged in electoral conflict advocated their claims less by appealing to a longstanding rhetoric of merchant virtue—a rhetoric that emerged from, and as a counterpart to, the traditional, public-hazard conception of commerce—and more by turning to a new conception of commerce as a natural and beneficent social function.

The first major electoral conflict for which extensive records have been preserved erupted in 1725.[90] At that time, the three lowest ranking guilds within the *six corps* (the furriers, hosiers, and goldsmiths) filed a petition with the monarchy—and, in particular, with the central *Bureau du Commerce*—requesting a restructuring of the Parisian Merchant Court and its electoral procedure. These guilds sought a ruling that would increase the number of consuls from four to six and that would require each of the *six corps* to supply either a judge or a consul.[91] The remaining position would be filled by a "celebrated trader" who was not a member of the *six corps*.[92] The top guilds firmly rejected this proposal and were soon joined by the furriers, who abandoned their initial demands. The result was an extended — and highly public — debate that gave lie to the myth of fraternal harmony among merchants. Taking the form of a war of printed pamphlets, in which each side claimed to have the public's support,[93] this debate prefigured the battles for public opinion that would come to dominate French political life during the second half of the eighteenth century.[94]

According to the petitioners, their demand to change the electoral procedure in order to increase their representation on the court was not an effort to change the status quo, and thus to disturb the peace, but to the contrary, an attempt to restore order by ensuring that harmony would reign once again among merchant brothers. Only by ensuring that each of the *six corps* would have one of its members serving on the court at all times would it be possible to "revive that ancient and perfect equality between the six brothers, among whom one did not at first distinguish any priority or posteriority other than that which the numerical order arbitrarily assigned."[95]

As the petitioners explained, the merchant court was an institution designed to police commerce. Indeed, it was created precisely because "the interest of the Prince and that of his subjects are united and require . . . that this important goal [of commerce] be well policed."[96] Who better to ensure that the court fulfill its policing function than those members of the *six corps* whose job it was to oversee these guilds' efforts at policing — namely, each guild's leaders? As the petitioners noted, "Each of the *corps* is governed by six subjects entitled *maîtres* and *gardes* . . . [who] are responsible for dealing with the statutes and regulations, with maintaining police and discipline within the *corps,* and with repressing the abuses that might creep in there."[97] Since the court was required to decide disputes regarding all areas of commercial activity, policing would be most effective if each guild had one of its leaders serving on the court — thereby maximizing the knowledge and experience on which the court could draw. Thus restructured to achieve its mission of properly policing commerce, the court would be able to "establish equality, peace, union between brothers,"[98] and to ensure that "half the brothers . . . [would] not have but a quarter of the inheritance."[99]

Not surprisingly, the leading guilds responded to the petitioners by arguing that it was the petitioners (and not the leading guilds) who — motivated by ambition — sought to change the status quo and thereby destroy the merchant harmony that the court was supposed to promote. As they observed, "It is sad that particular views and personal interests decide on steps for which the public does not ask, and that these same interests trouble the union among the *six corps* by dividing them and spreading confusion through the novelties which the two last *corps* want to introduce to the prejudice of the good order that one has always seen in the merchant court since its establishment."[100] Such self-interested behavior was contrary to "the good faith and the truth [which] are [supposed to be] inseparable characteristics of the merchant."[101]

On June 28, 1725, the King's Council resolved the conflict by declaring that the electoral procedure, as established in the Edict of November 1563, was to remain unchanged. Relying on this decision, the wine sellers' and printers' guilds filed suit against the merchant court in the *Parlement* of Paris, requesting an annulment of the election held on January 30, 1727. While the plaintiffs asserted similar demands to those previously raised by the lowest-ranking members of the *six corps,* they now did so on the grounds that the 1727 election failed to conform to the Edict of November 1563. According to the plaintiffs, the edict's clear meaning was that the judge and four consuls would be selected from among members of the *six corps* and the wine sellers' and printers' guilds "alternatively and successively, such that each *corps* can arrive . . . [into office] in its turn; and without there emerging from any of these elections, either for the judge or for the consuls, two subjects from the same *corps.*"[102] Contrary, however, to the edict (as interpreted by the plaintiffs), the merchant court was entirely dominated by the *six corps,* such that these guilds regularly placed their members on the court, to the exclusion of the wine sellers and printers.

As the lowest-ranking members of the *six corps* had previously argued, the wine sellers and printers now claimed that the refusal to provide them with sufficient representation on the court stemmed from a failure of virtue. But while the previous petitioners had confined themselves to relatively mild statements about their opponents' lack of brotherly feeling, the wine sellers and printers went further, asserting that their opponents were seeking to exercise an unlawful tyranny over the court. Making precisely the sorts of arguments that historians have associated with the rise of a democratic movement within the guilds, the plaintiffs asserted that they had no choice but to attempt to "cast off the tyrannical yoke of these ambitious *corps.*"[103] The *six corps,* they claimed, had achieved tyrannical rule by means of cabals, conspiracies, and corruption. Although the Edict of November 1563 provided that the current judge and consuls were to assemble sixty merchant electors, they typically called only the thirty-six leaders of the *six corps* and then "as concerns the other communities, only the number and the subjects that it pleased the judge and consuls to call; thus interpreting to their liking the provision of the edict."[104] Moreover, asserted the plaintiffs, "It is known that the leaders of the *six corps,* who . . . are always summoned to the elections, have held amongst themselves preliminary assemblies, where they gave their word not to name wine sellers: they have kept their word very exactly."[105]

According to the plaintiffs, such elections to the merchant court were clearly illegitimate, as "intrigue and cabals have obviously appeared there."[106] But since the leaders of each of the *six corps* were themselves selected through an electoral process dominated by corruption of one kind or another, it was hardly surprising that, in their capacity as merchant court judges, they then conspired to exclude all others from the merchant court. Moreover, the sad reality that "the office of guild leader [*garde*] . . . is bestowed most often through intrigue and favor" suggested that possession of such an office was not "a clear guarantee to the public of the talents, enlightenment, and qualities necessary to undertake the functions of consul with dignity."[107] Echoing the claim of the previous petitioners that they were being excluded from their fraternal share of their inheritance, the plaintiffs bemoaned that the end result of the *six corps'* tyranny was that "the printers' and wine sellers' guilds will be excluded from the merchant court, which they can nonetheless rightly call their patrimony."[108]

In thus arguing that the leaders of the *six corps* attained their positions in the merchant court by means of cabals and corruption, the wine sellers and printers were in one sense making a radical claim. Like the *modernes* and *jeunes,* who within particular guilds accused the *anciens* of exercising a despotic control illicitly obtained, these plaintiffs were challenging the merchant court's traditional power base and demanding democratic accountability. At the same time, it is important to recognize that the wine sellers and printers' accusations against the *six corps* were of a kind with the traditional rhetoric of merchant virtue, which was itself a counterpart to the longstanding public-hazard conception of commerce. In other words, just as the lowest-ranking members of the *six corps* had argued two years prior, the wine sellers and printers couched their demands in the assertion — now even more aggressive — that their opponents were lacking in virtue. As the electoral conflict continued, however, the merchant court and the *six corps* would come to defend the status quo, and thus their own power, by abandoning this rhetoric of virtue.

In the meantime, the *Parlement* of Paris dismissed the lawsuit filed in 1727 by the wine sellers' and printers' guilds. Citing the ruling issued by the King's Council in 1725, the *Parlement* held that the matter was within the council's jurisdiction, rather than its own.[109] The monarchy then sought to resolve the conflict once and for all by means of a declaration promulgated on March 18, 1728, in which it provided a new electoral procedure for the Parisian Merchant Court. Attempting a compromise, the declaration declined the plaintiffs' request to augment the number of consuls, but granted their request that no two members of the court be permitted to belong to the same guild. In addition, the declaration provided that, in selecting the sixty merchant electors, the current judge and consuls were to pick no more than five people from each of the *six corps,* the wine sellers' guild, and the printers' guild. The remaining twenty electors were to be selected from among other prominent Parisian merchants or *négociants.*[110]

Not surprisingly, the Declaration of March 1728 did not permanently resolve the conflict among the elite guilds for control of the Parisian Merchant Court. In 1738, the printers' guild filed suit once again in the *Parlement,* challenging an election held on January 28 of that year, and thus renewing its efforts to obtain greater representation on the court. By an order of February 3, the *Parlement* dismissed the suit and upheld the election.[111] Nonetheless, significant tension continued among the elite guilds concerning elections to (and thus control over) the Parisian Merchant Court. Consider, for example, the problem that arose when, in 1747, the court hired a sculptor, C. Pittoin, to create a sculpture representing autumn, to be placed on a large clock located near the court's entrance.[112] The sculpture that Pittoin initially produced was a head "coiffed with the attributes of vines and grapes."[113] However, as Pittoin noted in his final bill to the court, "the merchant court judges . . . [have] remarked that since this attribute is related to the wine seller, the building would appear to the public to belong to the wine sellers."[114] Horrified by the prospect that the court might be in this way associated with the wine sellers, whose claims to greater electoral power they had long rejected, the judge and consuls ordered Pittoin to redo the sculpture such that "the aforementioned head would instead be coiffed with [the attributes of the] oak."[115]

Despite Pittoin's misstep, significant conflict among the elite guilds regarding control of the Parisian Merchant Court did not reemerge until 1756, when the printers' guild, joined this time by the wine sellers' guild, brought suit yet again in the *Parlement.* The plaintiffs asserted that each of the *six corps,* the wine sellers' guild, and the printers' guild was entitled in turn to supply a judge or consul—and not simply to have its members serve as electors.[116] As their predecessors had done, the plaintiffs framed their arguments in terms of a failure of merchant virtue, complaining that their opponents had cast aside brotherhood and charity by means of tyrannical cabals. In contrast, however, the merchant court and the *six corps* appealed to a very different set of values.

Abandoning the traditional language of merchant virtue, the court argued that the problem with the plaintiffs' demands was not that these destroyed fraternal harmony among guilds, but rather that they restricted the freedom of the individual merchant electors to elect whomever they desired. If the plaintiffs were victorious, the merchant electors would be forced to pick candidates from those guilds whose turn it was to have representation on the court. But this was contrary to the Edict of November 1563, which in establishing the electoral procedure for the Parisian Merchant Court "leaves, as the essence of every election, the absolute and indefinite liberty of suffrage."[117] The primary criterion by means of which the electors should select the judge and consuls, claimed the merchant court, was not guild membership but individual merit—and, in particular, merit in undertaking commerce. As the court observed, "It is merit, probity, knowledge, experience concerning commerce that must decide the electors and determine their choice.[118] Accordingly, "the guild [*corps*] or the community does not enter into consideration."[119]

Underlying this argument that elections to the merchant court must be based on individual merit rather than corporate membership were the rudiments of a new understanding of the court's purpose. In the traditional view, the court, like the guilds to which it was linked, was an institution created to engage in policing—to oversee the morality and conduct of merchants and thereby ensure that they did not place greed and self-interest above the communal good. When, despite the efforts of guilds and police, conflicts nonetheless emerged, the merchant court simply stepped in to assist in maintaining order and harmony. As a kind of subsidiary and protector of the guilds, the court in essence mirrored them—serving as a kind of supra-assembly of the (elite) Parisian guilds. But by arguing that individual merit rather than corporate representation should be the deciding factor in selecting the judge and consuls, the merchant court suggested that it was an institution fundamentally distinct from the guilds—one that existed not to mirror and reinforce the guild system but instead to promote the interests of commerce as something apart.[120] As the court argued, "It is for the good of commerce, not for the decoration or vanity of certain merchant guilds [*corps*], in preference to others, that the court was established and that the elections of the judge and consuls should be done."[121]

The *six corps* made precisely the same argument in defending themselves and the merchant court that they dominated from this latest lawsuit. Rather than accusing the plaintiffs of disturbing the peace and sowing discord among brothers, the *six corps* complained that the plaintiffs were threatening the liberty of merchants to elect the best qualified individuals. This was contrary to the monarchy's intent, which through its declaration seeking to resolve the electoral conflict in 1728 "allowed to subsist . . . the ancient liberty of choosing among all the persons versed in commerce, those who would seem to be the most capable of filling the places."[122] According to the *six corps*, the relevant criterion in electing a judge and consuls was individual merit in commercial activity, rather than guild membership: "In an election that concerns the naming of judges for commerce [*juges au commerce*], it is not from this or the other guild [*corps*] that one must choose," but instead the choice should be of "the most capable from all the guilds [*corps*]."[123]

As suggested by their reference to the judge and consuls as *juges au com-*

merce, rather than the more habitual *juges des marchands,* the *six corps*—like the court itself—was grasping toward a new conception of the court as an institution designed to facilitate commerce, rather than as simply an extension of the merchant guilds. This is not to suggest, of course, that in opposing the demands of the wine sellers' and printers' guilds, the merchant court and the *six corps* were acting in a purely disinterested fashion, concerned only with promoting commerce for the sake of the public good, and untouched by any corporatist interest in maintaining the court as a power base. The judge and consuls of the merchant court were clearly protesting too much when they insisted that in defending the lawsuit "they concerned themselves only with their positions as judges, with motives of serving the public good, and with benefiting the court," and that they had "forgot[ten] their personal qualities, and lost from view the particular interests of the merchant guilds."[124] Similarly, it strains credulity to accept at face value the *six corps'* plea that they could not help the fact that merchant electors always recognized that candidates from the *six corps* were those "among whom fortune, the normal germ of education, is usually most abundant, and among whom, as a result, the knowledge acquired must be the most extensive and the most appropriate for the positions of judges of commerce."[125]

There is, in other words, no small irony in the fact that it was precisely in order to promote guild interests that the merchant court and *six corps* argued that the court was designed to facilitate commerce, rather than to promote guild interests. Significantly, however, with the onset of the Revolution, this as yet not fully developed vision of the court as a facilitator of commercial activity rather than guild interests—as a court of commerce rather than of merchants—would ultimately become reality. And, as we shall see, the unintended consequence of various royal administrative efforts was that it would become a reality not only for the Parisian Merchant Court but for merchant courts across France. Much, however, would transpire in the interim. The nature of commercial activity itself would change, thus forcing the court to reconsider its own relationship to commerce and to those who undertook it. In addition, as described in the remainder of this chapter, the Parisian Merchant Court's reconceptualization of the nature and purpose of commerce was driven in no small part by its intense jurisdictional conflict with the municipal government of Paris.

Like the conflict over the merchant court's electoral procedure, this jurisdictional conflict had elements of an inter-guild struggle, since it pitted the *six corps,* the wine sellers, and the printers, as advocates of the merchant court, against the water-based merchant communities, which supported the municipal government. And in this conflict as well, the merchant court was led to abandon its traditional self-conception as an institution of police designed to restore harmony among merchant guilds, and to appeal instead to a new view of itself as a facilitator of commerce. The merchant court's jurisdictional conflict with the municipal government was, however, distinct from the electoral conflict in that it forced the court to elaborate extensively on the nature of commerce, leading it ultimately to voice a strikingly modern theory of commerce as the free private exchange sustaining the social order.

Jurisdictional Conflict and the Merchant Court's Turn to a New Conception of Commerce

Throughout its existence, the Old Regime Parisian Merchant Court constantly engaged in jurisdictional conflict with competing seigneurial and royal courts. As noted above, the late-seventeenth-century monarchy tried and ultimately failed to abolish a number of seigneurial courts, which continued to operate in the various *lieux privilégiés* around Paris and to claim jurisdiction over the merchants and artisans who resided there. More threatening to the merchant court's jurisdiction, however, was the competition posed by various royal trial courts.

The royal trial courts consisted of a complex and overlapping patchwork of courts of general jurisdiction, authorized to hear the vast majority of civil and criminal disputes, and courts of limited jurisdiction, each of which was entitled to adjudicate only a particular type of dispute. The key trial courts of general jurisdiction were the *bailliages* or *sénéchaussées,* and the *présidiaux.* The *bailliage* and the *sénéchaussée*—identical institutions known by one or the other name, depending on the region—dated back to the Middle Ages, when the monarchy sent out bailiffs into the countryside to oversee local administration within a particular region or bailiwick.[126] In contrast, the monarchy did not establish the *présidiaux* until 1551, and it did so by declaring that certain existing courts (primarily *bailliages* and *sénéchaussées*) would henceforth function as *présidiaux.* In addition to providing new venal offices that could be sold to raise money for the fisc, the monarchy's goal in creating these courts was to ease the appellate burden on the *parlements.* Thus, the *présidiaux* were to hear appeals from the *bailliages* and *sénéchaussées* and, in certain kinds of cases, to serve as the court of last resort.[127] In Paris, there was no *bailliage* or *sénéchaussée,* but only a *présidial.* This was the famous *Châtelet,* known as such because of the fortified castle (*château fort*) in which it was established.[128] And while the *Châtelet* was authorized to hear civil and criminal, rather than commercial, disputes, it and the Parisian Merchant Court nonetheless battled one another for jurisdiction of various kinds, including notably the right to adjudicate bankruptcies—a form of jurisdiction that was a point of much dispute between ordinary, civil-law courts and merchant courts throughout France.[129]

Aside from the *Châtelet,* there were two royal courts of limited jurisdiction, which embraced commercial disputes of one kind or another and thus came into some conflict with the Parisian Merchant Court: the *amirauté de France,* or admiralty court, and the *bureau de la ville,* or municipal government. As the main judicial seat of the Admiral of France, the admiralty court served as a trial court and also had appellate review over the decisions of nine lower-level admiralty courts. Located within the building that housed the *Parlement* of Paris, its authority officially extended — pursuant to the Marine Ordinance of August 1681 — to matters of maritime law, including commercial contracts concerning merchandise transported by sea and disputes concerning maritime insurance.[130] Despite the relatively clear language of the ordinance, Old Regime commercial jurists — many of whom had served as merchant court judges — argued that the power of the admiralty court was less extensive than might otherwise appear to be the case. Thus, for example, in arguments akin to those, described below, concerning the municipal government, the jurist Philibert-Joseph Masson claimed that the merchant court's jurisdiction over bills of exchange and notes entitled it to hear disputes regarding bills and notes that had been drawn to pay for maritime insurance. Likewise, he insisted that the merchant court was entitled to adjudicate disputes concerning the sale of merchandise that "arrived by sea, once it was on land."[131] Arbiters' reports confirm that, as might be expected, since Masson was a former judge of the Parisian Merchant Court, the court embraced his expansive view of its jurisdiction, regularly hearing cases that in one way or another touched on maritime commerce. Nonetheless, the number of these cases was relatively small. This suggests that, to the extent that disputes arising from France's expanding international (and colonial) trade reached inland to Paris, many likely did go before the admiralty court.

Of all the jurisdictional conflicts in which the Parisian Merchant Court engaged, that with the municipal government of Paris proved to be the most intense and, as it turned out, the one that most profoundly shaped the court's sense of mission and identity. Historically, it had been the municipal government that had primary responsibility for the administration of Paris, including the key task of ensuring that its population was properly provisioned with fundamental necessities transported by means of river traffic. The municipal government arose in the twelfth century, and royal ordinances dating back at least as far as the fifteenth century endowed its officers with "the right of police and inspection on the rivers and ports where the commerce of the city of Paris takes place."[132] Over time, however, the municipal government lost much of its power. When the monarchy created the lieutenant general of police in

1667, the real business of governing Paris came to fall increasingly on this officer and his burgeoning staff.[133]

The establishment and growing prominence of the royal police led to perpetual conflict between it and the municipal government, regarding the authority to police Paris. In an effort to end this jurisdictional conflict, the monarchy issued an edict in June 1700 which reaffirmed the longstanding authority of the municipal government to police goods transported into Paris by water and entrusted to the royal police those goods transported by land.[134] While the edict failed in practice to end all jurisdictional disputes between the two institutions,[135] it firmly established the principle that goods arriving into Paris by water were within the police jurisdiction of the municipal government.

But what precisely was included in this jurisdiction? Some matters were clear. Numerous police ordinances dictated the amount, quality, and price of various goods that could and should be shipped into the city. When the municipal government discovered that such ordinances had been violated, it had the authority to punish the violation, including by means of criminal prosecution.[136] In order, however, to discover whether police ordinances had been violated, the municipal government needed to keep apprised of the nature of the sales undertaken at the ports.[137] How better to obtain this information, it concluded, than to adjudicate disputes between merchants regarding such sales, since during the course of adjudication information regarding the contract terms and the actual course of performance would necessarily surface? Accordingly, the municipal government insisted that, as part of its longstanding police authority, it was entitled to adjudicate contract disputes concerning goods transported into Paris by means of river traffic.

This brought the municipal government directly into conflict with the Parisian Merchant Court. Over the course of the eighteenth century, the merchant court tried increasingly to expand its jurisdiction by emphasizing its exclusive authority (as confirmed by its reading of the Commercial Ordinance of March 1673)[138] to resolve disputes involving negotiable instruments, such as bills of exchange and promissory notes. In so emphasizing, the court sought to take advantage of the rise of negotiability.[139] This recent and important change in commercial practice dramatically expanded the circulation of bills of exchange and promissory notes, and thus the opportunities for the court to exercise jurisdiction. Pointing to its exclusive authority over disputes concerning bills of exchange and promissory notes, the court argued that because most contracts for the sale of goods arriving into Paris (by both water and land) now involved payment by means of negotiable instruments, the litigation that arose over such contracts—which was quite sizable—fell within its exclusive jurisdiction.[140] This argument brought the merchant court into direct conflict with the municipal government, which continued to claim jurisdiction over all litigation arising between merchants regarding sales of goods transported into Paris by water.

The resulting jurisdictional dispute came to a head on December 14, 1735, with the filing of a lawsuit that in turn spawned a series of conflicting judgments and numerous appeals, all of which lasted at least thirty years. The events leading to the lawsuit occurred in December 1734, when Pierre Duclos, a brewer, went to purchase some lumber at a lumberyard located at the port and owned by Robert de Villamay. Duclos paid for the lumber by drafting to de Villamay's order two promissory notes for 300 livres each. The notes fell due in May 1734 and September 1735, respectively. Claiming that he had not received full payment for the lumber he had sold, de Villamay sued Duclos in the municipal government on December 14, 1735, for the sum of 514 livres.[141]

Rather than appearing before the municipal government and contesting the claim, Duclos summoned de Villamay before the Parisian Merchant Court on December 17, 1735. There he sought an order to the effect that the municipal government lacked jurisdiction over the suit, since "for lumber sold between merchants, and promissory notes endorsed between merchants, one can be summoned only to the merchant court, which has exclusive jurisdiction over such disputes."[142] In addition, Duclos requested that the merchant court enter judgment in his favor.

On December 19, 1735, the merchant court issued an order stating that it had exclusive jurisdiction over the lawsuit. The next day the municipal government responded by declaring Duclos' summons of December 17 unlawful, thus rendering invalid the merchant court's ensuing order of December 19. The government then entered an order stating that it had exclusive jurisdiction over the parties' lawsuit.[143]

On December 29, 1735, de Villamay again summoned Duclos to appear before the municipal government, and he again failed to appear. Accordingly, the government entered a default judgment against Duclos on January 11, 1736, ordering him to pay 514 livres for the lumber. Duclos then appealed this judgment, as well as the government's order of December 20, to the *Parlement* of Paris.[144] Around the same time, both the Parisian Merchant Court and the municipal government intervened in the lawsuit as interested parties. Thereafter, the individual litigants themselves largely disappeared from the conflict, which was instead continued by the two courts and the merchant guilds supporting them.

On January 17, 1736, the *Parlement* ordered a stay of all proceedings—including a stay in execution of the various judgments entered—pending its resolution of the jurisdictional question raised.[145] Several years later, on March 7, 1738, the *Parlement* finally issued its decision, ruling in favor of de

Villamay and thus upholding the jurisdiction of the municipal government.[146] More than a decade later, on March 10, 1751, the *Parlement* (under circumstances that are, unfortunately, unclear) reaffirmed its holding that the jurisdiction of the municipal government extended "even to [disputes over] bills of exchange whose cause is sales of merchandise."[147]

Disappointed by these rulings, the Parisian Merchant Court appealed to the King's Council to quash the *Parlement*'s decrees. The council responded on December 18, 1758, by entering an order stating that it intended to issue a ruling that would definitively resolve the jurisdictional conflict between the Parisian Merchant Court and the municipal government.[148] The council further directed each court to submit legal briefs setting forth its jurisdictional arguments. This directive led to a new flurry of published briefs, issued not only by the two courts but also by their respective merchant supporters. The *six corps de Paris,* the wine sellers, the printers, and the bankers all submitted briefs on behalf of the Parisian Merchant Court, while the associated merchants of the river and ports and the drivers of horse-drawn barges submitted briefs on behalf of the municipal government. These briefs continued to be published through 1767, about a decade after the council's initial order, but it does not appear that the council ever issued its promised jurisdictional ruling. Indeed, a litigation manual for merchants published in 1786 by Masson, a former judge of the Parisian Merchant Court, discusses de Villamay's lawsuit at length, but makes no mention of any ruling by the King's Council.[149]

As suggested by the large number of appeals and briefs filed, by the many merchant associations that chose to intervene, and by the extremely long duration of the litigation, the jurisdictional dispute between the Parisian Merchant Court and the municipal government was one of great importance to Old Regime merchants and jurists.[150] And it was particularly important to the Parisian Merchant Court. During the thirty or so years that de Villamay's lawsuit continued, the court published a series of legal briefs in which it constructed a comprehensive account of the legitimacy and utility of its jurisdictional demands — an account which it was thereafter unwilling to abandon.[151] This account was based on a new conception of commerce as private exchange, which paralleled to a remarkable extent that being developed elsewhere by the Physiocrats and by royal ministers interested in promoting administrative reform. But for the merchant court, unlike these elites, the conception of commerce as a self-regulating, beneficent social force was a tool to be deployed not in an effort to transform key social processes (including modes of production and taxation), but simply in an attempt to navigate the complex jurisdictional terrain of the Old Regime.

In arguing for jurisdiction vis-à-vis the municipal government, the Parisian

Merchant Court's key conceptual move was to distinguish between two categories that in the traditional logic of the Old Regime were integrally linked—namely, police and commerce. The longstanding conception of commerce as a public hazard implicitly called for policing, since it suggested that without proper regulation the individual pursuit of self-interest would lead to disastrous social consequences. Ignoring this traditional view, the Parisian Merchant Court advanced the radical claim that there was no necessary link between police and commerce—and that, indeed, the two categories were quite distinct.

Without fully theorizing the basis for this distinction, the court advanced several arguments, all of which hinged on the notion that, while police concerned matters of public welfare and regulation, commerce at its core depended on the credit supply, which in turn was governed largely by private decisions and conduct. From this perspective, commerce was not properly the subject of public law (either administrative or criminal), but was instead the subject of its own distinctive branch of private law—namely, private commercial law. Accordingly, private commercial disputes were appropriately judged not by the municipal government (a public regulatory institution) but instead by the Parisian Merchant Court (an institution akin to a private association of lay merchants functioning as the merchant litigants' peers).[152]

The first step in the merchant court's argument was to characterize the municipal government as a public regulatory institution, and thus one suited to focus exclusively on police matters. In this vein, the court argued that the "efforts of the municipal government" were appropriately directed at "that which is called *administration,*" which included such matters as "ceremonies, public buildings, bridges, festivals, management of public property, inspection of the fountains and aqueducts, collection of the poll tax, [and] lotteries."[153] The municipal government's police authority to ensure the proper provisioning of Paris was thus but one component of its broader administrative or police powers. But while the government's police powers were broad, these were its only powers. Indeed, according to the merchant court, the edict of June 1700, which sought to resolve the jurisdictional conflict that had arisen between the municipal government and the lieutenant general of police, confirmed that "it is solely policing . . . that is shared between the municipal government and the lieutenant general of police, who himself does not claim any jurisdiction other than that of *police.*"[154]

As concerns such police matters, the Parisian Merchant Court magnanimously observed that it in no way sought to interfere with the municipal government's authority: "Nothing prevents the municipal government from guaranteeing the quantity of basic commodities that must arrive by water;

from undertaking on-site investigations toward that end; from protecting navigation; from overseeing the arrival [of goods]; from inspecting the quality and nature of merchandise; from curbing the regulatory violations, theft, [and] violence that can be committed; from taking note of the greater or lesser quantity of merchandise; even from regulating prices; in a word, from embracing all that the administration of the police requires of the vigilance of municipal officers."[155] Indeed, the court assured the municipal government that it always did everything possible to preserve the latter's police authority. Thus, "where there appears before . . . [the merchant court judges] a dispute for the price of merchandise delivered to the ports, and the buyer who has the merchandise in his store complains about the price, weight, or poor quality that the seller had the shrewdness to conceal from him, the merchant court judges send the parties before the officers [of the police] and do not pronounce judgment."[156] If these officers discover that police regulations were, in fact, violated, they inform the relevant judges, whether of the municipal government or of the *Châtelet,* and these judges in turn "take great care to punish the violators."[157] In this way, "the order of the police is always maintained and conserved."[158]

Having thus confirmed the municipal government's police powers, the Parisian Merchant Court sought to demarcate these from the authority to adjudicate disputes among merchants for payment of goods transported into Paris by water. In order to do so, the court relied on the legal doctrine of contract novation, which provides that, under certain circumstances, parties to a contract may replace an existing contractual obligation with a new one. The court observed, in particular, that as a result of the growing prominence of negotiable instruments, most sales transactions—including for goods transported into Paris by water—were consummated by means of such instruments. But when a buyer purchased goods by drafting or endorsing a negotiable instrument, claimed the merchant court, the initial contractual obligation of the buyer to pay for goods received was extinguished. The seller, by accepting the negotiable instrument, agreed to a contractual novation, such that the original obligation to pay for goods received was replaced by a new credit obligation. This new credit obligation established that the buyer would repay the credit extended by the seller (and embodied in the negotiable instrument).[159] As the court explained, "every transaction is consummated by the delivery of merchandise; payment is deemed to have been made upon delivery; and if the seller accords a delay for payment, whether he takes . . . a promissory note or bill of exchange from the buyer, this is a new transaction, totally separate and independent from the first; in a word, there is a novation."[160]

According to the Parisian Merchant Court, the municipal government had a legitimate police interest in the initial contractual obligation to pay for goods received, but it had no such interest in the substituted credit obligation. In its words, "the municipal government cannot adjudicate a lawsuit for payment of the merchandise, given the novation that the extension of credit renders in any transaction."[161] The merchant court's reasoning was that the initial obligation to pay for goods received directly implicated the provisioning of Paris, as it was in exchange for such payment that sellers were willing to bring goods into the city. Accordingly, this initial obligation came within the municipal government's broad police authority to monitor such matters as quantity, quality, and price. But the second obligation was "alien to the provisioning of Paris, as well as to the policing of the rivers and their ports."[162] This second obligation concerned the extension of credit among merchants, *after* the goods had already arrived. As such, "this is a matter that concerns credit between merchants [and] commerce in general, as procured through bills of exchange or promissory notes, and the chain of their endorsements; in short, this is a matter purely for the merchant court."[163]

In thus claiming that the policing of payment for goods sold was distinct from the adjudication of disputes arising over credit obligations, the Parisian Merchant Court never denied that credit obligations had a bearing on the public welfare, including the provisioning of Paris. Indeed, to the contrary, the court insisted that they did. It was through private credit transactions that merchants were able to fund their endeavors and thereby ensure the production and supply of all kinds of goods. But crucially, the court argued, the conditions necessary to ensure that sales promote public welfare and those necessary to ensure that credit transactions promote public welfare were very different.

To ensure that sales promote public welfare (including the provisioning of Paris), it was necessary to guarantee the supply of a certain quantity and quality of appropriately priced goods, and this, in turn, required regulatory oversight in the form of policing. In contrast, to ensure that credit transactions promote public welfare (including the provisioning of Paris), it was necessary to expand the credit supply. This, in turn, did not require policing, but instead, a form of benign neglect, whereby merchants remained free to structure their credit transactions as they so chose, with the appropriate governmental authority stepping in simply to enforce the agreed-upon transaction in a rapid and inexpensive fashion. As the merchant court observed: "[The provisioning of Paris requires] at all times, in all seasons, that the *marchand forain* or the holder of a bill of exchange be assured of finding . . . at all hours, a [forum of] justice that is exact and free, a prompt and easy execution [of obligations] that ensures him the time and freedom necessary to conduct his commerce and that renders him capable of immediately attending to other matters, to new enterprises."[164] Only to the extent that merchants were assured an easy and effective means of enforcing credit obligations would they be willing to extend credit, thus ensuring that the credit supply would continue to flow to the benefit of all.

According to the Parisian Merchant Court, the fact that quick and secure debt enforcement was key to maintaining the credit supply meant that the municipal government must not be permitted to adjudicate disputes concerning credit obligations. This was, first, because, in contrast to the summary form of procedure applied by the merchant court, the municipal government used traditional civil procedure, which added significantly to the length and cost of litigation. To the extent that merchants became concerned that, as a result of such procedure, debt enforcement would prove too expensive and troublesome, they would be dissuaded from extending credit: "If . . . the bill of exchange that has as its cause *goods delivered to the ports* is subject to all the slowness of the ordinary judicial process and does not benefit from the advantages that other negotiable instruments receive in the institution of the merchant court, this paper will be devalued; people will not want to accept it anymore; bankers will refuse it; slowness and inaction will be introduced into an essential sector; the provisioning of the capital, which attracts with reason all the attention of the government and of high-level magistrates, will be the first to suffer from this disgrace."[165]

Perhaps more importantly, the Parisian Merchant Court argued, another problem with the municipal government was that its officers were incapable of understanding the fundamental importance of rapid and secure debt enforcement. Because the government focused on the policing of certain "things of primary necessity, such as wheat, wine, lumber, [and] coal,"[166] its officers failed to recognize that commerce was at a fundamental level universal, in that all commercial transactions—regardless of whether these concerned basic necessities or luxury items—hinged on the availability of credit. To ensure such a ready supply of credit, asserted the merchant court, what was needed was an institutional framework that would guarantee the quick and easy enforcement of *all* credit obligations. Accordingly, the merchant court observed, "We agree with the officers of the municipal government that to maintain abundance in the city, it is useful to ensure payment of the merchant who conveys merchandise," but "this guarantee is necessary [both] for those who convey luxury goods" and "for those who furnish items of primary necessity."[167] Since the municipal government traditionally concerned itself only with items of primary necessity, it failed to recognize this fundamental truth about the universal importance of credit.

A sad irony of the municipal government's limitations, suggested the Parisian Merchant Court, was that, in seeking to adjudicate disputes regarding credit obligations, the government actually worked to hinder the effective provisioning of Paris—its supposed aim and mission. As the merchant court explained, "Everything shows that the municipal government acts directly against the goal that it should care about most, that is, the provisioning of Paris, because this provisioning requires that the payment of merchandise be done promptly, without formalities, without charges."[168] Public welfare would suffer not only because the municipal government lacked the capacity properly to enforce credit obligations, but also because in focusing its attention on such obligations it would be distracted from its core policing duties: "If it is burdened further with the adjudication of commerce that it demands, it will be impossible for it to reconcile so many different tasks, and it will be necessary that it abandon one, in order to pursue the other."[169] Moreover, to the extent that the municipal government's unjustified jurisdictional demands were honored, this would lead to a "jurisdictional competition" that would in itself "inflict a mortal blow to commerce" by contributing to merchants' anxiety that they would be unable to enforce their debts.[170] The result would be the total destruction of the credit market: "The merchant will hesitate to sell on credit to other merchants; no one will want anymore to give cash in exchange for a promissory note or a bill of exchange; trade in bills of exchange and promissory notes will become disquieting and impracticable; all circulation will soon be interrupted."[171]

Not surprisingly, the Parisian Merchant Court concluded that it itself was the institution best suited to resolve disputes concerning credit obligations. In thus arguing, the court relied in part on the Commercial Ordinance of March 1673, which (per its interpretation) endowed merchant courts with exclusive jurisdiction over (1) disputes concerning negotiable instruments and (2) those concerning "sales made to merchants, artisans, and tradesmen so that they might resell or work in their profession," such as sales of wheat (to bakers) and lumber (to carpenters). Both wheat and lumber, observed the merchant court, among other items listed in this second jurisdictional provision, were frequently sold at the ports.[172]

But while emphasizing its formal legal entitlement to jurisdiction, the Parisian Merchant Court argued even more emphatically on the grounds of utility. Drawing on an unabashedly utilitarian language and logic that ought to give pause to those who presume that the French legal system has always placed (and continues to place) form above function, the court intoned: "If . . . it is a question of deciding on the basis of each institution's legal entitlement or current practice, it is clear that the balance tips in favor of the merchant court;

but it is [mainly] a question of determining in which jurisdiction it is useful for commerce that the disputes over these sorts of obligations be brought; that is the only thing that there is to discuss at this moment."[173] The court claimed that it was functionally superior to the municipal government because it employed a mode of summary procedure that enabled the fast and cheap resolution of disputes: "The merchant court is unique in the speed with which it administers justice. Its summonses require that the defendant appear the next day, and often that very evening; no appeals are allowed of sentences up to 500 livres; above 500 livres, and up to whatever amount sentences may extend, the appeal does not suspend execution of the judgment; and these prerogatives were accorded to the merchant court only for the purpose of favoring credit and facilitating trade in bills of exchange and promissory notes."[174] As the merchant court observed, by way of rhetorical question, these distinctive procedural advantages served to facilitate the circulation of credit: "Who decides to sell merchandise on credit and to take paper on the spot, if not with the guarantee of being fully paid when the paper falls due, or of receiving immediately a sentence from the merchant court condemning the debtor, regardless of all the privileges that the debtor might assert?"[175]

According, however, to the Parisian Merchant Court, the main reason why it was a superior forum in which to adjudicate disputes over credit transactions—and, indeed, the reason why it employed a more streamlined procedure—was its essentially private status. Whereas the municipal government was an institution endowed with public, police authority, the merchant court was little more than a private association of lay merchants concerned with resolving their own disputes. In thus arguing, the merchant court sought to deploy in its favor a conception of its jurisdictional status that, in other contexts, it vociferously disputed—namely, that it lacked the powers and prerogatives typically associated with royal courts, including most importantly, criminal jurisdiction.[176] This minimalist conception of the merchant court's jurisdiction is captured by the words of the famous eighteenth-century jurist Denisart, who explained that the merchant court "has no jurisdiction over all that concerns the public order."[177] It was, in fact, this widely held view that merchant court jurisdiction extended to matters of interest exclusively to merchants that explains the absence in these courts of a kind of official typically posted in the ordinary royal courts—namely, the "gens du roi," who were responsible for representing the royal (and thus public) interest.[178]

Ordinarily, the Parisian Merchant Court categorically rejected the traditional, narrow conception of its jurisdiction. Indeed, Old Regime merchant courts frequently railed against the way their opponents in status disputes sought to deny them precedence by characterizing their officers as mere private merchants, rather than royal judges.[179] In the context of its jurisdictional dispute with the municipal government, however, the Parisian Merchant Court suddenly discovered that there was much to be gained from its status as a private association of merchants. As compared with the municipal government, it emphasized, its distinguishing feature lay precisely in the fact that its judges were mere lay merchants—and thus, admittedly, lower in status than the "distinguished magistrate" who served as the municipal government's head (*prévôt des marchands*) and the four "notable bourgeois" who served directly under him as aldermen (*échevins*).[180] It was precisely because the merchant court judges were mere lay merchants that they possessed the expertise necessary quickly and correctly to resolve disputes among merchants concerning credit transactions. They were, the merchant court explained, "honest merchants, chosen, then elected by the *corps* of commerce to judge disputes, who after a year in office return to the class of simple citizens," and who were "more knowledgeable than others as a result of their experience."[181]

While seeking to defend and extend its jurisdiction on the basis of a new conception of commerce as free, private exchange, the Parisian Merchant Court and its judges never demanded an end to police regulation. Indeed, given these judges' positions as the leading members of Paris's leading guilds, it would have been quite surprising if they had. From the perspective of the individuals who served as merchant court judges, the arguments that they made in the context of the court's jurisdictional dispute with the municipal government had no bearing on their dealings as guild leaders with the royal police and with competing non-guild merchants. But while these individuals understood themselves to be operating in distinct institutional contexts, the municipal government was quick to recognize that the boundary between these contexts might prove permeable—and that, should this be the case, the merchant court's new conception of commerce had potentially radical implications.

According to the municipal government, the merchant court's efforts to distinguish between police and commerce necessarily implied a rejection of the traditional conception of commerce as a public hazard. Indeed, the merchant court, it seemed, was joining its voice to that of the Physiocrats, who beginning in the late 1750s appeared to be successfully propagating the new (and in the municipal government's view, dangerous) gospel that, given free rein, self-interest would somehow redound to the public good:[182] "If one should believe the ill-considered discourse of a certain public, the provisioning of Paris results from a necessary commerce and from the reciprocal needs of the capital and the provinces that surround it. The consumption of the capital is immense; farmers rush to exchange their products for the wealth that abounds in this city; the respective interest of each sustains this trade, independent of the magistrates, and without their efforts, one will always see in this capital an abundance of all that not only satisfies daily needs, but also that fosters luxury and the progress of the arts."[183] In the view of the municipal government, this notion that commerce was a natural, self-sustaining process was utterly foolish. Left to their own devices, self-interested individuals would attempt to satisfy their own needs and desires at the expense of all others. Accordingly, the municipal government announced, "It is time to lift the veil, to dispel a prejudice that is too widespread in a vulgar world, to prove that this same interest that is presented as the sole force behind the abundance of Paris will cause it the greatest calamity, if it is not subordinated to an administration that enlightens it always, encourages it sometimes, and represses it most of the time."[184]

As characterized by the municipal government, commerce was what it had long been in the Old Regime—a public hazard to be carefully regulated and contained. Failure to police commerce would result in merchants serving their own greed at the expense of the hapless consumer, such that Parisians—deprived of basic necessities or forced to procure them at exorbitant prices—would suffer to the point of running riot: "Nothing is more dangerous than abandoning the fate of the provisioning of this capital solely to the will of the traders whose attention to their personal interest is almost always contrary to the public interest; they enrich themselves during times of scarcity; they earn little during times of abundance."[185] Moreover, the municipal government observed, common sense suggested that, to the extent that Paris's population had grown in recent times—thus augmenting its needs—police regulation had become that much more crucial: "Through the passage of several centuries, the size and needs of the capital have grown in an immense progression such that there hardly remains the smallest trace of its former state; should we not today, if it is possible, multiply rather than reduce all the means . . . of ensuring the subsistence of its inhabitants, which becomes more difficult every day?"[186]

In rejecting the notion that commerce was a self-regulating process that naturally promoted the social good, the municipal government methodically attacked each component of the merchant court's argument—beginning with the claim that commerce is universal, in that all commercial transactions hinge on the credit supply. Commerce, the municipal government insisted, was not a single, universal process, but instead, multiple, different processes, each concerned with the production, distribution, and sale of a particular item. Because each item was unique, each required its own distinctive rules and regulations, whose formulation and enforcement constituted the art and science of police: "The range of commodities that contribute to this important goal [of provisioning Paris] requires, for each one, a particular vigilance and methods that cannot be usefully applied to the others; each one is, in effect, subject to its own laws and to the regulations that experience has necessitated."[187] Thus, for example, the policing of wheat entailed rules that "foresaw both natural and greed-driven manipulations" by "fixing the time and place of sales; . . . forbid[ding] certain persons from buying wheat . . . , merchants from associating, selling wheat en route, and raising its price."[188] Likewise, all "the other branches of the provisioning [of Paris]," including wine, lumber, and coal, each had its own distinctive police rules designed to address the natural and man-made hazards to which that particular type of commerce was susceptible.[189]

Along similar lines, the municipal government rejected the merchant court's effort to identify buyers' credit obligations as distinct from their obligations to pay for goods sold—and thus, removed from the framework of police regulation. It was absurd, the municipal government insisted, to suggest that "by converting into bills of exchange the debt that results from this delivery [of merchandise into Paris], there results a novation of the claim" and that "this second matter is alien to the provisioning of Paris."[190] The notion that the credit transaction enabling the initial purchase of merchandise rendered a novation of the sales agreement was a legal fiction that ignored the reality of the parties' actions and intent. To the extent that the buyer endorsed a bill of exchange to the seller's order, this was simply as a means of purchasing the goods provided by the seller. In this respect, the bill of exchange was no different from cash, or from the book debt that was traditionally used to finance sales transactions: "The supposed novation should make even less of an impression, since usually the bill of exchange is the original means of contracting; that is, the seller takes it from the moment of delivery."[191]

Furthermore, the municipal government suggested, even if one accepted the ridiculous claim that "the original debt was somehow denatured by the bill of exchange drawn afterwards, this new title would not be any less subject than the first to the jurisdiction of the municipal government."[192] This was because, even if the credit obligation was entirely new and separate from the initial obligation to pay for goods, it was still a key part of the chain of obligations that ultimately resulted in the production, distribution, and sale of goods essential for the provisioning of Paris. And, the enforcement of the police regulations required that "the municipal government be ready to follow the thread of the negotiation relating to this goal [of provisioning Paris]."[193]

According to the municipal government, to permit the merchant court jurisdiction over all disputes concerning credit obligations—including those arising from sales of items of primary necessity arriving into Paris by water—was to deprive the municipal government of a key tool in its efforts to detect the violation of police regulations: "The vigilance of the laws and that of the municipal officers will both be eluded, if the claim of the merchant court judges meets with some success."[194] One of the primary ways that the municipal government learned of violations of police regulations, it explained, was through adjudicating disputes among merchants regarding payment for sales of goods. In its words, its officers required "an exact knowledge of the offences" committed, and "they usually obtain such knowledge only to the extent that it is incidental to the disputes that are brought before them for the enforcement of sales or other agreements that may have been undertaken by those who compete and participate in the provisioning [of Paris]."[195] Accordingly, these lawsuits were not mere private disputes. To the contrary, they directly implicated the core public concern of policing commerce and thereby provisioning Paris.

In the view of the municipal government, it was precisely because these disputes over payment for the sale of goods were of such great public importance that entrusting their adjudication to the merchant court — an institution that was little more than a private association of lay merchants — would prove disastrous. The municipal government, in other words, dismissed the merchant court's efforts to deploy in its favor the oft-observed fact that it lacked a broad-ranging, public-law jurisdiction. As explained by the municipal government, commerce in goods necessary for the provisioning of Paris was a public police matter, and accordingly the merchant court's essentially private status necessarily deprived it of jurisdiction over suits for payment of such goods. In this vein, the municipal government argued that "these judges [of the Parisian Merchant Court] . . . have neither prosecutorial power nor criminal jurisdiction."[196] And for precisely this reason, they "can only order the enforcement of agreements."[197] But what if the parties' private agreement was of a kind prohibited by the police regulations — because, for example, the price exceeded the legal maximum? To enforce the agreement would be counter to the public good. And even if the merchant court declined to enforce the agreement, it lacked the public, police authority necessary to punish the contracting parties for their violation of the law. As the municipal government observed, "legal prohibitions will be vainly asserted before . . . [the merchant court judges]; they do not have the necessary authority to inflict the penalties that they pronounce; violators will thus have a sure way of shirking the penalties."[198]

The municipal government, in short, recognized that, taken to its logical extreme, the Parisian Merchant Court's efforts to distinguish between commerce and police implied a rejection of the traditional, public-hazard conception of commerce. And while the municipal government failed to predict the fundamental restructuring of social and commercial relations that would follow from the Revolution's embrace of the merchant court's new conception of commerce, it did foresee that there were radical implications to what the court had proposed. The merchant court itself, however, had no radical or revolutionary intent. As was true of the electoral conflict in which it engaged, the court's primary goal in its conflict with the municipal government was simply to promote an interest that was itself fully consonant with the institutional structure of the corporatist social order—in this case, defending and extending its jurisdictional turf. The judges of the Parisian Merchant Court, in other words, did not understand themselves to be in any way threatening the guild-based monopolies from which they—in their capacity as the leaders of Paris's leading guilds—benefited enormously and which through to the end of the Old Regime they continued aggressively to defend. But, as it turned out, they were wrong. When combined with the transformations in commercial practice and royal administration detailed later in this book, the efforts of the merchant court judges to promote their guild-based interests ultimately backfired, and they ended up undermining the very privileges that they sought to defend.

2

The Court's Self-Conception as a Bastion of Virtue: Relational Contracting and a Community-Based Approach to Procedure

> *The Procedure that is employed in the merchant court is most simple; all subtleties of law and unnecessary writings are banished from there; one seeks there only to discover the good faith of one party and the bad faith or chicanery of the other.*
>
> —[Couchot], *Le praticien des juges et consuls*

As important as they were, electoral disputes and jurisdictional conflict were not the only factors behind the Parisian Merchant Court's reconceptualization of commerce. Over the course of the late seventeenth and eighteenth centuries, commercial practices themselves developed in such a way that it became increasingly difficult to view commerce as an activity that could and should be restricted to those, like guild members, who possessed the legal status of merchants. But before considering these new commercial practices—including, notably, the rise of negotiable instruments—it is necessary to explore the traditional practices with which they came to coexist.

Throughout the eighteenth century, the majority of the lawsuits brought before the court were small-scale contract disputes concerning, most commonly, the sale of goods and services, but also employment and marriage. As these disputes often arose among individuals who engaged in repeat transactions with one another and who sought to create and maintain a long-term business relationship, they represent a form of what modern legal and economic scholars have termed relational contracting.[1] Even as new commercial practices emerged, these disputes regarding small-scale, highly relational contracts continued to appear before the court. Indeed, absent knowledge of the dates that such lawsuits were filed, it would likely be impossible to distinguish between those brought at the beginning and those at the end of the century.

The contract relations underlying these disputes were the foundation of traditional commercial practice and the bedrock upon which the court itself was based. Indeed, the court's adjudicatory methods—in particular, the various procedural mechanisms on which it relied—were premised on the assumption that the court's primary purpose was to resolve this kind of contract dispute by helping to resuscitate and strengthen the relationship between the parties. In this way, the relational contracting that characterized traditional commercial practice contributed to the emergence—and reinforcement—of the court's longstanding self-conception as an entity designed to promote virtue by restoring severed bonds of trust among merchant brothers.

Community, Reputation, and Book Debt

The world of commerce in Old Regime Paris was traditionally a highly personal one. Almost all commercial transactions were undertaken on the basis of credit. And credit—in particular, the relatively short-term credit that was key to commercial survival—was impossible to obtain without personal connections. Friends, family, and associates of one kind or another often advanced funds. They also provided information about potential debtors that was useful in determining whether the latter were creditworthy. Moreover, it was through such personal relationships that merchants developed the social status and reputation for moral probity that ensured potential creditors of their reliability.

A recent study has shown that there was a far more anonymous credit market at work in eighteenth-century Paris than was previously suspected. As the authors of this study were careful to emphasize, however, this was a market for long-term debt in the form of annuities (or *rentes*) brokered by notaries—and, thus, quite distinct from the short-term credit market on which commerce depended.[2] The short-term credit that fueled eighteenth-century commercial exchange arose not in the form of annuities, but instead through book debt, and increasingly as the century progressed, through negotiable instruments. The changes wrought by the increased use of negotiable instruments are discussed in a later chapter. For now, it is necessary to begin by exploring the highly personal world of the book-debt system, which even after the rise of negotiable instruments, remained an important source of credit, and in smaller-scale commercial activity, perhaps the primary one.

Book debt enabled the extension of credit for any number of purposes. Wholesalers granted credit to retailers in order to encourage the latter to purchase goods. Artisans who required primary materials or tools bought these on credit from suppliers. Merchants, whether engaged in the same or different trades, bought and sold goods to one another on credit when they found themselves in short supply. And both merchants and artisans often sold goods to consumers on credit and paid journeymen by means of credit.[3]

A book debt typically arose when buyer and seller made an oral agreement for the sale and delivery of goods, which they would then record in their respective accounting books. Typically, the buyer would pay the debt in installments, while at the same time purchasing additional goods on credit from the seller. Thus, the buyer's debt, while continuously amortized, was never paid in full.[4] Alternatively, if buyer and seller reciprocally bought and sold from one another, a purchase made by one would compensate for a purchase made by the other. Unless the goods were of identical value, however, one of the parties would always remain in debt to the other.[5] In either case, the buyer and seller would meet together periodically to do an accounting, creating a list of the goods sold and payments made, which both parties would then sign. At this meeting, the parties would usually also agree that the buyer was to pay a portion of the debt at a specified time. Generally, these accountings would occur not at predetermined, regular intervals, but every so often, when the parties decided it was timely and convenient. For example, if the buyer and seller were from different cities, a trip by one to the hometown of the other might serve as an occasion for doing an accounting.[6] When payments were made, they were generally in the form of either cash or promissory notes—with the latter serving to extend further the credit already granted.

The merchant-artisans who undertook purchases and sales in this manner focused their attention not so much on the individual transaction—on obtaining the best possible deal in the short term—but on building a long-lasting relationship with their contractual counterparts that would be to their mutual advantage over the long term.[7] Such relational contracting, common also among some modern-day commercial players, was particularly well suited to the economy of the Old Regime, which was plagued by the problem of unpredictable demand. Due largely to technological limitations on the availability and flow of information, men and women involved in commercial activity in eighteenth-century Paris had difficulty predicting how much of any given product they would be able to sell. Because demand was usually uncertain, and because economies of scale were far less significant in a preindustrial era, most merchant-artisans produced and sold goods that they made or obtained to order. Since production and sales were geared toward the short term[8]—toward requests that could be made at any moment—merchant-artisans needed to ensure that they would be able to obtain necessary inputs immediately upon demand. In a world in which the sellers of these inputs, like the buyers, were unlikely to have large stocks of generic goods on hand, this was no small problem. Moreover, since, as Michael Sonenscher has argued, goods were often produced to order through a complex network of subcontracting,[9] the problem of unpredictable demand could have particularly severe repercussions for the many who were linked together in such networks.

The solution found by eighteenth-century merchant-artisans was to build long-lasting relationships with their suppliers in the hope that the latter would come to their aid when necessary. The book-debt system, described above, facilitated the creation of such relationships by giving both buyer and supplier a personal interest in ensuring one another's success. The supplier, because he was owed money by the buyer, was that much more likely to supply the various inputs that the buyer required in order to make sales (and thereby become able to pay debts).[10] At the same time, the supplier could use the fact that a buyer was in his debt as a means of convincing the buyer to seek certain necessary inputs from that supplier. In particular, the supplier could promise to grant moratoria on repayment and/or additional extensions of credit in return for the buyer making further purchases. In this way, the book-debt system promoted long-term relationships between buyer and supplier, which were to the advantage of both in their efforts to deal with the chronic problem of unpredictable demand.

Such long-term relationships also proved valuable in addressing another recurrent problem in eighteenth-century commercial life—the difficulty of obtaining timely and accurate information regarding the reliability and creditworthiness of particular individuals. In a world without the vast informational infrastructure to which we today have become accustomed, search costs were very high. A buyer seeking a supplier who could provide the kind, quality, and number of goods that he sought—and who could be trusted to honor obligations—had to rely almost entirely on word of mouth. Similarly, a supplier seeking financially sound and reliable buyers also depended on gossip within the community. Finding the right people could thus be quite expensive for both buyers and suppliers. By developing long-term relationships with one another, buyers and suppliers minimized their need to search for new trading partners and thereby reduced search costs. Moreover, a long-term buyer-seller relationship was itself a source of valuable information about other merchants. Since the parties to such a relationship trusted one another and had a vested interest in each other's success, they were that much more likely to share vital information.

A key feature of the book-debt system was that individual transactions frequently took the form of oral agreements, with the parties committing these to writing only in their respective accounting books and in their periodic accountings. Although the merchant court regularly enforced such oral agreements, the civil law applicable in the ordinary, non-merchant courts required contracts to be made in writing. Indeed, the civil law prohibited the enforcement of oral agreements by disallowing the use of any evidence other than a writing to prove the existence of a contract. The common commercial practice of enforcing oral agreements was thus highly exceptional within the Old Regime legal system. It was, however, validated by the Procedure Ordinance of 1667, which specified that the civil-law rules mandating written contracts were not to apply within the merchant courts.[11]

The prevalence of oral agreements among Old Regime merchants makes good sense, given the logic of the book-debt system and, in particular, its focus on promoting long-term relationships. Since parties to such relationships expended a great deal of time and effort in their establishment, they had little reason to jeopardize them by shirking and thereby seeking one-sided, short-term gain. That there was little incentive to shirk suggests, in turn, that there was little reason to conform to the traditional civil-law requirements of contract formation, and in particular, the requirement of a writing. In fact, insistence on a writing might indicate a mistrustfulness corrosive to the goal of establishing a long-term, trusting relationship. Thus, Jean Toubeau, a prominent commercial jurist and former merchant court judge, wrote at the end of the seventeenth century that notaries—one of whose primary tasks was to witness and record the formation of written contracts—were necessary solely because of "infidelity." As Toubeau observed, "Writings . . . would still be useless, if merchants made it a point of religion to keep their word, as they must."[12] Likewise, Guyot, a noted jurist and author of a legal dictionary, explained in the late eighteenth century that merchant courts, unlike others, were willing to enforce oral contracts because "the danger of a few particular acts of fraud is preferred to that of destroying good faith and the ease of transacting by demanding too many precautions."[13]

The book-debt system did not, however, eschew writings entirely. The buyer and seller recorded transactions in their respective accounting books and did periodic accountings together. These written accountings were a means of agreeing on payments that were in the interest of both parties. Because such accountings were undertaken after the relationship was already formed, they were less disruptive than written contracts, which were often entered before a relationship was established. This is not to suggest, of course, that the process of undertaking written accountings was somehow immune from strife. Indeed, many of the disputes that came before the Parisian Merchant Court concerned such accountings. However, the use of oral agreements and written accountings enabled a flexibility that promoted amicable relations.

If intervening circumstances so required, a buyer and seller who made an oral agreement could more easily renegotiate the contract terms than if—as encouraged by the civil law applied by the ordinary, non-merchant courts—the contract took the form of a notarized writing. As discussed below, the civil law deemed notarized writings "full proof," thus all but ensuring their enforcement. To renegotiate the terms of such a contract was, however, relatively difficult, since this required the parties not only to rewrite the contract but also to have this new document signed, sealed, and filed by the notary. Merchants had relatively little incentive to incur these added costs associated with notarized, written contracts because they generally viewed litigation as a last resort—and because, in any event, the merchant court, unlike the ordinary courts, did not adhere to the Civil Law's strict Roman-canon rules of proof.

In the view of many merchants, oral agreements were preferable because they permitted renegotiation with relative ease. This renegotiation would then be reflected in subsequent accountings. Since both buyer and seller were subject to significant uncertainty, such flexibility was of great value to each. For example, if the seller was unable to deliver in a timely manner, or failed to deliver exactly what he had promised, the parties could easily renegotiate the price. Similarly, if the buyer proved unable to pay the amount on which he and the seller had initially agreed, the parties could negotiate a lower price or a longer payment schedule. And if the buyer discovered that he needed goods that differed in quantity and/or quality from those in the original agreement, the seller could deliver in accordance with the buyer's needs without the parties having to undertake a formal novation of contract. Indeed, the parties could even defer renegotiation of the price until they did an accounting together.

Although the book-debt system was shaped by concerns about building long-term commercial relationships that are shared by many merchants today,[14] it was particularly well suited to the highly interdependent social structure of the Old Regime.[15] In eighteenth-century Paris, most merchant-artisans were reminded daily of the extent to which they relied on one another through their participation in an active communal life grounded in a set of interlocking institutions. As we have seen, guilds and confraternities actively sought to inculcate merchants with a sense of fraternal loyalty and obligation to one another. Similarly, family, neighborhood, and parish church all served to reinforce interdependence.

Eighteenth-century French commercial life was rooted within a network of familial relationships. Indeed, such relationships could play a decisive role in a merchant's success (or failure). At the very beginning of his career, a young man generally obtained an apprenticeship through the assistance of his father, who in turn relied on relatives, friends, and neighbors to help find an appropriate placement.[16] Often, such placements involved a betrothal. The agreement to take in and teach the apprentice would include a promise that the young man would marry the daughter of his master as soon as his training was complete.[17] Thus, when the young man was prepared to begin his own business, he would be able to use the money he received from his new wife as a dowry.[18] In addition, his own parents typically supplied him with some capital.[19]

Once the young artisan-merchant became established, family ties would remain important, providing useful connections to other merchants, artisans, and customers.[20] Indeed, an individual's reputation depended not only on his own actions and achievements but on the reputation of his family as well. To be associated with a family of good standing was a great boon, and likewise any connection to a family of ill repute could prove disastrous.[21] Thus, for example, many within the small elite of *anciens* who served as guild leaders were related to one another through kinship and marriage—at least until the final decades of the Old Regime, when Turgot's brief abolition of the guilds in 1776 led to a restructuring of electoral procedures.[22]

The importance of personal relationships in commercial activity was further bolstered by neighborhood life. Many trades were concentrated within particular areas of the city, such that people who associated with one another through guild, confraternity, and family also lived in close physical proximity.[23] Such proximity was reinforced by the fact that the typical artisan-merchant lived and worked in the same apartment, using one room which faced the street as a store, another room as a workshop and a back room as living quarters.[24] In addition to encountering one another on the streets near their homes, male artisan-merchants were likely to see each other on a regular basis in such local establishments as the café and wineshop. Men often had lunch in the neighborhood wineshop on a daily basis, where they would exchange gossip and transact business in the presence of their colleagues, relatives, friends, and neighbors. For this reason, police regularly went to wineshops during times of crisis to listen to conversations and thereby learn what people were thinking.[25] While male artisan-merchants encountered one another in these ways, their wives usually met and shared gossip in the neighborhood stores.[26]

The parish church also played an important role in forging personal ties among Old Regime Parisian merchants. The lay administrators of Paris's parish churches, known as *marguilliers,* were often related to one another and belonged to highly respected families. These *marguilliers* ranged from noblemen to master artisans, depending on the status of the parish's inhabitants, but included many members of the *six corps de Paris* — the most esteemed of all the guilds and the power base of the Parisian Merchant Court.[27] And since many merchant confraternities were located within parish churches, such proximity provided further opportunities for guild and church leaders to interact.

The personal relationships underlying so much commercial activity in eighteenth-century Paris could lead to either great success or great failure. As described above, such relationships provided a vital source of capital and of information, and those with a good reputation reaped great benefits. Indeed, to some extent, success in navigating the complex hierarchy of Paris's interlocking communal institutions served in itself as evidence of an individual's moral probity, and thus of his creditworthiness. For example, as one plaintiff explained in a trial brief submitted to the Parisian Merchant Court, she was well aware that it seemed preposterous to charge the defendant with bad faith, since he served as a *garde* in his guild and as a *marguillier* in his parish church: "The widow Prud'homme is aware . . . that M. Aubin must be an honest man, that the offices of *garde* of [his] guild and *marguillier* of his parish with which he is honored bespeak his probity, [and] that he must therefore not have deceived."[28] To argue, as the plaintiff did, that the defendant was one of those rare individuals whose social status had no bearing on his moral worth was thus an uphill battle.

But while the merchant-artisan's dependence on a network of personal relationships could prove highly advantageous, it also made him tremendously vulnerable. In this world of interlocking social institutions, news spread rapidly, such that a person's reputation in one sphere was not confined to that sphere alone. A dispute with a neighbor, for example, could so destroy a merchant-artisan's reputation that both he and his family members would be shunned not only in their neighborhood but also in their guild, confraternity, and parish church.

Because of the vital importance of reputation for commercial success, eighteenth-century merchants and artisans were ever vigilant to cultivate and maintain their reputations, as well as those of the individuals with whom they were associated through bonds of family and friendship. Accordingly, as David Garrioch describes, many disputes over matters of honor arose among merchant-artisans in eighteenth-century Paris. Arguments over business matters sometimes escalated into public confrontation during which each party hurled insults at the other in an effort to destroy his or her opponent's reputation. These insults often consisted of claims that the person had conducted business immorally — for example, by engaging in fraud or being on the verge of bankruptcy.[29] Friends and neighbors frequently intervened, seeking to reconcile the disputants.[30] If neither party backed down, however, such public disputes might be followed by complaints to parish priests or to the royal police and demands that the aggressor retract his insults — and even that he pay damages. And if despite the mediation thus provided by priests and/or police the parties remained unable to settle their differences, they often decided to litigate.[31] Matters of honor and reputation, in short, were for most Old Regime merchants very serious business.

As concerns the many small, rural villages on the outskirts of Paris, less is known, unfortunately, than about Paris itself. It is clear, however, that the importance of personal relationships in commercial endeavors was, if anything, magnified in these tiny communities where it was that much more likely that people would have occasion to know one another and interact on a regular basis. Whether in Paris itself or in the surrounding countryside, traditional commercial practice, as epitomized by the book-debt system, presupposed a community life structured on the basis of interlocking institutions and governed by reputation.

Procedure and the Problem of Enforcement

As a formal matter, the Civil Procedure Ordinance of 1667 established the procedural rules to be applied by the French merchant courts. The ordinance's provisions in this regard were, however, extremely cursory, serving only to bolster such fundamental precepts as the requirement that the judge and consuls receive no fees[32] and the rule (so often ignored in practice) that the parties appear and represent themselves.[33] It was the Parisian Merchant Court itself, in the process of deciding actual cases, which seems to have developed much of its own procedure — though in doing so it clearly drew on elements of the Roman-canon tradition.

In developing procedure, the court sought to draw on the web of interlocking institutions and community ties underlying commercial activity in the Old Regime. As evidenced by a wide variety of its procedures, including especially arbitration, the court's reliance on communal ties served several purposes. In the Continental legal tradition, unlike that of the Anglo-American common law, courts themselves bore significant responsibility for investigating the facts relevant to the litigants' dispute.[34] But in a time when the administrative might of the state was far weaker than it is today, such investigatory work was particularly difficult and costly. For the Parisian Merchant Court, the solution to this problem was to rely on members of the merchant community — people who either had personal knowledge of the facts or at least knew where to look for them. As explained in a treatise on commercial litigation published in 1742, "the merchant courts . . . distinguish better than others between the man of good faith and he who wants to deceive," and this is because "one . . . knows [in these courts] most of the *négociants,* and if one does not know them, one finds out about them."[35]

Along similar lines, the fact that the power of the early-modern state was so limited meant that enforcement of court judgments posed a serious difficulty. By utilizing procedures that drew on community networks, however, the merchant court was able to minimize its need for costly, formal mechanisms of enforcement. Instead, it relied on the fact that, given the interlocking structure of the merchant community, there were significant reputation costs for those who failed to abide by the court's judgments, and thus significant incentives for self-enforcement.

Those granted judgment by the Parisian Merchant Court did have access to a number of formal enforcement mechanisms, but these were very limited in power and scope. Because the court was traditionally conceived as an extension of the merchant community, rather than a true royal court, it was deemed to lack jurisdiction over matters concerning the public order. In line with this view, the court had barely any enforcement personnel of its own. Although the court employed four bailiffs, or *huissiers,* their powers were very limited. They helped keep order in the courtroom[36] and served process—though in most cases plaintiffs had the option to pay for a process-server of their choice, and thus were not constrained to use those of the merchant court.[37] Victorious plaintiffs seeking to execute judgment by seizing defendants' property or by sending them to debtors' prison were long required to employ *huissiers* or *sergents* associated with the royal police located in the *Châtelet.*[38] In the late eighteenth century, however, the monarchy concluded that those chosen to execute judgment against debtors were often, in practice, mere thugs, who engaged in acts of "trickery, fraud . . . and violence."[39] At the same time (and perhaps more importantly), it decided that the longstanding prohibition on the arrest of debtors in their homes without special court authorization unduly hindered the ability of creditors to collect on their debts.[40] Accordingly, in November 1772, the monarchy created a small *corps* of ten officers—the *officiers-gardes du commerce*—who were exclusively charged with executing judgments against debtors.[41] While directed to respect debtors' rights to notice, these officers were also empowered to arrest debtors in their homes (except on Sundays and holidays).[42] Apparently concluding that more such officers were needed, the monarchy augmented their number to twelve in an edict of July 1778.[43] Given, however, the enormous size of the court's docket, it seems unlikely that even this augmented number was sufficient to ensure that all judgments would be executed.

To the extent that a plaintiff succeeded in arresting a debtor, such debtors were held in the ordinary royal prisons—though, unless they were found guilty of fraud or bankruptcy, they were generally separated from the criminal population.[44] Since creditors were required to pay for debtors' food throughout the entire period of imprisonment, this was, however, a costly proposition.[45] Moreover, because debtors behind bars could not engage in commercial activity, there was reason to doubt that imprisonment was the best way to recover on a debt—except insofar as it encouraged the debtor's solvent relatives and friends to come to his aid by paying the debt themselves. Accordingly, even to the (minimal) extent that arrest was feasible, it was often not desirable.

For these reasons, both the Parisian Merchant Court and the litigants who came before it had good reason to rely on alternative, more informal enforcement mechanisms—namely, procedures that augmented communal involvement in the process of adjudication and thus the reputational costs for failing to abide by the court's judgments. The court's reliance on the community, however, was more than just an efficient mode of administering justice. By encouraging community involvement in the process of adjudication (through such procedures as appointing arbiters of high standing and repute), the court also legitimated itself in the eyes of the community.

But while the court gained much from its use of community-oriented procedural mechanisms, it is important to recognize that it attained neither complete legitimacy nor perfect enforcement. As described above, the court's legitimacy was constantly under siege from the various merchant groups that felt it did not represent their interests. And while there is no record of the extent to which the court's final judgments were enforced, there is ample evidence that defendants frequently chose not to appear when summoned, thus leading to the entry of a default judgment.[46]

Docket records suggest that on the order of 200 to 350 cases were filed each of the three weekdays that the court was in session[47]—a number that accords with the estimate of the *Encyclopédie méthodique* that the court issued up to 56,000 sentences in a single year.[48] Indeed, according to estimates made in May 1790 by two deputies to the revolutionary National Assembly, the court disposed of an even larger number of cases in the final years of the Old Regime—namely, on the order of 60,000 to 80,000 cases per year.[49] As a result of the enormous size of its docket, contemporaries claimed that it often sat until midnight or even later.[50] Even so, the court was able to manage this docket only because it resolved a very significant proportion of the lawsuits filed—

sometimes more than 50 percent[51] — by entering default judgments. A former judge of the Parisian Merchant Court even complained that many parties or their attorneys who were found to have defaulted had in fact appeared in court, but because there were so many litigants, and thus "the audience is pretty noisy," they never heard their cases called.[52]

Among those defendants who chose to default, some surely filed suit in other jurisdictions that they believed were more favorable to their interests. Given the numerous overlapping jurisdictions of the Old Regime, as well as the limited enforcement personnel available to creditors, there were ample opportunities and incentives for defendants thus to seek to avoid merchant court jurisdiction. Indeed, some likely appeared before the merchant court solely for the purpose of challenging its jurisdiction through a procedure known as the *déclinatoire*. According to one commercial jurist, who wrote in the mid-eighteenth century, "*déclinatoires* . . . are frequently raised in the merchant courts."[53] Oddly, I have found no archival evidence that such challenges were made, but this is probably because the court decided these itself, rather than delegating them to arbiters.

It was in those cases in which the defendant chose to appear and defend on the merits that the merchant court was able to deploy the full panoply of its community-oriented and community-reinforcing procedures, including most importantly arbitration. The court, in other words, could devote resources to these procedures designed to reinforce values of fraternal harmony only because so many cases disappeared by means of default judgments (and perhaps also *déclinatoires*), which were, ironically, secured against the background of the court's constant (and highly unfraternal) jurisdictional conflict with other judicial entities. Thus, to some extent, default judgments gave the lie to the merchant court's claim that it promoted harmony among merchant brothers. At the same time, however, these judgments served as a means of demarcating the court's jurisdictional terrain, such that it could then insist as an internal matter — through the procedures that it applied to those cases that it did fully adjudicate — that it embodied and reinforced principles of merchant virtue.

Arbitration

Of the court's various procedures, the one that was most important in enabling it to manage its enormous docket and in bolstering its virtuous self-conception was its use of arbiters. Moreover, for the historian seeking to gain knowledge of how the court functioned as a legal institution — and, in particular, of the substantive and procedural law that it applied — the reports drafted by arbiters are the most useful of all extant archival records. While the official records of the court's judgments are fairly thorough and date from 1680 to 1792, they are not of much analytical value because they contain little more than the litigants' names and the party in whose favor the court found—and they are, furthermore, frequently illegible. In contrast, many—though by no means all—of the arbiters' reports explain the reasoning underlying the recommended decision. Accordingly, I draw extensively on the arbiters' reports, and it is worth pausing briefly to describe the scope and nature of these documents, as well as the ways in which I use them.

The reports date from 1702 through 1801 and fill a total of eighteen boxes, each containing roughly 300 reports—thus totaling about 5,400. Within the one hundred years that the reports span, however, coverage is far from even. Thus, the first box contains reports dating from 1702 through 1734, with many years—and, notably, the period from 1706 through 1722—lacking any reports at all. There also appear to be no extant reports for the years 1748–1757. Beginning in 1758 and continuing through 1791, coverage seems to be largely continuous, but becomes much more dense around 1773,[54] as of which time each box of reports spans at most a two- to three-year period. The last box covers the period from 1790 through 1801, with most of the reports clustering in the early 1790s.[55]

Given these significant lacunae in coverage, it is doubtful whether a comprehensive empirical analysis of all the arbiters' reports would be of substantial value. At the same time, this large corpus of reports is a remarkable and, thus far, largely ignored resource through which to explore significant aspects of the court's procedure and substantive law.[56] In an effort to utilize this resource as effectively as possible, I have approached the arbiters' reports in two ways. First, I systematically reviewed all the reports contained in one box, in an effort to gain a sense of the arbiters, parties, and disputes that most commonly appeared before the court.[57] This box contains 295 arbiters' reports, dating from 1783–1785. Second, I engaged in an extensive, more informal exploration of the remaining boxes, seeking to confirm that the box that I systematically reviewed was representative of the entirety, while also searching for cases of particular interest.

I did not draw a random sample from multiple boxes because, due to the great variability of types of dispute within any given box, this would most likely result in a distorted picture. Furthermore, since the range of years for which there remains a large number of arbiters' reports is fairly narrow (1773–1791), it seems unlikely that there would have been a very significant change in the arbiters, parties, and disputes that appeared before the court within this period. Accordingly, I concluded that the benefit to be gained from formally sampling across boxes within this thirty-year period was minimal.

This conclusion was confirmed by my more informal, but extensive exploration of the entire range of boxes. Moreover, to the extent that there were some minimal changes in the arbiters, parties, or disputes during this period, these would most likely follow from the speculative fever that consumed Paris in the 1780s. Accordingly, I decided to select a box dating from relatively late in the series.

Before turning to examine the ways in which the court relied on arbiters, a final word is in order regarding my use of the arbiters' reports. The judge and consuls were by no means obligated to adopt the recommended decisions proposed by arbiters in their reports. It is therefore possible that these reports do not provide an accurate reflection of the legal reasoning and rulings of the court itself. I do not, however, believe that there is a significant risk of such distortion. Cross-referencing of a number of arbiters' reports with the records of the judgments entered suggests that the judges appear usually to have adopted the rulings proposed by the arbiters.[58] Moreover, the sheer volume of litigation filed strongly suggests that the court's five judges would have had no choice but to delegate substantial decision-making power to the arbiters.

THE FUNCTIONS OF ARBITRATION

In 1560, shortly after it established the first merchant courts in Toulouse and Rouen,[59] the French monarchy issued an edict ordering merchants to settle their disputes through arbitration before three or more arbiters of their choice and commanding all royal courts to enforce such arbitral decisions.[60] However, the 1563 edict that created the merchant court in Paris and in several others cities made no mention of arbitration.[61] And while an arbitration requirement reappeared in the Commercial Ordinance of 1673, it was limited to partnership disputes.[62]

Despite the lack of clear statutory authority, arbitration played a fundamental role in the resolution of a wide variety of disputes that came before the eighteenth-century Parisian Merchant Court, including, but in no way limited to, those concerning partnerships. Although it is unlikely that the court concerned itself much with such matters, some doctrinal support for this practice can be found in the Procedure Ordinance of 1667, which provided that "if it is necessary to view the documents [*pièces*], the judge and consuls can name . . . a former consul or other merchant above reproach [*non suspect*] to examine them, and on his report, to enter judgment."[63]

Arbitration served two important functions. First, it offered the possibility of healing rifts that arose between the disputants and that threatened to sunder the personal ties that were so important for the successful practice of commerce in the Old Regime. Second, arbitration mediated the distance between decision-maker and disputant. An arbiter who was personally familiar with the disputants, or at least with their social and professional worlds, could more easily identify relevant witnesses and assess reputations. Such an arbiter was also more likely to inspire the litigants' trust and to bring communal pressure successfully to bear, thereby furthering his efforts to achieve reconciliation. Alternatively, if reconciliation failed, an arbiter who was personally linked to the litigants was more likely to recommend a decision (for the judge and consuls to impose) by which they would willingly abide.

Exactly when, why, and how the Parisian Merchant Court designated particular disputes for arbitration remains something of a mystery.[64] The many reports written by arbiters suggest that the court typically sent the more complex and time-consuming cases to arbitration. As one arbiter complained in a report to the judge and consuls, "I cannot imagine what claims were alleged at oral argument which convinced you to send this matter to arbitration; there has perhaps never been a simpler one."[65] Given the huge number of cases filed in the court, the ability of the judge and consuls to send the more complicated ones to arbiters was surely an important tool for managing the docket.

Arbiters were responsible for both fact-finding and adjudication. When assigned a case, they began by investigating and deciding the facts in dispute. For this purpose, they had full authority to interview the parties and any witnesses and to examine all relevant documents, merchandise, and other materials. In this respect, merchant court arbiters had far greater power than the judicial officers known as *commissaires-enquêteurs,* who served in the ordinary royal courts, such as the *Châtelet,* and whose job it was to assist in fact-finding by undertaking examinations of witnesses. Whereas the *commissaires-enquêteurs* were constrained to administer written questions drafted in advance by the parties themselves,[66] the arbiters (some of whom were also *commissaires-enquêteurs*)[67] posed their own questions, and were thus able to ask follow-up questions more easily than their civil-law counterparts. Such procedural flexibility was characteristic of the merchant court, which prided itself on being an institution that placed the pursuit of truth and justice above legal formalities. Consider in this regard, one arbiter's rather unsubtle attempt to flatter the court's pride. According to the arbiter, the defendant in the case before him was reluctant to answer questions for fear of giving fodder to the plaintiff. Indeed, the arbiter claimed, the defendant went so far as to bemoan his failure to remove the case to the *Châtelet,* since in that court, unlike the merchant court, only written questions were administered, and the truth was thus more easily avoided. As the defendant apparently informed the arbiter: "All your questions are quite astonishing; I had intended at first to have this lawsuit taken up by the *Châtelet;* one defends oneself there by means of writings and would not be asked a thousand questions like these."[68]

After undertaking fact-finding, arbiters were responsible for adjudication.

Here, they served two distinct roles. Their primary task was to try to reconcile the parties by helping them reach a compromise that they would embrace of their own free will. They served, in other words, as mediators. It appears that if the arbiters succeeded in reconciling the parties, the dispute did not come before the judge and consuls again.[69] If the arbiters failed, however, they were to write a report to the judge and consuls discussing their efforts and suggesting how the court should proceed.[70] Not surprisingly, given the extremely large number of cases that they were expected to decide, the judge and consuls usually seem to have adopted the judgments proposed by the arbiters.

The dual function of the arbiters as both mediators and magistrates paralleled the distinction in the Continental legal tradition between "arbitrators" and "arbiters." The arbitrator, also known as *l'amiable compositeur,* or amicable restorer, was supposed to reconcile the parties by proposing a compromise that they voluntarily chose to embrace. In so doing, he was free under principles of equity to ignore the letter of the law. In contrast, an arbiter's judgment was binding, and he was to decide the dispute strictly according to the law.[71]

From the modern perspective, the dual function of the arbiter as mediator turned magistrate seems peculiar. Efforts at voluntary reconciliation, it would appear, are necessarily illusory when the litigants know that failure to reach a "voluntary" compromise means that the arbiter can impose the compromise by proposing a ruling that the court will adopt. Unfortunately, since arbiters were required to write a report only when they failed to reconcile the litigants, there is no way to determine what compromises they proposed and whether, when they failed at reconciliation, the judgments that they recommended were merely the compromises that they had previously suggested. It seems likely, however, that—tracking the traditional distinction between arbitrators and arbiters—arbiters functioning as mediators had greater freedom to ignore legal rules than when they served as magistrates. Moreover, the fact in itself that litigants sometimes refused to be reconciled suggests that they had reason to hope that the judgment ultimately proposed to (and adopted by) the court would differ in some way from the compromise that they had rejected.

Ultimately, however, even if the arbiters' proposed rulings merely duplicated their proposed compromises, preliminary efforts at reconciliation were a crucial component of merchant court adjudication. Unlike mediation and arbitration today, which are valued primarily for saving disputants the time and expense of litigation,[72] the main purpose served by these mechanisms in the Old Regime merchant court was to restore the friendship and trust—the personal relationships—that were so crucial to the functioning of commerce. If the arbiter attained this end, then the parties would voluntarily embrace the compromise he suggested. This in itself was an achievement well worth the additional time and effort that the process of mediation required. As the jurist Toubeau observed, the judge and consuls of the merchant court "must try to reconcile disputes more than to judge them, . . . because their court is structured to attain a friendly restoration of the relationship [*l'amiable composition*]."[73]

THE IDENTITY OF THE ARBITERS

Who were the arbiters? As described above, I systematically reviewed a box of arbiters' reports dating from 1783 to 1785. Of these reports, most (86.8 percent) were written by a single author. A substantial number (10.8 percent) were penned jointly by the leaders of a particular guild—usually one that was implicated in the lawsuit, because one or both of the parties were members of that guild. The remaining reports (2.4 percent) were drafted by two individuals who were not guild leaders. Some individuals were repeatedly appointed as arbiters, thus suggesting that the court was particularly pleased with their services. Not all of these, however, enjoyed their popularity. As one arbiter observed, in order to comply with the court's request that he recommend a judgment in the case before him, he would have to interview a number of witnesses and review the parties' accounting books, all of which would require "a considerable amount of work."[74] Accordingly, he beseeched the court to send the case "to an arbiter other than myself, because my business and frequent travels absolutely do not permit me to take on continued responsibility for this litigation, which along with the others that you have successively assigned me, has occupied me greatly, and as a result, hindered me in my own business affairs."[75]

Although certain arbiters were reluctant repeatedly to serve because they lacked the time to do so, an occasional few refused to serve even once, for fear that any association with the merchant court—and thus with commercial endeavors—would tarnish their honor. For example, in a lawsuit between two art dealers regarding the sale of a painting, the court asked the Royal Academy of Painting and Sculpture to designate several of its members to serve as arbiters.[76] The academy, however, firmly refused. As explained in a letter drafted by its secretary, "The association unanimously decreed that it neither can nor must defer to the wishes of messieurs the judge and consuls."[77] "Pursuant to its constitution," the secretary asserted, the academy is permitted "to give its opinion concerning the quality of works of art . . . [but] in this litigation the degree of beauty of the painting is absolutely not in question."[78] The litigation concerned instead the details of the parties' contractual agreement—a base, commercial matter that was beneath an institution devoted to promoting high-minded, artistic endeavors.

While certain individuals and groups were reluctant to serve as arbiters, the voluminous number of arbiters' reports that have survived suggests that, in general, the court had relatively little difficulty recruiting such assistants. As observed in 1767 by the associated merchants of the river and ports and the drivers of horse-drawn barges—admittedly not great supporters of the merchant court but perhaps therefore more willing to acknowledge the truth—"most of . . . [the court's] rulings consist of referrals to arbiters."[79]

The profession or social status of those who served as arbiters is, unfortunately, often difficult to determine. While many arbiters chose to provide such identifying information in their reports, even more chose not to do so. Of the reports in the box that I systematically reviewed, 62.6 percent provide no identifying information—or, on occasion, are so illegible or damaged that it is impossible to determine whether such information was provided.[80] Given the large percentage of reports for which there is no readily available information about the arbiters' identities, it is not clear that the reports in which arbiters chose to identify themselves are representative of the whole. Nonetheless, analysis of these reports provides the best available indication of the range of the arbiters' social and professional identities. Among the reports in which the arbiters' professions can be identified, the profession that appears by far the most frequently is that of parish priest. Priests wrote 11.5 percent of these reports. Also significantly represented were saddlers (8.8 percent of the reports), barristers (7.1 percent), and royal administrators of various kinds (6.2 percent).[81]

As these numbers suggest, a significant proportion of arbiters appointed by the Parisian Merchant Court were not merchants at all. Notably—and largely ignored in the scholarly literature[82]—the judge and consuls often appointed the local priest, who knew one or both of the parties as his parishioners. As observed by Philibert-Joseph Masson, a contemporary commentator on merchant court practice and former judge and consul of the Parisian Merchant Court, "Arbiters hear witnesses and inform the judges about that which they were able to discover. It can be said on this subject that messieurs the parish priests render services that are essential."[83] Indeed, as late as May 1790, a deputy to the revolutionary National Assembly advocated the preservation of the merchant courts by observing that their judges seek "to inquire into the litigants down to their mores and their habits" and that one of the primary ways that they do so is by "send[ing] them . . . before the parish priest."[84] Those who were less sympathetic to the court were not so enthusiastic about its appointment of priests as arbiters, but they too acknowledged that it was common practice. Recognizing that the court frequently named priests to serve as arbiters, the associated merchants of the river and ports and the drivers of horse-drawn barges queried, "What relationship do ecclesiastics have to commerce?"[85]

The Parisian Merchant Court tended to select parish priests as arbiters when one or both of the parties resided in a small town or village outside Paris, where the priest had his parish. In contrast, parish priests from within Paris were very rarely selected to serve as arbiters.[86] One likely reason that priests outside Paris were employed as arbiters—and that priests within Paris were usually not—was administrative convenience. When the parties to a dispute lived in a town outside Paris, it was surely much easier to have the local priest arbitrate the dispute than it was to send a busy, Parisian merchant all the way to the town or to require the parties to travel to Paris. In addition, while the judge and consuls were acquainted with the prominent merchants in Paris, they were unlikely to know those outside the city. Thus, it was probably simplest to send the parties before the local priest.

Priests, however, were more than a second-best choice. As suggested by an arbiter who was not a priest, arbiters were required "to read into the depths of the litigants' consciences"—a task that was supremely difficult, since ultimately "it is only for God to know what is truly in the litigants' consciences."[87] By virtue of their profession, priests were particularly well suited to this task. Moreover, at least in the small communities outside Paris, priests were in an especially good position to know or identify the relevant facts and to reconcile the disputants. Such a priest was likely to have known his parishioners for many years, if not from birth, and even to have taken their confessions. He also learned many things about his parishioners—or at least, his parishioners' reputations—by listening to the stories and complaints of their relatives, friends, and neighbors. And since he was often asked by people involved in everyday disputes to serve as a mediator, the role of the merchant court arbiter was quite familiar.[88]

It was thus partly because of the distinctive knowledge and skills that they possessed by virtue of their profession, and not exclusively as a matter of administrative convenience, that priests in the villages outside of Paris were appointed as arbiters. Significantly, however, priests within eighteenth-century Paris were much less likely to possess such knowledge and skills. By this time, parishes within Paris had grown so large that it was no longer possible for the priest to know all of his parishioners, even by reputation. As a result, the role of the parish priest as the community mediator—the person to whom Parisians went to make complaints and seek advice regarding family, friends, and neighbors—was increasingly usurped by officers of the police.[89] This, in turn, helps account for the fact that parish priests from within Paris were rarely appointed as arbiters.

That priests were selected as arbiters, at least in part, *because* they were priests is suggested by the fact that, in their reports to the court, they commonly referred to information that they had acquired about the litigants in a sacerdotal capacity. For example, the priest of Chatou recommended that the court find for the plaintiff, because "the conduct that he has always demonstrated in our parish . . . [is] among the most honest."[90] Likewise, the priest of Chevilly concluded in favor of the plaintiff, because she is "a person who leads a good life and has good morals and is known by everyone as such and . . . , according to my own knowledge and that of the inhabitants of my parish where she was born and has always lived, she has never failed to pay a debt."[91] Similarly, in a report regarding a lawsuit brought by a day laborer for payment of wages, the priest of Vincennes emphasized that "this is not today the first lawsuit in which Girard, a plasterer from Vincennes, has been involved against the workers who work for him . . . and concerning the question of paying them; this is at least the fifth or sixth since I have been the parish priest of this place."[92] Moreover, the arbiter-priest informed the court, the plaintiff "is an honest man, whom I believe is incapable of asking for something that is not due him, and Girard on the other hand, is a man who probably lacks order, and who can quite easily be mistaken, or whose memory has failed."[93] Accordingly, the arbiter suggested, the plaintiff was probably entitled to judgment.

Parish priests were so well-informed that, long before legal disputes arose, merchants sometimes contacted them to inquire about the moral character and business activities of people with whom they were considering doing business. This, for example, is what Nicolas François Viennos did after just entering a business deal with a man named Berthin.[94] Viennos was a farmer from Vincennes, whose friend Claude Launoy, a teamster from the faubourg Saint-Antoine, recommended that he purchase some oats from his friend Berthin. Viennos did not know Berthin, who lived in Dronay en Champagne. However, Launoy vouched for him, and, on the advice of his friend, Viennos agreed to buy some oats from Berthin. The total price was 300 livres, of which Viennos paid 120 as a cash deposit. When Berthin failed to deliver the oats as agreed, Viennos became nervous and wrote a letter to the priest of Dronay, Berthin's hometown, explaining his situation and asking for any information that the priest could provide about Berthin's character and activities. As explained by the arbiter, himself a priest, who was appointed in the lawsuit that eventually arose, "the aforementioned priest . . . responded [to Viennos] that the aforementioned Berthin was in the habit of doing mischief under the pretext of deals similar to the one that Viennos described, that Berthin was in debt for considerable sums of money, that Berthin owed him some money, and he exhorted Viennos to console himself for the 120 livres that he lost, along with many others who lost a lot more than he."[95] As the community's confessor and, interestingly, as someone who had been personally duped by Berthin, the parish priest knew, perhaps better than anyone else, Berthin's reputation as a scoundrel who frequently promised more than he could deliver and who regularly failed to meet his obligations.

Through pastoral activities, priests not only gained knowledge of their parishioners' character and conduct, but also grew accustomed to promoting virtuous behavior and encouraging people to place community above self-interested gain. Moreover, because of the Catholic Church's highly successful, seventeenth-century movement to reform the clergy, most parish priests in the following century enjoyed a high status within the village community.[96] As a result, when priests served as arbiters, they exercised a moral authority that encouraged litigants to heed their call to compromise. And strikingly, litigants were often willing to compromise as directed, even when doing so required them to foreswear legally valid claims for payment and thus, it would seem, their own (at least short-term) financial self-interest.

Consider, for example, the compromise proposed by the parish priest from the town of Champlan, who served as arbiter in a dispute between two cousins, Jean and Denis Meusnier, both of whom were his parishioners.[97] Jean, a tavern keeper, sued Denis, a fruit seller, claiming that his cousin had long owed him sixty livres, which he refused to pay. After failing to reconcile the parties, the priest decided to have a talk with Jean on his own: "I took Jean Meusnier, the plaintiff, aside."[98] By pointing out the defendant's "lack of affluence" and the plaintiff's "wealth, in contrast," the priest was able to convince Jean that he ought to be more generous to his less fortunate cousin.[99] Pressured by the moral authority of the priest, Jean agreed to reduce the amount of his claim and to grant Denis a long moratorium on payment of the debt.

Despite the priest's unique powers of persuasion, he did not always succeed in convincing the parties to agree to a compromise. Indeed, in the dispute between the Meusniers, the defendant remained steadfast in his claim that he had already paid the debt and refused to agree to any moratorium. When the priest failed to reconcile the litigants, however, the judgment that he recommended to the court was likely to carry particular weight. Because cases turned to such a significant extent on the credibility of the parties and witnesses, priests — who possessed a wealth of information about their parishioners' reputations — were at a distinct advantage in opining about which litigant was entitled to judgment. Moreover, the high moral stature of arbiter-priests was such that those litigants who were dissatisfied with the judgments that they recommended found it especially difficult to persuade the court to hold otherwise.

This was the plight of a journeyman watchmaker named Flamant, who filed suit against his master, Sarget.[100] The precise grounds for Flamant's lawsuit are unfortunately not evident, but likely included the failure to pay wages. As the parties were both from Vaugirard, on the outskirts of Paris, the judge and consuls initially appointed the local parish priest to serve as arbiter. The priest wrote a report to the court recommending that it find in favor of the defendant. Dissatisfied with this recommendation, Flamant urged the court to appoint a second arbiter to decide the matter, arguing that the priest had denied him a fair hearing. The court apparently agreed and thus appointed a second arbiter—a man by the name of Déyeux, upon whom it called frequently for assistance in arbitration, but whose professional identity is not clear. In his report to the court, Déyeux explained that he had at first been "seduced by Flamant's speeches" into concluding that "Monsieur the parish priest of Vaugirard had neglected to pursue the necessary investigation."[101] Since then, however, he had obtained and read the arbiter-priest's report to the court, as well as a letter addressed to him by this priest, and concluded that "the criticism made against . . . [the priest] could not be more ill founded."[102] As Déyeux explained, "I do not know, Messieurs, if Monsieur the parish priest of Vaugirard has the honor of being known by you, but to judge from the large number of cases that you have sent him over the last twenty years, I have reason to believe that he has earned your trust. To suspect that he could abuse it by finding against Flamant without having provided him with sufficient opportunity to be heard would be to insult him, and . . . those who know him know that he is incapable of having any part in the smallest injustice. . . . [He] know[s] Flamant and Sarget, since they are both his parishioners; he knows the reasons that led [them to act as they did]."[103] In Déyeux's view, in short, the priest's character was such that he was incapable of acting unjustly. Moreover, since both parties were his parishioners, he was in the best position to know who between them was truthful and deserving. Accordingly, Déyeux concluded, the arbiter-priest's judgment was entitled to deference.

Although priests enjoyed a privileged position in the village community that permitted them unique access to information about their parishioners' character, reputation, and activities, they were not the only arbiters who knew litigants personally or at least knew of them. The position of the parish priest at the fulcrum of an information network within the village in some ways paralleled that of guild leaders within Paris. As we have seen, gaining membership in a guild was a long and arduous process, which tested not only artisanal and mercantile skill but also moral character. The successful candidate was one who for many years lived and worked within the same guild community, such that almost nothing about him—either professional or personal—remained unknown. Since guild leaders stood at the pinnacle of the guild hierarchy, they were likely to have the best access to this wealth of information about guild members.

Just as parish priests were often appointed as arbiters in disputes involving their parishioners, guild leaders were frequently named arbiters in disputes involving members of their guilds.[104] As discussed later in this book, the disputes in which guild leaders served as arbiters usually concerned either the sale of goods or the payment of wages, and in their role as arbiters they helped to reinforce the guild system, whose claim to ensuring order and harmony among merchants was threatened by the outbreak of litigation.[105] Moreover, by calling on guild leaders to assist in resolving such disputes, the court was able to draw on their superior knowledge of the litigants and of the merchandise or labor at issue.

For example, in a lawsuit brought by Antoine Manjard, a journeyman cartwright, against his master, Chopard, the court appointed three leaders of the cartwrights' guild to serve as arbiters. Manjard argued that he was entitled to payment for seventy-eight days of work and that he and Chopard had agreed on wages of forty-two sous per day.[106] Chopard, however, insisted that Manjard had worked only seventy and a half days and that they had agreed to wages of thirty-six sous per day. In the process of fact-finding, the arbiters relied, in part, on information that they were particularly well suited to obtain because of their status as guild leaders — namely, the testimony of two other masters in the cartwrights' guild. These were Madame Lerat, for whom Manjard had worked prior to entering Chopard's employ, and Monsieur Laval, for whom he was presently working. As the guild leaders reported to the judge and consuls, both these masters had nothing but positive things to say about Manjard's work and confirmed that they both paid him the forty-two sous per day that he now sought from Chopard. Drawing on their personal knowledge of Lerat and Laval, the guild leaders observed that they were "both very honest members of our guild community, and in whom faith ought to be placed."[107] Accordingly, the guild leaders concluded that the fair value of Manjard's labor was, indeed, forty-two sous per day. However, since Chopard's accounting books established that Manjard had worked only 70.5 days, and Manjard evidently had no written proof to the contrary, the guild leaders recommended that Chopard be ordered to pay for only 70.5 days of work.

Even when arbiters were neither priests nor guild leaders, they sometimes knew, or knew of, the litigants through connections within the merchant community. In one case, an arbiter who was a former consul of the merchant court recommended that the court order a long moratorium on payment, because he had personal knowledge that the defendant was deserving.[108] As the arbiter explained, he was "personally aware of . . . [the defendant's] honesty and of the impossibility of his paying in shorter intervals."[109] Likewise, he had personal knowledge of the fact that "this individual enjoys in his town . . . the public esteem that his good conduct has earned him."[110] By thus vouching for the defendant's character and conduct, the arbiter used his own reputational capital to help secure the moratorium.

In some cases, arbiters knew the disputants so well that they were actually witnesses to events at issue in the litigation. Consider, for example, the arbiter in the case of *Bayard v. Botté*.[111] This arbiter, who unfortunately did not identify his profession, reported a conversation that occurred between him and the plaintiff on the very day that the plaintiff's claim arose—long before the plaintiff brought the lawsuit. The plaintiff, Bayard, was a Parisian merchant who purchased some goods and had them delivered to him by a teamster named Botté. Bayard paid Botté for his services immediately upon delivery, but according to Bayard he accidentally paid too much and consequently brought a lawsuit seeking restitution. In his report, the arbiter found for Bayard, relying heavily on his own personal knowledge of the events in question. Essentially serving as a witness, the arbiter wrote that Botté had delivered goods to him, the arbiter, just a few minutes after he had made the delivery to Bayard. Apparently, Bayard realized that he had overpaid shortly after Botté left and, according to the arbiter, "[he] came [to my place] to find out if the teamster had already left and told me of the mistake that he and his wife had just made."[112]

That arbiters had this kind of personal connection to the litigants may be quite surprising. Like all judicial officers today, arbiters are viewed as neutral decision-makers and are therefore prohibited from having a personal relationship with the litigants. Given the nature of commercial activity in the Old Regime, however, a personal relationship between arbiter and litigant was sometimes viewed as an asset, rather than a liability. In a world of tight-knit, interlocking institutions, who was better suited to restore bonds of friendship and trust between the disputants than someone who knew them personally, who was perhaps a friend or adviser, or at the very least enjoyed good standing in the community?

Witness Testimony

In reaching a decision, arbiters relied not only on their personal knowledge of the litigants and their reputations but also on the testimony of witnesses. Authorized by the Procedure Ordinance of 1667 in cases in which "the parties disagree about the facts,"[113] witness testimony served two functions.

First, witnesses testified to relevant facts in disputes, based on either personal knowledge or hearsay. Second, they served as experts, opining about the quality, and thus value, of the goods or services at issue in the litigation. In either case, the witness's credibility, and thus reputation and social standing, were crucial in determining how much weight to give to his or her testimony. In one suit, for example, an arbiter determined that a witness to the formation of an oral contract ought to be believed, because in the town where the defendant lived and where the contract negotiations took place, he "enjoys . . . the reputation of an honest man."[114] Similarly, in a lawsuit in which the value of some cobblestones was at issue, the arbiter-priest called upon a paver from his parish to provide an estimate and informed the court that this paver's opinion should be trusted because he is a "man who is very capable in his trade and who enjoys the trust of the canton."[115]

Witnesses to disputed issues of fact played a particularly important role in litigation over oral contracts, which, as discussed above, were enforceable in the merchant court as long as some evidence could be proffered proving their existence. Often such evidence took the form of witnesses to the contract's formation. As noted by Masson, a former judge and consul of the Parisian Merchant Court, "If . . . [sales contracts] are not written, which definitely happens often, they are denied by the party who has an interest in doing so, [and] it is necessary to return to the place where the contract was made in order to hear witnesses."[116] For this reason, merchants frequently took pains to negotiate in public.

This, for example, is what Herbelle and Ferret, parties to a contract for the sale of rope, chose to do.[117] Herbelle, a rope merchant from Paris, reached a sales agreement with Ferret, a farmer from the town of Choisy-le-Roi, which they recorded in a signed contract. The contract specified that Ferret would have the choice to purchase one of two ropes, and the weight and length of each was noted. As was common in the Old Regime, the contract included an extension of credit. Ferret promised to pay half the purchase price immediately in cash and the other half in three months. Shortly after the contract was signed, Herbelle began pressuring Ferret to buy both ropes. Over dinner in a Parisian restaurant, Herbelle promised that if Ferret took both ropes, he would extend more credit and grant him an even longer period in which to pay. Ferret remained undecided, so a few days later they met over lunch in another restaurant. They were joined this time by a carpenter named Bergerat, who was also from Ferret's town of Choisy-le-Roi. After lunch, the three men went to a café and, according to Herbelle, he and Ferret then orally agreed that Ferret would buy the second rope and that he would have an entire year to pay. Ferret, however, disputed Herbelle's account. According to Ferret, the oral agreement that they reached was made conditional on the second rope being delivered to him in Choisy-le-Roi and on his satisfaction upon weighing and measuring the rope. As the parties failed to resolve their dispute, Ferret filed suit in the Parisian Merchant Court.

In support of their respective claims, the parties called on different witnesses. Ferret relied on the testimony of Bergerat, a "man who is recognized for his probity,"[118] and who was with the parties in the café when they made the oral agreement.[119] In contrast, Herbelle relied on the statement of the café owner, a woman named Louvault, who said that she had overheard the formation of the oral contract. That Bergerat supported Ferret and Louvault supported Herbelle is likely not accidental. Ferret must have asked Bergerat as a friend, respected merchant, and fellow townsman, to join him in Paris during his negotiations with Herbelle. Similarly, Herbelle, the Paris resident, surely chose the café to which to take his out-of-town guests and was in all likelihood well acquainted with Louvault and her establishment. Both Ferret and Herbelle, in other words, sought to undertake their negotiations in the presence of friendly witnesses, and they succeeded. Upon determining that both Bergerat and Louvault were of good repute, the arbiter was at a loss to decide which party was telling the truth about the terms of the oral agreement. Unable to make up his mind, he simply told the judge and consuls that he could not advise them and preferred to trust in their wisdom.

While some merchants benefited from negotiating in public, others would have preferred to keep their negotiations secret but, because of the communal nature of Old Regime life, were unable to do so. This was the experience of Derient, a master cobbler in Paris, who had the misfortune of speaking too freely in a cabaret one evening, and shortly thereafter found himself the defendant in a lawsuit, which he then lost.[120] Derient owed a significant sum—slightly over 1,158 livres—to another master cobbler by the name of Gossé for various goods that the latter had supplied him. Derient had given Gossé a written acknowledgment of this debt. However, since Gossé was about to travel on business, he went to Derient's home to request that this acknowledgment be converted into a promissory note, which—as a negotiable instrument—could be used by Gossé to make purchases on his travels. Derient agreed and made a promissory note to Gossé's order. But while waiting for the ink to dry, the two cobblers "drank a bottle of wine together" and Gossé then departed, forgetting to take the promissory note with him.[121] When Gossé finally discovered his mistake and asked Derient to return the note, Derient and his wife made every effort to avoid doing so. Finally, Gossé managed to corner Derient, who persuaded the latter to go with him to a cabaret, where they "would talk about business."[122]

When they arrived at the cabaret, they "entered into a room in which there were two individuals at another table."[123] Gossé then asked Derient why he was refusing to return the promissory note, to which Derient apparently responded: "I know well what I owe you, but I do not want to make promissory notes."[124] When Gossé continued, however, to insist on payment, Derient changed his tune, asserting "that he does not owe him anything, and pronounc[ing] many invectives."[125] Thereafter, Gossé "called as witnesses two individuals who were present."[126] The two witnesses, both of whom were grocers, testified to the arbiter, and in the presence of the defendant, Derient, that "they had heard . . . [Derient] say that he was in the plaintiff's debt and that he would settle up."[127]

To Derient's horror, a third witness—one who had not been identified by Gossé—also appeared before the arbiter to testify against him. This was the widow Chevalier, a Parisian seamstress, who "entered with a servant . . . to dine in the cabaret at the time of the quarrel."[128] According to the widow, she had overheard the argument between the parties. Convinced that Derient owed the money, she had apparently marched up to him and told him "it is clear, Monsieur, that you are in debt, because you are completely pale and disfigured; you would do better to admit it and you would be calmer; it is disgraceful to disclaim one's debts."[129] Although Chevalier evidently believed herself to be fully entitled to intervene in her neighbors' affairs, Derient, not surprisingly, responded to this advice by informing her that "this was not any of her business."[130] Knowing full well, however, that Chevalier could prove quite dangerous as a witness against him, Derient went to her home that very evening to ask her what she had heard. Apparently dissatisfied with her answers, he then sent his wife the next day "in order to tell her bad things about the plaintiff."[131]

That Derient and his wife were thus able to locate Chevalier's home and to secure two separate meetings with her serves to highlight the community's expansive reach and power—power that, as it turned out, Derient had good reason to fear. As deployed by Gossé in his lawsuit against Derient, the three witnesses who had happened to overhear the parties' negotiations proved quite compelling. Confronted with all this testimony, it was clear, the arbiter concluded, that the court should find for Gossé.

Accounting Books

The examination of merchants' accounting books was another means by which the Parisian Merchant Court brought community ties to bear in the adjudicatory process. By law, merchant-artisans were required to keep accounting books that recorded their transactions.[132] As these books provided key evidence as to whether payments had been made, they were cited frequently in disputes before the merchant court. Since the examination of accounting books was necessarily a time-consuming process, the court typically ordered arbitration when such an examination proved necessary.

Merchants kept a variety of accounting books,[133] the most important of which were the *brouillard,* the *livre-journal,* and the *grand livre.* Stemming from the verb *brouiller*—to mix or muddle up—the *brouillard* was the book in which merchants recorded all their transactions as they occurred or as they remembered to do so. As its name suggests, the *brouillard* was not supposed to be an orderly presentation of the merchant's affairs, but was simply a place for voluminous details to be noted, so as not to be forgotten. After recording all transactions in the *brouillard,* a merchant would use this information to write the *livre-journal,* or daily book, which was a chronological record of all business transacted each day. Once information was entered into the *livre-journal,* it could then be entered into the *grand livre,* or great book, which set forth the merchant's various accounts with other individuals—including both merchants and consumers. Within each account, transactions were recorded chronologically.[134]

When merchants relied solely on oral contracts, as was frequently the case, accounting books were often the only written evidence of the sale and of payment (or nonpayment). Moreover, even when parties produced a written contract and/or receipts of delivery and payment, accounting books were generally considered the decisive piece of evidence. Whereas an individual piece of paper, such as a contract or receipt, could be forged fairly easily as the occasion demanded, there were more stringent obstacles to the forgery of accounting books.[135] In particular, because both *livres-journaux* and *grands livres* were to be kept in strict chronological order—and because merchants were prohibited from skipping pages, writing in the margins, and crossing out entries[136]—it was very difficult to forge transactions in a properly kept accounting book. For this reason, even when other written evidence was available, accounting books were often deemed dispositive in disputes over payment.[137]

Accounting books were considered to be important evidence not only for the technical reason that they were difficult to falsify, but also because they were viewed as a testimonial to the merchant's character. A merchant who properly maintained his accounting books was a person with nothing to hide, one who on a daily basis sought transparency in his dealings and took responsibility for his obligations. In contrast, the merchant who did not keep accounting books at all or who failed to maintain them in the prescribed manner was a person who, at best, did not sufficiently appreciate the weight of his obligations and, at worst, was actively engaged in chicanery. As the noted jurist Philippe Bornier remarked, any deviation from the strict rules for maintaining accounting books, including "poor ordering or lack of chronological continuity, is a mark of bad faith."[138] Indeed, the state of a merchant's accounting books, as revealed over the course of the litigation, could profoundly shape his reputation, which, in turn, would have a significant effect on the merchant's professional prospects.

The case of *Colon v. De Sainte Beuve* illustrates the moral weight accorded to accounting books.[139] Colon was a locksmith and mechanic who for several years provided various services to De Sainte Beuve, a goldsmith. Colon worked on credit, and every so often De Sainte Beuve paid Colon part of what he owed him, while at the same time giving him more work and thus incurring further debt. After several years, the parties did an accounting, which they recorded in a writing stating that De Sainte Beuve owed Colon 1,326 livres. According to Colon, De Sainte Beuve never paid him any of this amount, and thus he was forced to bring suit two years later. In his defense, De Sainte Beuve claimed to have paid most of his obligation in the form of promissory notes for the sum of 1,200 livres. Colon, however, denied ever receiving the notes.

In seeking to resolve the dispute, the arbiter examined both parties' accounting books. In part, this examination focused on the particular facts at issue in the case—namely, whether Colon had ever received the notes. Thus, the arbiter noted that Colon's accounting books recorded money received from De Sainte Beuve in prior years, but did not list any money received for the particular services in question. This, he suggested, was evidence that De Sainte Beuve had never paid Colon for these services. The accounting books, however, served the arbiter as evidence not only of the fact of nonpayment but also as evidence of the parties' moral character, and thus, of which was likely to be speaking the truth. De Sainte Beuve, the arbiter noted, possessed one sole "imperfect book" with recent entries totaling only three or four written pages.[140] Furthermore, this sole accounting book recorded only De Sainte Beuve's sales transactions and contained no information about his obligations to people he hired. While De Sainte Beuve presented these shoddy books, continued the arbiter, "Colon, in contrast, presented to me books that reveal careful administration and good faith."[141] Based significantly on this evidence as to character, the arbiter concluded that the court ought to grant judgment to Colon.

In its analysis of merchants' accounting books, the court's reasoning was strikingly circular. Just as properly maintained accounting books were prima facie evidence of good faith, so too a reputation for good faith was reason to believe a merchant's accounting books. In fact, according to some contemporary jurists, accounting books could be accepted into evidence only if the merchant propounding them enjoyed a good reputation in the community. As Toubeau explained, paraphrasing Bornier, accounting books could be used as evidence only if the following conditions were met: "It is necessary that the merchant has the reputation of an upright and loyal man; that he himself keeps his accounting books; that he has the reputation of recording only that which is legitimately owed him; and that, finally, one can judge from other circumstances that he is a good man."[142]

In practice, and contrary to what Toubeau's statement might imply, the Parisian Merchant Court always accepted merchants' accounting books into evidence. The weight given by the court to the accounting books, however, depended on the merchant's reputation in the community. Thus, the court typically analyzed a merchant's accounting books (or lack thereof) against the background of a more general assessment of the merchant's character. In the case of *Gornier et Dardrieu v. Chandon,* for example, the plaintiffs sued the defendant, a seller of linens, for payment of various items of clothing that they had sold her.[143] Examining the plaintiffs' accounting books, the arbiter observed that they were in perfect order and that "fraud is not presumed when accounting books are in order."[144] In addition, the arbiter suggested that the plaintiffs' reputation was so good that it was simply unimaginable that they had committed fraud: "The plaintiffs seem infinitely above such a suspicion."[145] The plaintiffs' accounting books were to be believed, in short, not only because they were well ordered, but also because of the plaintiffs' stellar reputation. In this way, the community's judgment of a merchant's character entered even into the court's seemingly cut-and-dried assessment of accounting books.

Oaths

The oath was yet another procedure employed by the Parisian Merchant Court that was designed to assess the litigants' moral character. As the commercial jurist Toubeau explained, "In the merchant court, where more than in any other court good faith reigns, judges, and decides lawsuits, affirmations by oath are used and relied on more than in other courts."[146] Like the ordinary, civil-law courts of the Old Regime, the merchant court regularly required litigants to take a decisory oath, which as its name suggests, determined the litigation's outcome. If a party who was asked to take the oath did so, he won the lawsuit, but if he refused, he lost. Although from the modern perspective it seems extraordinary that the outcome of a lawsuit could turn solely on a litigant's oath,[147] in the world of the Old Regime an oath made to God on penalty of eternal damnation remained a serious matter. As Toubeau remarked, "If God, who is the avenger of perjury, does not punish perjurers visibly as he did in the past, they are no less grievously chastised, because we do not know from where our miseries, losses, sudden death, etc. come. But what must give us even greater fear is the eternal damnation that such an enormous sin merits."[148] For eighteenth-century merchants, whose lives were structured around a constant series of religious rituals, God was in a literal sense omnipresent. Indeed, this was the experience even of those who, like the glazier Ménétra, became very critical of the Church. Within the merchant court itself, as noted above, each sitting began with attendance at Mass, and the court held numerous special Masses for the repose of the souls of various departed judges and consuls. In this context, people who pledged their souls in taking an oath to God were likely to think twice before lying.

Although the decisory oath was in no way unique to the merchant courts, it was administered differently in these courts than it was in the ordinary, civil-law courts.[149] In the civil-law courts, a party could be asked to take the oath only when the party who bore the burden of proof failed to meet the evidentiary standard of full proof, which consisted either of "authentic" written evidence (such as a notarized document) or some combination of half-proofs. "Private" written evidence (such as an unnotarized document) and a witness's testimony each constituted a half-proof.[150] Thus, for example, if a plaintiff seeking payment on an alleged contract offered as evidence only an unnotarized document, the judge might require either the plaintiff or the defendant to swear an oath as a means of completing the proof. In determining the party to whom to "defer the oath," as this procedure was termed, the judge was supposed to consider such factors as which party might be more likely to know any relevant information, as well as the status and reputation of the parties.

If the party who bore the burden of proof failed to proffer any evidence at all, however, the judge was required to defer the oath to his opponent.[151] Thus, in the typical scenario, when a plaintiff filed suit without mustering even a half-proof, the defendant would take the decisory oath swearing that he was under no obligation or that he had fulfilled it. The plaintiff's suit would then be dismissed. As a contemporary commentator explained, dismissal on the basis of the defendant's oath was appropriate because it was that for which the plaintiff himself had bargained: "[The plaintiff] relied on [the defendant's] faith; this is the title to property that the alleged creditor chose for himself; he therefore cannot seek to eschew it."[152] Rather than demanding a writing or other evidence, the plaintiff had decided to place his trust in the defendant's good faith, and it was thus only right that the plaintiff's claim should be resolved by the defendant's taking an oath in which he pledged his faith.

Given that the traditional theory behind the decisory oath was that it supplied a means of completing incomplete proof, Toubeau's assertion that it was used more frequently in the merchant courts than in the ordinary, civil-law courts is at first glance surprising. The Parisian Merchant Court—despite some contemporary jurists' suggestions to the contrary[153]—does not appear to have followed strict Roman-canon rules of proof, and thus would seem to have had no need for the decisory oath as an evidentiary gap-filler.

Because the merchant court relied so much on accounting books, it was impossible for it to adhere firmly to the Roman-canon law of proof. The traditional rules of proof divided evidence into the categories of written and oral, and then subdivided the written category into authentic or public writings, on the one hand, and private writings, on the other. Authentic or public writings were governmental, including judicial decisions, as well as documents signed and witnessed before a notary public. Private writings were documents that were written and signed by the parties on their own, without the involvement of a notary. While accounting books were clearly written evidence, they did not fit neatly into either the public or private subcategories. As unnotarized documents, written and maintained by the parties themselves, accounting books would not seem to be public writings. But unlike such private writings as unnotarized contracts, which were drafted for the benefit of the parties to the contract, a merchant's accounting books were kept—by order of the monarchy and its Commercial Ordinance—for the benefit of all who considered transacting business with the merchant. In Toubeau's view, accounting books formed their own category of written proof located somewhere between "public writing" and "private writing" and appropriately termed "intermediate writing."[154]

Since accounting books did not belong within any of the traditional categories of proof, it was difficult to apply to them the Roman-canon rules quantifying proof. Thus, Guyot, author of a contemporary legal dictionary and prominent jurist of the Roman and canon-law traditions, was clearly confused about what evidentiary weight to accord accounting books and noted with some shock that the commercial jurist, Toubeau, seemed to regard them as full proof: "Accounting books when they are kept in good order become . . . a beginning of written proof, and in some sense a half-proof. Toubeau even seems to want the court to give full faith to these books, especially when the merchants to whom they belong are of good reputation."[155] In fact, Toubeau never addressed the question of how to quantify the evidentiary value of accounting books but simply indicated that such books are an important source of evidence in the merchant court. Toubeau's assessment of the evidentiary role of accounting books dovetails with the reports written by merchant court arbiters, who relied heavily on the books without attaching a quantifiable value to them—or to any other form of evidence.

Because the merchant court's approach to weighing evidence was much more flexible than the traditional rules of proof would permit, it would seem to have had no need for the decisory oath as an evidentiary gap-filler. Nonetheless, the oath played a very important role in the merchant court—and according to Toubeau, a more important one than in other courts. This was for two reasons. First, although the merchant court did not concern itself with the technical question of whether accounting books constituted full proof or half proof, it relied on such evidence extensively and sought a means of ensuring that its reliance was justified. By requiring the party who wished to enter his accounting books into evidence to take the decisory oath, the court helped ensure that the faith it placed in the books' accuracy was justified by the party's willingness to pledge his own faith. Second, since the decision to defer the decisory oath to a party was premised on a determination that he possessed knowledge of the facts at issue and, more importantly, a good reputation, the oath was also a means of ensuring that reliance on accounting books was justified by the knowledge and reputation of the merchant who prepared them. As explained by Rogue, a commercial lawyer at the Merchant Court of Angers, "In choosing to which party to defer the oath, the judge must consider the status of the litigants, [and also] which is the party who is worthier of faith or who is likely to have greater knowledge of the facts."[156] In this way, administration of the decisory oath by the merchant court judge was yet another vehicle for the community's judgment to enter into the litigation and into the adjudicatory process.

That the oath was a means for the merchant court to help ensure that victory was granted only to litigants reputed to be of good faith is evident from the distinctive way in which it administered the oath. In contrast to the procedure followed in the ordinary courts, the merchant court required all plaintiffs to take an oath attesting to the truthfulness of their claims, even when they proffered what was indisputably full proof—namely, a notarized contract. Likewise, defendants raising affirmative defenses were required to back these defenses by an oath. In Toubeau's words, "The appearance of litigants in person before the court, which is so valued by our edict [the Commercial Ordinance of 1673], is designed not only so that the parties can speak for themselves, but also so that they can affirm by oath their claims or their defenses; thus a merchant court does not find for a plaintiff, even if the defendant defaulted by failing to appear, and even if the plaintiff has a written contract as evidence, unless the plaintiff affirms by oath that what he claims is truly owed him."[157] That the merchant court required plaintiffs to take the decisory oath even when they proffered full proof clearly indicates that the oath's function in commercial adjudication went far beyond its civil-law role of evidentiary gap-filling. In the merchant court, its primary purpose was instead to highlight the fact that, as Toubeau explained, "in the merchant court . . . more than in any other court good faith reigns."[158] To win a case in the merchant court, it was not sufficient for the plaintiff to satisfy a technical legal requirement concerning the sufficiency of the evidence. His claim had to be true—so true, in fact, that he was willing to pledge his eternal soul and good reputation on its merit.

Like the relationship between accounting books and reputation, the relationship between the decisory oath and reputation was circular. The party who swore the decisory oath pledged his faith and thereby proved that he was a person of good faith. A judge, however, decided to which party to defer the oath based largely on the parties' reputations for good (or bad) faith—a determination sometimes deemed synonymous with social standing. As one arbiter explained, in recommending that the court defer the oath to the defendant: "In these sorts of cases one considers the status of the litigants . . . ; . . . the [defendant] appears to have tipped the scales; he enjoys a certain rank in society, he is well established; the [plaintiff] is without any status [and] lacks a domicile other than an inn; it is, thus, in my view, to the [defendant] that the oath must be deferred."[159]

It was thus the perfect conjunction of accounting books, reputation, and decisory oath that would be most advantageous for the litigant. Among such fortunate litigants was a wholesaler from Mâcon, who sued a Parisian wine merchant, demanding payment for wine that he claimed to have sold the defendant.[160] Based largely on the plaintiff's accounting books and on the defendant's total lack thereof, the arbiter concluded that the court ought to find for the plaintiff. In so recommending, however, the arbiter also suggested that the court defer the decisory oath to the plaintiff in order to be sure that it was deciding correctly. Paraphrasing the work of a contemporary jurist, the arbiter advised that it was the plaintiff, as the party with properly maintained accounting books and a good reputation, who ought to swear the decisory oath: "In one word, the order in which accounting books are kept, the reputation of the parties, and the most apparent good faith must always enter into consideration in determining to which party to defer the oath."[161]

Even those litigants who proffered no accounting books or other evidence, however, could win based exclusively on their reputations and willingness to swear the decisory oath. Consider, for example, Jean Desbordes' lawsuit against his relative Jacques Desbordes, who, he claimed, owed him over 234 livres.[162] Neither party kept accounting books, and Jacques denied that he owed the money. Jacques did admit, however, that he had at one time verbally acknowledged that he owed Jean 100 livres. He insisted, however, that since he and Jean had made no writing memorializing their transaction, he was not bound by this verbal acknowledgment. Given the dearth of evidence, the arbiter concluded that the only way to resolve this contest of credibility was to defer the decisory oath to one or the other of the litigants.

Deeming Jacques' effort to escape liability on the grounds that there was no written contract proof of his bad faith, the arbiter decided that the court must defer the decisory oath to Jean: "Given the bad faith of Jacques Desbordes, who now denies owing a sum, which he admits to having previously verbally recognized that he owed, and only because there is no written promise on his part, the undersigned believes that it is appropriate to take the oath of Jean Desbordes that all claims in his brief are true and exact."[163] Thus deployed, the oath was a way for the court to demonstrate its commitment to promoting the community's sense of justice—and, in particular, its commitment to ensuring that, no matter the state of the evidence, good faith would triumph over bad.

Sentimental Legal Reasoning

Arbiters sometimes employed a sentimental, narrative-based form of reasoning that lent itself particularly well to a jurisprudence designed to ensure that good faith would always trump bad. The sentimental style elided the distinction between law and fact, such that the judgment recommended seemed to follow naturally, indeed necessarily, from the highly melodramatic presentation of facts. Like all melodrama, such reports presented a narrative in which virtue and vice—merchants of good and bad faith—confronted one another.[164] By recommending judgment in favor of the merchant of good faith, the arbiter resolved the plot in a way that ensured the triumph of virtue. Reports penned in this sentimental, melodramatic style are characterized first and foremost by their narrative form. In relating a narrative account, the arbiter presented the particular transaction at issue in the context of the parties' respective characters and lives. In extravagant prose, the arbiter commented on the litigants' various virtues and vices, noting the ways in which these contributed to the formation of the transaction in question. In this way, the arbiter's judgment as to which party should win the lawsuit appeared to emerge directly from his assessment of the parties' moral character.

Such narratives could be relatively brief. For example, this was the case in the arbiter's report prepared in a lawsuit brought by a business association ("the associated purchasers of the forest of the Parc de Meudon") against a man named Castel, seeking payment on two promissory notes that he had made to its order.[165] The arbiter began his report by musing on the nature of a certain class of less than honorable debtors to which Castel apparently belonged: "You are surely not surprised, messieurs, to encounter debtors who, finding it impossible to fulfill their obligations, and in order to gain time, create difficulties and obligate you . . . to send them before arbiters."[166] Having thus set the stage, the arbiter then introduced the main character: "I present to you Monsieur Castel, as one of those debtors who, in order to elude, invent a large number of arguments and present them only gradually as they believe them necessary for their advantage."[167]

The arbiter next turned to examine Castel's three defenses. Two of these consisted of assertions that he had, in fact, paid a significant portion of the debt — an argument that the arbiter rejected. As concerns Castel's first defense, however, the arbiter refused to reveal what it actually was, thus drawing on his readers' imagination to supply horror to the unknown: "With your permission, I will conceal the first; it is odious."[168] Having thus portrayed the defendant as an untrustworthy character who had said or done something too heinous to be mentioned, the arbiter drew the obvious conclusion: "Monsieur Castel clearly and legitimately owes" money to the plaintiff.[169] Moreover, in sharp contrast to Castel, the members of the plaintiff business association were, as depicted by the arbiter, models of virtue: "These Messieurs [are] always ready to help the unfortunate and to grant them opportunities."[170] In this way, the plaintiffs' charity and kindness served to highlight Castel's lack thereof and to legitimate their demand for judgment. Moreover, the arbiter suggested that, because the plaintiffs were so virtuous, they were willing to grant Castel a substantial moratorium on payment. It was on this hopeful note — as the virtuous plaintiffs sought to redeem the wicked defendant — that the arbiter concluded his narrative.

In contrast to this fairly succinct narrative, others were sometimes quite a bit more extensive. The arbiter's report in the case of *Blaincourt v. Dubois et Dubuisson, entrepreneurs* is an example of the sentimental style of reasoning in its most fully elaborated form.[171] In this case, a man named Blaincourt sued Dubois and Dubuisson, the owners of a starch factory, for money that he claimed they owed him for his services as their agent. Dubois had discovered a secret process for making starch out of spoiled flour. As a result, he obtained an authorization from the King's Council to build his own starch factory employing this secret process. Lacking the funds to undertake this venture himself, Dubois enlisted Dubuisson as his associate, who provided the necessary financial backing. Dubuisson then made an agreement with Blaincourt, the exact terms of which were the subject of the lawsuit, but which provided generally that Blaincourt would be responsible for the daily operation of the factory whenever Dubuisson had to leave town.

Believing that he had been remunerated insufficiently for his services as their agent, Blaincourt sued Dubois and Dubuisson after five months had passed. In response, Dubuisson argued that he had no formal agreement with Blaincourt establishing the latter as his agent. Instead, he claimed, he had allowed Blaincourt to help him during his absences, in return for some money, purely out of kindness. Dubuisson had already been very charitable with Blaincourt, giving him money on many past occasions, and his decision to allow Blaincourt to oversee the factory while he was away was but one more act of charity. Furthermore, Dubuisson continued, he had already given Blaincourt more than he deserved, since Blaincourt was extremely negligent in overseeing the factory and thereby caused him and Dubois to lose a great deal of money. In addition, Dubuisson claimed that he had given Blaincourt more money than Blaincourt was now willing to acknowledge. No response from Dubois is reported, presumably because whatever deal existed with Blaincourt was made by Dubuisson.

The arbiter concluded the report by recommending strongly that the judges find in favor of Dubois and Dubuisson. In his view, not only should Blaincourt's claim be dismissed, but in addition Blaincourt should be made to pay Dubuisson back for the money that he claimed he never received and for which he could not account. The way in which the arbiter arrived at this conclusion was through the presentation of a narrative in which the virtues and vices of the various parties are so readily apparent that no doubt was possible concerning who should win. The arbiter began his report by stating that before he explained the parties' respective claims and supporting arguments, "it is very essential to give you an idea of the characters [*personnages*] and of their position."[172] As the term "characters" would suggest, what follows is a description of the parties that reads as if it were excerpted directly from a novel:

> M. Dubois is a former officer for whom fortune serves above all to furnish the mediocre necessities; he has applied himself forever to chemistry and this art, which is most often fatal to those who try to make discoveries, provided him with knowledge of means to fabricate high-quality starch from all kinds of spoiled flour; thus, after different experiments conducted in the presence of the commissioner of the [Royal] Academy [of Sciences] and upon the commissioner's certification, Dubois was authorized by decree of the [King's] Council to set up a starch factory. This authorization, though potentially profitable, did not eliminate his incapacity to provide the necessary capital; he had only talent and needed money, thus an associate; but new enterprises rarely find proselytes; it is necessary to find men who, blind with ambition, are willing to risk their fortune on their faith in the experiments, whose success does not guarantee profit; we are about to see who is the man whom the most gratifying hopes seduce.

> M. Dubuisson is the valet of the king's barber; he was born with that tender soul that often causes generosity to degenerate into a shortcoming and that, due to an inability to discern those on behalf of whom feeling must weep, transforms a virtue into a weakness; having besides a too credulous spirit, with an ambition too eager to seize upon the first projects that might satisfy it, Dubuisson resides in the country, where he lives without spending much money.
>
> M. de Blaincourt is one of those beings who, after having passed through different places in the army and lived from day to day, turned up during a time of peace in the capital, where tumult serves to disguise to some extent their unhappy existence, where after having spent the year, they find themselves astonished by the miracle that enabled them to subsist and hope that it will enable them to survive the next year; pillars of the cafés, trying to convince themselves that they have dined because they find themselves in the cafés during the hours when others occupy themselves with precipitating digestion, nourishing themselves with the fumes of hope; amateurs in business; among those beings, in conclusion, whom unhappiness renders as crafty as ingenious and whom it is impossible to approach without their producing a very strong shock, like a jolt of electricity, that makes itself felt by all those who dare to touch them.[173]

The arbiter's description of these characters at the beginning of his report left little doubt concerning how the narrative would develop and to whom the arbiter would grant victory. Dubois, the scientific genius, was unfit for all practical endeavors. While he understood the abstruse complexities of science, he lacked the worldliness necessary to undertake commercial activity. Not surprisingly then, the arbiter turned to Dubuisson, and thereafter Dubois' role in the establishment and running of the starch factory all but disappears from the report. Dubuisson, in contrast, possessed common sense, but he suffered from the Achilles heel of an overtrusting and overly generous nature. A kind man, living simply in the countryside and eschewing the falseness and luxury of the city, he embodied traditional, Christian ideals of simplicity and charity. As one would expect, Dubuisson was the inevitable dupe of Blaincourt, a man so corrupted by the vileness of the city—so obsessed with luxury and so accustomed to idleness—that he was a danger to all who approached him. The arbiter's decision in favor of Dubois and Dubuisson and against Blaincourt followed directly from this opening narrative account of the parties' moral character. Hardworking, productive, generous, and honest, Dubois and Dubuisson necessarily had to triumph over the lazy, selfish, and duplicitous Blaincourt.

The sentimental narrative style that characterized the arbiters' reports in the lawsuits brought by "the associated purchasers" (in 1784) and by Blaincourt (in 1773) is strikingly akin to the literary style identified by Sarah Maza and

David Bell as characteristic of late-eighteenth-century French legal writing.[174] According to these authors, lawyers in the 1770s and 1780s, who wrote trial briefs, or *mémoires judiciaires,* which were also published as pamphlets for public distribution, began self-consciously to borrow stylistic elements from the new, melodramatic theatrical form the *drame bourgeois.* Maza and Bell suggest that lawyers adopted this style for a variety of reasons, but primarily as a means of galvanizing public opinion in the wake of the Maupeou coup of 1771, which abolished the *parlements* and thereby engendered a growing fear of despotic rule. But while the legal briefs that these historians have examined may have been influenced to some extent by late-eighteenth-century political events and literary styles, the example of these arbiters' reports—which were never published and publicly distributed—cautions against neglecting the fact that legal discourse does serve distinctively legal functions within distinctively legal institutions. Sentimental legal reasoning, in short, was a mode of adjudicating legal disputes—a mode that enabled the adjudicator to harness the community's moral sensibilities, thereby reinforcing these, while at the same time legitimating the adjudicator's own exercise of power. As such, it was a mode of adjudication that was particularly well suited to early-modern society, which was characterized by a relatively weak state apparatus, on the one hand, and relatively powerful religious and communal norms, on the other. Along these lines, it bears emphasis that, as James Whitman has argued, a sentimental mode of legal reasoning appears to date back in France at least to the early seventeenth century.[175]

But while there is good reason to suspect that sentimental reasoning was employed across early-modern French judicial institutions, it is a mode of legal argument that was of distinctive importance for the Parisian Merchant Court. More than any other court, the merchant court understood its primary function to be, as Mercier claimed, discovering "the good faith of one of the litigants and the bad faith of the other."[176] By transforming contests of legal claims into battles between virtue and vice, sentimental legal reasoning bridged the distance between legal and moral judgment and thereby enabled the merchant court to act in accordance with its self-conception as a bastion of merchant virtue.

3

An Equity-Oriented View of Contract: The Court's Resolution of Disputes Concerning Sales, Employment, and Marriage

*There is nothing that better suits human faith than doing what one has promised, and nothing that conforms better to the law of the merchant courts [*droit consulaire*], because all lawsuits between merchants should be resolved summarily and equitably.*

—Toubeau, *Les institutes du droit consulaire*

Disputes concerning small-scale, highly relational contracts long were and remained the Parisian Merchant Court's primary focus. Such disputes usually involved two litigants, tied together in a relatively long-term, contractual relationship, framed by repeated extensions of credit, rather than by formal written contract. The court's self-conception as an institution designed to enforce virtue by restoring severed bonds of trust was based to a significant extent on the fact that it was primarily these kinds of relational contract disputes with which it was accustomed to dealing. Indeed, it was relational contracting that lay at the root of the court's approach to procedure—an approach that sought to draw on the web of communal institutions and structures within which merchants lived and worked. But what substantive law did the court apply?

This chapter explores how the Parisian Merchant Court resolved the contract disputes that came before it—disputes concerning primarily the sale of goods and services, but also employment relationships and marriage contracts.[1] In so doing, it touches on the complex interrelationship in such cases between procedural and substantive law. However, before turning to the cases themselves, it is necessary briefly to consider the sources of the law applied by the court, not only in these contract disputes but also in those concerning business associations and negotiable instruments, analyzed in later chapters.

Sources of the Law

To inquire into the nature of the law applied by the merchant court is to approach a topic about which much has been written but remarkably little is known—namely, the history of the law merchant. To what extent did the procedural and substantive law applied by the Parisian Merchant Court accord with the standard account of the law merchant?

THE STANDARD ACCOUNT OF THE LAW MERCHANT

The standard account of the law merchant is one that Charles Donahue Jr.—borrowing the phrase from Wyndham Anstis Bewes's eponymous classic—has aptly termed the "romance of the law merchant."[2] According to this account, the law merchant first emerged in Europe around the twelfth century, during the period of economic recovery and social and political restructuring that attended the rise of the early Continental monarchies. The standard account suggests that, beginning at this time, and lasting well into the early-modern period, merchants across Europe developed common, customary practices designed to facilitate commercial development. Because these customs ran counter to the traditional procedural and substantive law applied in ordinary, noncommercial courts, merchants eschewed the latter and developed their own merchant-run courts in which to apply their merchant custom. As argued by one proponent of the standard account, the law merchant was "voluntarily produced, voluntarily adjudicated, and voluntarily enforced," and in its absence, "the commercial revolution of the eleventh through fifteenth century that ultimately led to the Renaissance and industrial revolution, could not have occurred."[3]

This merchant custom, we are told, was characterized by both universality and dynamism. The law merchant was universal in that it applied to all merchants across Europe; indeed, it was precisely this universality that was so valued by merchants seeking to trade with one another across borders. But while universal, this body of law was also dynamic, such that it constantly changed to meet evolving merchant interests. According to the standard account, the law merchant was able to be both universal and dynamic, because unlike the formal law, which was created and amended by sovereign authorities, the law merchant consisted simply of merchant custom and thus took root wherever merchants happened to be and changed naturally in accordance with their needs and desires.

What precisely was this merchant custom? While the standard account provides some indication of the law merchant's approach to procedure, it is remarkably vague about the substantive content of this body of law. In the words of J. H. Baker, "The obscurity begins with the very concept of the 'law merchant,' which has been differently understood by different writers and continues to be used in widely divergent senses."[4] As concerns procedure, the standard account emphasizes that the law merchant prioritized speed, cost-minimization, and expertise in adjudication—goals that it promoted through such methods as limiting the need for written pleadings and proof and relying on merchant judges. As concerns the substantive law, however, the standard account offers varying, somewhat unclear, and not entirely consistent depictions.

In some versions of the standard account, we are told simply that "the Law Merchant enforced commercial standards, mercantile values and trade interests,"[5] but no particular standards, values, and interests are identified. The implication is that whatever these standards, values, and interests may have been, they were all offshoots of a presumably universal merchant interest in promoting trade and economic growth over and above other values. Other versions of the standard account are more precise, suggesting that the law merchant consisted of a particular set of practices that ultimately gave rise to modern commercial law—including, notably, those practices underlying the bankruptcy system and negotiable instruments.[6] How precisely these practices arose is a question that the standard account leaves unanswered. As such practices are assumed to facilitate merchants' supposedly universal and predominant interest in promoting economic growth, the question of how they arose is evidently deemed one of mere mechanics and thus of little interest. Finally, yet other versions of the standard account of the law merchant suggest that merchant custom consisted of particular norms or customs existing between particular types of traders engaged in particular types of transactions—such as, for example, norms about whether the buyer or seller of a certain type of good was required to arrange for delivery. In the absence of a contractual agreement concerning delivery, the law merchant would supply the applicable default rule by looking to such norms. Accordingly, "customary law and contract law [we]re closely related."[7]

Although these three versions of the substantive content of the law merchant differ in significant respects, they share two common assumptions. First, they assume that the law merchant is the product exclusively of merchant norms and practices. Second, they assume that the law merchant arose in a way that was clear and incontrovertible, such that merchants at all times knew what the law merchant was—and, in fact, they knew what it was, because it facilitated what they all understood to be their interests.

One of the most remarkable features of the standard account of the law merchant (in all its forms) is that it is based on relatively little historical evidence. In support of their claims, proponents of this account rely significantly on citations to other secondary scholarship written in the same vein—and, in particular, to the classic works of Levin Goldschmidt and William Mitchell.[8] As for the primary sources cited, these are largely published treatises and statutes, rather than archival court records. Moreover, because the driving theme of the standard account is that the law merchant was the same throughout Europe and across many centuries, proponents sometimes deploy these published sources in strikingly ahistorical ways. For example, one author bases his description of procedure in the supposedly pan-European, medieval law merchant largely on a single treatise, written by the late-seventeenth-century French jurist Toubeau—a treatise concerning the French merchant courts of Toubeau's own era.[9] In addition, while the standard account relies on published primary sources only minimally, and often poorly, it largely ignores archival records from actual merchant institutions. The absence of such archival evidence is due, no doubt, in part to the inherent difficulty of archival research, but is also likely due to the nature of the standard account itself. Since the law merchant is presumed to have been the same everywhere, and since merchant interests are presumed to be universal, unchanging, and self-evident, why bother to explore how the law merchant actually operated in particular institutions at particular moments in time?

The standard account of the law merchant has a long history,[10] which has been given new life in the last several decades by two groups of scholars. First, legal scholars advocating the establishment of a transnational commercial order created by and reflecting the interests of merchants have called for a return to the law merchant.[11] Second, some of the economists instrumental in developing the field of institutional economics were inspired to trace the institutional foundations of the modern Western economic and political order—and, thus, perhaps to transplant these in the developing world—by the history of the law merchant.[12] Notably, however, a prominent institutional economist has recently published a book challenging the validity of institutional analysis undertaken without sufficient historical information and contextualization, and in so arguing, points explicitly to unsupported claims that have been made about the history of the law merchant.[13] Moreover, the standard account of the law merchant has been subject to growing criticism in recent years from legal historians who have argued, among other things, that the law applied by merchants to resolve their disputes varied significantly across jurisdictions, that sovereign rulers played an important role in its development, and that there was, in fact, no coherent body of customary rules and practices that could be said to constitute "the law merchant."[14] These critics have focused, however, largely on English developments, and many questions remain unanswered. In short, more research—and especially archival research—is needed to elucidate the history underlying the standard account of the law merchant.

This book's account of the eighteenth-century Parisian Merchant Court seeks, in part, to address this need for further research. It bears emphasis, however, that its contribution in this regard is necessarily modest. Because the standard account asserts that the law merchant was the same across Europe for many centuries, it must be tested through research conducted into many different institutions operating in different locations at different time periods—including both merchant-run courts and ordinary, civil courts. This book focuses exclusively on the eighteenth-century Parisian Merchant Court and thus cannot provide such a comprehensive overview. It can, however, contribute to the broader project of undertaking studies of individual institutions, which read together, will one day provide the comprehensive perspective that we are currently lacking.

Another reason that this book's contribution to evaluating the standard account of the law merchant is necessarily modest is that it explores the eighteenth century. Proponents of the standard account have focused primarily on the Middle Ages, arguing that, as nation-states began to take clear shape in the early-modern period, the universal scope of the law merchant began to falter. Yet, precisely because many such proponents have sought to demonstrate the continued viability of the *lex mercatoria,* they have also been reluctant to suggest that the law merchant disappeared in the early-modern era. Thus, for example, Bruce L. Benson claims that, while in the early-modern era the law merchant "bec[ame] less universal and more localized under state influence," it "did not die" and "merchant custom remained the underlying source of much of commercial law in Europe."[15] Likewise, Leon E. Trakman asserts that, to the extent that early-modern rulers codified commercial law, they were simply incorporating merchant custom into the law of the state, such that, to take the French example, "customs and usages of merchants were embodied in French law, while the Law Merchant was recognized as a reality in the French legal System."[16] Because the standard account of the law merchant, though focused on the Middle Ages, runs well into the early-modern period, this book's study of an eighteenth-century merchant court bears on the validity of this account.

THE LAW APPLIED IN THE PARISIAN MERCHANT COURT

What then was the law applied by the Parisian Merchant Court? Was it, as the standard account would have us believe, merchant custom, developed to promote merchant interests, and thereafter encapsulated in the monarchy's statutory law, such as the Commercial Ordinance of 1673? The short answer is that, while some aspects of the standard account seem to be accurate, others do not. Historical reality, in sum, was far more complex than the standard account would suggest.

Procedural Law

As for the procedure applied by the Parisian Merchant Court, much of this was, as the standard account asserts, developed by merchants themselves with the aim of adjudicating disputes in a rapid, low-cost, and expert manner. It is clear, however, that a great deal of the court's procedure derived from the learned tradition of the Roman-canon law, as well as from statute. Moreover, it was designed not only to promote efficiency and expertise but also to advance a very different set of goals concerning both status and morality.

The court's procedural law was based on three separate sources: (1) the Procedure Ordinance of 1667; (2) the *ius commune,* or common law, which emerged in Europe beginning in the twelfth century and, combining Roman and canon law, was applied (to differing extents) throughout the Continent, when no local statute or custom was on point; and (3) the merchant court's own daily experience deciding cases. That the court's procedure was based, in part, on the Procedure Ordinance and the *ius commune* suffices to indicate that, at least as of the early-modern era, merchants themselves were not exclusively responsible for its development.

Proponents of the standard account of the law merchant do generally recognize that the early-modern state came to play some role in the formation of this body of law. They argue that the state began to incorporate merchant custom into the formal law—an argument for which the example of the Parisian Merchant Court provides some support. Since the court was first established in 1563, and the Procedure Ordinance was not drafted until more than a century later, it is likely that the court had to develop most of its own procedure, aspects of which were then codified in the ordinance. Significantly, however, and contrary to what proponents of the standard account have usually suggested,[17] much of the procedure that merchants thus developed was borrowed from the learned tradition of the *ius commune.* To note but a few examples, the decisory oath, the practice of arbitration, and the enforcement of *nuda pacta,* or mere agreements (such as oral agreements), were all elements of the *ius commune.*[18]

As for the goals served by the Parisian Merchant Court's approach to procedure, these included, but were not limited to, speed, cost-minimization, and expertise. As we have seen, the merchants who ran the court and appeared before it also placed great weight on promoting what they perceived to be virtue and developed procedure in furtherance of this goal. While they certainly had reasons of economic self-interest for seeking to be perceived as virtuous—namely, the desire to be deemed creditworthy—they were motivated by other factors as well. In a society that was highly status-oriented and in which commerce was traditionally disdained, merchants had every incentive to demonstrate their virtue as a means of defending and promoting their personal honor and reputation. Moreover, for those who were true believers, it was important not merely to be perceived as virtuous but, for the sake of their own spiritual well-being, to behave virtuously as well. For all these reasons, the merchant court deployed procedure not only with the aim of achieving efficient and expert dispute resolution but also with that of encouraging such merchant virtues as charity, leniency, and harmony.

Substantive Law

As concerns the substantive law applied by the Parisian Merchant Court, the sources of this law varied depending on the nature of the dispute. It is clear, however, that, unlike postrevolutionary France, where judges are (at least in theory) deprived of law-making powers,[19] merchant court judges themselves made a great deal of the law that the court applied. This was true of all commercial law but especially of contract law, since there were so few statutes or treatises on point that might limit judicial discretion.

To some extent, the discretion of the merchant court judges was constrained by the *Parlement* of Paris, which was authorized to hear appeals from the merchant court in decisions in which the amount in controversy exceeded 500 livres.[20] But according to Masson, a former judge of the Parisian Merchant Court, the right of appeal "is hardly used . . . because [merchant court] judgments are enforceable notwithstanding the appeal."[21] When the losing party did appeal, the rulings of the *Parlement* were, in theory, binding and final. In reality, however, the merchant court had quite a bit of room to maneuver around rulings with which it was dissatisfied. Sometimes, it directly challenged the *Parlement* by appealing to the King's Council, as it did in its jurisdictional dispute with the municipal government. At other times, however—as in its development of a law of negotiable instruments that departed significantly from the Ordinance of 1673 and from established custom—the court appears simply to have ignored the dictates of the *Parlement,* which usually sought to enforce the letter of the law.[22] In short, because of the complexity of the Old Regime's jurisdictional terrain and the limited nature of the state's enforcement power, the *Parlement*'s authority was much greater in theory than it was in practice.

Contract Disputes The merchant court itself developed much of the law that it applied in contract disputes. That merchants thus played a predominant role in developing the law in line with the standard account of the law merchant. In contrast, however, to what this account has tended to suggest, much of this law was not particularly "lawlike." With some exceptions detailed below, the court did not resolve contract disputes by applying fixed, generally applicable rules, but instead by making a highly fact-dependent assessment of what equity required in the particular case. As the commercial jurist Toubeau explained, merchant courts "base their judgments almost exclusively on natural law" and "only good sense and reason must preside in these courts."[23] To the extent that equitable reasoning played such a key role in the resolution of contract disputes, it is far from clear that there was a body of law—"the law merchant"—that the court applied. Instead, the outcome of such litigation depended far more on how individual arbiters weighed the relevant equitable considerations—and thus ultimately, on the process or procedure of dispute resolution.

The court's determination of the equitable outcome in any given case was profoundly influenced by the prevailing norms and values of the community. To the extent that certain values were commonly held, they tended to manifest themselves in the court's holdings, regardless of the identity of the arbiter helping to decide the case. For example, because familial relations were universally recognized to be important, most arbiters attempted to decide intrafamily disputes in ways that would preserve family unity. In contrast, some values were held (or held particularly dearly) by only certain segments of the community. In cases implicating such values, the identity of the arbiter could prove decisive in how the litigation was resolved. Thus, guild leaders serving as arbiters sought to decide intra- and inter-guild disputes in ways that would reinforce the status of their guilds and their own power within them. And priests serving as arbiters were especially committed to deciding cases in ways that would promote Christian ideals of charity and leniency.

Importantly, as this brief exposition of some of the values animating the court's adjudication of contract disputes suggests, and as developed in greater detail below, the standard account has substantially oversimplified its depiction of the interests that the law merchant supposedly sought to advance. Merchants in all times and places have not, in other words, shared the same predominant interest in promoting economic growth above all other values. At times, the Parisian Merchant Court sought to further values of charity and leniency—by means, for example, of the doctrine of just price—with apparently little concern for the economic consequences of doing so. It is possible that, in so acting, the court understood itself to be reinforcing communal institutions and values that were key to the effective functioning of a market that was so heavily dependent on relational contracting.[24] But even if this is so, the court's concern with advancing charity and leniency cannot be reduced exclusively to such economic considerations. In short, for all the reasons described above, the court was also motivated by the desire to promote virtue.

The court's value-laden and outcome-oriented approach to resolving contract disputes was informed and supplemented to some extent by legal rules derived from three sources. Two of these—the *ius commune* and the *Coutume de Paris*—were, contrary to what the standard account of the law merchant would suggest, not developed by merchants themselves. The third source was commercial custom of the kind that figures prominently in at least one version of the standard account.

As developed by legal scholars over the course of many centuries, and most especially by the great jurists of the sixteenth century, the *ius commune* offered a set of background principles against which all contract disputes could be resolved.[25] These were very basic principles, such as the related requirements of cause, consent, and good faith, which functioned to establish the conditions necessary to form a valid contract. Of these three requirements, only that of good faith was directly litigated in the merchant court. But while arbiters did not usually discuss cause and consent explicitly, these well-established contract requirements seem to have informed arbiters' efforts to promote an equitable outcome. This makes sense, since the requirements of cause, consent, and good faith arose within the *ius commune* as part of an effort to guarantee the moral legitimacy of contracts. Accordingly, they were particularly well suited to an institution like the merchant court, which was so concerned with promoting virtue.

As developed by jurists of the canon law, the requirement of *causa* was a means of ensuring that parties to a contract undertook their contractual obligations for a reason, or cause—thus, of their own free will—and that this cause was morally legitimate.[26] Consent, a requirement implicit in the notion of a freely chosen "cause," was rooted in the Roman-law tradition. Roman law identified four kinds of "consensual contracts"—including the commercially crucial contracts of sale and partnership—which were based entirely on the parties' consent, rather than on any procedural formalities, and were therefore unenforceable if they had arisen through error, fraud, or duress. Because parties to these consensual contracts obligated themselves simply through an informal expression of their intent to do so, the Roman law deemed it appropriate to impose on them a requirement of acting with the utmost bona fides, or good faith.[27]

In addition to these general contract principles derived from the *ius commune,* the merchant court drew on specific rules of law that originated in the *Coutume de Paris.* As contemporaries understood the term, customary law referred to the local customs of various regions of France, which were recorded in the sixteenth century in regional codifications, known as the *Coutumes.*[28] The most important of these was the *Coutume de Paris,* on which arbiters appear to have relied primarily for two relatively narrow but important rules of law. First, they cited it as authority for the *saisie et revendication,* a form of replevin, discussed below, which was intended as a remedy for the seller who sold goods on credit and then, before receiving payment, discovered that the buyer was insolvent.[29] Second, arbiters regularly permitted the *action redhibitoire,* a cause of action originating in Roman law (the *actio redhibitoria*) and subsequently codified in the *Coutume de Paris.* The *action rédhibitoire* permitted buyers of horses and other draught animals to demand the return of their money if the animal had certain defects, and if suit was brought within nine days of delivery.[30]

Specific legal rules were also supplied by a third source of law: commercial custom. It was this kind of custom that, in at least one version of the standard account, constituted the core of the law merchant. These were the default rules that evolved over time among particular types of merchants to establish, in the absence of an applicable agreement, the respective responsibilities of the parties. Consider, for example, the Parisian Merchant Court's use of such a customary rule to decide the case of *Ibert v. Moreau.*[31] Ibert, a master draper, purchased some cotton cloth at the merchant fair in Saint–Denis. After buying the cloth, Ibert paid a teamster, Jean Louis Moreau, to have it delivered to the central office of the drapers' guild in Paris. When Ibert went to the office to collect his cloth, however, he could not find it, nor any record of its having been delivered. Accordingly, he sued the teamster for the price of the cloth. In analyzing the case, the arbiter concluded that the relevant question was how a teamster discharged his delivery obligation and thereby avoided liability. Since the parties did not negotiate this point, a default rule was necessary, and the arbiter looked for this in commercial custom. According to the arbiter:

> It is the custom that packages coming from Saint-Denis during a fair, containing either drapery or cloth, are driven directly to the market and deposited at the [guild] office, which must collect the duties [imposed by the guild on the goods].
>
> It is also the custom that at the time the goods are delivered, the teamster must inscribe in the register the number of packages and the names of the merchants for whom they are intended. Once this formality is completed, the teamster has discharged his duties, and the guild administration becomes responsible for the packages and for any errors that may be committed.[32]

Only by doing all of this would a teamster properly complete his delivery obligation, thereby shifting liability to the guild's administration. Applying this customary rule, the arbiter concluded that, because Moreau had failed to inscribe the delivery of the packages in the register in the drapers' guild, he remained liable for anything that happened to them.

While customary rules of this kind occasionally surfaced in the arbiters' reports, they did so only rarely, and thus seem to have played a fairly small role in deciding the cases that came before the merchant court. Contrary, in other words, to what at least one version of the standard account of the law merchant would suggest—and consistent with the views recently expressed by a number of modern-day commercial law scholars[33]—customary default rules were a relatively minor source of law. The reason for this seems to be that, even in the fairly tight-knit and insular world in which eighteenth-century merchants lived and worked, customary practice often proved too vague and imprecise to be of much use. Consider, for example, how difficult it was for the court to define the applicable commercial custom in a suit brought by a farmer to receive payment on some wheat that he had sold.[34] As the court determined, it was the custom of Parisian bakers to pay millers a lump sum to purchase wheat from farmers and then grind it into flour. In the case at hand, a Parisian baker gave money to a miller in the accustomed fashion, and the miller negotiated with a farmer from the town of Juilly to purchase wheat. After receiving the wheat, however, the miller failed to pay the farmer. Because the miller was declared insolvent, the farmer decided to sue the baker in the Parisian Merchant Court.

Upon receiving this case, the judge and consuls wrote directly to the parish priest in Juilly, asking him whether it was the customary practice among farmers, bakers, and millers from Juilly to permit recovery against the baker in such a situation. The priest responded in a letter, which he began by noting that he learned of local commercial custom "through the testimony of various farmers."[35] According to the priest, these farmers explained that when a farmer was not paid, the customary rule in Juilly was that he could demand payment from the baker, even if the baker claimed to have given the money to the miller. However, the priest reported, it was also the custom in Juilly that bakers always accompanied millers when they went to purchase wheat from farmers. The puzzle for the priest was that, in the case at hand, the baker-defendant was Parisian, and he had followed the Parisian custom of not accompanying the miller. Thus, the priest had to decide whether the two customs from Juilly—namely, the baker being held liable when the farmer was not paid, and the baker accompanying the miller to purchase wheat—were linked, forming in essence a single, customary norm. If the two customs were linked, then the baker would be held liable only if he had accompanied the miller (and thus was presumably involved in the negotiation for the purchase of the wheat). If instead they were distinct, then the baker would be held liable, no matter whether he had accompanied the miller.

Since the defendant baker had not accompanied the miller in the case at hand, the outcome of the litigation hinged on defining the applicable norm correctly, but unfortunately this norm was anything but clear. As custom did not simply reveal itself, the priest was forced to make the kind of outcome-oriented, equitable judgment that characterized so much of the merchant court's jurisprudence. Accordingly, while the priest recommended that the baker be held liable, his basis for doing so appears to have been that, in his personal judgment, this would be the fairest outcome. In this respect, the use of such merchant custom in the Parisian Merchant Court may, in fact, parallel its role in modern-day commercial adjudication, where according to at least one legal scholar, "appeals to custom . . . often turn out to be appeals to a kind of moral reflection,"[36] requiring the decision-maker ultimately to make a normative judgment about which outcome seems most equitable.

Disputes Concerning Business Associations and Negotiable Instruments

Before exploring in depth how the merchant court resolved the contract disputes that came before it, it is necessary to say a word about the law applied by the court in other disputes that it adjudicated. While the court resolved contract disputes largely, though not entirely, through case-by-case, equitable reasoning, other areas of commercial law—including notably, the law of business associations and of negotiable instruments—were somewhat less within the court's direct control. The Commercial Ordinance of 1673 codified both these areas of the law.[37] Nonetheless, as discussed later in this book, the court came to deviate significantly from many provisions of the ordinance.[38] In this sense, the standard account of the law merchant has been right to emphasize the predominant role played by merchants in developing their own law.

At the same time, it bears emphasis that Roman law provided an important foundation for the court's approach to the law of business associations. So too did modern natural law theory, the era's predominant school of legal thought. Most importantly, in adjudicating disputes regarding both business associations and negotiable instruments — like those regarding contracts — the court brought to bear a complex panoply of values and interests, not all of which are reducible to a concern with promoting efficient economic growth. And while it is true that, as the eighteenth century progressed, the court's development of these areas of the law — and, in particular, the law of negotiable instruments — became increasingly focused on the goal of creating an efficient market, its movement in this direction was contested by many and was at times faltering. Thus, the story of the law merchant — in which the rise of the negotiable instrument has long figured prominently — is fraught with much more internal dissension, debate, and resistance than has been recognized.

A Note on Codification and Treatise Literature While, in practice, the court often departed from the requirements of both the Procedure Ordinance of 1667 and the Commercial Ordinance of 1673, codification was nonetheless significant. As we shall see, codification was an important component of the royal effort to rationalize and centralize the administration of commerce, whose ultimate (and unintended) consequence was in turn to cause merchant courts and chambers of commerce across France to recognize and unite in furtherance of common interests, even against the monarchy itself. For present purposes, however, it suffices to emphasize that codification played a key role in giving rise to a body of treatise literature, which sought to explicate the royal ordinances.

Because treatise literature tended to focus on those areas of the law that were codified — namely, procedure, business associations, and negotiable instruments — merchant court arbiters and lawyers tended to cite such literature when questions arose relating to these areas of the law. Thus, occasional references to treatises — and in particular to those of Philippe Bornier and of the former Parisian Merchant Court judge Philibert-Joseph Masson — appear in arbiters' reports and legal briefs.[39] Such citations were, however, few and far between. This is likely due, in part, to the fact that the court tended to focus on achieving an equitable outcome in the particular case and thus had little interest in treatises, which by their nature seek to describe fixed legal rules. Furthermore, treatises often adhered closely to the structure of the ordinance and were updated infrequently at best. Thus, to the extent that the court readily departed from the provisions of the statutory law and regularly reconfigured its own judge-made law in significant ways, treatises were likely of limited utility.

There is, however, reason to believe that treatises—and, in particular, those written by commercial jurists, who were themselves merchants—had some influence on the merchant court's development of the law. As noted above, citations to such literature, while rare, did occur. In addition, there are parallels between some of the court's arguments and those set forth in the treatise literature that strongly suggest the court's reliance on this body of work, even when it failed to cite it. For example, as discussed in a later chapter, when the monarchy issued an edict in 1759, which limited the geographic scope of merchant court jurisdiction, the Parisian Merchant Court developed in opposition a complex argument based on the premise that its jurisdiction derived from the subject matter of commerce, rather than the merchant status of the defendant.[40] As this highly sophisticated premise was developed at length in treatises written by contemporary commercial jurists, it seems certain that the court was intimately familiar with such literature. Indeed, Jean Toubeau, the author of what was perhaps the most famous commercial treatise of the late seventeenth and eighteenth centuries—*Les institutes du droit consulaire, ou les elemens de la jurisprudence des marchands*—asserted that there was significant demand for commercial treatises among contemporary merchant court judges.

A successful merchant from Bourges, Toubeau had served both as the city's *prévôt des marchands* and as judge of the local merchant court. In seeking to adjudicate the disputes that came before him, he apparently realized that there was no comprehensive account of the law applicable in merchant courts and thus decided to write one for his own benefit. After doing so, however, he discovered that there was great demand among merchant court judges throughout France for such a treatise and, accordingly, decided to publish it as an aid for them as well: "All the judges and consuls, in the discussions that I had with them, in person and by letter, made me know that they have the same need for this book, [and] they displayed to me their impatience to have it."[41] First published in 1682, the treatise was subsequently reissued in 1700, in a new edition augmented by Toubeau's son. As demonstrated by Jacqueline L. Lafon's analysis of the correspondence between the monarchy's *Bureau du Commerce* and merchants throughout France, Toubeau's strategy for making "consular law [*droit consulaire*]" available and understandable to merchants nationwide proved quite successful. According to Lafon, his treatise was one of the primary resources to which eighteenth-century merchants turned in seeking guidance on matters of commercial law.[42]

Litigation Concerning Sales of Goods and Services

SUITS BROUGHT BY SELLERS

Most of the lawsuits filed in the Parisian Merchant Court concerned the sale of goods and services,[43] and many of these were brought by sellers seeking payment. Such suits were largely between merchants—perhaps in part because, as Michael Sonenscher argues, there was a great deal of subcontracting between merchant-artisans in the Old Regime.[44] The sellers in such lawsuits included *négociants* from cities throughout France, members of Parisian guilds, Parisian merchant-artisans who worked outside the guild system, and merchants, artisans, millers, and farmers who lived in the villages outside of Paris. Merchant litigants from outside of France appeared relatively rarely in the court,[45] and when they did, this was usually in higher stakes litigation concerning negotiable instruments, rather than sales.[46] Nonetheless, *négociants* from abroad did occasionally litigate contract disputes in the merchant court, as for example, when a *négociant* from Brussels and a painter from Liège became embroiled in a lawsuit regarding the sale of what the parties claimed to be the Rubens masterpiece *The Assumption of the Virgin.*[47] Although sellers suing for payment were usually merchants of one kind or another, such suits were also brought by individuals who, in the traditional lexicon of the Old Regime, were not considered merchants—including members of the clergy and nobility who appear to have sold goods cultivated on their land, such as wine and lumber.[48]

Like the sellers who initiated such lawsuits, the buyers seem to have been largely merchants, of the kinds described above. Sellers, in other words, do not appear to have sued consumer purchasers. The absence of suits against consumers likely stemmed from concern that merchant court jurisdiction did not extend to such nonmerchant defendants. The notion that nonmerchants could be forced to appear before the court as defendants, while embraced by many commercial jurists, was rejected by most ordinary, civil-law jurists, and thus remained very controversial.[49]

Assessing the Just Price

At issue in much of the litigation brought by sellers was the question of how much, if anything, the buyer owed. Resolution of this question did not generally turn, as a modern-day lawyer might expect, on the precise contours and content of the contract. Given the kinds of long-term, informal, and often oral contracting in which merchants traditionally engaged—exchanging goods and payments over an extended period of time and meeting occasionally to undertake accountings—questions regarding the moment of formal contract formation arose only infrequently. The court's focus was, instead, on examining what should be done to ensure an equitable outcome—namely, that the seller obtain all to which he was entitled and no more. Entitlement in this context often hinged, in turn, on the court's ex post assessment of the value of the goods that the seller had delivered.

An issue that commonly arose in suits brought by sellers for payment was whether the price charged for the merchandise—as established in contracts, accountings, witness testimony, and the like—was in fact fair or just. Embraced widely by canon lawyers in the Middle Ages, the doctrine of the just price had deep roots in the *ius commune*. It is generally argued, however, that this doctrine had little real bite by the eighteenth century and was applied only in contracts for the sale of land.[50] A contract for the sale of land could be rescinded on the grounds of *lésion*, meaning that the land had been sold for less than half the just price. But in contracts for chattels, *lésion* was supposedly not deemed grounds for rescission.[51]

This established view is based on treatise literature from the Old Regime, which in turn cited royal edicts and rulings of the *parlements* that thus sought to limit the applicable scope of *lésion*. Evidence from actual court records, however, demonstrates that, contrary to the standard wisdom, failure to pay the just price did indeed remain an actionable claim in the eighteenth century—at least in the Parisian Merchant Court. Claims that the price of goods sold was unjust could take one of two forms. On occasion, a seller complained that the price of the goods was too low—that they were worth significantly more than the amount paid and that a *lésion* had therefore occurred. More frequently, the buyer asserted as a defense that the price was too high and that the seller was therefore demanding more than the goods' true value. That such claims concerning the just price were in fact actionable was consistent with the merchant court's long-standing commitment to promoting such merchant virtues as charity and leniency and with the established jurisprudential principle—grounded in the canon-law idea of "cause"—that "equality is the general law of all commercial contracts."[52] The actionability of such claims in the merchant court also accorded with the court's foundations in (and efforts to promote) the guild system, in that pricing was one of the guilds' primary interests.

What then was the just price? And how was it calculated? There are no easy answers to these questions. The arbiters' reports themselves typically state simply that the arbiters examined the goods in question and determined that the price charged was just, or if not, that the price should be lowered (or occasionally raised) by a particular amount. They offer no explanation for how this alternative amount was calculated. It seems likely, however, that the just price was determined, at least in part, by reference to the price controls established by police and guild regulations. These prices in turn were shaped by a complex amalgam of concern with levels of supply and demand (for both the goods themselves and the cost of labor), on the one hand, and a tendency to view merchandise as possessing an inherent, objective value, on the other.[53]

By examining contract prices in order to ensure that they conformed to the just price, the merchant court and its arbiters were thus, to some extent, reinforcing the guild system and its efforts at regulation. Not surprisingly, given the guild interests at stake in these suits, the court frequently appointed as arbiters the leaders of the guild to which the seller who produced the goods in question belonged.[54] These guild leaders had knowledge of the goods at issue and were thus able to opine as to the justness of the price charged. As explained in a mid-eighteenth-century treatise on commercial litigation, "the judge and consuls are in the habit of sending valuations to be done . . . to a senior master [*ancien*] of the trade at issue; for example, to an *ancien* master carpenter when carpentry is at issue, to a master locksmith for matters concerning the locksmith's trade, etc."[55] Thus, for example, in a suit for payment brought by a master cartwright against the widow of a master saddler, the defendant-buyer argued that the plaintiff-seller's demand for 135 livres for components of a cabriolet was "an exorbitant sum."[56] The court appointed as arbiters four leaders of the cartwrights' guild, who together examined the components in question and determined that the amount requested by the seller—one of their own members—was indeed "excessive."[57] Accordingly, they reduced the price to 96 livres.

While the court often appointed the leaders of the seller's guild as arbiters, it sometimes appointed the leaders of a different guild. This is what it did, for example, in *Darnaudery v. Desgranges,* a lawsuit that arose as the result of an informal agreement that Darnaudery, a button merchant, and Desgranges, a button maker, reached in October 1783.[58] Pursuant to this agreement, Darnaudery was regularly to supply Desgranges with the funds necessary to produce and deliver buttons. This arrangement continued until March 1784, when Desgranges decided that he wanted to end it. The parties then met to do an accounting and discovered that they had sharply different views concerning the price of the buttons that Desgranges had produced. Desgranges therefore filed suit, arguing that the prices that Darnaudery assigned to the buttons that he, Desgranges, had produced were far below their true value—resulting in a *lésion,* which Darnaudery could make right only by paying more money for the buttons. As Desgranges argued, he was the victim of an "onerous bargain [*marché onéreux*]," since "there was in these prices an obvious *lésion.*"[59] Darnaudery responded by claiming that he had supplied Desgranges with funds exceeding the value of the buttons that he had received and by asserting a counterclaim that Desgranges return these excess funds. Resolution of the lawsuit thus hinged on assessing the true value or just price of the buttons in question.

Rather than appointing the leaders of the button makers' guild to serve as arbiters, the court appointed, instead, seven leaders of the goldsmiths' guild. These arbiters decided to call on the assistance of two button makers in examining the buttons produced by Desgranges. Thereafter, they concluded not only that there had been no *lésion,* but that in fact Desgranges had charged more than the buttons' fair value: "We were amazingly surprised to discover not only that Desgranges' claim was ill founded, but also that Darnaudery had paid a great deal more than the ordinary and profitable [*avantageux*] prices."[60] Accordingly, they ordered Desgranges to compensate Darnaudery for the excessive prices he had charged.

As for why the court opted to appoint the leaders of the goldsmiths' guild as arbiters in this case, we can only speculate, but a number of possibilities present themselves. First, the arbiters refer to Desgranges, the seller, as a "button worker" (*ouvrier en boutons*) and Darnaudery, the buyer, as a button merchant (*marchand boutonnier*).[61] Neither of these men, in other words, possessed the status of master, journeyman, or apprentice that would suggest that he was a member of the button makers' guild. Accordingly, the court perhaps concluded that there was little reason to believe that leaders of the button makers' guild would exercise significant persuasive authority over these parties.[62] Indeed, given the very high status of the goldsmiths' guild, the court may have concluded that the parties would be more likely to bow to its authority. More importantly, the court's appointment of the leaders of the goldsmiths' guild may have been in accordance with these leaders' own desire to serve as arbiters. Since the goldsmiths were authorized to police the various trades using their metals, including the button makers' guild (and presumably those merchant-artisans unlawfully competing with this guild), they had a significant police interest in the prices charged by Desgranges.[63]

At other times, and for reasons that are unfortunately unclear, the court appointed an individual or several individuals, rather than a guild's leaders, to serve as arbiters in suits brought by sellers for payment. These individual arbiters also seem to have been selected in part for their professional knowledge of the goods at issue. Consider, for example, a lawsuit brought by Tournu, a master gilder, against Fabre Duborgnes, a *négociant,* for payment of goods, in which the court appointed two individual arbiters, and then later a third.[64] Since Duborgnes, the buyer, argued that Tournu demanded an excessive price, the two arbiters first appointed by the court undertook to assess the goods' value. Although these arbiters concluded that the price charged was just, Duborgnes insisted that they "have not assessed the items [*ouvrages*] at their just value."[65] Accordingly, before entering judgment on behalf of Tournu, the court appointed a third arbiter to undertake yet another analysis of the goods. He too, however, concluded that judgment for Tournu was appropriate, since in his view the previous arbiters had "assessed the items [*ouvrages*] at their just value."[66]

When the individual arbiters appointed did not have professional knowledge of the goods produced by the seller, they seem to have consulted with other merchants who possessed such knowledge. This is what the goldsmiths serving as arbiters in *Darnaudery v. Desgranges* did. Similarly, in a lawsuit in which the defendant, a master roofer, raised the counterclaim that the plaintiff had not paid him for "a wooden fountain plated in lead," the arbiter called upon "members of that trade [*gens de l'état*]" to determine its fair value.[67] Likewise, an arbiter adjudicating a dispute between a cattle merchant and a laborer over payment of a bull asked two farmers to determine the price of the bull.[68]

As these cases suggest, the Parisian Merchant Court frequently had occasion to name a price when the parties themselves failed to agree on one. A common feature of the practice of long-term, informal, and oral contracting in which merchants regularly engaged was that buyer and seller did not establish a price term at the outset. The seller simply delivered the goods requested and the parties left it to their periodic accountings to agree on a price. But there were times when such agreement was never reached, and instead litigation ensued. That merchants would regularly fail to agree on price terms might seem quite surprising to the modern-day reader. But since the price of many goods was regulated by guild and police rules, such merchants probably had some sense of the default price that would ultimately be imposed by the court, if litigation proved necessary. And since they were accustomed to the notion that price terms could be imposed by third-party regulators—namely, the guilds and police—they likely had little difficulty accepting the prospect that the merchant court might also exercise such power.

There were occasions, however, when the parties did agree on a price—often when undertaking an accounting, rather than at the initial moment of contract formation—and thereafter one or both challenged it as unjust. Here too, arbiters reviewing the price were willing to declare it unjust—even though this meant not simply supplying a missing term but actually modifying the terms of the contract. For example, in one unfortunately terse report, an arbiter who identified himself as a former guild leader considered a dispute between two guild members in which the seller sued the buyer for payment.[69]

The parties had previously met to do an accounting, at which time they agreed in writing that the defendant owed 688 livres for the merchandise at issue. Upon examining the merchandise purchased by the defendant, the arbiter concluded that the price demanded by the plaintiff and on which the parties had agreed was unjustly high. On this basis, he reduced the price to arrive at the "just value": "I examined the aforementioned merchandise, which is listed in the parties' written accounting at 688 livres, the value of which I estimated, and I reduced the price to the sum of 645 livres, the just value."[70]

In ordering that defendant-buyers pay plaintiff-sellers, arbiters usually focused exclusively on the value of the goods sold. On occasion, however, they also considered whether the seller had suffered any incidental damages as a result of the buyer's failure to pay, such as damages incurred in having to warehouse and transport goods that a buyer refused to accept. Reports in which arbiters considered the possibility of such incidental damages are rare—likely because such damages were themselves rare. In most cases, sellers sued for payment after they had already delivered goods, and thus they did not incur incidental costs for post-breach transportation and warehousing. When sellers did incur such costs, however, arbiters considered awarding these.

For example, in *Fouches v. Huguet*, a butcher sued a tanner for breach of a one-year agreement that they had entered verbally on April 17, 1783, on the understanding that they would thereafter commit the deal to writing.[71] Pursuant to this agreement, Fouches was to sell to Huguet "all the cowhide and calfskin originating in his slaughterhouse from last Easter through next Easter."[72] Moreover, the parties also agreed on prices. On May 3 Huguet put the agreement into writing and presented it to Fouches. Claiming that one of the items was listed in the written contract at a price lower than that on which they had verbally agreed and thus that "the defendant [Huguet] did not fulfill the agreement," Fouches "ceased to deliver merchandise to . . . [Huguet] and . . . requested rescission of the deal."[73] The arbiter proposed resolving the lawsuit by permitting Fouches henceforth to sell to whomever he wished and by requiring Huguet to compensate Fouches solely for the goods that Fouches had thus far delivered. As concerns those goods, the arbiter appears to have determined their value simply by splitting the difference, such that Huguet would pay a price that was precisely in between that to which he and Fouches claimed they had agreed. Before thus concluding, however, the arbiter also considered Fouches' claim that he was entitled to incidental damages for the cost of the additional salt he was required to purchase "to put on the cowhide that was at his place in order to prevent it from going bad."[74] Presumably, because he decided simply to split the difference, the arbiter ultimately denied Fouches such incidental damages.

While arbiters' reports suggest that incidental damages could be awarded, the same cannot be said of lost profits. The remedy of lost profits presumes that the seller possesses many identical items in stock, such that a buyer who breaches by failing to accept goods that he promised to purchase causes the seller's total volume of sales to decrease. In the Old Regime, where most merchant-artisans produced and/or sold goods on demand, they rarely carried a standardized series of items in stock. As a result, if a buyer refused to purchase items, thereby breaching a contractual agreement, the seller could simply sell these goods to someone else. Such a seller would likely not be injured by a decrease in volume of sales, and thus would not need a remedy for lost profits.

It is important to emphasize, however, that failure to request and grant the remedy of lost profits resulted from the nature of commercial practice, rather than from any conceptual lack of sophistication. Eighteenth-century jurists and merchants were no strangers to the concept of lost profits. Jurists of the *ius commune* had long recognized and embraced the notion of *lucrum cessans* as a legitimate form of damages.[75] Likewise, the Parisian Merchant Court willingly granted the remedy of lost profits in those relatively rare situations—not involving sales of goods—in which such damages existed and were calculable. For example, when an amphitheater built to house spectacles at Saint Ovide's fair (located at what is now the *place de la Concorde*) collapsed during the first show, and seven to eight hundred audience members all rushed out, demanding return of the ticket price, the arbiter recommended that the court permit the spectacle's producers to recover lost profits from the negligent builder.[76] In so concluding, however, the arbiter suggested that the amount of lost profits to which the producers were entitled was much lower than that which they claimed: "We cannot prevent ourselves from observing that the show was only able to attract those of low social standing [*le petit peuple*], and . . . given this [among other reasons], . . . [the producers] should not have expected a profit as considerable as . . . [their] demand would suggest."[77]

Granting Delays

Once arbiters determined the amount that the defendant buyer owed and confirmed that this amount was just (or changed the price accordingly), the next question that they typically considered was whether the buyer was able to pay this amount. Indeed, in many suits brought by sellers for payment, the debtor-defendants acknowledged the obligation but claimed that they simply did not have the money to pay. In such cases, the arbiter usually recommended that the debtor be granted a delay and often proposed a payment schedule, which divided the total debt into a certain number of equal payments due in regular intervals. Like the decisory oath, such a delay was not unique to the merchant courts, but was instead a fixture of the *ius commune,* called the *délai de grâce,* or delay of grace.[78] In the merchant courts, as elsewhere, it was purely in the judge's discretion to grant or refuse a delay. But in the Parisian Merchant Court, at least, delays appear to have been almost universally granted. Furthermore, according to the former merchant court judge Masson—and as substantiated in the arbiters' reports—the merchant court often granted delays exceeding the three-month limit permitted all courts by an ordinance of August 1669, enacted as a supplement to the Procedure Ordinance of 1667.[79]

The merchant court's willingness to grant delays stemmed, in part, from economic considerations. Long-term creditor-debtor relationships were an important and highly valued component of traditional commercial practice. When the debtor was experiencing difficulty, the best way to maintain such relationships was to grant the debtor a delay in which to pay. To condemn a debtor to pay his entire obligation at once, when this was impossible or nearly so, would be to no one's advantage. The creditor would not receive the money that he was owed and the debtor, having failed to obey a court order, would suffer serious injury to his reputation and perhaps be deemed insolvent. Moreover, to the extent that, as was probable, this particular creditor and debtor were each obligated to others, there was always the further risk that one business failure would lead to another, resulting in a chain of insolvencies that might endanger the credit market as a whole.

Sometimes, but by no means always, the granting of a delay was tied to the debtor's ability to provide a surety[80] or to pay interest. Consider, for example, a lawsuit brought for payment of goods by Joseph Tasslin, a merchant from Orléans, against the widow of a Parisian used-clothes dealer named Masson.[81] Since Masson acknowledged the debt, there was no disagreement regarding the amount owed. As the arbiter explained, "the only question is the time to accord for payment of this debt."[82] Because Masson's business had failed, her only (and very small) source of income was money earned from renting out her house. Accordingly, she requested eight years in which to pay the debt. While Tasslin "wanted to be paid in full a great deal sooner," he agreed to this extensive delay, upon being "appealed to" by Masson's brother—and on the condition that he would receive both a surety and interest.[83] As for the surety, the arbiter concluded that Tasslin "must, as an old friend of . . . [Masson], and as a way of taking into account [*entrant dans*] the smallness of her fortune, content himself with" eight bills of exchange drafted by Masson.[84] Masson would draft these to the order of "her brother, or any other person recognized as solvent," who would then endorse them to Tasslin, thereby making himself liable for their ultimate payment. Moreover, as authorized by the November 1563 edict that established the Parisian Merchant Court, the arbiter recommended that Masson be required to pay interest.[85] Such interest was to accrue from the day judgment was entered until the debt was repaid.

Like many other aspects of the court's jurisprudence, its decision to order that the defendant provide a surety and/or pay interest was largely equitable — dependent, in other words, on the particular facts of the case rather than on specific legal rules. Arbiters, however, seem to have been more likely to order interest payments when the delay granted was very long, as in the case just discussed, or when the buyer's failure to pay was attributable to bad faith. Take, for example, the lawsuit brought by Ganal, a merchant of some unspecified type, against Rainfray, an ironsmith, demanding payment for goods sold.[86] The arbiter summoned Rainfray to appear before him on three occasions, and each time the defendant failed to appear. Without identifying the source of his information, the arbiter concluded that "Monsieur Rainfray is entirely capable of paying and can offer as a reason not to do so only bad will, which has been sufficiently proved by his conduct."[87] On these grounds, the arbiter recommended that the court order Rainfray to pay interest on his debt. Similarly, in a suit brought by a tithe collector for payment of some sheep that he had sold to a butcher, the arbiter ordered that the defendant pay interest on the amount owed since, in his words, "the silence of . . . [the defendant] and his failure to appear have made me suspect his sincerity."[88]

The willingness of arbiters to grant delays — and to grant delays exceeding the official three-month time limit — stemmed, however, from more than narrow economic considerations. As Masson observed in describing merchant court procedure, "Humaneness is only too prepared to grant a delay to the unfortunate debtor."[89] The arbiters' reports reveal a frequently resurfacing moral concern that it was wrong for a rich person to demand money from someone who could not afford to pay, even though the latter was legally bound. Not surprisingly, among all the arbiters, the parish priests seem to have been the most concerned with the moral implications of forcing the poor to pay the rich.

Consider, for example, the arbiter's opinion in a lawsuit brought by Simon, a carpenter, against a married couple by the name of Dubreuil.[90] Simon had performed various services for the defendants over the years, all on credit as recorded in his accounting books. After waiting a long time for the defendants to pay, Simon finally sued for an amount exceeding 456 livres. The defendants for the most part did not deny their obligation, stating only that the plaintiff's claim should be reduced by twenty livres because they had given him a horse worth that amount. Their main defense was simply that they were too poor to pay their debts. They claimed that they could not afford to pay more than thirty livres per year—a proposed payment schedule that amounted to a delay of approximately fifteen years, rather than the official three-month limit. The arbiter-priest succeeded in convincing the plaintiff to grant a delay, but not for as long as the defendants wanted. The priest thus asked the court to decide how long a delay to order. In so doing, however, he depicted the defendants' plight in the most sympathetic terms. He remarked on "the state of poverty to which . . . [the defendants] have been reduced," noting that "they were obliged to quit the bakery trade and to become day laborers, even hiring themselves out to carry sacks in the market."[91] Clearly, in the arbiter-priest's view, the defendants, by virtue of their poverty, should be granted the longest delay possible.

Concern with requiring the poor to pay the rich is even more apparent in the arbiter's report written by a parish priest in the case of *Meusnier v. Meusnier.*[92] Jean Meusnier, an innkeeper from the small town of Champlan, sued his cousin, Denis Meusnier, a fruit seller from the same town, for a debt of sixty livres that he claimed Denis had never paid. Denis insisted that he had already paid Jean this amount and that he no longer owed him any money. After examining several witnesses, the arbiter-priest remained uncertain as to which party was telling the truth, but concluded that the plaintiff was probably in the right because two witnesses "seem to prove the deception of Denis Meusnier."[93] Despite his conclusion that Denis did in fact owe Jean the money, the priest nonetheless tried to convince Jean to grant Denis a reduction in purchase price and a one-year delay because Jean could so easily afford to do so and because Denis was so poor: "We spoke to the aforementioned Jean Meusnier, plaintiff, in private and did our best to get him to agree to reduce the obligation of the aforementioned Meusnier, defendant, in consideration of his lack of affluence and the well-being, in the contrary, of the aforementioned Jean Meusnier, plaintiff."[94] Although Jean ultimately agreed to a reduction in price and to "content himself with . . . a one-year delay," Denis refused, insisting that he had already paid his obligation and would not pay twice.[95] Unable to reconcile the cousins, the priest recommended to the court that it find for Denis, the defendant, because it was wrong to hold a debtor to his obligation when the debtor could not afford to pay and the creditor could easily afford to lose the money. In the priest's words, "In our view, given the state of poverty of Denis Meusnier and, in contrast, the affluence of Jean Meusnier, we think the misery of the former obliterates his debt and it is not to be supposed that Jean Meusnier, who is more comfortable, would be capable of wanting to be paid . . . by his cousin, who is less comfortable than he."[96]

It was not only priests, however, who proved extremely sympathetic to the plight of the poor debtor in arrears to the rich creditor. In the case of *le comte de Colincour v. Bequet,* a colonel in the royal army, who had sold a mare to a Parisian horse merchant, sued for payment.[97] The arbiter, who identified himself as a merchant who regularly provided expert testimony in litigation brought before the lieutenant general of police,[98] sought to reconcile the parties by convincing the plaintiff to grant the defendant a two- to three-month delay in which to pay. The plaintiff, however, refused. In his report, the arbiter berated the colonel for his hard-heartedness, remarking that he was steadfast in his refusal "despite the representations that the aforementioned defendant honestly made to him concerning the large number of horses that remained on his hands."[99] According to the arbiter, the court should simply order the delay that the defendant had requested because it would cost the colonel so little, while helping the defendant enormously. In his opinion, he explained, "Colincour, being above such a little concern, should have easily accorded this delay to his debtor."[100] Since he refused to do so, however, "the aforementioned defendant must have recourse to your justice as concerns his situation."[101]

Such empathy for the unfortunate is also readily apparent in the report drafted in *Vasinelle v. Blin* by an arbiter who unfortunately failed to identify his profession but who was therefore likely not a priest. Vasinelle, an iron merchant, sued Blin, a locksmith, for payment of goods.[102] Having failed to reconcile the parties himself, the arbiter informed the court that the defendant, Blin, owed the plaintiff slightly over 768 livres. The arbiter, however, strongly urged the judge and consuls to grant the defendant a long delay in which to pay the debt. As he intoned, the defendant had suffered a "considerable loss," and if he were forced to pay the debt at once, he would lose the funds necessary to remain in business.[103] The results would be tragic, given "the large family for which Blin is responsible, having eight children, whose needs recur daily [and] to which he cannot attend without the help of his profession [*état*], which it is crucial that he retain."[104] Sparing no effort in his attempt to pull on their heartstrings, the arbiter concluded by declaring to the judge and consuls that the delay "is a humane undertaking [*un oeuvre d'humanité*] to which [I] commit you."[105]

Ordering *Saisie et Revendication*

In addition to ordering payment, there was one other remedy that the Parisian Merchant Court sometimes granted to sellers who had not been paid. This was the remedy of *saisie et revendication,* an odd term combining the feudal concept of *seisin,* or a possessory interest distinct from full ownership, with the Roman concept of *revendication,* or the reclaiming of an undivided property interest. *Saisie et revendication* was essentially an order of replevin—

namely, a remedy entitling the rightful owner of goods to recover them from a wrongful possessor. It was intended as a remedy for the seller who had sold goods on credit and had still not been paid when he discovered that the buyer was insolvent.[106] If the court granted the remedy, it would authorize the seller to arrange for seizure of the property in question. *Saisie et revendication* was thus founded on an underlying security interest granted to sellers in the goods they sold on credit. When the buyer was declared insolvent, the seller could exercise his security interest in the goods and reclaim them.

For the merchant court, the process of determining whether to grant *saisie et revendication* entailed relatively few complications. Once the debtor-buyer was declared insolvent, the creditor-seller had an automatic right to the return of the goods as long as they had been sold on credit, had not been paid for, and remained in the debtor's hands. Thus, a decision whether to grant the remedy of *saisie et revendication* generally required only a few rather mechanical factual assessments. It was necessary to examine the litigants' accounting books to determine whether the goods had been sold on credit and whether payment had already been made. In addition, a decision-maker had to discover whether the buyer was still in possession of the goods. Finally, a determination had to be made whether the particular items claimed by the seller were in fact those goods that he had sold on the occasion in question to this particular buyer. Such a determination was possible because merchant-artisans usually marked goods that they produced for sale with their own distinctive marks. As part of the typical sales transaction, both buyer and seller recorded these marks in their accounting books as a means of identifying the items involved in the transaction.

Since the decision whether to grant the remedy of *saisie et revendication* involved a time-consuming factual investigation, it was well suited for delegation to an arbiter. Often the Parisian Merchant Court delegated the case to a member of the seller's guild, who was presumably in a particularly good position to make the required factual assessments. As Masson, the jurist and former merchant court judge, explained, it is the custom of the merchant courts to send the litigant seeking *saisie et revendication* before a merchant from his own guild "in order to determine the identity of the reclaimed merchandise and to report on it."[107] This is precisely what the court did, for example, in the case of *Granjaquart v. Laurent.*[108]

When Laurent, a grocer, was declared insolvent, Granjaquart, another grocer who had sold him a bottle of olive oil on credit and had never been paid, petitioned the Parisian Merchant Court for *saisie et revendication.* The court appointed Peraut, a former leader of the grocers' guild, to decide whether the remedy should be granted. Peraut examined the bottle of oil and saw that it was marked "OB." He then looked at the invoice Granjaquart had received when he purchased this and five other bottles of olive oil from *négociants* in Rouen. The invoice listed all six bottles as containing the mark "OB." In addition, he looked at Granjaquart's accounting books, which recorded the purchase of all six bottles, marked "OB," and noted that bottle number 6 had been sold to Laurent on credit. Finally, he went to Granjaquart's cellar to examine the five bottles that, according to his accounting books, he had not yet sold and saw that all of these were also marked "OB." Based on this investigation, Peraut determined that the bottle of oil in Laurent's possession had, in fact, been sold to him on credit by Granjaquart, that he had not paid for it, and that, therefore, the court should order *saisie et revendication.*

The Problem of Inter-Guild Disputes

In general, arbiters appointed by the Parisian Merchant Court to help adjudicate lawsuits brought by sellers seeking payment had little difficulty recommending a judgment. However, underlying tensions between the guilds implicated in a lawsuit could cause an otherwise fairly orderly adjudicative process to break down. This is what happened, for example, in *Vadaux v. Pleyard.*[109] Over a period of twenty years, from 1757 to 1777, Vadaux, an engraver, engraved various pieces of jewelry for Garand, a master goldsmith. As was common practice, Vadaux provided services to Garand partially on credit, by means of book debt. Thus, the parties recorded their transactions and every so often Garand would pay Vadaux part of the debt he owed him. At the same time, Garand would continue hiring Vadaux to do more engravings such that his debt to him was never fully extinguished. Finally, in 1778 Vadaux sued Garand to receive the 4,487 livres that he claimed he was owed for all these years of work. At this time, the court appointed a former consul to serve as arbiter. But before the arbiter reached a conclusion, Garand died.

This put an end to Vadaux's suit, until 1782, when he sued Garand's widow and heiress, as well as her new husband—another master goldsmith by the name of Pleyard—on the same grounds. For reasons that are unfortunately unclear but that likely included the acrimony that had developed between the parties, the court did not, as previously, send the litigants to a single arbiter. Instead, the court appointed as arbiters both a former leader of the goldsmiths' guild and a master engraver. The court probably hoped that by thus enlisting the two guilds implicated in the lawsuit it could more easily pressure the parties into reconciliation. When, for unspecified reasons, the leader of the goldsmiths' guild resigned his position as arbiter, the court replaced him with another master goldsmith. Despite their efforts, the two arbiters could not agree on what should be done, and the case dragged on for about six months. Finally, in order to resolve the deadlock, the judge and consuls appointed a third arbiter, a former leader of the goldsmiths' guild. Although the arbiters' reports do not explain why the court chose another goldsmith as the tie-breaker, an important factor in the decision was surely that the goldsmiths' guild was one of the *six corps de Paris* and thus a very powerful force within the court—certainly more powerful than the engravers' guild.

As might be expected, the two arbiters who were goldsmiths recommended judgment for the Pleyards, the goldsmith-defendants, and the one arbiter who was an engraver recommended judgment for Vadaux, the engraver-plaintiff. Unable to agree, the arbiters finding for the defendants and the arbiter finding for the plaintiff wrote separate reports. Moreover, the two reports present strikingly different—indeed, irreconcilable—factual accounts. The arbiters finding for the goldsmith-defendants claimed that the court could not possibly rely on the accounting-book records that Vadaux, the engraver-plaintiff, kept of the work he had done for Garand. These accounting books, they stated, were so disorderly that they clearly bespoke Vadaux's bad faith. In particular, they were not kept in chronological order, and as a result engravings he did in one year were interspersed in a listing of engravings that he had done in another year. Furthermore, they continued, "we have noted there a large quantity of blank pages mixed in everywhere."[110] In the view of the arbiter finding for the engraver-plaintiff, however, "the registers of Monsieur Vadaux, being in order . . . establish title in favor of Monsieur Vadaux, as against Monsieur and Madame Pleyard."[111]

That these three arbiters were ultimately unable to reach agreement, and in fact presented very different accounts of the underlying facts at issue in the dispute, ultimately followed from the court's method of resolving contract disputes—a method concerned not with enforcing fixed, predetermined rules of law but instead with reaching an equitable outcome, as determined on a case-by-case basis. Such determinations of necessity gave expression to the values of the merchant community. But despite the merchant court's efforts to portray merchants as a unified brotherhood, there was no single merchant community to whose shared values and norms arbiters could easily turn. The guild system on which the court was based and which it sought to reinforce was rife with tensions and conflict. By giving voice to these tensions and conflicts, the arbiters in *Vadaux v. Pleyard* were thus in a certain sense true to their mission of representing the merchant community and its values, in all its multifaceted, conflict-ridden complexity.

SUITS BROUGHT BY BUYERS

Litigation over sales of goods and services also took the form of suits brought by buyers. As in the litigation initiated by sellers, a broad array of merchants appeared in these suits—ranging from elite wholesalers to farmers living in the Parisian outskirts. Unlike the suits brought by sellers, however, consumers made regular—though still not very extensive—appearances in buyer-initiated suits.[112] Indeed, it is possible to read in some of these cases traces of the consumer revolution that historians now agree occurred during the Old Regime, as ordinary men and women grew increasingly prosperous and items once reserved largely for the nobility (including, notably, dresses and watches) began to be produced for and sold to a much wider public.[113]

Suits brought by buyers generally raised one of two claims: failure to deliver or delivery of nonconforming goods. However, likely due to the prevalence of informal, relational contracting, such buyer-initiated litigation seems to have arisen less frequently than litigation initiated by sellers. To the extent that merchants exchanged goods informally on an ongoing basis, meeting periodically to do accountings and make payment, they expected—and indeed sought—contractual flexibility regarding the date of delivery as well as the quantity and quality of goods delivered. Perfect timeliness of delivery was thus often not of great moment, and a buyer might find it more cost-effective in the long run to wait for delivery (and maintain a good relationship with the seller) than to file suit. Moreover, to the extent that the goods delivered deviated in some respect from the agreement, a dissatisfied buyer could seek redress by attempting to negotiate a lower price at the time the parties met to do an accounting. When such negotiations failed, the buyer would simply decline to pay, thus leaving it to the seller to initiate litigation.

There were times, however, when as described below, the seller never made (even a belated) delivery, or the buyer simply could not use the goods proffered and thus refused to accept them. Such buyers then filed suit, seeking either specific performance of the contract or its rescission. Not surprisingly, buyers were more likely to raise such claims in those situations in which the contract at issue was more formalized (such that the nonconformity was clear and important), or where the goods in question deviated greatly from applicable guild and police regulations.

Claims of failure to deliver were often brought by consumer purchasers, rather than by merchants. The case of *Monsieur et Madame Bienchi v. Chaffenere* is represenative.[114] The Bienchis, a couple whose status the arbiter's report does not identify and who were thus likely not of very high social standing, sued a Parisian seamstress. They asserted that the seamstress failed to deliver a dress that she had agreed to refashion—evidently for Madame Bienchi's use—and with which they had entrusted her. Upon her failure to deliver the dress, the Bienchis confronted the defendant, and she acknowledged that she no longer had it, because someone had taken it from her. The Bienchis then filed suit, and the court appointed an arbiter of undisclosed professional status, who concluded that the consumer contract should be rescinded and the parties restored to their precontractual positions. Since the defendant no longer possessed the dress and thus could not return it, she was required to pay the Bienchis its value as determined in a formal estimate (presumably undertaken by other seamstresses).

In another consumer-initiated suit, the plaintiff was a widow who identified herself as a *bourgeoise de Paris*[115] — a title that was easily assumed, but that in theory entitled the holder to certain privileges akin to those of the nobility.[116] The plaintiff sued a master watchmaker for failure to deliver a watch that she had purchased for her son and to fix a second watch that she had left for repair. The arbiter appointed by the court, who unfortunately did not identify his profession, recommended that, as requested by the plaintiff, the court rescind the contract. The defendant watchmaker, in other words, was to return the watch he had agreed to fix as well as the funds that the *bourgeoise* had advanced for purchase of the new watch.

More common than these suits for nondelivery were suits brought by buyers who claimed that the seller had delivered, but that the goods or services were nonconforming. In the Old Regime there were two ways in which goods could be nonconforming. First, as in the present day, a nonconforming good was one that did not conform to the parties' agreement. Second, a nonconforming good was one that did not conform to guild standards. In litigation raising either kind of nonconformity, the court often appointed as arbiters individuals who hailed from the same guild as the seller (or from a related trade) and who thus possessed the expertise necessary to assess whether the goods conformed to the contract and/or to guild regulations. Among the individuals thus appointed were the guild's leaders, who had an important interest in maintaining the guild's reputation for supplying the goods that buyers ordered, and more importantly, in ensuring that the goods conformed to applicable guild standards.

Consider, for example, a lawsuit in which the buyer, a writer, sued a master printer for printing a defective version of his book and thus for furnishing goods that failed to conform to both the contract and guild regulations.[117] The court appointed two arbiters, both of whom had served as leaders of the printers' guild and one of whom was also a former merchant court consul. The plaintiff, Nicholas Duval, had written a book entitled *Pratique Universelle des Sciences* and hired Alexis Xavier Mesnier, a master printer, to print a section of the book. The parties memorialized their agreement in a written contract. The edition that Mesnier printed, however, was full of errors and, as the arbiters explained, this was a violation both of the parties' contract and, more importantly, of the statutes establishing and regulating the printers' guild: "[The section is] very defective, which is contrary to the [parties'] agreement and to the regulations of the printers' guild, and in particular to that of February 28, 1723, article IX, which establishes: All printers will print books with attractive font on good paper and [the books will be] correct."[118]

Given the gravity of the defect at issue, which made the book essentially unusable and tarnished the reputation of the printers' guild, the arbiters recommended the remedy of specific performance. Mesnier, in other words, was to be directed by the court to perform his obligation as contracted and thus to reprint the section at his own expense. In this way the guild leaders serving as arbiters ensured that the guild would provide what was in essence a warranty of the goods' quality. In addition, however, the arbiters ordered Mesnier to bring the defective pages to the "royal and syndical chamber of the printers of Paris" so that, in the presence of the guild's leaders, as well as that of the litigants, they could be sold as paper by the ream.[119] Money from the sale of the paper was to be given to Mesnier, who was to deduct this amount from the sum Duval still owed him for the printing. This was a remedy ordered not so much for the benefit of the plaintiff but primarily for that of the guild, whose reputation had been injured by the misconduct of one of its members. As the arbiters explained, only the destruction of the offensive pages would ensure that defective copies of the book would not be distributed to the public.

Even when the court did not appoint the leaders of the seller's guild as arbiters in buyer-initiated lawsuits, those arbiters that it did appoint often invited the leaders of the seller's guild to dispose of goods that failed to conform to guild and police regulations and thus posed a threat to public well-being. Consider, for example, a lawsuit brought by Antoine le Fuesn against a man named Eloy, who had sold him 120 packets of pepper, as well as some handkerchiefs.[120] Both parties appear to have been merchants, but the arbiter does not identify in his report the precise nature of their professions or his own. Fuesn claimed that the pepper tasted terrible and thus did not conform to the standards imposed by the grocers' guild. Moreover, "fearing that he would be equally deceived" concerning the handkerchiefs, he had refused to accept delivery of these.[121] Fuesn then filed suit, seeking an order that would rescind the contract, thus entitling him to return of the funds he had already paid and discharging him from any obligation to pay more in the future.

The arbiter tasted one of the 120 packets of pepper in question and concluded that the powder that Eloy had sold as pepper was in fact "a bad mixture," which consisted of at most "a sixteenth of pepper."[122] He then concluded that to permit this sale to go forward by enforcing the contract and denying Fuesn's claim would be "to risk that the plaintiff deceive the public by selling this so-called pepper."[123] In other words, if Fuesn were forced to pay for the corrupted pepper, then in order to recoup his costs he would be tempted to sell it to consumers. This, however, would result in a public-health disaster, because "the consumption [of this powder] can only be dangerous and even spoil food."[124] For precisely this reason, the arbiter noted, "police regulations prohibit the sale and retail of adulterated pepper."[125] Moreover, the arbiter observed, the testimony of one witness—the doorman at the residence where the litigants reached their agreement—indicated that the seller-defendant, Eloy, was well aware of these regulations. Prior to reaching the agreement with Fuesn, the witness claimed, Eloy had consulted with a retailer, who informed him that "he must not risk selling this pepper in Paris, but instead in the provinces, and that if she [the retailer] wanted, she would have it seized."[126] Accordingly, the arbiter concluded, Fuesn was entitled to the relief he sought—namely, rescission of the contract. However, it was crucial that he be required to deposit the "fake pepper" at the office of the grocers' guild, "so that at the behest of the responsible leaders, and pursuant to the regulations that they must enforce, that which justice requires will be ordered."[127]

As suggested by these cases, buyers suing for failure to deliver or for the delivery of nonconforming goods could obtain either specific performance (requiring the defendant-seller to provide conforming goods) or rescission (restoring the parties to their initial, precontractual positions). Although it is not entirely clear why arbiters selected one remedy rather than the other, they seem to have based the decision on some combination of the buyer's preference and their own sense of equity. In addition, arbiters sometimes recommended that the court reduce the purchase price. This is what happened, for example, in a lawsuit brought by one wine seller against another for the sale of poor quality wine, which failed to conform to the contract and to the standards of the wine sellers' guild.[128] The court appointed an arbiter, who unfortunately failed to identify his profession, but who was almost certainly a wine seller. The buyer was in possession of the wine, because, despite the fact that he "always refused to accept it," the seller had nonetheless delivered it to him.[129] Importantly, however, not all of the wine delivered was bad. The arbiter tasted the wine that was allegedly nonconforming and concluded that, as the buyer claimed, "this wine that I was made to taste does not even merit the name."[130] Presumably because some of the wine delivered was conforming, however, the arbiter recommended that the court resolve the dispute by directing the buyer to pay only for the conforming portion of the delivery.

Notably, the arbiters' reports do not, to my knowledge, discuss cases in which the aggrieved buyer requested or was granted money damages designed to place him in as good a position as he would have been had the seller not breached. When arbiters recommend that the defendant-seller be ordered to pay money, this was not as damages but instead in conjunction with an order of rescission, which required the defendant to restore any funds advanced, thereby returning the parties to their precontractual positions. The absence of a damages remedy may well be due to buyer preference. To the extent that buyers sought the enforcement of the contractual obligation, rather than rescission, they likely preferred specific performance to money damages, since the latter would not provide buyers with the actual merchandise that they sought. And since most eighteenth-century merchant-artisans produced and sold goods on demand, a buyer who had been sold defective merchandise would be hard-pressed to replace these in a timely fashion by purchasing conforming goods from a different seller. There was a good chance, in sum, that the time it would take for a buyer to obtain the goods elsewhere would exceed the time required for the original seller to cure. This is likely also the reason that the arbiters' reports reveal no cases in which a buyer who received nonconforming goods "covered" by purchasing the items from another seller.

In accounting for the absence of a damages remedy, it is also important to recognize the force of longstanding juristic tradition, and in particular that of the canon law. Due in no small part to the influence of canonists, French contract law long deemed specific performance preferable to money damages, since the latter permit the breaching party to escape obligation.[131] While likely fading (and clearly observed more in theory than in practice) this preference for specific performance continues to this day and stems from the fact that, as Barry Nicholas has argued, "French law treats breach of contract as a form of moral wrongdoing"—a viewpoint that contrasts with the tendency of the Anglo-American "common law [to] look[] more to commercial considerations."[132] Given the efforts of the eighteenth-century Parisian Merchant Court and its arbiters to demonstrate their commitment to promoting virtue, they likely shared this preference for specific performance. As Toubeau explained, it was a central maxim of the merchant courts that "merchants perform simple, informal agreements among themselves, just as if they were formal contracts."[133] When merchants failed thus to honor their word, the merchant court could not implicitly condone such misconduct by permitting the parties to buy their way out of their obligations. The court's proper role was, instead, to direct the parties to do as they had promised.

Litigation Concerning Employment Relationships

While most of the contract disputes that appeared before the Parisian Merchant Court concerned sales of goods and services, a significant number involved employment relationships.[134] This in itself is a point that bears emphasis. The one major work to date that broadly explores litigation within the eighteenth-century trades emphasizes that there was a "relatively centralised system of judicial provision affecting the trades."[135] In particular, it argues that litigation in Paris concerning the trades was centered entirely in the *Châtelet* (with appeals to the *Parlement*). In reality, however, as concerns guild-related litigation, like most other kinds, the Old Regime judicial landscape was characterized by extensive jurisdictional overlap, rather than by centralization. Thus, as described below, the merchant court played an important role in addressing conflict within the trades—though the nature of the disputes that it resolved appear to have differed in certain key respects from those filed in the *Châtelet.*

The employment-related suits filed in the merchant court were initiated by individuals and framed in the language of contract. Most were brought by workers seeking payment for work that they had performed, but employers sometimes also sued for violation of employment contracts and guild rules. In contrast, suits filed in the *Châtelet* were often brought by coalitions of masters or journeymen and raised broad questions of police regulation, such as the wages to be paid to all journeymen engaged in a particular type of work.[136] In this sense, the jurisdictional boundary between the merchant court and the *Châtelet* conformed, to some extent, to the distinction between commerce and police—or private ordering and public administration—that the merchant court developed in its ongoing jurisdictional conflict with the municipal government of Paris.

But just as the municipal government argued in that conflict, the theoretically clear distinction between commerce and police tended to collapse in practice, since individual contracts necessarily arose in the context of a broader system of police regulation. In other words, even though the merchant court's jurisdiction was limited to the particular employment contract at issue in the lawsuit before it—and even though it lacked the police authority to enforce guild regulations—it could not help but observe whether this contract complied with applicable guild regulations. Accordingly, despite the fact that the merchant court, unlike the *Châtelet,* was not an institution of the police, the employment-related disputes that it addressed implicated significant guild interests. Indeed, at the most fundamental level, such employment-related lawsuits were of great interest to guilds for the simple reason that they threatened the conceptual underpinnings of the guild system. Since one of the primary purposes of the guilds—and thus one of the main justifications for their power and privilege—was to ensure harmony within the world of work, the very existence of such lawsuits implied that the guilds were failing in their mission.

Given the guild interests at stake in these employment-related lawsuits, the judge and consuls, not surprisingly, often appointed guild leaders as arbiters.

This was so particularly in the case of lawsuits brought by apprentices or journeymen against their masters. The court presumably believed that, called before their guild leaders in the guild's central office,[137] the parties were more likely to defer to the leaders' authority and reconcile as directed. Moreover, if the arbiters failed to reconcile the parties, they determined which party was entitled to judgment by the usual method of examining written proof (including employment contracts and accounting books), interviewing witnesses, and assessing the parties' and witnesses' credibility. For all the reasons previously discussed, guild leaders were at a distinct advantage in this process of fact-finding.[138]

Since the court often appointed guild leaders to resolve disputes between members of the same guild, a question arises as to why parties bothered to file suit in the first place, rather than submit their disputes directly to the guild leadership. Although here we can only speculate, it seems likely that apprentices and journeymen opted to sue when they failed to obtain relief directly from guild leaders. Moreover, there were times when, for reasons that are not clear, the court appointed individuals other than guild leaders as arbiters.[139] But whatever the motivation of the apprentices and journeymen who filed suit, it is evident that when guild leaders were asked to serve as arbiters, they had good reason for doing so. Such service enabled them to enlist the support of the merchant court in disciplining errant guild members and thereby reinforcing their power.

Consider, for example, how the guild leaders in *Manjard v. Chopard* utilized their position as arbiters to call for the court's help in controlling one of their wayward members.[140] Antoine Manjard, a journeyman cartwright, sued his master, Chopard, demanding payment for seventy-eight days of work and claiming that they had agreed on wages of forty-two sous per day. According to Chopard, Manjard worked for only seventy and a half days, and they had agreed to wages of thirty-six sous per day. The court appointed three leaders of the cartwrights' guild to serve as arbiters. In seeking to resolve the dispute, these arbiters—much like those in sales disputes—focused much less on the specifics of the parties' ex ante agreement than on achieving fairness ex post. In particular, they attempted to make their own, objective assessment of the fair value of Manjard's work. Thus, they observed that "taking into account Manjard's youth, which is well-known to augment one's strength in working," there was good reason to think that he was entitled to the higher wages of forty-two sous per day, rather than the thirty-six sous that Chopard wished to pay.[141]

In so concluding, the arbiters also relied on information that they were particularly well suited to obtain because of their status as guild leaders—

namely, the testimony of two other masters in the cartwrights' guild. These masters, one of whom was Manjard's present employer and the other his employer prior to Chopard, confirmed the arbiters' view that the fair value of Manjard's labor was forty-two sous per day. However, since Chopard's accounting books established that Manjard had worked only seventy and a half days, and Manjard evidently had no written proof to the contrary, the guild leaders recommended that Chopard be ordered to pay for only seventy and a half days of work.

Having thus recommended a judgment, the guild leaders did not, however, conclude their report. Instead, they took the opportunity to call for the assistance of the judge and consuls in disciplining Chopard. Chopard, they complained, lacked sufficient respect for the guild leadership and, indeed, was publicly expressing his treasonous views. In plaintive tones, they implored the judge and consuls to remind Chopard of his place: "We beg . . . Messieurs the judge and consuls to order Monsieur Chopard to be more circumspect vis-à-vis the guild in the future and also not to suspect its officers of partiality."[142] The guild leaders were particularly aggrieved by Chopard's suggestion that they were overly sympathetic to journeymen, such as Manjard. Such a claim was absurd, they argued, since they concerned themselves only with doing justice, and quite frequently this meant finding against those journeymen who failed to work as required. As the guild leaders explained, they made it "a duty scrupulously to mete out justice to whomever it belongs, because far from supporting and empowering journeymen, the guild has always . . . deployed justice against those who failed to show up at the homes of the masters and widows of masters where they worked."[143]

Moreover, the guild leaders complained, Chopard had failed to appear before them when they initially summoned him and had ultimately appeared only when so directed by the merchant court. Chopard's failure to appear, they observed, not only violated his duty to obey the guild leadership, but also caused great harm to the poor journeyman-plaintiff, who had to appear before the guild leaders "six or seven times, which caused him to lose a good third of the day each time."[144] The leaders thus pleaded with the judge and consuls "to order Monsieur Chopard, when he will have similar disputes with his journeymen, to appear in the office of his guild every time that he is summoned there."[145]

By serving as arbiters, the guild leaders in *Manjard* were thus able to enlist the merchant court's support to bolster their position of authority within the guild itself. Significantly, however, in the process of trying to empower themselves, they found on behalf of the journeyman-plaintiff and against the master. Indeed, in a significant number of the lawsuits brought by apprentices and journeymen seeking wages from their masters, guild leaders serving as arbiters decided for the plaintiffs.[146] This is a point that bears emphasis, as it runs counter to the tendency to view guilds and their leadership as more likely to serve the interests of masters than those of workers. In line with this tendency, it is commonly argued that the reason why guilds mandated uniformity in wages was to prevent competition for labor, which would lead to wage increases and thus be to the overall detriment of masters.[147] But while the example of *Manjard* confirms that guilds sought uniformity in wages—and that they frequently failed to achieve this goal[148]—it also suggests that such uniformity was not always deployed in service of masters' interests. A rule mandating uniformity in wage levels could redound to the great benefit of journeymen at times when the labor market was glutted, such that competition would tend to push wage levels downward. And as *Manjard* reveals, guild leaders were willing to enforce uniformity in such circumstances as well—not only when it was masters who stood to benefit. This is not, of course, to suggest that the guild system was a net benefit to apprentices and journeymen, however this might be measured. The point is simply that we ought to be attentive to the ways that the complex institutional landscape of Old Regime France (of which the merchant court was part) sometimes enabled workers to deploy the guild system in their favor. By filing suit in the merchant court, and thus calling for its assistance, workers could at times forge alliances between themselves and their guild leaders against oppressive masters.

But while apprentices and journeymen sometimes benefited from litigation before the merchant court, this was not always so. Masters seeking to discipline wayward workers also found welcome support from the court and, in particular, from the guild leaders appointed as arbiters. Why masters thus seeking to discipline workers opted to bring litigation in the merchant court, rather than simply appealing directly to guild leaders or to the royal police for assistance is something of a mystery. Perhaps such litigation was brought because a favorable court ruling was thought necessary (or at least helpful) in instigating action by the guild leadership or the police. But whatever their reasons, masters did occasionally file suit in the merchant court, seeking to obtain its assistance in forcing apprentices and journeymen to abide by guild rules and regulations. And when appointed as arbiters in these master-initiated lawsuits, guild leaders were perfectly willing to find against workers. Their focus, in short, was not on promoting the interests of either masters or workers, but instead on enforcing guild rules and fortifying their own power.

This certainly describes the frame of mind of the six leaders of the shoe and boot makers' guild, appointed to serve as arbiters in *Chainboy v. Laurent.*[149] Chainboy, a master boot maker, and Vincent Laurent had entered a long-term contract, whereby Laurent was to serve as Chainboy's journeyman for an eight-year period. Laurent, however, left Chainboy's employ three years before the contract was to terminate. Immediately thereafter, Laurent established his own competing boot shop very close to that of his former master and employed a number of Chainboy's apprentices. Apparently meeting with some success, he attracted several of Chainboy's customers to his new store. Chainboy was infuriated by what he viewed as a betrayal and filed suit against Laurent. The court, he argued, should enforce the contract that they had entered and direct Laurent to comply with guild rules prohibiting a journeyman from thus competing with his master.

In sharp contrast to modern notions about the limits of the law's power to mandate labor, the guild leaders serving as arbiters had no doubt that "Monsieur Laurent . . . [should be] made to honor the commitment set forth in the contract that he signed and to obey guild regulations, [thus] remaining with his master and providing him with knowledge of his practices without any dissimulation."[150] Should Laurent refuse to abide by the contract and insist on maintaining his own business in violation of guild rules, then according to the guild leaders, he should be forced to compensate Chainboy for all the losses that he caused. Moreover, it was the guild leaders themselves who would make this damages calculation: "[Laurent] should be condemned to pay whatever damages and interest that it pleases Messieurs the arbiters to order, and all costs."[151] Finally, the guild leaders concluded, if further conflict arose between the parties, the court should decline jurisdiction and instead direct the parties "to appear before the police," whose involvement was ultimately necessary to enforce guild rules and regulations.[152]

It was thus guild leaders themselves, in their capacity as arbiters—and not the masters or workers who came before the merchant court as litigants—who were best assured of being able to use the court to their advantage. Indeed, guild leaders utilized their appointment as arbiters to enlist the court's help in disciplining not only masters and workers but also non-guild competitors. Consider in this regard the efforts of the five leaders of the wig makers' guild, appointed to serve as arbiters in *Sallier v. Lasserre.*[153] Lasserre, though not a master wig maker, had employed Sallier to serve as his apprentice. For reasons that are, unfortunately, unclear, Sallier subsequently sued Lasserre in the merchant court—presumably for payment of wages. As for the claims at issue in the litigation, the guild leaders serving as arbiters reported simply that they were unable to determine the truth and that they therefore committed these entirely to the discretion of the judge and consuls. They concluded their report, however, by emphasizing that, since Lasserre was not a master wig maker, he had no authority to employ an apprentice and thereby commit to teaching the art of wig-making. Evidently seeking to obtain the support of the judge and consuls in upholding guild rules, the guild leaders intoned: "We observe only that Monsieur Lasserre should not have taken on Sallier . . . to make an apprentice of him, because not being a master wig maker, he has no standing [*n'a aucune qualité*] to do so."[154]

In a similar case, *Persant v. Besse,* the four leaders of the cartwrights' guild, serving as arbiters, sought to reinforce the sanctity of the guild system and its privileges by portraying those who violated guild rules as unsavory characters deserving of the court's condemnation.[155] As the guild leaders presented it, greed and self-interest were the underlying causes of the litigation. Besse was a master saddler, who decided to manufacture and sell carriages. The process of manufacturing a carriage, however, involved various kinds of expertise, each associated with a different guild, including not only Besse's own guild (the saddlers), but also those of the cartwrights and the carpenters.[156] To pursue his plan, Besse therefore had to employ both cartwrights and carpenters. Like all guild members, however, he was permitted to hire only members of his own guild. Eager to earn a profit, and evidently unable (or unwilling) to obtain a royal privilege that would permit him legally to combine different trades within a single enterprise,[157] Besse decided to ignore this rule and employed four individuals—two cartwrights and two carpenters, who while practicing these trades, were themselves not guild members (and perhaps for this very reason were willing to work for a master saddler). One of these cartwrights was Persant, the plaintiff named in the litigation.

Having employed these four individuals, Besse "had built at his place, and in secret, all kinds of vehicles and of different types."[158] Unfortunately, for Besse, however, his secret enterprise ultimately became known to the cartwrights' guild. As the guild leaders explained, "The guild of master cartwrights, having learned of Monsieur Besse's ventures, went to his place with a police commissioner and a bailiff, and it seized all the new items of the cartwright trade that it found there."[159] At the time of this surprise visit and the seizure of the unlawfully produced goods, Persant declared to the police officer writing the official report that Besse owed him wages. As recorded in the police report, Besse, who was also present, denied Persant's claim, insisting that Persant "was a rogue and that it could have been only he who had denounced him to the guild and that sooner or later he would make him pay."[160] Thereafter, Persant filed suit in the merchant court, seeking the wages that he claimed he was owed.

In their effort to recommend a judgment to the court, the leaders of the cartwrights' guild were stymied by the fact that both parties had evidently broken guild rules, which suggested that neither's word could be trusted. On the one hand, Besse had threatened to take revenge against Persant for denouncing him to the cartwrights' guild. Thus, Besse might be refusing to pay Persant's wages simply as a means of exacting revenge: "Monsieur Besse, still convinced that it is Persant who gave him away and who arranged for the seizure of goods by the guild, would like as a result to avenge himself and make Persant lose his earnings."[161] Moreover, the leaders observed, they had no choice but to admit that, while Persant was not actually a journeyman within their guild, he had produced "some extraordinary work," such that "we cannot prevent ourselves from doing justice to Persant."[162] On the other hand, Persant himself had worked as a cartwright without being a member of the cartwrights' guild and knowingly agreed to perform such work in the service of someone who was not a master cartwright. Thus, it could well be the case that "having worked for someone who lacks the proper qualifications [*n'avoit point de qualité*], he wanted to benefit from this circumstance by having himself paid more than that which he is owed."[163]

As neither party had proven himself trustworthy, the leaders of the cartwrights' guild advised the judge and consuls to hear the parties themselves and to reach their own judgment as to which was speaking the truth. In the end, the guild leaders' primary concern was not to resolve the litigation but instead to utilize their position as arbiters to reinforce their guild's monopoly privileges. In this, moreover, they were quite successful. It was through their role as arbiters in the merchant court that they discovered the violation of guild rules. And while the court itself lacked enforcement authority, the guild leaders were able easily to call on the police to intervene where the court itself could not.

Marriage Contracts and Other Intrafamily Disputes

Because of the crucial role of the family in Old Regime commerce, the Parisian Merchant Court and its arbiters tried hard to reconcile those engaged in intrafamilial squabbles. Such squabbles took any number of forms, ranging from ordinary litigation regarding sales to disputes over marriage contracts. When the survival of the family was at stake, the court's general concern with promoting amicability among merchants took on a heightened urgency.

Such was the case in *Duhamel v. Flamand,* a lawsuit in which the arbiter concluded that the goal of family unity was a more important value than the legal requirement of the prescription period—namely, the time period within which the lawsuit could be brought.[164] In December 1785, a Parisian *négociant* named Jacques Duhamel sued M. and Mme. Flamand, demanding payment for purchases that Mme. Flamand had made over the years for use in her business. Although Mme. Flamand had made payments occasionally, these became so infrequent that three years prior to suing, Duhamel ceased providing her additional goods. Attempting to conceal her debts from her husband, Mme. Flamand begged Duhamel to be patient and to help guard her secret. She also promised to pay him when she received an inheritance she claimed to be expecting from a relative in Germany. But no such inheritance existed. Mme. Flamand had fabricated the story simply to gain time.

The arbiter appointed by the court recommended that it find for Duhamel. In so doing, he noted that, "If Monsieur Duhamel has made a mistake, it is to have ceased supplying goods three years ago without bringing suit; but too much indulgence, Messieurs, is not grounds for dismissing his suit."[165] Though unstated, the arbiter's concern here seemed to be that the court might consider the plaintiff's claim time-barred. According to the Commercial Ordinance of 1673, merchant-artisans were supposed to bring suit within one year of the sale and delivery of the items giving rise to the dispute.[166] However, as an arbiter involved in an unrelated lawsuit explained, "everyone knows . . . that the merchant court does not allow prescription in suits between one merchant and another," despite the language of the ordinance.[167] But while the court's practice was thus to ignore the letter of the law, the arbiter in *Duhamel v. Flamand* was nonetheless anxious that the suit might be deemed time-barred—perhaps because Duhamel's three-year delay so greatly exceeded the official one-year prescription period. Eager to eliminate any such possibility, the arbiter insisted that to impose the prescription period would be to punish Duhamel for the very laudable "indulgence" that he had exhibited toward Mme. Flamand. As he explained, "The indulgence of Monsieur Duhamel is praiseworthy, since it serves to preserve in a household the peace that . . . [M. Duhamel] was later forced to destroy, because he saw, too late, that he had been fooled."[168] For the arbiter, in other words, Duhamel's indulgence was highly commendable because it stemmed from his desire to help maintain peace in the Flamands' marriage, and this goal of family unity was far more important than any technical requirement about when suit must be brought.

As it turned out, Duhamel's concern that the Flamands' marriage would be endangered if the wife's debts were revealed proved to be prescient. Upon learning of the suit brought by Duhamel, M. Flamand's attitude toward his wife was less than charitable. As the arbiter noted somewhat facetiously: "Monsieur Flamand, [having discovered his wife's debts] . . . knows neither his name nor that Madame Flamand is his spouse; thus, Messieurs, he is no longer named Flamand, and the person known for the past thirty years as his spouse is today no longer his spouse."[169]

As the case of *Duhamel v. Flamand* suggests, family was such an important value in the commercial world of the Old Regime that efforts to preserve family unity could play a role in deciding even those cases that did not directly present a conflict between family members. But when the litigation was directly between family members, arbiters' efforts to achieve reconciliation were that much greater—and the failure to restore sundered family ties could lead them to exhibit great animosity toward the litigant deemed responsible for the conflict. A classic example of this phenomenon is provided by the arbiter's report in the dispute that arose between the widow Noël and her son-in-law, Cheret.[170] The widow Noël, like many Old Regime women who lost their husbands, was anxious to find a man to take over the family business.[171] After her husband died, she contracted a marriage for her daughter with a man named Cheret and agreed in the contract to make her son-in-law an equal partner in her business for a period of ten years beginning on the day of the marriage. Just eight months after they signed the marriage contract, however, the relationship between the widow Noël and her son-in-law had so deteriorated that she brought suit in the Parisian Merchant Court, seeking the dissolution of their partnership.

After listening to the parties' respective claims, the arbiter determined that reconciliation was impossible and resigned himself to determining how exactly to divide the partnership property. In making this determination, he was guided not only by the various contract provisions concerning dissolution but also by his perception of which party was more to blame for the disintegration of the relationship. In the arbiter's view, Cheret was largely at fault because he failed to show the proper respect to his aged mother-in-law, the woman to whose good graces he owed his entire fortune: "The facts are pretty grave as to the way Cheret treated his mother-in-law; swearing, lack of respect, the mother and the son-in-law ready to kill one another at every moment, and finally things were pushed to a point that it is impossible for the partnership to continue."[172] Moreover, the arbiter observed, Cheret's claim for 4,500 livres was so obviously excessive, and thus so distasteful, that he was tempted to abandon the parties to their own devices. Recognizing, however, "the necessity of ridding the aforementioned widow Noël of a matter that constitutes the unhappiness of her days," the arbiter decided that "charity forces me to return to assisting them."[173] If the court failed to preserve familial relationships, then, in his view, it was required to identify those responsible for their disintegration and to come to the aid of the unfortunate individuals who had been made to suffer at the hands of such malfeasants.

Animosity toward the litigant deemed responsible for destroying family unity—and concomitant compassion for the litigant attempting to preserve it—might be so great as to overcome what would otherwise be clear presumptions governing resolution of a dispute. This appears to have been the case in the lawsuit brought by M. Jeauly, a wholesale grocer from Versailles, against his brother-in-law, M. Lemoine, a retail grocer, who at the time of the lawsuit resided in the town of Saint-Germain-en-Laye.[174] M. Jeauly had supplied M. Lemoine with merchandise worth more than 4,275 livres. Claiming that M. Lemoine had failed to pay him, M. Jeauly filed suit in the merchant court. As always, the arbiter appointed by the court began by examining the parties' accounting books. While he deemed the state of M. Jeauly's records—and in particular the fact that he possessed only a single accounting book—less than ideal, he nonetheless observed that M. Jeauly did possess some written proof. In contrast, M. Lemoine presented no accounting books or other documentation.

As the merchant possessing superior accounting records, M. Jeauly would normally be entitled to swear the decisory oath, affirming that M. Lemoine had failed to make good on his debt and, thereafter, to receive judgment in his favor. The arbiter, however, was unable to reach this seemingly obvious conclusion, because M. Lemoine offered a compelling explanation for his failure to proffer written records—namely, his efforts to maintain good relations with his brother-in-law. According to M. Lemoine, his older sister—M. Jeauly's wife—had raised him like a mother. As the arbiter explained, Mme. Jeauly "raised him from his most tender youth, . . . she took care of his education and thereafter helped establish him [in life]."[175] Accordingly, the arbiter observed, M. Lemoine "always had for this sister all the respect that . . . he owed her . . . [and] he ceaselessly exhibited toward his sister an awe and timidity without parallel."[176] Indeed, the relationship between Mme. Jeauly and her younger brother, M. Lemoine, was so close that, when their parents died, M. Jeauly, the plaintiff, was appointed M. Lemoine's guardian.

Thereafter, the Jeaulys and the Lemoines began transacting business with one another. The Jeaulys, as wholesalers, supplied goods to the Lemoines. According to M. Lemoine, he and his wife asked M. Jeauly for receipts whenever they paid him money, but M. Jeauly repeatedly suggested that he was offended by the implication that the Lemoines did not trust him. As M. Lemoine explained: "When it was I who brought him money and I asked for a receipt, Monsieur Jeauly said to me, come now my brother, you do me little justice, don't you know that I want your well-being and not your loss, rest assured; when it was my wife, he told her the same and added, you are quite suspicious regarding our account, rest assured, we will have no more differences concerning our commercial activities than we will have concerning the account of the guardianship that I must provide you, we will all be satisfied. The only option was to leave, rather than to incur their enmity."[177] In order not to offend his brother-in-law, M. Lemoine suggested, he had no choice but to accept M. Jeauly's refusal to provide receipts. Thus, while M. Lemoine had improperly disregarded the requirement that merchants maintain records, and while technically he had no evidence in support of his defense, this was largely because of his commitment to maintaining his relationship with the brother-in-law whom he trusted.

Torn between the technical requirements of the law—including, the long-standing presumption that a merchant's failure to maintain accounting records was itself evidence of bad faith—and his compassion for M. Lemoine's efforts to maintain familial unity, the arbiter could not decide what judgment to recommend. He had no choice, he explained, but to leave the ultimate decision to the judgment of the judge and consuls—even though "it is costing a great deal of my self-respect [*amour propre*] not to be able to give you a definitive decision today."[178] The problem was that this dispute, "as sensitive as it is thorny," pitted against one another "two brothers-in-law, . . . in whom there ought to be found feelings of probity as solid as a rock, and nonetheless there is bad faith in one of the two."[179] But the facts were such that it was impossible to determine which was the party who had acted in bad faith, and the risk of hazarding the wrong guess was too painful to contemplate: "It would be too harmful to my sensitivities if I dared to recommend a holding, while fearing that my judgment might be wrong."[180] Was it M. Lemoine who engaged in bad faith behavior by failing to maintain accounting records? Or was it instead M. Jeauly who acted in bad faith by demonstrating an utter lack of respect for familial obligations—obligations that were all the more sacred since he had been formally appointed M. Lemoine's guardian? Unable to decide, the arbiter placed his faith in the judge and consuls: "I dare to flatter myself that the members of your tribunal, in joining together and each sharing their views with one another, will discover the false claimant and render justice to whom it is due."[181] As the leaders of a court devoted to protecting and promoting merchant virtue, the arbiter concluded, they had no choice but to succeed where he had failed.

Ultimately, for this arbiter, as for so many Old Regime merchants, it was in fact merchant virtue itself that was at stake in disputes that threatened to tear the family asunder. Family unity was, of course, deemed important for the simple reason that, as discussed above, good familial relations often proved a crucial component of commercial success. In addition, however, merchants sought to preserve familial harmony because they viewed the family as a model for the kinds of trust-infused, long-term relations that they embraced as the foundation of commercial practice and the epitome of merchant virtue. A merchant who failed his own blood brother, in short, could hardly be expected to behave any better in his dealings with mere merchant colleagues, while one who exhibited proper loyalty and respect toward his relatives might be more easily trusted to do the same in his nonfamilial interactions. Indeed, as we will see, it was precisely this tendency to equate familial and commercial relations that underlay traditional understandings of one of the primary institutions of merchant practice: the business association.

4

Société *and Sociability: The Changing Structure of Business Associations and the Problem of Merchant Relations*

God has rendered necessary for all . . . [men's] needs the mutual employment of their industry and labor and various kinds of trade. . . . Thus, for the employment of industry and labor, they associate.

—Jean Domat, *Les loix civiles dans leur ordre naturel*

While Old Regime merchants insisted that all commercial endeavors were infused with a spirit of brotherly love, it was the business partnership, they claimed, that best epitomized merchant virtue. Such claims drew on the writings of highly influential natural-law theorists, who pointed to the partnership, or *société,* as evidence of an innate human sociability. Taking this line of reasoning one step further, merchants asserted that commercial *sociétés* evidenced a distinctive, merchant sociability and thus disproved the prevailing view that theirs was a profession of avarice and cunning.

As commerce expanded over the course of the eighteenth century, merchants experimented with forms of business association other than the general partnership. These included both limited partnerships and organizational forms that approached modern-day *sociétés de capitaux*—namely, institutions akin to the Anglo-American corporation in their bureaucratic governance structure and division of capital into readily transferable shares. But while the traditional partnership was conceived as an association of equal, interdependent brothers united to promote their mutual advantage, the same could not so easily be said of these newer, more complex forms of business association. Accordingly, the model of the *société* as the embodiment of fraternal charity was undermined, and merchants were left to wonder how they would henceforth structure their relations. In order to understand these merchant concerns, it is necessary to begin by exploring how commercial *sociétés* were traditionally formed and conceived.

The Partnership Relationship

The distinction between general and limited partnerships in eighteenth-century commercial theory and practice was less clear-cut than it is today. As a general rule, however, partnerships in which all partners contributed both capital and labor were deemed general, such that each partner was able to obligate the partnership and was held jointly and fully liable for its debts. In contrast, those in which one partner contributed only capital and the other only labor were deemed limited, and the capital-contributing partner, while standing to lose only his initial contribution, was unable to obligate the partnership.

Whether general or limited, most of the partnerships that appeared in disputes before the Parisian Merchant Court were formed among a small number of people—two or, at the most, three. Partners were frequently members of the same family or practiced the same or similar trades. And even when partners were not related to one another by kinship or profession, the personal bond they shared was a defining feature of the partnership and largely inseparable from their business relationship.

PARTNERSHIPS BETWEEN FAMILY MEMBERS

Family was of key importance in the commercial culture of the Old Regime. This is precisely why, as we have seen, arbiters appointed by the Parisian Merchant Court devoted so much effort to restoring sundered familial ties. Indeed, the family was traditionally the focal point of commercial activity. The master-artisan and his family generally lived and worked in the same apartment, with the back room serving as a residence and the front room(s) as a workshop and/or store. In most families, the man of the house was the guild member, and as such he produced and/or procured the merchandise, while his wife aided in bookkeeping and in running the store.[1] There were, however, a number of guilds whose members were exclusively women—including those of the seamstresses, linen makers, hairdressers, and midwives.[2] In theory, it was only these women, known as *marchandes publiques*, who were permitted to bind themselves contractually and thus to run businesses entirely on their own. Indeed, well-established legal doctrine provided that married women who were not *marchandes publiques* required special authorization from their husbands to enter binding agreements of any kind.[3]

In reality, however, arbiters reports filed with the court indicate that married women regularly signed contracts, bills of exchange, and promissory notes without such special authorization. Moreover, the court readily enforced these obligations against both the wife and her husband—a practice that was essential to enabling women to play the key role that they did in the family business. As one arbiter observed in a report to the judge and consuls, urging them to disregard arguments that a married woman could not bind herself without her husband's express permission, "You are . . . messieurs in a better position than any merchant or *négociant* to know that . . . without special authorization, many wives of *négociants* and merchants . . . draft, endorse negotiable instruments, pay such instruments on protest, sell daily, receive deliveries of merchandise."[4] While a comprehensive analysis of the court's jurisprudence regarding women is beyond the scope of this book, it bears emphasis that the merchant courts of Old Regime France—recognizing the key importance of family in commercial activity—seem to have granted women the legal capacity of which they were elsewhere deprived.

While the married couple was the fulcrum on which business life hinged, familial success also depended on the development of more extended and intergenerational relationships.[5] But relationships between generations and across families that were joined through marriage could be difficult to establish and sustain. The formation of partnerships provided a means of strengthening such familial ties. Partnerships between parents and children, in-laws, and siblings formalized, and thereby reinforced, bonds of mutual dependence. Moreover, at moments of intergenerational transition, when the family's continued survival was at greatest risk, partnerships resolved potential problems arising from the need to transfer power in the family business.[6]

Because family partnerships played such an important role in intergenerational transitions, they were often memorialized in marriage contracts. The case of *Brice LeChauve v. Accau de Nainville* is indicative of many of the common reasons that family partnerships were formed.[7] As the recipient of a royal pension [*pensionnaire du roy*], Accau Sr. was, by the standards of the Old Regime, a fairly wealthy man, intent on seeing his nineteen-year-old son well established in life. To ensure their son's success, Accau Sr. and his wife sought to arrange an advantageous marriage, ultimately selecting as the bride-to-be the daughter of a Parisian architect named Le Clerc.

After much negotiation, the parents of the young couple agreed to the following financial arrangements in relation to the marriage. The bride's parents would give their daughter 4,800 livres as a dowry—1,800 to be paid at the time of the marriage and the remaining sum within three years from the wedding date. The groom's parents, in turn, promised that when they died, their children would all receive equal shares of their estate. In this way, the groom (and his future bride) were assured some inheritance. In addition, the Accaus agreed to enter two partnerships with their otherwise penniless son. The first of these was a farm run by Accau Sr., in which the groom was to receive a one-half interest, "without requiring that he contribute any funds or capital advances."[8] The second partnership was a horse-trading business, which the groom was to establish upon marrying. The Accaus agreed to "undertake a one-third interest in the business."[9] Since young Accau had no money of his own, the marriage contract specified that his parents would supply all the funds necessary to start the business, and the son would invest, at least initially, only his time and labor. To protect their interests, the parents reserved the right to withdraw from the partnership whenever they chose, as long as they gave one month's notice. Since no limitation on liability was specified in the parties' agreement, the partnerships were presumed to be general.

The two partnerships established between the Accaus and their son cannot be meaningfully distinguished from the family relationships on which they were based and which they were intended to promote. Formed as clauses of a marriage contract, rather than as separate agreements, these partnerships were designed to restructure the family at a crucial moment of transition—when aging parents had to begin preparing for old age and their adult child was ready to establish his own family. In both partnerships, the Accaus guaranteed their son a significant share of profits without requiring him to commit any money up front. These are not terms to which investors interested only in making a profit would likely have agreed. Rather than earn an immediate profit, the Accaus sought to help their son establish himself in the world of commerce, and thereby promote his chances of contracting a good marriage—which, in turn, would further advance his commercial interests.

For both the Accaus and their son, the formation of these partnerships was preferable to a gift of money. By associating with his parents, Accau Jr. could benefit from their connections and good reputation to obtain both credit and information. Indeed, because the partnerships were general, merchants knew that they could hold the parents fully liable, and thus were far more likely to extend credit to Accau Jr. At the same time, the partnerships were advantageous for the Accaus because, unlike a gift of money, they were an investment in which they could maintain some control. This proved important since, as it turned out, Accau Jr. was not well suited to the horse-trading business. As planned, he began the business on August 1, 1782, immediately after his wedding. From the very start, however, it was a disaster. After several months, during which Accau Jr. lost all the money invested and failed to earn a profit, the Accaus concluded that the business was a hopeless failure and decided to exercise the right they had reserved to withdraw from the partnership.

Upon dissolution of the partnership, the need arose for the first time to distinguish between family and business, and it proved to be quite difficult. Who exactly was liable for the partnership's debts—only those who were legally members of the partnership or, more broadly, those who were linked to the partnership through familial ties? Although the bride's family members were not partners, the Accaus seemed to believe that their participation in liquidating the partnership's assets was imperative. Thus, the Accaus sent an urgent letter to the parents and uncle of their daughter-in-law, asking them to come to their home to discuss liquidation. The bride's family accepted the invitation, and on Christmas Day, the two families met to do a final accounting. At this time, they determined that the partnership had sustained losses of over 2,080 livres. The Accaus recognized that, as general partners, they were fully liable for the business's losses and promised to pay all the debts, with one exception—a promissory note for 648 livres that Accau Jr. had given his wife's uncle in return for a cash loan to the business.

While willing to pay all debts owed to third parties, the Accaus apparently believed that the bride's family members were responsible for some share of the business's losses, even though they were not officially partners. The bride's uncle, however, did not agree and sued Accau Sr. in the Parisian Merchant Court, demanding payment on the note. As required by the law, the arbiter found for the uncle. Because Accau Sr. was a partner in the horse-trading business and the bride's uncle was not, it was Accau Sr. who was liable for the business's debts, including the promissory note made to the uncle. That the Accaus so fervently believed that the uncle was obligated is a telling measure, however, of the extent to which contemporaries viewed the business partnership not as an artificial, legal entity but as a natural extension of the family with all its informal, personal obligations.

Similar concerns regarding intergenerational transition led the widow Noël and her son-in-law, Cheret, to form a partnership.[10] Noël was the mother of three children and, after her husband's death, the sole proprietor of the business that they had established together. When her eldest child, a daughter, came of age, she sought to arrange her marriage and thereby resolve many financial difficulties. Once her daughter married, Noël would cease being responsible for her upkeep. More importantly, Noël's future son-in-law might take over her business. Although widows in Old Regime France, unlike married women, were officially permitted to obligate themselves legally and thus to transact commerce independently,[11] most nonetheless thought it advantageous to find a man to take over the family business. This man might be the widow's son, when he came of age, a new husband, or, as in Noël's case, a son-in-law.[12] But while widows like Noël had much to gain by joining forces with a man, they also had a great deal to lose in thus relinquishing complete independence. By forming a partnership with the man she selected, Noël was able to minimize the risks to her and her children. In particular, she retained an ownership interest in—and thus some control over—her family business. In this way, for Noël, as for the Accaus, partnership was a means of negotiating a very difficult period of transition in the family structure.

In the contract arranging her daughter's marriage, Noël agreed to provide a dowry and to establish a partnership between herself and her future son-in-law, Cheret, which was to begin on the day of the marriage. The dowry was worth 1,500 livres, 1,100 of which would consist of a half ownership interest in "the carriage, horses, and tools for use in the business of the aforementioned Mme. Noël."[13] The remaining 400 livres would take the form of furniture, linens, and cash (in unspecified proportions), all to be distributed the day before the wedding. As for the partnership, the contract stated that it was to last ten years from the date of the marriage and that, upon dissolution, Noël and Cheret would split any profits or losses equally. In addition, the partners were to do an accounting every three months and to divide profits immediately thereafter. If the widow Noël lent money to the partnership to purchase a cart, horses, tools, or merchandise of any kind, the debt the partnership thereby accrued to her would take priority over all other claims against it. If the partnership's debts to Noël remained outstanding for more than three months, she would be entitled to interest of 5 percent.

Interspersed among such contract terms regarding the partnership's duration and the division of profits were others that seem to have been more directly concerned with issues of family than of business. The marriage contract specified that the partners would live and do business in Noël's home. In return for the rent-free use of her home, the partnership would feed Noël's two other children, "which will serve as compensation."[14] If Cheret and his new wife had children, they would be personally responsible for their children's upkeep, "as long as the business [*la maison*] does not earn profits."[15] If and when the partnership started earning profits, it would undertake to provide for these children.

As Noël and Cheret soon discovered, it was precisely the intersection of business and family—the intersection that made partnership so desirable—that could also easily prove its downfall. Shortly after the wedding, Noël and Cheret realized that they could not bear working together. Claiming that her son-in-law was insolent, Noël withdrew from the partnership and Cheret responded by demanding "a profit proportional to that which he could have expected over the course of the aforementioned ten-year period."[16] In particular, he claimed entitlement to lost profits of 4,500 livres, plus 1,500 livres for the value of his wife's dowry. Noël rejected the claim for lost profits as extravagant and argued that, even if it were justified, she would be unable to pay because "her entire fortune consists of a house, her horses, the tools needed for her business; and of the credit that she has established with the merchants with whom she deals [*ses correspondants*]."[17] Unable to reach an agreement with Cheret, Noël asked the Parisian Merchant Court to decide on the terms for liquidating the partnership.

The arbiter determined that Cheret had indeed been insolent and that such behavior on the part of a son-in-law toward a widowed, vulnerable woman who had given him so much was without justification. Accordingly, the arbiter proposed that Cheret reduce his demands for lost profits to 2,400 livres. Cheret initially agreed to the arbiter's proposed settlement, but then changed his mind and rejected all compromise. Accordingly, the arbiter recommended that the judge and consuls impose the settlement by means of a court order. In order, however, to protect Noël from her ingrate son-in-law, the arbiter concluded that the court must further direct that Noël retain all partnership property and that Cheret depart from her home within the month.

That the arbiter, despite his animosity toward Cheret, thus favored granting him some lost profits bears emphasis. While lost profits seem not to have been requested or granted as a remedy for breach of a sales agreement, they were evidently available for breach of a partnership agreement—a difference that is itself a measure of the distinctive interdependence of partners. Partners responsible for running the partnership were generally expected to devote all their time to it, thus abandoning any prior business ventures and becoming completely financially dependent on the partnership.[18] As argued by one partner suing for breach of a partnership contract, she was entitled to lost profits because, in order to form the partnership, she had "neglected her factory in Brussels."[19] Lost profits compensated for the significant opportunity costs that followed from the nature of the partnership as a kind of formalized but all-encompassing brotherhood.

PARTNERSHIPS BETWEEN MERCHANTS IN THE SAME OR SIMILAR TRADES, AND BETWEEN MERCHANTS AND NONMERCHANTS

While many merchants formed partnerships within the family, others established partnerships with friends and colleagues engaged in the same or a similar trade, or even with nonmerchants. These partnerships, like those among family members, were characterized first and foremost by significant interdependence among the partners.

The partnership offered several advantages to working alone. First, it enabled individuals to expand the resources available to them. For example, by pooling capital, partners could save on the fixed costs of doing business, such as tools and a workplace. And though guild rules generally prohibited the formation of inter-guild partnerships, arbiters' reports filed with the Parisian Merchant Court suggest that merchants regularly formed such partnerships as a means of leveraging one another's distinctive skill sets. Generally, arbiters made no mention of the fact that such partnerships were technically impermissible, and when they did, it was with little concern. Thus, for example, when a hairdresser and a wine seller from Paris formed a six-year partnership to sell wine and the hairdresser then sued the wine seller for breach, the arbiter wrote several pages analyzing the plaintiff's various claims and concluded that he was entitled to judgment on each.[20] It was only after thus recommending that the court find in the plaintiff's favor that the arbiter ended his report by observing, as an afterthought, that "all wine sellers are prohibited by guild regulations from making any partnership to trade in wine with someone other than a wine seller."[21] At no point did the arbiter suggest that because such an inter-guild partnership was prohibited, the court should decline to enforce the agreement establishing it. That arbiters were more likely to insist on enforcement of guild regulations in employment-related lawsuits than in those related to business associations probably stems from the identity of the arbiters typically appointed in the two types of litigation. As we have seen, guild leaders were frequently appointed as arbiters in employment-related litigation. While the identity of the arbiters in disputes concerning business associations is unclear, it is evident that these individuals were usually not guild leaders[22]—and thus presumably had less incentive than such leaders would to seek to enforce guilds rules.

A second advantage of the partnership is that it greatly reduced monitoring costs. Merchants who worked alone often had to hire assistants, but since such employees had little personal stake in the business, they had to be carefully monitored for fear that they might not use their best efforts. Partners, in contrast, had a stake in the business, since they invested capital and shared in both profits and losses. By taking on a partner, rather than hiring an employee, merchants were therefore able to forgo extensive monitoring and its costs. Finally, as discussed below, limited partnerships provided investment opportunities for wealthy merchants and nonmerchants, who sought to make use of idle capital without becoming actively involved in the running of the business. At the same time, such partnerships afforded those with time and talent but little money an opportunity to capitalize on their skills.

Serteur, Guérin, and Texier, three lumber merchants, established a partnership largely for the purpose of saving on monitoring costs.[23] Prior to doing so, Serteur and Guérin, who lived in the hamlet of Beaumarchais, formed a partnership to buy and sell wood and to manufacture bowsprits, a component in shipbuilding. Seeking to expand their business, they contacted Texier, a lumber merchant in the village of Staims, near Saint-Denis, and asked him to join the partnership. Since Texier resided near Saint-Denis, they would be able to buy and sell in Saint-Denis without having to travel there themselves or to rely on an agent. This would save them a great deal of money. And because Texier, as a partner, would have a personal stake in potential profits and losses, they had reason to trust him more than someone to whom they paid a salary.

Unfortunately for Serteur and Guérin, they quickly discovered that this benefit of partnership entailed a significant, parallel drawback—namely, that while Texier's interest in the partnership was identical to theirs, so too was his power. Shortly after joining the partnership, Texier sold some wood on credit to a man named Delacroix, concerning whom he later explained to the arbiter, "he sought information, [and he] seemed good."[24] Texier, however, was misinformed. Soon after the sale, Delacroix was imprisoned for failure to pay his debts—including the debt he owed for his purchase from Texier. Furious that their new partner had made such a poor choice, Serteur and Guérin sued Texier in the Parisian Merchant Court, claiming that the loss fell on him alone, rather than on the partnership as a whole, because he had not been authorized to extend credit without their permission. Texier responded by citing the well-established principle that, absent a provision to the contrary in the partnership agreement, a partner has full authority to act on behalf of the partnership: "As a partner, he had the right to sell on credit, just as for cash, and he did this sale, as he would have done any other, only for the benefit of the partnership."[25] Not surprisingly, the arbiter agreed and recommended that the court issue an order declaring that the loss fall on the partnership as a whole.

While the goal of saving on monitoring costs led to the formation of the Serteur-Guérin-Texier partnership, Baudry and Albert formed their partnership as a means of pooling, and thereby expanding, resources.[26] Baudry was a manufacturer of printed fabrics [*toiles peintes*]—textiles in the style of the highly popular patterned cottons imported from India—and Albert was a master tailor. As a master artisan, Albert had considerable capital, which he was prepared to invest, but he did not know the technique for producing printed fabrics. Baudry, in contrast, knew how to produce such fabrics—perhaps having learned to do so while in someone's employ—but he had no money. Accordingly, they agreed to form a partnership in which Albert would supply all necessary capital and Baudry would be responsible for establishing and operating the business.

As Serteur, Guérin, and Texier discovered, however, the interdependence that was the great benefit of partnership could also prove a significant drawback. Baudry's complete dependence on Albert for financing placed him in a desperate situation when Albert was imprisoned for fraud. While in jail, Albert ceased supplying funds, and Baudry had to turn to Albert's wife and to the partnership's debtors to obtain the money necessary to keep the business afloat. Although Baudry managed to save the business temporarily, it ended when, shortly after being released from jail and having no money, Albert fired all the employees. Baudry then filed suit in the Parisian Merchant Court for breach of the partnership agreement, and the arbiter found in his favor.

Although partnerships among those who were not family members were motivated largely by financial concerns, they, like family-based partnerships, were structured such that there was little distance between the personal and the professional. Since members of a general partnership were fully liable for the debts incurred by one another in the partnership's name and had full authority to act on its behalf, they had a significant incentive to know and trust each other. And while the members of a limited partnership were less interdependent, they too had reason to seek to protect their (more limited) investments by developing close personal relationships with one another. Such financial incentives promoting friendship and trust were furthered by the terms of the partnership agreement, which often provided that the partners live in the partnership's place of business and that the partnership provide them with basic necessities.[27] For example, the Albert-Baudry partnership was responsible for the partners' physical maintenance, including the cost of housing, heating, lighting, and food.

The extent to which personal considerations shaped partnerships, even among those who were not family members, is suggested by the partnership formed between Dujardin and Lejeune.[28] Dujardin, a Parisian bourgeois, and Lejeune, a man trained as a goldsmith but lacking a guild mastership, agreed to become partners in a gold and jewelry business, for which the former would supply the capital and the latter the labor. The would-be partners recognized from the outset that the success of their business relationship hinged on their ability to maintain a good personal relationship—and, in particular, on whether their wives would support or undermine that relationship. As explained by the arbiter appointed to resolve the dispute that eventually arose, "We have recognized that the contracting parties, who knew without a doubt the unsociability of their wives, tried to take precautions to temper their disposition to quarrel and deceive one another."[29] In particular, Dujardin and Lejeune included in their partnership agreement, or *acte de société,* a clause providing that an insult leveled by either partner's wife against the other partner was not grounds for dissolution, and that the only remedy for such an insult was for the insulted partner to lock the offending wife out of the workshop: "To prevent any disturbances, profits will be divided between the partners, without the wife of one being able through greediness, or other chicanery, to rail against the other, and allowing only that the partner who was verbally abused by the other's wife be permitted to keep her outside the workshop."[30]

Despite their best intentions, however, the partners failed to insulate their business relationship from their personal life. Less than a year after forming the partnership, Dujardin sued for dissolution, arguing that Lejeune had breached the partnership contract by locking him out of the workshop. While admitting that he had locked Dujardin out, Lejeune claimed that he was entitled to do so by the *acte de société* because "he was grievously injured in his honor and his reputation by the . . . reiterated invectives of Mme. Dujardin, who lavished him with the most disgraceful epithets."[31] Consistent with the *acte,* Lejeune did not request the dissolution of the partnership. Instead, "he forbade his partner from entering the laboratory in order to oblige him to force his wife to make reparations for the injury to his honor, that is to say through a document made before a notary, through which, in addition to the reparations he demands, M. Dujardin would undertake responsibility for any new injuries that his wife might do to him."[32]

The arbiter observed that Lejeune — by locking out M. Dujardin, rather than his wife — had failed to comply with the provisions of the partnership agreement and thereby caused its "rupture."[33] However, he concluded, strict enforcement was improper, because the agreement was based on an error so fundamental as to vitiate the consent underlying it — namely, the mistaken assumption that it was possible to maintain a partnership despite the personal animosity between the partners' wives. The friendship and trust on which partnerships were necessarily premised could not possibly be sustained if the partners' wives despised one another: "If the partners proved through this clause the desire they had to live in harmony, it must also be admitted that they did not reflect sufficiently on the physical and moral impossibility of keeping peace between two women, who are prejudiced toward one another, and whose interests are always daily motives for dispute."[34] Because the preservation of friendly, harmonious relations among partners was of the utmost importance, the arbiter decided that "the intemperance of [Mme. Dujardin's] tongue" must be considered "like a rupture of the partnership, which presupposes a great deal of harmony to prosper."[35] Concluding that "there are thus wrongs on both their parts," the arbiter ordered the dissolution of the partnership.[36]

Sociétés *and the Natural Law Tradition*

The intersection of the personal and the professional that was the defining feature of most partnerships that came before the Parisian Merchant Court had a long history. This history dated back to the Roman-law conception of *societas,* as subsequently transformed and endowed with new significance by the rise of the seventeenth-century, modern natural-law tradition. Writing at the end of the seventeenth century, the noted commercial jurist Toubeau described partnerships in terms suggesting the importance of both its Roman and natural-law heritage: "Partnership is a contract of law and good faith within the law of nations [*Droit des Gens*] and it is, of all the contracts that law has made available to men, that which is the most natural to him and which he should desire the most."[37] True to Roman law, Toubeau characterized the partnership as a contract of the "law of nations" or *ius gentium.* True to natural-law jurisprudence, he claimed that the partnership is "the most natural" of all contracts.

In classical Roman law, the partnership or *societas* was deemed an institution of the *ius gentium,* or the law common to all peoples, rather than unique to the Romans.[38] This classical Roman-law definition of the partnership as an institution common to all people was predated, however, by a peculiarly Roman form of partnership—one which profoundly shaped the later, classical conception of *societas.* The preclassical Roman form of partnership was modeled on the *consortium,* an institution of family law. When the *paterfamilias* died, the family's property passed automatically into a community, or *consortium,* consisting of his sons and their families. Property owned by this community did not belong to any of the heirs individually but to the community as a whole. Eventually, individuals who wished to pool their resources were permitted to form a partnership resembling the *consortium,* in which they were to behave as if they were in fact blood brothers. In this first kind of partnership recognized by Roman law, the *societas omnium bonorum,* each partner placed the entirety of his property into the partnership and no distinction was drawn between that which belonged to the individual partners and that which belonged to the partnership as a whole.[39] Because such partnerships permitted no personal property to exist separate from that of the partnership, the law reinforced a brotherly identification between individual and partnership interests. Under such a property regime, self-serving actions designed to promote the interests of one partner as against those of the other were greatly minimized since the law automatically attributed any property acquired by the individual to the partnership.

Because of the tremendous risks involved in pooling all assets in this manner, Roman law came to recognize another kind of partnership which distinguished between personal and partnership property. The *societas omnium bonorum* and this more modern business form subsequently merged to create the classical Roman-law conception of the *societas* as a contract of the *ius gentium.* The *societas* was established simply by mutual consent of the partners, who were free to combine as many or as few of their assets as they desired.[40]

Because of its origins in *consortium*—a legal and mystical union of brothers through which the *familias* continued beyond the father's death—the classical Roman *societas* was viewed as a sacred fraternal union. Many centuries later, this conception of the partnership as fraternal union was embraced by modern natural-law jurists, who viewed the partnership as a key piece of evidence supporting their claim that the legal and social order emerged from immutable laws of human nature. The extent to which they succeeded in widely perpetuating the view that the partnership was an institution of natural law is suggested by the following comment made by Robert-Joseph Pothier. Writing in the mid-eighteenth century, this classically trained civil-law jurist stated that "the partnership contract is a contract of natural law that is formed and governed by the simple principles of natural law."[41]

The leading French exponent of natural law—and, moreover, the leading jurist of the age of Louis XIV—was Jean Domat. His *Les loix civiles dans leur ordre naturel,* published in 1689, remained the most important text on French law until it was supplanted by the treatises of Pothier a century later. As its title indicates, Domat, much like his German contemporary Samuel Pufendorf,[42] sought to bring the civil-law tradition into accord with divinely established principles of human nature. But while natural-law jurisprudence proved highly influential throughout seventeenth- and eighteenth-century Europe, there were, not surprisingly, significant regional differences. Thus, Domat's work was profoundly shaped by two traditions that were particularly French: Cartesianism and Jansenism.

Domat began his masterpiece with a distinct, self-contained *Traité des lois,* in which he set forth a general framework for understanding the relationship between law, human nature, and the divine. In classically Cartesian fashion, he opened the *Traité* with a discussion of method. According to Domat, law is a science, and thus knowledge of the law, like knowledge of the natural sciences, is to be gained through Descartes' new method of systematic doubt. Rejecting Scholasticism, Descartes had set out to identify those few principles whose truth was beyond all doubt and which could therefore serve as firm ground for the development of human knowledge. Just as Descartes deduced the existence of God and the material world from the indisputable principle of his existence as a thinking being, Domat set out to deduce the entire body of human positive law from one indisputable principle. Only by developing a system of law on the foundation of such a fundamental, unquestionable truth would it be possible for the first time to know that all law was valid. As Domat explained, "Since . . . there is nothing more necessary in sciences than to possess the first principles of them, and that every science begins with establishing its own principles, and setting them in such a light as may best discover their truth and their certainty, that they may serve for a foundation to all the particular laws which are to depend upon them; it is of importance to consider what are the principles of laws, in order to know the nature and firmness of the rules which depend on them."[43]

While Domat's method was Cartesian, the indisputable truths he adopted as the lynchpin of his system derived as much from faith as from reason—in particular, from Jansenism. In recent years, historians have increasingly recognized the centrality of Jansenism in the ferment of Old Regime political and social culture that ultimately gave rise to the Revolution.[44] The term "Jansenism" derives from the name of the bishop of Ypres in the Spanish Netherlands, Cornelius Jansenius, whose 1640 publication, *Augustinus,* launched a great debate about the nature of free will and the necessity of divine grace. The *Augustinus* revived Saint Augustine's deeply pessimistic belief that human nature is fundamentally corrupted by original sin and that redemption absent God's grace is impossible. As such, the *Augustinus* was an implicit critique of the view, associated primarily with the great Spanish Jesuit Luis Molina, that people can choose to accept or reject God's grace and that free will therefore plays some role in redemption.[45] In the debate that ensued in France, the most vocal defenders of the *Augustinus* were a group associated with the Convent of Port-Royal and its spiritual leader, the abbé de Saint-Cyran, who were dubbed "Jansenists" by their opponents.[46]

Although there were significant differences of opinion among these seventeenth-century Jansenists, they shared certain key beliefs. Like Jansenius, they embraced a fundamentally Augustinian view of human nature as inherently corrupt. Humankind's corruption expressed itself primarily in *amour-propre,* a tendency to love oneself and to place one's own self-interest above love of God and fellow man. Opposed to *l'amour-propre,* was *la charité,* a spirit of selfless love originating in love of God and reflected in love of others. By grace of God, some people were elected to undergo a conversion, such that, in their souls, *la charité* came to dominate *l'amour-propre.*[47] These converts were absolved of their sins, and thereby redeemed.[48]

While all Jansenists agreed that humankind is fundamentally sinful and prone to *amour-propre,* some—most notably Pierre Nicole—believed that *amour-propre* is a force for social cohesion. In his *Essais de morale,* first presented to the public in the 1670s, Nicole argued that *amour-propre,* informed by reason, taught human beings living in society that the best way to further their self-interest was to act as if they were in fact motivated by *charité.*

Whereas the person who nakedly pursued self-interest engendered resentment and dislike, the person who seemed to act on behalf of others was rewarded with reciprocal acts of kindness and affection. Deception was socially useful in this way because, unlike God, who could look into a person's soul and determine whether he was motivated by true *charité* or mere *amour-propre,* human beings lacked this capacity to distinguish between actions and their motivating force.[49]

In his *Traité des lois,* Domat, a devout Jansenist,[50] set forth a theory of the relationship between *amour-propre* and social cohesion essentially identical to Nicole's. According to Domat, the first principle of law is that human beings are "formed to know and to love God."[51] This principle was true beyond doubt and able to serve as the foundation for an entire Cartesian system of law because it was a self-evident fact of human nature. By examining his own nature every man could see that God endowed human beings with the capacity to reason so that they might understand, and to will so that they might love; and furthermore, that God alone was a worthy object of human understanding and love. From this first principle of law, Domat argued, there necessarily follows the second, which is that human beings must love one another: "This [first] law, which commands man to search after and to love the sovereign good, being common to all mankind, it implies a second law, which obliges them to unity among themselves, and to the love of one another."[52] Society and all the laws establishing it are, in turn, the direct results of this second law, requiring humans to unite in love of God and one another: "The several ties which engage [man] to [society] from all parts . . . are consequences of the destination of man to the exercise of the first two laws, [and] are at the same time the foundation of the particular rules of all his duties, and the fountain of all laws."[53]

Because love of God and fellow man are the two original principles of law, Domat concluded that "whatever we see in society that is contrary to order is a natural consequence of the disobedience of man to" these principles.[54] Rather than loving God and other human beings above all else, people have devoted themselves to the pursuit of material goods. Unlike love of God and fellow man, such goods "cannot be possessed by all; and . . . cannot make the happiness of any one," and thus the love of such goods results in divisiveness.[55] According to Domat, this love of the material is an aspect of *amour-propre,* because "he in whom this love reigns, seeks only after those goods which he makes entirely his own, and which he loves in others only in so far as he can draw advantage out of them to himself."[56] Thus, in characteristically Jansenist fashion, Domat attributed all social ills to the triumph of *amour-propre* over mutual love: "It is therefore the disorder of love that hath disordered society."[57] For Domat as for Nicole, however, the conclusion that *amour-propre* is victorious left a puzzling anomaly. If *amour-propre* was such a socially corrosive force, how could its triumph be reconciled with the evident fact that society continued to exist and, indeed, to prosper? This anomaly made it necessary "to inquire in what manner it is that God supports society in the deluge of evils which are produced in it by self-love."[58]

Domat's explanation was precisely Nicole's. *Amour-propre,* under the guiding force of human reason, serves a socially cohesive function: "From so bad a cause as our self-love, and from a poison so contrary to mutual love, which ought to be the foundation of society, God hath made use of it as one of the remedies for preserving it in being."[59] Reason teaches that the individual cannot survive on his own and that the forthright pursuit of self-interest at the expense of others will engender their hatred and retribution, rather than their support. In this fallen world, "no man being sufficient of himself to procure the necessaries and conveniences of life, the diversity of wants engages men in an infinite number of ties, without which they could not live."[60] Driven by *amour-propre,* the individual therefore feigns a virtuous love of God and fellow man in order to attain the help he requires: "This [fallen] state of mankind induces those who are governed only by a principle of self-love to subject themselves to labors, to commerce, and to ties which their wants render necessary. And that they may reap advantages from them, and preserve in them both their honor and their interest, they observe in all these intercourses integrity, fidelity, sincerity; so that self-love accommodates itself to every thing, that it may reap advantage from all things. And it knows so well how to adapt its different steps to all its views, that it complies with all duties, and even counterfeits all virtues."[61] In this way, sinners animated by *amour-propre* manage to live together in society.

Although Domat's Cartesian and Jansenist emphases were peculiarly French, he shared the central tenets of his philosophy with the modern natural-law tradition as a whole. Like all natural law thinkers—including Samuel Pufendorf, the most influential of all—he believed that positive law could and must be based on immutable principles of human nature. Similarly, both Domat and Pufendorf placed great emphasis on self-love as a driving force in the emergence of human society. Whereas Pufendorf viewed self-love more as scientific fact than as sin, he too thought that individual self-love, combined with the rational awareness that mutual assistance was necessary for survival, was key to the formation of society. Thus, he observed, "In investigating the condition of man we have assigned the first place to self-love . . . because man is so framed that he thinks of his own advantage before the welfare of others."[62] Self-love, guided by reason, Pufendorf explained, teaches that "the power of individual men is so slight that they need the assistance of many things and men if they are to live well and comfortably."[63] It is, therefore, a first law of nature that men must be sociable to one another—which is to say, that each person must understand that he is "bound to the other by kindness, peace, and love, and therefore by a mutual obligation."[64]

Significantly, both Domat and Pufendorf sought support for their natural-law accounts of the social order in the existence across cultures of common—and, in their view, naturally arising—institutions that hinged on sociability. For example, they both argued that the institution of the family was key evidence that human beings are intended by God to live in society. According to Domat, the especially close ties linking together husband and wife, parents and children, and to a lesser extent all relatives, provide an early and sustained lesson in the importance of loving one's fellow man by "engag[ing] [family members] to a continual practice of the several duties of mutual love."[65] Similarly, Pufendorf rejected the Hobbesean state of nature, in which isolated individuals are in a perpetual state of war, by arguing that humankind descended from a single family: "The race of man never did live at one and the same time in a simple state of nature, and never could have, since we believe on the authority of the Holy Writ, that the origin of all men came from the marriage of a single pair."[66]

Likewise, according to both Domat and Pufendorf, friendship was another manifestation of the natural law of mutual love. As Domat explained, "As friendships arise from the several ties which bring men together, so they are at the same time the sources of an infinite number of good offices and services, which keep up those very ties, and which contribute a thousand ways to the order and uses of society, both by the union of friends among themselves, and by the advantages which each person may find in the ties which are between his friends and other persons."[67] Along similar lines, Pufendorf suggested that friendship is a natural extension of the obligation of mutual love, and he thus defined the sociable attitude that all human beings are required to have toward one another as a kind of "general friendship."[68]

For Domat and Pufendorf there was yet a third social institution, which, like family and friendship, revealed and fortified the natural law commanding all men to love one another. This was the partnership, or *société*. The *société,* in fact, so embodied the natural law of sociability that, in their view, it was a kind of microcosm of civil society as a whole.[69] Moreover, just as family and friendship were key to sustaining civil society, so too these all-important institutions were essential in the life of the partnership. Appealing to a commercial reality in which, as described above, the boundaries between family, friendship, and business were largely indistinguishable, Domat described partnership in language evoking both brotherhood and friendship. According to Domat, partnership is "a liaison, which is a type of brotherhood."[70] Yet, unlike familial relationships, in which "there be no choice of persons in this love,"[71] a partnership "can be contracted only by consent of all the partners, who must choose and please one another."[72] Like true friends, partners are motivated at least in part by genuine, reciprocal love, such that each seeks "to act on the other's behalf as. . . . [he] would do for himself."[73] Because partners are obligated to one another like brothers, but love one another like friends, the partnership is, for Domat, the human institution that offers the greatest hope for the reign of true mutual love among people in society.

For Pufendorf, like Domat, the partnership is key evidence of humankind's fundamental sociability and thus of its ability to sustain peaceful, prosperous coexistence in civil society. While Domat equated partnership and civil society by emphasizing the importance to both of family and friendship, Pufendorf simply took the standard legal definition of the partnership as his definition of civil society. Both a partnership and civil society, he suggested, are contracts of association whereby the parties agree to promote the interests of the association above their own and to share all profits and losses. Thus, he argued, "among those who are united by no other bond than a common humanity, this general sociable attitude and peace should be fostered, which consists in the *avoidance of unjust injuries* and in the *mutual advancement and division of advantages and profits.*"[74] Similarly, Pufendorf relied on the language of partnership—and the dual meaning of the word *société*—to establish that individual self-interest is fully consistent with social coexistence: "Even though a man, when he joins himself to any special society, holds before his eyes, first of all, his own advantage, and after that the advantage of comrades since his own cannot be secured without that of all, yet this does not prevent his being obligated so to cultivate his own advantage, that the good of the society be not injured, or harm offered its different members; or at times to hold his own advantage in abeyance and work for the welfare of the society."[75]

Like so many contemporaries, commercial-law jurists were deeply influenced by natural-law theory and its conception of society as a realm in which conflicting self-interests are harmonized in a manner promoting the general welfare. Included in this number was Jean Toubeau, a successful merchant, who as we have seen, was among the most influential commercial-law jurists of the Old Regime. In his 1682 publication *Les institutes du droit consulaire ou les elemens de la jurisprudence des marchands,* Toubeau related a narrative of the rise of society and its relationship to commerce that clearly derived from the prevalent discourse of natural law. According to Toubeau, human beings in a state of nature, as first created by God, lived in families, each of which was a self-sufficient economic and political unit: "After the creation of the world . . . our first fathers satisfied with their hands all their desires without competition, without ambition, received neither law nor justice other than from the father of the family."[76] With time, however, people came to realize that they had much to gain by joining together in society. By pooling their labor and resources, they established a common defense against aggression and developed an integrated economy sustained by commerce and the division of labor: "Almost everywhere the law of nature and of community was not long in effect; because men grew bored of living so narrowly, they left this solitary life, and seeing that society would give them the means not only to support, maintain, and defend themselves, but also to advance and to grow, they began to look for one another, to approach, to receive, to give a hand, to progress, to love, to recognize one another, to negotiate, to traffic, to do for one another, they built cities: Behold, the first rudiments of commerce."[77] Rooted in trade, society afforded benefits that were not only material, but also spiritual. People, in other words, came "to advance and to grow," but also "to love, [and] to recognize one another."

Although Toubeau did not employ terms like *amour-propre* or self-interest, he, like Domat and Pufendorf, argued that God made human beings weak by nature in order to ensure that they would need one another and thus have reason to engage in commerce and form society: "God wanted to render commerce necessary. . . . [H]e did not want the earth to be fertile everywhere in all things, so that men, having need of one another, would be obligated to communicate with one another."[78] In this way, need or self-interest was translated into that quintessential Christian and merchant virtue—namely, a charitable love of one's fellow man. As Toubeau explained, "After having made known the necessity of commerce, I want to demonstrate its utility. One of the principal ends of commerce is not only to have that which we lack, but also to help others with that which they need, and thus to exchange [*nous entrecommuniquer*] all our goods . . . [T]here is nothing more charitable than that."[79] Thus, while self-interest was innate, so too was sociability.

To the extent that commerce was an integral component of this natural-law narrative of the origins of society, following from human nature itself, the law of commerce was synonymous with the law of nature. In other words, since commerce was an expression of divinely created principles of human nature—principles of self-interest or necessity, on the one hand, and sociability or charity, on the other—it was these very same principles that should govern its practice. For this reason, in describing his years of service as a merchant court judge, Toubeau wrote, "I found myself in a tribunal in which effectively one judges almost only according to natural law, and where it is said that it is only good sense and reason that must preside."[80]

While all commercial law was a form of natural law, the law governing commercial partnerships was, in Toubeau's view, particularly natural. Like Domat and Pufendorf, Toubeau defined partnership and society in almost identical terms. At its root, society is the joining together of individuals to engage in exchange. Likewise, the partnership, or *société commerciale,* is "an agreement between two or several people, who put together either their money, or their industry, in order to be able to do a greater commerce, earn a greater profit, and with greater ease."[81] Accordingly, Toubeau praised partnerships as being "of all the contracts that law has made available to men, that which is the most natural to him and which he should desire the most."[82] Partnerships are the "most natural" of all contracts because, like society, they are an expression of a sociability innate to human nature. Similarly, they are the contracts which humankind should "desire the most" because, like society itself, they further the individual's self-interest, while at the same time benefiting others: "Partnerships are advantageous to the individual, but they are even more so to the public, which cannot subsist without commerce, which being immense and infinite, an individual whose strength is extremely limited, either in terms of money or of attention, vigilance, and efforts, cannot alone attend to a huge traffic."[83]

While agreeing with the natural-law jurists that partnerships are evidence of a human sociability that led to and sustained civil society, Toubeau took this line of reasoning one step further, suggesting that they are also an expression of a unique merchant sociability. If commerce is a prime example of human sociability in action, he argued, then surely those individuals most responsible for commerce—namely, merchants—best exemplify the qualities of love and faithfulness at the core of such sociability.[84] On the basis of this reasoning, Toubeau rejected the traditional conception of the merchant as an avaricious promoter of material and worldly interests. He bemoaned the fact that "many people keep their distance from commerce because, being regarded as the lot of base souls, . . . one has always had a bad idea of it, one considers it more as an object of men's avarice, than as a mark of their generosity, [an object] in which luck and recklessness often play a greater part than industry and prudence."[85] While it was true that some merchants did not undertake "commerce as religiously as they should, nor with all the necessary sincerity,"[86] the majority were motivated by a spirit of charitable love. For precisely this reason, "commerce has furnished the Church with many great and illustrious saints, . . . [w]hich makes us see again that commerce, far from being incompatible with religion, contributes on the contrary to its growth."[87]

Because partnerships are such a useful, other-serving endeavor — the most natural of an entire body of natural, commercial law and practice — Toubeau insisted that they, more than any other form of commercial activity, demonstrate the inherently moral, sociable character of merchants. Thus, in a particularly striking turn of phrase, he claimed that "the name of *société* and of *associé* . . . are names of honor, which have in themselves some type of saintliness."[88] Borrowing from the language of honor traditionally associated with the nobility, Toubeau subverted the longstanding view that honor is incompatible with the base, material practice of commerce, suggesting instead that, through participation in a partnership, a kind of saintliness is attained. In thus asserting that commerce was an honorable undertaking, Toubeau echoed the early-seventeenth-century mercantilists studied by Henry Clark, who argued in a similar vein that commerce was worthy of respect because it "contribute[d] to the inculcation of virtues normally associated with the noble ethos."[89] But Toubeau took this argument even further, elaborating a fully developed theory of how historical transformations in the structure of the French state necessitated that a sizable portion of the nobility begin to engage in commercial activity. As discussed in a later chapter, he thus anticipated by more than a half-century l'abbé Coyer's provocative claims on behalf of a *noblesse commerçante*.[90]

Contrasting merchant sociability, which was productive and charitable, with noble "idleness," Toubeau decried the fact that noblemen disdained the practice of commerce. In his account, as in Coyer's, it was the nobleman who epitomized the vice of narrow-minded selfishness of which merchants were traditionally accused: "As idleness cannot reside in great souls, gentlemen must not stay in their castles, just like rats, . . . nor at court, languid and dull, behaving like children who run after butterflies."[91] The nobleman, he concluded, would acquire true virtue only by abandoning his slothful, avaricious ways in favor of a productive, commercial existence. Merchant sociability, in short, would have to supplant noble honor.

The Regulatory Regime

The belief that the *société* epitomized an ideal of merchant sociability — that partners were bound together by ties of friendship and trust even stronger than those that were supposed to link all merchants — led to the imposition on *sociétés* of certain unique legal requirements. As explained in the *Encyclopédie méthodique*, "There are hardly any contracts in which probity and good faith are more necessary than in those establishing a business association; . . . the law deems null those that are formed contrary to equity."[92] Unlike all other commercial contracts, the contract establishing a *société* had to be in writing and a summary of it had to be publicly posted. Furthermore, unlike all other disputes between merchants, partnership disputes were supposed to be resolved, not by the merchant court, but rather by arbiters selected by the parties. In practice, however, as was often the case in the commercial culture of the Old Regime, these legal requirements were regularly ignored.

THE FORMATION OF *SOCIÉTÉS*

As a general principle, commercial contracts were exempt from the rule requiring that all civil (namely, noncommercial) agreements be in writing.[93] The Commercial Ordinance of 1673, however, created one very important exception to this exemption. All commercial associations were to be formed through a written agreement—usually called an *acte de société,* but sometimes a *traité de société*—which could be either notarized or privately signed. Furthermore, testimony regarding what the partners allegedly said "before, at the time of, or after the writing of the *acte* [*de société*]" could not be used to contradict any term of the *acte* or to add additional terms, even if the agreement had a financial value of less than one hundred livres.[94] This was in contrast to the rule applicable to other commercial contracts that were formed orally, which provided that those for less than one hundred livres were enforceable, and that, as Toubeau explained, "oral proof [could be used] against a writing."[95] Indeed, the requirement that contracts establishing *sociétés* be in writing was in striking contrast to the generally applicable principle that merchant good faith necessitates the enforcement of all agreements, regardless of such formalities as a writing.

The writing requirement was imposed on *sociétés* because, in comparison with other contracts, an agreement establishing a *société* gave rise to a particularly powerful bond between the contracting parties—and thus to a particularly intensive duty of mutual good faith. Ironically, however, the crucial role of good faith in the agreement to form a *société* dated back to the Roman-law conception of the *societas* as a "consensual contract," which required no writing or other procedural formalities. In fact, it was precisely because the *societas,* as a consensual contract, was established entirely on the basis of the parties' informal agreement—such that the parties had only each other's word on which to rely—that the Roman law imposed a requirement of *bona fides,* or good faith.[96] In an interesting twist, the Old Regime monarchy reversed the logic of the Roman law, identifying the good faith that was so central to the *société* as grounds for requiring the procedural formality of a writing. As discussed below, however, contemporary merchants proved far less capable of abandoning the historic connection between the duty of good faith and contractual informality, and thus regularly ignored the ordinance's requirement of an *acte de société.*

The duty of good faith, while important in all *sociétés,* was particularly crucial in the *société générale,* or general partnership, because there each partner bore full, joint liability for any obligation undertaken by the others in the partnership's name. The traditional rule of the *ius commune* was that joint liability could never be presumed, but instead had to be the subject of a specific, written agreement.[97] Absent such an agreement, each partner was liable only for that which he had contributed. Over time, however, merchant practice led to a radically new default rule—namely that, unless otherwise agreed, partnerships were assumed to be general, such that each partner bore full, joint liability for partnership debts.[98] The Commercial Ordinance of 1673 embraced this new default rule, providing that "all partners will be held jointly liable for the debts of the partnership."[99] By mandating that all agreements to form a *société* be made in writing, the ordinance sought to ensure—much like the traditional rule of the *ius commune*—that joint liability would not be enforced absent at least some indication that the parties intended it.

The particularly intimate nature of the partnership relationship meant not only that partners incurred a unique set of obligations toward one another, but also that they incurred a unique set of obligations toward the public as a whole. It was for this reason as well that the commercial ordinance mandated a written *acte de société.* Pursuant to the ordinance, a summary of the *acte de société* had to be registered with the merchant court and posted in public.[100] The summary was to contain, at a minimum, the partners' names, their profession and status [*qualités*], the dates on which the *société* was to begin and end, and any "unusual clauses" limiting the capacity of a partner to obligate the partnership.[101] Any changes made to the provisions of this registered and posted summary were to be themselves registered and posted.[102] Failure to comply with the registration and posting requirements would result in the "nullity of legal acts [*actes*] and contracts entered between the partners, as well as with creditors and legal successors."[103] In other words, the penalty for ignoring these requirements was that the *société* would be deemed not to exist, such that any claims against it—brought by an *associé* or by a third party—would have to be made, instead, against the *associés* in their individual capacities.

Notifying the public of the contract establishing the *société* and of certain of its terms was deemed so important because such contracts were viewed as implicating the public interest in ways that other commercial contracts did not. When a third party transacts business with a partner (who acts on behalf of his partnership), the third party enters a relationship not only with that partner but also with all the other partners, as they each bear liability for the partnership's debts. Accordingly, it was thought that such third parties were entitled to the information necessary for them to reach accurate judgments about the reliability and creditworthiness of each and every partner, and thus of the partnership as a whole. As the jurist Boutaric explained, access to such information was necessary "so that the public would not be deceived by partnerships, whose terms were unknown to it."[104]

For example, should an unscrupulous individual on the verge of bankruptcy seek to induce a hesitant third party to trade with him by falsely claiming that some pillar of the merchant community was his partner, the third party would be able to determine that no summary of an *acte de société* had been posted, and thus that no such partnership existed. Likewise, if a partnership went bankrupt, and one of the partners denied he was a partner so as to escape joint liability, third parties who had transacted business with the partnership could rely on the posted summary of the *acte de société* to prove he was lying. In Toubeau's words, the commercial ordinance imposed a registration and publication requirement because: "Our great monarch saw that his subjects, to the prejudice of the ordinances, of public safety and of commerce, formed in his kingdom the types of *sociétés* in which there appeared a very considerable amount of capital and in which, furthermore, there were sometimes only one or two of the partners who were known and who signed the letters, bills of exchange, notes, and other things; that upon fraudulent or other bankruptcies occurring, those that did not appear disappeared; and like M. Bornier says, one thereby stole from the public the knowledge of other partners and participants, and the creditors had recourse only to the goods of those who were known and who signed."[105]

Fascinatingly, as Toubeau's comment suggests, the public interest furthered by the registering and posting requirements was deemed to hinge primarily on the identity of the partners, and not on the capital structure of the partnership. Thus, the commercial ordinance mandated that the posted summary of the *acte de société* list the partners' names, their profession and status, and their powers within the partnership, but not information about the partnership's capital. As Bornier explained, "it is not necessary that the terms concerning the capital that each has put in the partnership, nor those concerning their share, be included in the summary and known by everyone; but only those concerning the public."[106] The amount of money each partner had contributed and how the partners intended to divide profits and losses was considered to be of interest primarily to the partners themselves and not to the public. This was not a belief that survived the passing of the eighteenth century. Reflecting the increasing importance placed on capital—and the awakening view that the *société* possessed its own legal personality and thus its own capital, distinct from that of the *associés*[107]—Napoleon's *Code de Commerce* of 1807 required public notification of such basics of the *société*'s capital structure as the amount of money each partner contributed.[108]

Despite jurists' best efforts, it was widely recognized by the mid-eighteenth century that *sociétés* of all kinds were typically formed and enforced without proof that the ordinance's writing, registering, and posting requirements had been observed. As Boutaric stated in 1743, "registering is judged as unnecessary today with respect to the public, as it is with respect to the partners; however wise the rule contained in these articles [of the ordinance], the contrary usage has prevailed."[109] Similarly, Pothier, writing in 1764, claimed that he had been informed by a colleague with greater knowledge of commercial law and practice that no one bothered to comply with the registering and posting requirements.[110] Even the requirement of a written *acte de société* was widely ignored. The jurist Daniel Jousse, for example, observed that no *société* is ever deemed null for lack of an *acte de société,* as long as its existence can be established through some kind of written documentation, "either by letters or by other documents formed between the parties or with their creditors."[111] And Masson, a former judge of the Parisian Merchant Court, claimed that witness testimony would suffice.[112]

Arbiters' reports from the Parisian Merchant Court reveal that oral partnership agreements were regularly enforced.[113] Consider, for example, the agreement between Baudry and Albert, discussed above, to establish a partnership that would produce and sell printed fabrics. Their contract consisted entirely of "verbal agreements," though they decided that they would commit these to writing "upon the first demand of either of the two."[114] When Baudry sued for breach of the partnership agreement, there was no *acte de société* to which he could point to establish the partnership's existence, and so he had to rely on other means. In particular, he proffered documents with the address of the fabric factory printed under the name *Albert et Baudry;* an official stamp with the same name; and evidence that he, Baudry, had been sued by a third party in his capacity as a partner of the partnership entitled *Albert et Baudry.* Based on this evidence, the arbiter concluded that there was an "oral partnership made under the seal of good faith between the aforementioned Albert and Baudry."[115] Finding that Albert was responsible for "the interruption of all work," he ordered him to pay six hundred livres in damages for breaching the partnership agreement, and declared the partnership dissolved.[116] At no point in his analysis did the arbiter mention the commercial ordinance and its writing requirement.

Lévy-Bruhl persuasively argues that merchants failed to comply with the writing, registering, and posting requirements because of a combination of negligence, illiteracy, and the desire of those of high status to hide their participation in commercial activity.[117] All these factors were surely significant. According to a former merchant court judge, the fact that "there are so many who become involved in commerce without knowing either to write or to read" helped explain the fact that *sociétés,* along with many other contracts, were often not established in writing.[118] And as discussed below, nobles or would-be nobles frequently sought to conceal their involvement in commercial activity, which in turn led them to form limited partnerships, or *sociétés en commandite*, and to avoid entering written partnership agreements. Such noncompliance must also be viewed, however, in the context of a broader tradition of merchant practice that placed greater emphasis on equitable considerations of good faith than on strict compliance with the law. As we have seen, reliance on oral agreements was common, and writings were often viewed suspiciously as an implicit challenge to good faith. Indeed, according to one commercial jurist, it was precisely because of "the trust that merchants have in one another" that they so often failed to comply with the ordinance's writing, registering, and posting requirements.[119]

While the intimate nature of partnership and the public interest it implicated led the monarchy to impose greater formalities on the *acte de société* than on other commercial contracts, it was precisely these characteristics that made the partnership the embodiment of merchant sociability. This, in turn, suggested to many that partnership disputes were properly left to the tried and true informal regime of trust that (at least in theory) was supposed to govern commercial relations.

ARBITRATION AND COURT PROCEDURE

Promulgated in 1560, the Edict of Fontainbleau provided that all disputes between merchants concerning merchandise were to be resolved by three or more arbiters, whom the disputants were to select.[120] Just three years after requiring arbitration in all merchant disputes, the monarchy issued an edict creating the Parisian Merchant Court, which made no mention of arbitration at all.[121] A century later, the Commercial Ordinance of 1673 mandated arbitration once again, but limited its use to partnership disputes.[122]

Pursuant to the ordinance, every *acte de société* had to contain a clause naming arbiters responsible for resolving all disputes between the *associés.*[123] Absent such a clause, the parties were to name arbiters at the time the dispute arose.[124] Arbiters were to adjudicate based on the briefs and documents proffered by the parties, "without any legal formality."[125] All such arbitral decisions then had to be formally ratified by the merchant court.[126]

Why would arbitration, originally required in all merchant disputes, later be considered necessary only in disputes between *associés?* One answer is that, to some extent, all merchant disputes *were* sent to arbitration. The merchant court, in other words, delegated a great many of its cases to arbiters. The kind of arbitration regularly used in the merchant court differed significantly, however, from that which the ordinance required in partnership disputes. The arbiters regularly employed by the court were not selected by the parties, but instead by the judge and consuls. Furthermore, while the court was free to accept or reject the recommended decisions of its own arbiters, it had little choice (at least in theory) but to ratify those of the arbiters selected by the parties in partnership disputes.

The question thus remains why a unique arbitration procedure was deemed necessary for disputes between *associés*. The answer here, as with so much of partnership law, is once again the unique, quasi-sacred status of partnership agreements vis-à-vis all other commercial contracts. Given the view that *sociétés* epitomized the spirit of friendship and brotherhood on which merchants prided themselves, the idea of partners litigating against one another was particularly disturbing. For one partner to sue another was the antithesis of every ideal that a partnership was supposed to embody—and implicitly contradicted the claim that the institution of partnership manifested an innate human, and merchant, sociability. As one eighteenth-century *négociant* observed, "Nothing ruins us in commerce as completely as a lawsuit between *associés*."[127] Indeed, the jurist Toubeau explained the commercial ordinance's requirement of an arbitration clause by noting that "*associés* must always treat one another honestly, and not deal with each other and sue one another like thieves, for the smallest of blames; that is unworthy of the name of *société* and of *associé,* which are names of honor, which have in themselves some type of saintliness."[128] Arbiters selected by the *associés* in their initial partnership agreement would serve as extensions of the *associés* themselves, rather than as delegates of the court. This—along with the fact that the court was required to ratify the arbiters' decision—would minimize any suggestion that the partners failed to reconcile of their own accord and that the friendship and trust so central to the partnership relationship had been in any way compromised.

But while the commercial ordinance required the merchant court to rubber-stamp the decisions reached by arbiters named by the parties, the reality is that the court regularly resolved partnership disputes through its standard arbitral procedure. At the same time, the percentage of (known) arbiters' reports concerning business associations in the box of reports that I systematically reviewed is relatively small—only 8.2 percent.[129] Given the prominent place in Old Regime commercial life ascribed to *sociétés* by contemporary jurists and merchants, it seems likely that the percentage of total disputes concerning business associations was actually higher, but that many of these were in fact—as per the dictates of the commercial ordinance—successfully settled out of court. Nonetheless, it is also clear that a significant number of *associés* disregarded the ordinance and chose to litigate.

That such litigation regularly occurred may be due, in part, to the fact that the commercial ordinance imposed no penalty for failing to include an arbitration clause in the *acte de société* or for failing to honor such a clause when it was included. As a matter of commercial practice, arbitration clauses typically provided that noncompliance would result in payment of a fine. As a result, any partner who sought to litigate was free to do so—at a price. For example, the *acte* establishing the "*société en commandite* for the concern of the factory of braids and ribbons" contained a clause providing that all disputes between *associés* were to be resolved by two *négociants,* one chosen by each disputant, that these arbiters would name a third should they fail to reach agreement, and that the disputants would obey the arbitral decision "like a judgment of a sovereign court."[130] The only consequence of refusing to honor the arbitral decision was that the obstinate *associé* would have to pay (an admittedly hefty) fine of three thousand livres to the *hôpital général,* the primary workhouse and charitable institution of eighteenth-century Paris.[131] Similarly, an arbitration clause was included in the *acte de société* establishing a partnership to run a tax farm encompassing the towns of Versailles and Marly.[132] The penalty for failing to abide by the arbiters' decision was a 5,000-livre fine, half of which was to be paid to the partner who had agreed to abide by the decision, and the other half to the *hôpital* located in Versailles. That penalties were to be distributed at least in part to charity reflects the moral significance ascribed to the partnership relationship and thus its breach, and the concomitant pressure to restore a semblance of virtue, where it had evidently failed.

Another factor that likely contributed to the application of standard court procedure to partnership disputes was that many partnership agreements were oral and thus did not contain the mandatory arbitration clause. Although the ordinance specified that, in the absence of such a clause, the partners were to select arbiters at the time of the dispute, it appears that in many such cases lawsuits were filed just as in any nonpartnership dispute. For example, after three brothers from Vincennes formed a partnership to run a butchery—presumably through oral agreement—one filed suit against the others, claiming that they had used partnership funds for personal matters.[133] The court applied its standard procedure, appointing the parish priest of Vincennes to reconcile the parties and directing him, in case of failure, to file a report recommending judgment.

It may also be the case that, as Lévy-Bruhl suggests, partners submitted to private arbitration but then, dissatisfied with the decision reached, used the ordinance's requirement of court ratification as a (technically unlawful) means of appeal.[134] Indeed, some partners, evidently foreseeing the possibility of such an appeal, sought to cripple the court by burning all documentation concerning the partnership. For example, when two pork merchants agreed to dissolve their partnership, they undertook an accounting in the presence of "individuals who convinced . . . [them] to come to a compromise [*transiger entre eux*]."[135] In order to ensure that neither partner would be able successfully to challenge the settlement thus reached, "all documents concerning the account and the partnership were burned."[136] Similarly, when a tax farmer and a merchant from Normandy agreed to dissolve the partnership that they had formed to trade in livestock, they undertook an accounting, which concluded with the statement that they renounced the "power to inquire directly or indirectly into matters concerning . . . [the partnership and its dissolution]."[137] Moreover, "to remove the means to do so, the parties declare . . . that the documents concerning this account have been torn to shreds and thrown into the fire."[138]

Ironically, despite these parties' efforts to foreclose litigation, the archival evidence concerning these partnerships is available today precisely because, in both cases, lawsuits were eventually filed. Furthermore, the arbiters appointed by the court did not recommend dismissal. Instead, after acknowledging the difficulties in adjudication that stemmed from lack of documentation, they suggested that the court might rely on witness testimony. Nonetheless, the fact that merchants thus sought initially to resolve partnership disputes on their own—without the court's assistance—suggests that, while ignored by some, there were others for whom the distinctive private arbitration requirements imposed on *sociétés* continued to resonate.

The Problem of the Limited Partnership

While fully compatible with the general partnership (*société générale*), the natural-law conception of the *société* as a quasi-sacred union of brothers did not lend itself so well to the limited partnership (*société en commandite*).[139] Indeed, as argued below, the prevalence and power of this natural-law paradigm of the *société* may help explain the strange fact that, while both the Commercial Ordinance of 1673 and contemporary jurists distinguished between *sociétés générales* and *sociétés en commandite*, the arbiters' reports and legal briefs submitted to the Parisian Merchant Court refer to all partnerships simply as *sociétés*. The term *société générale* was, to my knowledge, never used in these documents. And on the rare occasions in which the term *société en commandite* appears in the court's archives, it is employed to designate not a partnership at all, but rather what I call a proto-*société de capitaux*—a business association with a larger capital base and more complex governance structure than either a general or limited partnership.

The two crucial, identifying features of the natural-law ideal of partnership were the equality and interdependence that were supposed to characterize relations between partners. In the general partnership, as it developed through centuries of merchant practice,[140] such equality and interdependence manifested themselves in the fact that each partner could obligate the partnership and bore full liability for the partnership's debts. In contrast, in the limited partnership, it was only the general partner who could obligate the partnership and who bore full liability for its debts. The limited partner was not authorized to act on behalf of the partnership and stood to lose only his initial capital investment. In this sense, the limited partnership could not be said to embrace the equality and interdependence that were the defining features of the natural-law model of partnership.

That Old Regime merchants and jurists understood there to be a significant tension between the limited partnership and the fraternal ideals of *société* is evident in their tendency to associate the lawful *société en commandite* with the unlawful *société léonine.* A *société léonine,* or *societas leonina,* as it was termed in Roman law, is a partnership in which one party bears all the losses without any share in the profits.[141] Because such a method for dividing profits and losses was contrary to the Roman conception of the partnership as a brotherly association of equals, the *societas leonina* was prohibited under Roman law. During the emergence of the *ius commune,* and under the influence of the canonical prohibition on usury, the *societas leonina* came to be seen as illicit for the further reason that it permits the earning of interest on capital without risk. The partner who stands to gain everything and bears no risk of loss makes a usurious profit. As the jurist Boutaric cautioned: "There is a partnership known by the name *société léonine,* and which is contracted with the condition that all the loss will be one side and without any profit, and all the profit on the other without any loss; such a partnership is condemned by the law."[142]

Because the *société en commandite* ensures that one party bears a significantly greater risk of loss than the other, some jurists feared that it might be deployed as an unlawful *société léonine.* Toubeau, for example, was a great advocate of *sociétés en commandite,* arguing that they are "advantageous to the public and to the individual, to the big and to the little, to the rich and to the poor, and give them the means to produce and to advance."[143] For the rich, such partnerships offer an important avenue of investment, and for the poor, they provide an otherwise unavailable opportunity to gain an ownership interest by means of talent and skill alone. But despite his enthusiasm for *sociétés en commandite,* Toubeau cautioned that the wealthy who invest in such partnerships must be careful not to create *sociétés léonines,* in which they enjoy all the profits and force their poor associates to bear all the losses: "It is necessary that they [*sociétés en commandite*] be made in an orderly fashion and that the rich do not consider that there is nothing that equals their gold. . . . [T]he industry and intelligence of a clever and capable trader is more valuable and can produce infinitely more than their gold and their silver. . . . Thus, the rich must not render themselves insatiable for gain and oblige the poor to contract partnerships with them in which they have all the profit and all the satisfaction, and a poor merchant all the anxiety and the loss of his time and his efforts. These types of partnerships are prohibited by divine and human laws, policy cannot tolerate them, the canonists and casuists deem them usurious, the jurisconsults call them *sociétés léonines.*"[144]

While jurists wrote extensively about *sociétés en commandite,* the arbiters' reports and legal briefs filed with the Parisian Merchant Court fail, as noted above, to distinguish between general and limited partnerships, and instead refer to both as "*sociétés.*" Accordingly, it is more difficult to discern the way in which those who actually formed business partnerships perceived the *société en commandite.* Nonetheless, there are indications that commercial jurists were not alone in their concern that the lawful *société en commandite* was sometimes hard to distinguish from the unlawful *société léonine.* Consider, for example, the arguments advanced by the parties to a lawsuit concerning a partnership formed to run a tax farm.[145] Tax farms, which were central to the Old Regime tax system, were operated by private financiers, who advanced the monarchy substantial sums in exchange for a monopoly license to collect various taxes within a particular region. The tax farm at issue in this lawsuit covered the towns of Versailles and Marly, and the plaintiffs were the heirs of one of its partners, who had recently died. After this partner's death, an agent was appointed to manage the partnership's daily operations. When the agent declared bankruptcy, having lost much of his own and the partnership's funds in the royal lottery, the plaintiffs sued the remaining partner. According to the plaintiffs, all losses stemming from the agent's mismanagement should fall on the defendant, rather than on the partnership as a whole.

In support of their claim, the plaintiffs argued that the clauses of the *acte de société* pursuant to which the agent was appointed unlawfully deprived them of the power to participate in managing the partnership business. Such a limitation in the managerial powers of an owner — a feature that would also characterize the traditional *société en commandite* — was, they suggested, impermissible. Indeed, they claimed, because the offending clauses of the partnership agreement thus limited the power of those with an ownership interest, they "establish a *société léonine*."[146] In reality, as the arbiters appointed to resolve the dispute recognized, it was well established that membership in a partnership ceased upon the partner's death. A partner could transfer to his heirs his ownership interest, but not his status as a partner and its concomitant powers. Nonetheless, the fact that the plaintiffs thought to argue as they did suggests that any business association that departed from the equal sharing of powers, profits, and losses that characterized the general partnership—namely, any *société en commandite*—was potentially suspect, and thus a ready target for criticism. In fact, in countering the plaintiff's argument that he was solely liable for the agent's mismanagement, the defendant appealed to precisely the same suspicions regarding the *société en commandite*. According to the defendant, the losses stemming from the agent's mismanagement should fall on the partnership as a whole, rather than on him alone, because it was impermissible to depart from a strictly equal sharing of profits and losses. As the defendant insisted, "the profits that . . . [the partnership] produced were for the partnership's account, and . . . it is indecent to want that the same not be true of losses; . . . that would be a *société léonine* prohibited by our mores."[147]

That lingering doubts thus persisted about the legitimacy of *sociétés en commandite* may help account for the surprising fact that the term itself appears in contemporary statutory law and treatises but not in documents filed with the Parisian Merchant Court. Those who formed partnerships may, in short, have preferred to avoid openly embracing an organizational form of questionable legitimacy, and thus chose to identify all partnerships—whether general or limited—simply as *sociétés*. Also significant, however, was the fact that contemporary merchants and nonmerchants seem not to have viewed liability structure as an issue of prime importance in partnership formation. Accordingly, when limited liability arose, it was often not because the partners had agreed to it up front, but instead because the court imposed it during subsequent litigation. To the extent that the court ordered limited liability of its own accord, on a case-by-case basis, contemporaries would have had little use for distinguishing ex ante between different categories of *sociétés* (and thus between the different liability rules that these entailed).

While we now take limited liability to be the central, defining feature of the limited partnership,[148] eighteenth-century merchants and nonmerchants appear to have valued the institution much more for the partial separation of ownership and management that it afforded. Accordingly, in entering partnerships, they sometimes agreed that one partner was to provide capital and the other labor, without specifying limited liability. This is particularly surprising given that the medieval Italian *commenda*—from which the *société en commandite* derived—appears to have been employed precisely for the limited liability that it afforded. In particular, the *commenda* enabled merchants to secure maritime insurance at a time when bottomry loans, though available, remained harshly criticized as usurious and thus contrary to the teachings of the Church.[149] By means of the *commenda,* those with capital to invest would supply a navigator with the funds necessary to undertake maritime commerce, receiving in return the lion's share of the profits but bearing exclusive liability for any losses.[150] Over time, as Roman law was rediscovered, the *commenda* was deemed a form of business association, in the family of the Roman *societas* or partnership.[151] Gradually, this new form of partnership began to be used across continental Europe, not just in Italy, and for purposes other than maritime commerce.

The social and cultural context in which the *société en commandite* came into frequent use in seventeenth- and eighteenth-century France[152] was such, however, that the limited liability it offered was not a primary consideration. As commerce rapidly expanded over the course of the eighteenth century, the nonmerchant elite, including noblemen and the many who hoped to attain noble status, increasingly sought commercial investment opportunities. But in a world where commerce was still commonly viewed as a less than honorable endeavor, those with money to invest had good reason to worry about keeping their involvement in a commercial enterprise secret. Indeed, noblemen who undertook conduct that was not in accordance with their noble status—including commercial activity—continued to incur the risk that they would be legally stripped of their nobility and thereby made to suffer *dérogation.*[153] Thus, investors turned to the *société en commandite* not so much for the limited liability that it afforded but more importantly because it permitted a separation of ownership and management that enabled them to shield their commercial activities from public view. As explained in the *Encyclopédie méthodique,* the *société en commandite* is "useful for the state and the public in that all kinds of people, even nobles and magistrates [*gens de robe*] can contract to establish one as a means of investing their money, which then benefits the public through its circulation."[154]

Consider, in this regard, Toubeau's definitions of the terms *société générale* and *société en commandite*. The *société générale,* he argued, is an enterprise "in which commerce is done in the name of all the partners, through their individual names or collectively."[155] In contrast, the *société en commandite* "is contracted between two or several people, in which one . . . does nothing other than contribute his money and the other gives his name, his money, and his industry, or his name and his industry only."[156] Toubeau thus suggested that the fundamental difference between the *société générale* and the *société en commandite* is that the latter permits a partial separation of ownership and management, such that some partners, though owners, are not required to contribute their efforts and names to the partnership business. It is only many pages after setting forth these definitions that he noted that, pursuant to the Commercial Ordinance of 1673, partners who do not give their names to the *société en commandite* have limited liability.[157] For Toubeau, in other words, the limitation on liability was only one—and perhaps even a secondary—feature of a form of association that could also be distinguished from the *société générale* by the existence of partners who are hidden from the public because they do not participate in management.

In similar fashion, Jousse offered a definition of the *société en commandite* in which the limitation on liability appears as but one of its three distinguishing features: "The . . . *société en commandite* . . . is made between several partners, in which one furnishes only his money and the others give their money and their work, or their work only. . . . Those who have thus associated in a *société en commandite* are not held jointly liable for the partnership's debts: they are content to furnish their money without undertaking any other function and without appearing in any way in the purchases and sales, obligations, notes, or other documents concerning the business; but they participate only in profits or losses, up to the limit of the part and share that they have in the partnership."[158] That the limited partners do not contribute their labor and can keep their participation secret is at least as important to Jousse's definition of the *société en commandite* as the limitation on liability.

The emphasis that Old Regime jurists placed on the secrecy afforded by *sociétés en commandite* is particularly apparent in their analysis of how the commercial ordinance's registering and posting requirements apply to such partnerships. While, as discussed above, jurists generally favored the requirement that *actes de société* be registered in the merchant court and publicly posted, they insisted on an exemption for *sociétés en commandite*. To publicize that nonmerchants are partners, Toubeau argued, would be contrary to the purpose of the *société en commandite*, which was to provide an avenue for rich nobles or would-be nobles to invest idle capital without becoming actively involved in a commercial endeavor and thereby risking *dérogation*. In Toubeau's words: "Partnerships are extremely advantageous to the state and to the public, because by this means, commerce, which is its wealth, is greatly swollen, since without this means, a lot of money would remain in the coffers and would not move; because through such partnerships the nobility and magistrates [*Gens de Robe*], in good conscience and without losing their title [*sans déroger*], can make the most of their money and enjoy all the advantages of commerce, without being saddled with efforts and hard work."[159] Agreeing with Toubeau, Boutaric argued that the ordinance's registering and posting requirements, by their own terms, apply only to *sociétés* in which all the partners are merchants [*marchands*] or *négociants.* Since "those who form *sociétés en commandite* [are] for the most part neither *négociants* nor merchants," Boutaric concluded that the registering and posting requirements do not apply to *sociétés en commandite.*[160]

Similarly, Bornier insisted that, even though the registering and posting requirements were key to protecting the public from fraud and should therefore be applied to all forms of business organization, applying them to *sociétés en commandite* would likely cause noblemen to cease participating in such ventures. For this reason, he concluded that these requirements must be applied only to those *sociétés en commandite* consisting exclusively of merchants and *négociants*: "As concerns other people who are not merchants and *négociants*, and who formed *sociétés en commandite* with another who is, the ordinance does not require these people to have the summary of the agreement registered, because this would put an end to the use of *sociétés en commandite,* since people who are not of the mercantile profession would perhaps not want the public to know that they are associated with merchants, nor that their names be displayed in a public place."[161]

While from today's perspective the advent of limited liability appears to be a defining moment in the rise of modern commercial society—a development that proved crucial for the efficient placement of capital[162]—many Old Regime merchants and jurists seem to have viewed it instead as a necessary *moral* consequence of the separation of ownership from management. To the extent, in other words, that a partner played no role in managing the business, he could not be said to have made decisions of his own free will that caused its failure, and thus it seemed wrong to make him bear full liability for its losses. This was the clear implication of modern natural-law theory, as propagated by Domat and others, which sought to ground all law in man's nature as a rational being with free will.

That limited liability was often viewed as an appurtenance to the separation of ownership and management—one that followed as a kind of moral necessity—can be seen perhaps most clearly in contemporary legal practice. Pursuant to the Commercial Ordinance of 1673, a partnership was presumed to be general, such that "all partners will be held jointly liable for the debts of the partnership."[163] A *société en commandite,* in contrast, had to be created through the express, written agreement of the parties. However, even when the *acte de société* was silent as to liability and the partnership should therefore have been deemed general, arbiters sometimes imposed limited liability based on their own equitable, ex post determination of fairness under the circumstances.

The case of *Dupont de la Hallière v. Despres, père et fils* is a good example of how limited liability arose ex post through the court's decision that it would be morally unjust to impose full liability on a partner who played no role in management and thus bore no responsibility for the partnership's losses.[164] Dupont de la Hallière, a Parisian banker, and Despres and Son, manufacturers of emery and varnish, agreed to form a partnership to manufacture emery and varnish. According to the terms of the partnership agreement, Despres and Son were to "limit themselves to the manufacture and sale of merchandise, [and] to the keeping of the books," while Hallière "will alone maintain the proceeds of the sold merchandise and will alone keep the enterprise's cash-box."[165] The agreement established no limitation on liability and, pursuant to the Commercial Ordinance of 1673, could therefore be presumed general. The arbiters presiding over the partnership's eventual liquidation, however, did not apply the default rule of full, joint liability. Instead, presumably relying on the fact that Despres and Son had primary responsibility for running the business, the arbiters decided that they should be held solely liable for all the debts contracted by the partnership and for which Hallière might be sued. Hallière would lose only the capital he had already furnished. The arbiters, in other words, determined that because Despres and Son were alone responsible for managing the business and Hallière was involved only insofar as he possessed an ownership interest, it would be unfair to hold Hallière fully liable for losses he played no role in causing.

In an environment in which the availability of limited liability was not a primary consideration in the decision to invest in a partnership and in which the court sometimes decided on liability rules ex post—with little attention to the parties' ex ante agreement—it is hardly surprising that those who formed partnerships seem to have referred to all of them simply as *sociétés*. For many Old Regime merchants and nonmerchants, in other words, there was little, if anything, to gain from devoting the effort necessary to agree on whether they wished to form a *société générale* or a *société en commandite*. And for those who did actually seek limited liability, the longstanding ideal of the partnership as a sanctified fraternal union—and the concomitant tendency to associate the limited partnership with the unlawful and usurious *société léonine*—provided ample additional reason to eschew the term *société en commandite*.

New Forms of Commercial Association

The greatest challenge to the longstanding conception of the *société* as a fraternal union epitomizing merchant sociability came ultimately not from *sociétés en commandite* but rather from *sociétés de capitaux*. The late seventeenth and eighteenth centuries witnessed the emergence of two kinds of business association that differed significantly from the traditional *société générale* and *société en commandite* in both their capital base and their governance structure: the *société anonyme* and the *société en commandite par actions.* As described below, the distinctive features of the new *sociétés de capitaux* implied a conception of the *société* as a juridical entity separate and apart from the individual *associés* who composed it. This conception of the *société* was fundamentally at odds with the traditional view that the *société* embodied a set of particular, personal relationships — a view that led to its embrace as the quintessential institution of merchant sociability. This, in turn, made it difficult to reconceptualize the *société* as an institution in which abstract relations of capital were more important than those between particular, flesh-and-blood persons. Significantly, it was not until the nineteenth century that French law officially deemed *sociétés* (of all kinds) juridical persons[166] and that the term *société de capitaux* was invented. New forms of commercial practice, however — including both the *société anonyme* and the *société en commandite par actions* — preceded such reconceptualization.

The *société anonyme,* which arose in the mid-eighteenth century,[167] is comparable to a corporation in Anglo-American law — an association of individuals, all of whom have limited liability, whose ownership interest in the business takes the form of negotiable stock certificates, and who participate in corporate governance through shareholder assemblies. The owner of a negotiable share may assign his property interest simply by endorsing the stock certificate and conveying it to the recipient. And the good-faith purchaser for value of a negotiable instrument (including a negotiable share) has an enforceable interest even if the prior holders have a legitimate defense against enforcement.[168] The security thus afforded holders of negotiable shares promotes rapid and extensive trade in such shares, thereby facilitating investment. Accordingly, the speculative boom that consumed Paris in the 1780s was fueled in no small part by trade in negotiable stock. And many of the biggest businesses at the end of the Old Regime, including especially mining companies and arms manufacturers but also the new *Compagnie des Indes* created in 1785, are considered to have been *sociétés anonymes.*[169]

Another new form of business association to arise in the Old Regime was the *société en commandite par actions,* which dates back to the late seventeenth century[170] and is a kind of hybrid between a limited partnership and a corporation.[171] Like a limited partnership, the *société en commandite par actions* is owned partly by individuals with unlimited liability and partly by individuals with limited liability. Like a corporation, however, ownership interests in this type of *société* consist of negotiable shares, and its governance structure is more bureaucratic and complex than that of a limited partnership. John Law's *Banque générale,* created in 1716, was structured as a *société en commandite par actions.*[172] Likewise, many of the business associations formed to undertake Atlantic trade, including with France's colonial empire in the Caribbean, took the form of *sociétés en commandite par actions.*[173]

Despite the fact that there were clearly *sociétés anonymes* and *sociétés en commandite par actions* operating in eighteenth-century France, commercial jurists of the time never acknowledged their existence. Eighteenth-century commercial-law treatises addressing issues of business organization, ranging from Toubeau's *Les Institutes du droit consulaire,* as augmented and reissued in 1700, to Pothier's *Traité du contrat de société,* published in 1764, make no mention of any form of business organization other than the partnership. This may be due, in part, to the fact that the largest and most well-known *sociétés de capitaux* were owned in some significant measure by the monarchy. For example, the monarchy contributed upward of 20 percent of the capital invested in such colonial companies as Law's famous *Compagnie des Indes.*[174] Because of the significant royal investment in these companies, they may have been perceived as implicating matters of public, rather than private, law and thus not appropriate for inclusion in commercial-law treatises. Indeed, since disputes involving *sociétés de capitaux* could appear to raise issues of public law, they were at times deemed to be beyond the jurisdiction of the merchant court—an institution commonly viewed as lacking any public-law authority.[175] Thus, for example, when in 1778 a group of speculators employed falsified bills of exchange as part of a scheme involving the sale of stock in the *Caisse d'Escompte*—an entity that served much like a national bank—the monarchy prohibited the Parisian Merchant Court from deciding the resulting lawsuits. Per the monarchy's order, these were adjudicated instead by a special commission headed by the lieutenant general of police.[176]

Just as contemporary jurists failed to make mention of *sociétés anonymes* and *sociétés en commandite par actions,* so too did the arbiters' reports and legal briefs filed with the Parisian Merchant Court.[177] This does not mean, however, that only partnerships appeared before the court. To the contrary, many kinds of complex (nonpartnership) *sociétés* were involved in merchant court litigation. Indeed, the variety of these organizational forms was such that the two categories of *société anonyme* and *société en commandite par actions* do not suffice to describe them. Merchants themselves referred to all these business associations simply as *sociétés* or, on rare occasions, as *sociétés en commandite.* The variety of organizational forms, along with the absence of legal categories any more precise than *société* (or *société en commandite*), suggest that the *société anonyme* and *société en commandite par actions* had yet to solidify as fully established forms and were thus but two options among the many new types of business association—which I term proto-*sociétés de capitaux*—that were in the process of emerging.

While varying widely, the many types of proto-*sociétés de capitaux* that appeared before the Parisian Merchant Court shared a number of key characteristics. The one common, defining feature that distinguished them from most partnerships was that their capital was divided into shares. These shares were generally called *sols,* rather than as in modern parlance, *actions.* The term *sol* derived from the method of calculating shares that existed prior to the Revolution's institutionalization of the decimal system. The *société*'s capital was equated with the standard unit of currency, the livre, which consisted of twenty sols (or sous). The sol, in turn, consisted of twelve *deniers.* Companies would thus typically sell shares consisting of some number of sols (up to twenty) and/or deniers (up to 240).[178]

Consider, for example, the capital structure of "the men interested in peat," a *société* formed in 1747 to extract charcoal from peat.[179] Pursuant to the *acte de société,* shares were initially distributed to eight individuals. Of these eight, only five actually purchased their shares: Heron de Courgis, three sols, six deniers (3–6); Jacquemin Demontlis (6–6); Harvouin (2–6); Noel Famin (2); and Carrand de la Fabrice (1). The remaining three individuals were given shares known as *sols sans fonds* or *sols non faisant fonds,* which, as indicated by their name, were distributed to those who had not made capital contributions but who had otherwise furthered the company's interests. Thus, four sols, three deniers were given to Porro as compensation for having obtained a decree from the King's Council, giving him and his legal successors a twelve-year privilege to extract charcoal from peat and then sell it. Three deniers were "awarded to two lords for favoring the enterprise."[180] These last individuals would seem to be among the noblemen described by Lévy-Bruhl, who lent companies their good name and connections—their *crédit* in the broad sense of the word. In exchange, they received an ownership interest in the enterprise, but sought to keep their involvement secret in order to avoid any risk of *dérogation.*[181]

Shares in such proto-*sociétés de capitaux* differed from modern *actions* not only in the manner that they were calculated but more importantly in that they were often not negotiable, and thus could be transferred only by consent of the *société.* Take, for example, the method employed to transfer shares in the "*société en commandite* for the concern of the factory of braids and ribbons," a company established on September 1, 1747.[182] When a shareholder, named de Beauvillé, decided to dispose of his two sols in the *société,* he first had to sell them back to the *société* through a formal *acte de rétrocession.*[183] After paying him for his two sols, the *société* was free to sell them to others as it deemed fit. At a meeting held on December 1, 1749, the assembled shareholders agreed to sell one of the sols to a Saint-Julien. But since the shareholders never sold the second sol to anyone else, this share remained unissued.

Why divide the *société*'s capital into shares if these were not negotiable? One possibility is that, as Lévy-Bruhl argues,[184] the division of a *société*'s capital into sols and deniers — a system of quantification familiar to all Frenchmen from their currency — made for easier calculation. Assigning each partner a certain number of sols was a particularly helpful way to calculate the division of profits and losses when, as was frequently the case, each *associé*'s share was equated to the proportion of the *société*'s capital that he had contributed. This seems to have been a motivating factor for Millin de Grandmaison, Duchesne, and Normans de Mezieres.[185] When on March 23, 1757, these three individuals established a *société* for the purpose of undertaking "various speculations on the commodities necessary for the subsistence of the king's army" during the Seven Years' War, they decided to divide its capital into shares.[186] As per the *acte de société,* the *société*'s capital was deemed to consist of twenty sols, of which eleven went to Grandmaison, and four sols, six deniers each to Duchesne and de Mezieres. Profits and losses were to be shared by each partner "according to the relative share of each one's interest."[187] Presumably, the division of the capital into shares would assist in the process of thus distributing profits and losses on a pro rata basis.

The division of a *société*'s capital into shares was most useful, however, for those *sociétés* that differed from partnerships not only in that their capital happened to be divided into sols, but also in that they had a larger number of *associés* and a more complex governance structure. The traditional partnership had just two or three partners, and the responsibility for running the business fell directly on these individuals — either on all of them (in a general partnership) or on some of them (in a limited partnership). The small number of *associés,* and the significant powers wielded by each, meant that their personal relationships with one another were important elements of the partnership's survival and success. Thus, when a partner decided to abandon the partnership, the partnership would automatically dissolve, unless the remaining partners unanimously agreed to continue the partnership without him or to replace him with some third person. Such an agreement to continue the partnership or to replace the exiting partner was, however, essentially an agreement to form a new partnership.

In contrast to the partnership, the proto-*société de capitaux* might have upward of ten *associés.* The large number of *associés* encouraged a more bureaucratic governance structure, involving a significant division of labor.

Daily operations were generally assigned to managers who might be shareholders or simply employees, while important, long-term decisions were undertaken by vote of the assembled shareholders according to some formula of representation decided upon in the *acte de société*. Because ownership and responsibility for management were spread across so many individuals, no particular one was crucial for the business's survival. As a result, it was relatively easy for such *sociétés* to survive the departure of an *associé* —and thus to permit the ready transfer of ownership interests. The bureaucratic governance structure of proto-*sociétés de capitaux*, in short, led them to appear as unified corporate entities distinct from the individual *associés* who composed them.

Consider, for example, the "*société en commandite* for the concern of the factory of braids and ribbons,"[188] which was established in 1747. The *société*'s capital was to be "composed of a livre consisting of thirty-six sols," such that there were a total of thirty-six sols.[189] Pursuant to the *acte de société*, daily management was to be entrusted to the Bertholon brothers, shareholders who jointly owned two sols and who were required to live in the *société*'s place of business in Sainte-Perrine de la Villette in order to oversee operations. If the Bertholon brothers themselves or the other shareholders decided that they should relinquish their management posts, they would step down after six months notice and remain *associés*. The shareholders would then decide through a simple plurality of votes who was to replace them.

While the *acte de société* entrusted daily operations to the Bertholon brothers, it stated that all significant, long-term decisions were to be made by the shareholders. The shareholders were required to assemble at least twice per month, at a time and place to be later decided, to deliberate on such matters as what merchandise to manufacture, the price at which to sell the merchandise, and how much to pay workers. Their decisions would be valid and enforceable only if recorded in a written document of *délibération*, signed by a minimum of eight *associés*.[190]

This bureaucratic governance structure enabled shareholders to abandon both managerial positions and ownership interests in the *société* with relative frequency and ease. Pursuant to the company's *acte de société*, the Bertholon brothers began serving as managers of the business in Sainte-Perrine de la Villette. After some time, however, they informed the other shareholders that they wished to resign. In the process of seeking a replacement, the shareholders decided to open a store in Paris. Henceforth, the merchandise would continue to be manufactured in Sainte-Perrine de la Villette but would be sold in Paris.

The decision to divide operations in this manner necessitated two different sets of managers to oversee the two locations. The shareholders appointed de Beauvillé, to whom they then sold two sols, to run the business in Sainte-Perrine de la Villette, with the aid of two other *associés,* Humel and Kornbeck. They selected the Delaleu brothers to manage the store in Paris and sold them two sols as well. Subsequently, de Beauvillé, Humel, and Kornbeck resigned their management positions and sold their shares back to the company. The remaining shareholders agreed to employ someone named Soutivier to run the business in Sainte-Perrine de la Villette without making him a shareholder. Shortly thereafter, however, "those with a financial interest in the factory" concluded that "a manager who does not have a personal interest in the *société* does not have the same zeal."[191] In *délibérations* undertaken on December 12, 1750, they therefore decided to confide management to a shareholder. Consequently, they sold two sols to a man named Vierne and appointed him to replace Soutivier. The Delaleu brothers then resigned their positions as managers of the Paris store, giving rise to various disputes that eventually led them to sue the other shareholders in the Parisian Merchant Court.

It is not clear from the archival records how the administration of the business was thereafter handled. The important point for present purposes, however, is that unlike most partnerships, this proto-*société de capitaux* was able to change managers and owners at least three times in a three-year period with relatively little difficulty and without jeopardizing the business's continued survival. Indeed, the appeal of the proto-*société de capitaux* as an institutional form was precisely the (relative) stability it managed to achieve, as well as its concomitant ability to attract capital by ensuring potential investors of a viable exit strategy. At the same time, these advantages did not come without drawbacks. The proto-*société de capitaux* represented a significant break with the traditional conception of the *société* as an entity coextensive with — and indistinguishable from — the bonds of family and friendship uniting its members. And this, in turn, gave rise to serious problems of governance.

If the associates were not (literally or figuratively) brothers, required to deal with one another as equals and obligated to sustain a long-term relationship, then how exactly were they to treat each other? Which shares or shareholders, for example, were entitled to vote and which were not? How many votes were required to make a decision binding the *société?* And did proxies representing those shareholders with voting rights have the authority to vote on their behalf?

The problems of governance to which the new, proto-*sociétés de capitaux* gave rise are readily apparent in a lawsuit filed on March 4, 1771, by Mignon, an *associé* in "the men interested in peat." Mignon charged four of his fellow *associés* with conspiring in "the plan to make themselves its despotic masters."[192] In particular, he asserted that these defendants had made major decisions on behalf of the *société* as a whole — including the decision to dissolve it — without having the authority to do so. How could it possibly be legitimate, he queried, that in a *société* consisting of ten *associés,* the assembled defendants "numbering only four, and sometimes three, represented . . . the company?"[193]

"The men interested in peat," a company which, as discussed above, was devoted to extracting charcoal from peat, was established in 1747 through a written *acte de société.* As per the *acte,* eight individuals were given shares, but only six of these were deemed *associés* — and only these *associés* had the right to vote in shareholder assemblies. The two shareholders who were not given voting rights received their shares in return for extending their "*crédit*" to the company, rather than by purchasing them. The *acte de société* further provided that "*délibérations*" made by the assembled shareholders would be valid only if signed by four of the *associés,* including a man named Harvouin.[194]

Over time, the *société* sold additional shares to new *associés.* In addition, several of the existing *associés,* including Harvouin, sold their shares to other people and left the *société* entirely. Thus, as of 1757, there were ten *associés,* not including Harvouin, who had by this time sold his shares. Between 1757 and 1763, when the assembly of shareholders began making decisions that Mignon deemed "despotic," five of these ten *associés* ceased attending shareholder assemblies — three because they died, one because he left Paris, and one because he lost a lawsuit he had brought against the *société* and wanted nothing more to do with it. The interests of the four *associés* who had died or left were represented by proxies who agreed to everything decided upon in the shareholder assemblies by the remaining *associés.*

According to the arbiters' report, the *société* "was always unfortunate."[195] Having never earned a profit in the many years of its existence, it continued to borrow money, and each year its debts increased. Finally, at an assembly held on February 26, 1763, the remaining *associés* agreed that the *société* would significantly cut back on the scope of business because "one ran the risk of increasing the company's debts without hope of being indemnified in any way."[196] Mignon did not sign this *délibération* or any others made during subsequent shareholder assemblies. Shortly thereafter, on March 10, the *associés* decided to cease operations entirely, and in the months that followed they reached several agreements for the sale of the *société*'s property. Finally, on July 18, 1767, an assembly was called, and the remaining four *associés* (plus proxies) wrote an *acte de dissolution,* which provided that certain designated arbiters would undertake the liquidation of the *société* and that an accounting done by one of the *associés* would be presumed "universally approved," unless views to the contrary were expressed.[197]

Having withheld his signature, Mignon challenged the validity of the *acte de dissolution,* as well as that of the various *délibérations* made during the shareholder assemblies in 1763, which provided for the sale of the *société*'s property. According to Mignon, who was one of five remaining *associés* in 1763, the other four conspired in "the plan to make themselves [the *société*'s] despotic masters" by making unauthorized decisions on its behalf—including the decisions to sell the *société*'s property and then to dissolve it.[198] Under the *acte de société,* he claimed, *délibérations* signed by four *associés* were valid only if Harvouin was among the four. Since none of the *délibérations* he challenged were signed by Harvouin—who had long since sold his interest in the *société* —they were, in Mignon's view, invalid. Although Mignon did not specify how many *associés* would have to sign to render a *délibération* valid, he suggested that this number must bear some relation to the total number of *associés.* Thus, he claimed that, absent Harvouin, "the *délibérations* of four can no longer be valid, as long as the *société* consisted of ten."[199] Since four out of ten was insufficient, a majority of the *associés* or at least half would presumably be necessary. Furthermore, even if the signatures of four *associés* sufficed to render a *délibération* valid in the absence of Harvouin, this would be true only of those *délibérations* that "lead to the good of the *société* and do not result in its ruin."[200] According to Mignon, the 1763 *délibérations* and the *acte de dissolution* led to the *société*'s "ruin," both in the literal sense that they enabled its dissolution and in the more figurative one that they were contrary to the *société*'s best interests. For this reason, he argued, the provision of the *acte de société* validating *délibérations* signed by four *associés* was inapplicable, and "the participation of all the *associés* was necessary."[201]

Defending themselves against Mignon's claims, his fellow *associés* insisted that there was nothing despotic in the *délibérations* they had undertaken. In 1763, they asserted, during the "period of the alleged despotism," there were only five *associés* left, including Mignon, and all but Mignon signed the *délibérations.*[202] Mignon's failure to sign was not evidence that he had been in any way excluded from the shareholders' assemblies or denied the right to vote. Indeed, Mignon "was summoned by notice to all assemblies, [and] . . . he was almost always found there and voted like the others."[203] Furthermore, after the shareholder assemblies were held, one of the defendants "took to Mignon's house the minutes of all the *délibérations* that he had not signed [and] . . . he still has them in his possession."[204] Although Mignon clearly knew what his fellow *associés* were deciding and had every opportunity to join in the debate and vote, argued the defendants, he not only refrained from signing the *délibérations* but also voiced no opposition whatsoever. In this context, his silence could only be interpreted as approval: "Since not unaware of anything, he made no protest, . . . his silence is a tacit approbation of that which was done."[205] Because Mignon was fully aware of and present during the shareholder assemblies, the *délibérations* were not products of a despotic conspiracy unlawfully to usurp power. Finally, the defendants emphasized, the *délibérations* were signed not only by themselves but also by the proxies of those other *associés* who had died or left Paris.

After lengthy consideration, the arbiters decided in favor of the defendants. It was true, as Mignon argued, that the *acte de société* contained a provision (article 8) requiring the signature of four *associés,* including Harvouin, to validate a *délibération.* However, Harvouin had left the company before Mignon ever became an *associé,* and "since his leaving until the present no change was made in article 8 of the *acte de société* to increase the number of four *associés* designated by that article as necessary to render a *délibération* valid."[206] Not only was this provision left unchanged, but in the years after Mignon joined the company and before 1763, plenty of *délibérations* had been signed by only four *associés* and subsequently implemented, without Mignon ever objecting to their validity. By failing to object during all this time, Mignon tacitly accepted that the provision had been amended through customary practice, such that it now permitted the signing of *délibérations* by four *associés, not including Harvouin.*

The arbiters also rejected Mignon's argument that, even if four signatures sufficed for most decisions, unanimity was required for those tending to the company's "ruin." According to the arbiters, the challenged *délibérations,* while dissolving the company, did not ruin it, because they were clearly in its best interests: "The abandonment of the enterprise and the dissolution of the *société* were not only an absolute necessity, but even . . . should have been done earlier for the general good of the *associés.*"[207] Finally, the arbiters concluded, it was clear that the defendants had not despotically usurped Mignon's power because "we are convinced that M. Mignon had full knowledge of all that was decreed in the aforementioned *délibérations.*"[208]

In deciding against Mignon and his claim that (at least for certain core decisions) all *associés* were entitled to vote, the arbiters recognized that the governance model appropriate for the general partnership was not suited to the proto-*société de capitaux.* The *associés* in "the men interested in peat" were not and were never intended to be entirely equal and interdependent. Indeed, the value of the proto-*société de capitaux* was precisely the bureaucratic governance structure that, while facilitating ease of entry and exit, was premised on the *associés'* possessing unequal powers and interests and remaining fundamentally independent of one another.

But to recognize that *associés* were unequal and independent was not to decide the question of how they were obligated to relate to one another. While in the case of "the men interested in peat" the arbiters decided against Mignon's demand for, inter alia, universal shareholder suffrage, numerous alternative governance structures were imaginable, and their validity remained to be tested. It was only in the nineteenth century that comprehensive answers to the kinds of questions posed by Mignon's lawsuit would be found—and that, indeed, the type of business association created by "the men interested in peat" would be given a name. But while no definitive solution to the practical and conceptual problems posed by the rise of *sociétés de capitaux* was found in the eighteenth century, the fact that these problems arose is in itself significant. The proto-*société de capitaux* and the new problems of governance that it raised marked the decline of the traditional, natural-law model of the commercial *société* as an entity coextensive with a particular set of personal relationships and thus as the embodiment of a distinctive merchant sociability.

It was in the context of a different set of disputes—those concerning negotiable instruments—that Old Regime merchants had occasion directly to address the question of what relational model would replace the traditional paradigm of merchant sociability. And as we shall see, the model that they ultimately embraced as the new foundation for merchant relations was, in their eyes, embodied in the negotiable instrument. As epitomized by the negotiable instrument, merchants came increasingly to view themselves as relating to one another (as well as to others in society) through anonymous credit networks, fueled by private exchange.

Before turning to negotiable instruments, however, it is tempting briefly to speculate on one final implication of the demise of the traditional model of the *société*. In addition to raising questions regarding merchant relations, the demise of this model touches on the broader question of social governance writ large. David Bien has provocatively suggested that traditional corporate bodies, like guilds, played an important role in the rise of liberal democracy. Because these bodies were governed by assemblies in which each member's vote was equal to that of all others and the majority decided, they embodied the principle that government is legitimate only when it is based on equality and liberty, while also providing important lessons in assembly rule.[209]

Along similar lines, it may well be the case that the kinds of complex governance questions posed by proto-*sociétés de capitaux* caused these institutions to serve, in part, as (unintended) laboratories of democracy. Indeed, unlike Bien's guilds, where all masters had identical property rights through purchase of the guild office, the proto-*sociétés de capitaux* directly posed the question that would come to haunt the Revolutionaries, as well as nineteenth-century advocates of democracy throughout the West—namely, how to link differing property interests with voting rights. Thus, around the same time that Comptroller General Turgot — the reforming minister and frequent ally of the Physiocrats — was attempting to ground a theory of representative government on the foundation of (landed) property ownership,[210] Mignon and his co-*associés* were asking themselves what kind of ownership interest a shareholder must have in order to obtain voting rights. Given the conceptual link forged by natural-law jurists between the commercial *société* and civil society, it is difficult not to wonder — though well beyond the scope of this book to address — whether and to what extent proto-*sociétés de capitaux* and their shareholder assemblies provided Frenchmen with a practical education in the workings of representative, democratic government.

5

A Crisis in Virtue: The Challenges of Negotiability and the Rise of a New Commercial Culture

It would be very desirable for the form and use of bills of exchange to be subject to the empire of law that is general and uniform throughout commercial nations, for the terms of endorsements not to be susceptible to any interpretation in any tribunal in Europe, and for the protest [of a bill for failure to pay] . . . to have the same effect in all countries.

—Jacques Accarias de Sérionne, *Les intérêts des nations de l'Europe, dévélopés relativement au commerce*

The use of negotiable instruments in eighteenth-century France posed a serious challenge to traditional commercial culture and its structuring norms of morality and community. Even apart from negotiable instruments, of course, these norms were, as described in previous chapters, sometimes belied by the harsh reality of self-interested conflict. Nonetheless, the Parisian Merchant Court sought to resolve most contract and partnership disputes by reinforcing what it understood to be an ethic of fraternal harmony. And while *sociétés en commandite* and proto-*sociétés de capitaux* strained traditional conceptions of merchant sociability, they did not compel a serious rethinking of merchant relations. In the case of *sociétés en commandites,* limited liability continued to be imposed according to the court's longstanding, equitable, and ex post approach. As for proto-*sociétés de capitaux,* these had yet to emerge as clearly defined forms by the end of the eighteenth century. In contrast, negotiability and the practices associated with it directly undermined the court's traditional ex post approach, as well as its ability to appeal to norms of brotherly love. Firmly rooted in France long before the century's end, the widespread use of negotiable instruments forced merchants to confront new fears of market anonymity, bad faith, and usury.

The anxieties to which the use of negotiable instruments gave rise are detailed in this chapter, but they are perhaps best introduced by a contemporary merchant's account of a remarkable lawsuit concerning a bill of exchange. This account appears in *Le négociant patriote*[1]—a description of merchant life published in 1779 and then again in 1784 by an anonymous *négociant*. The author, subsequently identified as Bedos, claimed to be from Languedoc[2] and to have served as president of the local chamber of commerce[3] and judge in the regional merchant court.[4]

According to Bedos, the lawsuit was brought by a woman demanding payment of a bill of exchange for ten thousand livres, which had been drafted in red ink. The plaintiff claimed that she had given the defendant value in return for the bill, but that the person on whom the defendant had drawn the bill refused to pay it when it fell due. Moreover, she insisted, the bill was written in strict accordance with the Commercial Ordinance of 1673, such that her entitlement to payment was clear. That it happened to be written in red ink was of no matter, since the ordinance said nothing about ink color. In response, the judge stated firmly but gently, "Yes, miss; but have you always observed the ordinance of modesty?"[5] At these words, the plaintiff suddenly collapsed. Apparently, the judge understood that the value the plaintiff had given in exchange for the bill was the use of her body and that, as the defendant later admitted, the red ink consisted of his own blood, which he obtained by sticking a pin into his vein.

For Bedos, the lesson of "The Red-Ink Case" was clear: Negotiable paper threatened to commercialize the most sacred of all human relationships, and in the process, to drain humanity of its lifeblood. The solution to this threat, he suggested, was to reinforce traditional merchant virtue, relying on the longstanding role of the merchant court as a bastion of morality and community. Accordingly, in Bedos' account, the court resolved the lawsuit not by applying the ordinance, the technically applicable law, but instead by actively seeking to promote virtue. Indeed, the court's motto, as Bedos explained, was that "humanity is the primary law."[6] Thus, after ordering the clerk to come to the aid of the grief-stricken plaintiff, the judge turned to the defendant and said, "Here, sir, is where you have led her; she sinned out of weakness and you by setting the trap: tell her that you will marry her; her restored honor will call her back to life."[7] Properly chastened, the defendant agreed that he ought to marry the plaintiff and promised God that he would make her happy. At this point, the plaintiff immediately revived and recovered sufficiently to ask the court to keep the bill until the day following the marriage, upon which it could be returned to her then husband. Thus assisted by the merchant court in their efforts to remain virtuous, the litigants departed, presumably to live happily ever after: "These poor children withdrew satisfied."[8]

But while in Bedos' account the challenges posed to traditional merchant culture by negotiable instruments could be addressed simply by calling on the merchant court to help reinforce that culture, reality was, in fact, more complex. As this chapter explores, and as Bedos suggested in his recounting of the Red-Ink Case, the rise of negotiability and associated practices threatened to restructure the way credit was extended and, in the process, the nature of relationships among merchants and nonmerchants alike. To understand this threat, however, it is necessary to begin by examining how negotiable instruments were used and how these uses changed over the course of the eighteenth century.

A Brief History of Bills of Exchange and Promissory Notes

There were two principle kinds of negotiable instruments in eighteenth-century France: bills of exchange and promissory notes.[9] Although these instruments differ somewhat in formation and operation, they share the fundamental characteristic of negotiability. Like a written contract, a negotiable instrument is a writing by which one party promises to pay another. It can be distinguished from a contract, however, by two crucial features. First, while in Old Regime France an interest in a contract could be assigned only upon the assistance of a notary, the holder of a negotiable instrument assigns his interest simply by endorsing the instrument and conveying it to the recipient. Accordingly, rights in a negotiable instrument can be easily and quickly transferred from one person to the next.

The second way that a negotiable instrument differs from a contract is that it offers an especially high degree of protection to the holder who purchased it for value and in good faith—namely, without knowledge of any defenses against its enforcement or of additional claims to it. Such a holder has a right to payment even if the person from whom he acquired the instrument has a legitimate defense against its enforcement. By thus providing potential holders with a guaranteed right of payment, this feature of negotiability promotes rapid and extensive trade in negotiable instruments. In contrast, the rights of someone who has been assigned an interest in a contract are identical to those of the assignor, such that a defense preventing the assignor from enforcing the contract would be fully applicable against the assignee as well.[10]

Although negotiability did not arise in France until the middle of the seventeenth century,[11] the two main types of instruments that became negotiable—namely, promissory notes and bills of exchange—have a long history dating back to the Italian city-states of the twelfth and thirteenth centuries. Both of these instruments were originally types of contract, typically witnessed and signed before notaries. As early as the fourteenth century, however, many of these instruments ceased being notarized.[12] The promissory note was simply a written promise by the maker to pay the payee within a certain amount of time. It was used primarily in small-scale, local transactions as a means for sellers to extend credit to buyers. The bill of exchange, then called a *contrat de change,* had a more complicated purpose and structure. Like promissory notes, bills of exchange enabled merchants to purchase goods on credit. In addition, however, they were a means of making purchases across significant geographical distances without transporting specie. This was of great value because transporting specie exposed the merchant to a serious risk of theft and was very costly. Furthermore, when merchants who transacted business with one another were from cities that employed different currencies, bills of exchange also enabled a currency exchange.

Structurally, this early form of the bill of exchange usually involved four parties.[13] The *donneur,* or giver of value, purchased the bill with a cash payment in local currency, and the *tireur,* or drawer, drew the bill in return for the *donneur's* cash payment. The *bénéficiaire,* or beneficiary, was named as the person to whom the bill was to be paid, and the *tiré,* or drawee, was named as the person who was supposed to pay the bill. Typically, the giver of value and the beneficiary, and similarly the drawer and the drawee, had ongoing relationships as principal and agent.[14] For example, a merchant who purchased a bill of exchange in Paris (the giver of value) would name his agent in Bruges as the beneficiary. In this way, the Parisian merchant could transfer money to his Belgian agent without having to transport specie. Similarly, the drawer in Paris would name his agent in Bruges as the drawee. By having his agent in Bruges pay his obligation, the Parisian drawer could use his money abroad to dispose of his debt, also without having to transport specie.

As Raymond de Roover suggests, the bill of exchange served not only to avoid the transport of specie and to exchange currencies, but also to extend credit at interest.[15] In the Middle Ages, and as described below, to some extent even in the early-modern world, the Church's injunction against usury was a barrier to the extension of credit. Merchants who wanted to lend or borrow money at interest sought to conceal the true nature of the transaction, by means of bills of exchange. What enabled the bill of exchange to mask interest was the drawer's promise that he would have the drawee pay the obligation *at some future date.*[16] Because the purchaser of the bill of exchange had to forgo the use of his money during the period before it fell due, argues Roover, he typically demanded that the bill be for a sum that exceeded the amount he originally paid, and thus that included interest.[17] Because exchange rates fluctuated, however, there was always a risk of loss. According to Roover, it was precisely this element of risk that made the bill of exchange acceptable to the Church, since usury was long defined as the *risk-free* profit on a loan.[18]

Although by the fourteenth century bills of exchange ceased being notarized, they continued to be viewed as a form of contract—hence the name *contrat de change.* Because this early form of the bill of exchange was viewed as a contract, rules of privity applied which greatly limited the recourse available to the holder in good faith.[19] This meant that, in case of nonpayment, the beneficiary of the bill could sue neither the giver of value nor the drawer, but only the drawee who had "accepted" the bill by agreeing to pay it.[20] When the negotiable bill of exchange emerged around the mid-seventeenth century, it was far more favorable to the beneficiary who was a holder in good faith, permitting him to collect not only from the drawee but also from the drawer and from all other individuals who had endorsed the bill.[21]

Over the course of the seventeenth century, as commerce expanded and merchants sought new sources of credit, a shift occurred in the number of people who were generally involved in creating a bill of exchange.[22] In the three-party bill of exchange, the drawer drafted a bill ordering the drawee to pay a certain sum to the beneficiary. One of these three parties, in other words, also served as the giver of value. For example, the drawee who was a banker might function as the giver of value when he extended credit to the drawer by allowing the drawer to draw a bill directly on him. As James Steven Rogers persuasively argues in his fascinating account of the English history of bills and notes, the emergence of the three-party instrument marked a shift around the mid-seventeenth century from an "era of exchange transactions" to an "era of bills of exchange."[23] In the era of exchange transactions, the bill of exchange was simply the physical representation of an underlying exchange contract—namely, the obligation of the drawer to pay for the funds he received from the giver of value. In contrast, in the later era the bill of exchange became the drawer's original and only obligation. In this new era, the drawer drafted the bill, not in exchange for funds that he received from a giver of value but simply as a means of using funds located elsewhere (with the drawee). This new way of deploying bills, suggests Rogers, was associated both with the rise of negotiability and with the increased use of such instruments by large numbers (and types) of people, rather than exclusively by merchant experts. Indeed, it seems likely that the disappearance of a distinct giver of value furthered the rise of negotiability, by undermining the conception of the bill of exchange as a contract between the giver of value and the drawer.

Along with negotiability, there arose the practice of discounting.[24] To discount a bill was to buy it before it fell due at a price lower than face value. Since, in this situation, the seller of the instrument received payment before the law required, it was necessary to compensate the buyer for the time value of his money. In other words, the buyer was loaning money to the seller and the diminution in price served as interest on this loan, ensuring that when the instrument fell due, the buyer would receive more than he had paid. Although the development of negotiability appears to have spurred the practice of discounting, there is much scholarly debate about when discounting became common practice. Roover suggested that discounting emerged around the mid-eighteenth century.[25] More recently, however, economic historians have taken issue with Roover's timetable, arguing that discounting was practiced widely as early as the second quarter of the eighteenth century[26] or even the second half of the seventeenth century.[27]

Uses Served by Negotiable Instruments

Of the arbiters' reports contained in the box that I systematically reviewed, 20.9 percent (of the known disputes) concern negotiable instruments.[28] Since some sales-related cases were resolved by arbiters who recommended that one party pay a particular sum without identifying the nature of the underlying debts, it may well be the case that the percentage of cases involving such instruments was actually higher.

As revealed by the arbiters' reports, bills of exchange and promissory notes were used in eighteenth-century France by many different types of people for a wide variety of purposes. Merchants of all kinds, ranging from the small-scale artisan-retailer to the international *négociant* and banker, employed negotiable instruments. So too did farmers, officeholders, and noblemen. Those who appear in the arbiters' reports include such figures as Boutin, a nineteen-year-old military officer and son of the treasurer of the navy;[29] Richard, an employee in the king's library;[30] and Noel, a professional musician.[31] As observed in the December 1760 installment of the monthly *Journal de Commerce*, "for *négociants*, it is a great advantage that bills of exchange pass through hands other than their own," since if they circulated only among merchants "lending at interest" would be "destroy[ed]."[32]

Although the jurisdiction of the French merchant courts was generally limited to disputes between merchants over merchandise-related matters, one of the main exceptions to this rule concerned bills of exchange. According to the Commercial Ordinance of 1673, anyone who signed a bill of exchange was subject to the jurisdiction of the merchant courts.[33] As concerns other forms of negotiable instrument, the ordinance provided that disputes regarding exchange notes — namely, notes drafted as payment for a bill of exchange — were not subject to merchant court jurisdiction if these notes were "between nonmerchants, . . . or where [*négociants* and merchants] do not owe the value."[34] In contrast, disputes concerning exchange notes "between *négociants* and merchants, or where they do owe the value," were subject to merchant court jurisdiction.[35] While the ordinance made no mention of promissory notes, contemporary courts, jurists, and merchants widely interpreted these provisions concerning exchange notes to apply to promissory notes as well.[36]

The precise meaning of the ordinance's rather ambiguous provisions concerning exchange notes was, as Jacqueline Lafon demonstrates, a subject of extensive debate within the Old Regime. The *Parlement* of Paris interpreted these provisions so as to narrow the scope of merchant court jurisdiction. Thus, it ruled in July 1733 that, pursuant to the ordinance, merchant court jurisdiction extended only to exchange notes drafted between merchants, where the note's maker remained in debt, and to those promissory notes that were both drafted and held by merchants.[37] In contrast, commercial jurists, along with the merchant deputies of the royal *Bureau du Commerce,* insisted that the ordinance granted merchant courts jurisdiction over all exchange notes (regardless of whether the maker remained in debt) and over all promissory notes drafted by a merchant (regardless of the holder's identity).[38]

As might be expected, arbiters' reports reveal that the Parisian Merchant Court adopted the view of the commercial jurists and the merchant deputies of the *Bureau du Commerce,* rather than that of the *Parlement.* As suggested by the cases described below, the court failed to distinguish between exchange notes and promissory notes and regularly adjudicated disputes concerning notes whose holders were nonmerchants. Contrary even to the writings of the commercial jurists and merchant deputies, it displayed little concern to determine whether those who had drafted such notes were themselves merchants. Relying on its clearly established jurisdiction over bills of exchange, the court succeeded to a remarkable degree in extending its jurisdiction to encompass negotiable instruments of all kinds, regardless of the identities of those engaged in their negotiation. Thus, by the second half of the eighteenth century, it was widely accepted that, whatever the niceties of legal doctrine, cases concerning negotiable instruments were generally heard by the Parisian Merchant Court. As observed by Louis-Sébastien Mercier in his contemporary commentary on Parisian life, the court's jurisdiction consisted "especially . . . of bills of exchange and promissory notes, which have so multiplied in our time."[39]

DEVELOPMENTS PROMOTING THE WIDESPREAD USE OF NEGOTIABLE INSTRUMENTS

Several institutions that were new or newly transformed in the eighteenth century greatly facilitated trade in negotiable instruments. Among these was the Parisian exchange, or *bourse de Paris,* which was founded by the monarchy in 1724, after the demise of John Law's disastrous Mississippi Scheme.

Law's scheme united in a single entity a royal bank and a colonial trading company, such that the public debt came to be financed largely through sale of the company's shares. The latter, in turn, became the object of an intense speculative fever, which peaked in 1719. The following year panic ensued and the market crashed. Among the many far-reaching consequences of the Mississippi Bubble was that it significantly reinforced what was, as we will soon see, a longstanding distrust of commercial paper, while also leading to widespread disdain of those *agioteurs* who devoted themselves to financial speculation. Although concern about royally backed paper and the financiers who traded in it was particularly great—and has long been cited as a key factor in explaining France's relative delay in establishing a national bank[40]—private commercial paper did not escape untainted.

A further consequence of the Bubble and its collapse was that the monarchy thereafter attempted to subject financial speculation to greater regulation by replacing the unofficial exchange that had emerged during the Bubble[41] (fig. 2) with the first officially established bourse. Thus, in the 1724 statute establishing the bourse, the monarchy granted a monopoly for brokering the purchase and sale of negotiable instruments to licensed brokers, called *agents de change.*[42] In practice, as the arbiters' reports reveal, people other than *agents de change* often served as brokers, and it is therefore far from clear that the monarchy succeeded in achieving its regulatory aims. Nonetheless, the establishment of the bourse and the *agents de change* increased the information regarding potential instruments and endorsers available to merchants and nonmerchants alike, thereby facilitating market expansion.

Also important in expanding the market for negotiable instruments were the many private banks that emerged in Old Regime Europe. Ever since the commercial growth of the medieval Italian city-states, men known as *marchands-banquiers* sold goods to one another and, in the process, provided banking services. At first, they offered only deposit and transfer banking, but over time,

Fig. 2 The *hôtel de Soissons,* established for trade in commercial paper in 1720 (Antoine Humblot, *L'hôtel de Soissons,* 1720. Courtesy of British Museum.)

as bills of exchange developed, the *marchands-banquiers* began to offer these as well, drawing bills to the client's order on colleagues located elsewhere.[43] And when negotiability arose, they started to serve as brokers, arranging purchases and sales of negotiable instruments in return for a fee, while also engaging in financial speculation on their own behalf. From the late seventeenth century onward, as a growing number of these *marchands-banquiers* came to specialize exclusively in such banking services, manuals describing currencies, exchange rates, and the complex mechanics of bills of exchange began to appear, including perhaps most famously Barrême's *Le grand banquier* (fig. 3), but also Bouthillier's *Le banquier françois* and Bléville's *Le banquier et négociant universel.*[44] In Paris alone, there were on the order of fifty banking houses in the first quarter of the eighteenth century, and about seventy by the third.[45] The availability of such bankers was key to fueling the market for negotiable instruments.

In the final years of the eighteenth century, yet another institution emerged that promoted trade in negotiable instruments: the *Caisse d'Escompte.* Created in 1776 and generally viewed by economic historians as France's precursor to a national bank, the *Caisse d'Escompte* proved quite successful. As of 1787 it had amassed a total capital of 100 million livres—an amount far exceeding its initial capital of 12 million livres.[46] By placing government debt with private investors, it played an important role in financing the monarchy and its activities. More importantly in this context, its discounting of bills of exchange and other negotiable instruments at the low rate of 4 percent[47] facilitated the widespread trade in such instruments.[48]

As an institution that promoted trade in both public and private debt, the *Caisse d'Escompte* is notable for bridging what remained, to some extent, two distinct markets.[49] Although there was some overlap, the community of individuals concerned with royal finance was largely distinct from that involved in the private credit market. Financiers were mostly French, Catholic, and engaged almost exclusively in finance activities. Bankers, in contrast, were often actively involved in mercantile trade and were sometimes—though by no means always—foreign and Protestant.[50] Moreover, since the monarchy frequently defaulted, participation in the public debt market was not for the risk averse, and thus not for the traditional merchant and banking community with its moralistic antipathy to excessive self-interest and financial speculation.[51] As explained by a *négociant* from Lyon in February 1761, "commerce . . . [is] the first and most noble of all professions [*états*] . . . [as] it does not know . . . the odious surprises of finance."[52]

Merchants and financiers, however, may have interacted more than has at times been suggested. It is notable, for example, that while the Parisian Merchant Court operated largely under the control of elite merchants and bank-

Fig. 3 *The Book of Foreign Currencies, or the Great Banker of France, Dedicated to His Lordship Colbert* (Frontispiece to François Bertrand de Barrême, *Le grand banquier,* 1696. Courtesy of Stanford University Libraries.)

ers, financiers—such as tax farmers—sometimes litigated before it.[53] And some of the interaction between merchants and financiers was of a kind that may well have served to expand trade in negotiable instruments. For example, as a number of historians have observed, merchants sometimes issued commercial paper drawn on the accounts of financiers, such as tax receivers.[54]

USING NEGOTIABLE INSTRUMENTS AS A SUBSTITUTE FOR SPECIE

Aided by these institutional developments, the use of negotiable instruments increased rapidly over the course of the eighteenth century.[55] But for what purposes were such instruments used? One possibility is that they served, in part, as a substitute for specie, because (1) the value of specie was unstable, and/or (2) specie was in short supply.

Under the monetary system that prevailed in Old Regime France, and that dated back to the Carolingians, there were two different systems of currency in operation. The currency of payment, or real currency, consisted of the actual gold, silver, and copper coins—such as *louis* and *écus*—used to make payment. The currency of accounting, in contrast, was purely theoretical, consisting of the *livres, sous,* and *deniers* used in making contracts and undertaking accountings. The monarchy was responsible for fixing the relationship between the two forms of currency, and until January 1726 it did so frequently, causing France to suffer until this date from great monetary instability. Such instability may have led contemporaries to prefer bills of exchange to specie, since like contracts and accountings, bills of exchange referred to the invariable currency of accounting rather than to real currency.[56]

Whether eighteenth-century France suffered from a shortage in specie, and if so, how this was related to the use of negotiable instruments, is a matter of dispute among economic historians. According to some, shortages in the money supply were severe, leading merchants to embrace commercial paper.[57] Others, however, have suggested that any such shortage was minor, and at any rate had little effect, since merchants actually preferred negotiable instruments to cash, due to the credit extension that such instruments afforded.[58] But whether it was because of a dearth of coins in circulation or because of merchant preference, most commercial transactions in the Old Regime were undertaken on the basis of some form of credit—including not only negotiable instruments but also book debt. Specie was employed for only a very limited number of purposes, such as small-scale consumer purchases, payments made by master-artisans to their employees,[59] and taxes owed to the monarchy.[60]

USING NEGOTIABLE INSTRUMENTS TO OBTAIN CREDIT

Aside from a possible role in substituting for specie, one of the key functions that negotiable instruments served in eighteenth-century France was as a means of obtaining credit. Within the context of a sales transaction, negotiable instruments were commonly used to make payments on book debt, and thus as a component of the traditional book-debt method of extending credit. A merchant or nonmerchant buyer who had purchased goods on credit and whose debt was recorded in the seller's accounting books would make payments on this debt by means not only of cash but also of negotiable instruments.[61] In this way the buyer obtained additional credit, while the seller could, by negotiating the instrument, convert the debt into ready cash.

Rather than using negotiable instruments to settle book debt, a merchant or nonmerchant buyer could also use them to make an initial or one-time purchase. This would be of interest to the buyer or seller who did not seek to enter into a long-term creditor-debtor relationship — perhaps because trust had not yet developed, or because repeat transactions were unlikely. Unlike book debt, a negotiable instrument had to be paid by a fixed date, and once the instrument was paid, the creditor-debtor relationship was over. The rise of negotiability made the use of bills of exchange and notes to make one-time purchases particularly desirable since the seller who received the instrument could negotiate it and thereby gain almost immediate access to the instrument's cash value (less the discount rate).[62]

Negotiable instruments could also serve as a source of credit without being linked to a sales transaction. Anyone seeking to obtain credit could obligate himself on a bill of exchange or note and thereafter negotiate the instrument at a discount and acquire a loan. Merchants of all kinds, but particularly large-scale wholesalers and *négociants,* who had long traded with one another, paying their debts through bills of exchange, were able to extend their activities to include the buying and selling of negotiable instruments.[63] In addition, nonmerchants relied on brokers to assist them in discounting negotiable paper and thereby obtaining a loan.[64]

USING NEGOTIABLE INSTRUMENTS TO MAKE INVESTMENTS

Negotiable instruments served not only as a means of obtaining credit but also as a means of investing idle capital, either by purchasing an occasional instrument or by engaging in market speculation. Indeed, anyone with the requisite funds could purchase a negotiable instrument as a means of earning interest — namely, by charging the discount rate. While the private discount rate in eighteenth-century Paris appears to have fluctuated around 5 percent, it varied widely, sometimes peaking in excess of 10 percent,[65] and thus providing plenty of opportunities for speculation.

Facilitated by the establishment of the *Caisse d'Escompte* in 1776, speculation on a range of financial instruments, including government debt, reached fever pitch in the 1780s.[66] Driving this speculation were rival syndicates of bears and bulls, who successfully deployed press campaigns and political connections to manipulate public opinion. Commonly (and disparagingly) described as *agioteurs,* many of these speculators were Protestants from Amsterdam and Geneva and had little to do with the traditional Parisian merchant and banking community.[67] Nonetheless, the speculative boom that they engendered led to a significant expansion in the market for commercial paper, which benefited Parisian bankers by enabling them to increase the commissions they charged.[68] At the same time, this expansion also meant that those individuals who chose not to engage in speculation themselves sometimes came to hold instruments that had arisen as part of such activity. In these circumstances, bankruptcies abounded, and many bankers, merchants, and nonmerchants found themselves holding paper that was of little or no value. As the contemporary nobleman Bachaumont observed, when it was discovered in December 1786 that a group of *agioteurs* had falsified numerous bills of exchange and then discounted them widely, these malfeasants "have infected the public with [their fraudulent paper]."[69]

Challenges Posed by Negotiable Instruments

That the use of negotiable instruments had become widespread by the latter half of the eighteenth century is readily apparent in the popular culture of the time. Indeed, contemporaries seem to have viewed the negotiable instrument as one of the main symbols of the rising power and prominence of commerce in social and political life. Consider, for example, the popular theatrical form that emerged in the 1760s—the *drame bourgeois,* or as its progenitor Diderot termed it, the *genre sérieux.* Rejecting the traditional genres of tragedy and comedy as outdated, overly stylized, and morally pernicious, Diderot and his followers argued that the *drame* would serve a moralizing mission, by depicting how ordinary individuals coped with trying circumstances and chose of their own free will to act virtuously.

In line with the Enlightenment program of the *philosophes, drames* often lampooned the nobility and its conception of honor as acquired by lineage and sustained by luxurious display. Identifying the virtuous man as the one who is useful and productive, such plays embraced the long-disdained figure of the merchant—and especially that of the large-scale *négociant*—as the new embodiment of other-serving virtue, or *bienfaisance.*[70] As explained by the author of a classic work on eighteenth-century French theater, playgoers beginning in the 1760s "grew more and more accustomed to hearing people on stage talk about profits and losses, inventories, promissory notes, redemption dates, and bankruptcies."[71] And of all the activities in which the *négociant* engaged, it was for many authors trade in negotiable instruments that best epitomized his remarkable power to spread wealth, and thus well-being, across the globe. This was the case, for example, for Diderot's friend and ally Michel Sedaine, whose *Le philosophe sans le savoir* premiered at the Comédie-Française to great acclaim[72] on December 2, 1765, and enjoyed long-running success. In this prototype of the highly popular *drame,* the main character is a *négociant* named Vanderk, who points to negotiable instruments in his effort to persuade his son that commerce is an honorable profession: "What a profession [*état*]... [is] that of a man who, with a stroke of the pen, makes himself obeyed from one end of the universe to the other! His name, his signature do not require, like the coins of a sovereign, that the value of metal serve as a guarantee of his mark...: he has signed, that suffices."[73]

Notably, however, in their efforts to glorify bills of exchange and notes as instruments of virtue, *drames* sometimes significantly distorted the reality of contemporary commercial practice. Indeed, in such plays as *Le philosophe sans le savoir,* as well as Beaumarchais' *Les deux amis, ou le négociant de Lyon* (1770) and Dampierre de la Salle's *Le bienfait rendu, ou le négociant* (1763), negotiable instruments are depicted not as instruments of credit or speculation — as merchants in fact used them — but instead as instruments of charity.[74] To continue with the example of *Le philosophe sans le savoir* — by far the most popular of these three plays, and indeed, among the most successful of all the era's *drames* — the *négociant* Vanderk displays his virtue by refusing to accept a discount in cashing a bill of exchange.

The denouement of the play occurs when, at the very moment that Vanderk's son is engaged in a duel with a man named Desparville, Desparville's father arrives in Vanderk's office and asks him to cash a bill of exchange. Desparville Sr. explains that he needs the money so that his son will have the wherewithal to flee upon killing his opponent — a man whom he does not understand to be Vanderk's son. Although Vanderk does understand this fact, and moreover during their discussion acquires the news (later proven false) that his own son has been mortally wounded, he nonetheless agrees to purchase the bill. Indeed, he vehemently disapproves of those *négociants* who, recognizing that Desparville Sr. was desperate, "demanded to charge a large discount rate."[75] And when Desparville Sr. insists that Vanderk take some percentage as a discount, Vanderk proudly states, "I do not take any discount, that is not my commerce."[76] Thus tested and proved, Vanderk's virtue is ultimately rewarded and the play closes with him surrounded by his family and friends, including the son who, as it turns out, survived. Speaking for all, Desparville Sr. praises him as "the most decent [*brave*] man, the most, the most...."[77]

Sedaine's decision to make Vanderk's virtue turn, in part, on his refusal to charge a discount rate in cashing a bill of exchange is remarkable. While Vanderk insists that it is not in the nature of his commercial activity to discount bills of exchange, this is simply not credible. Late-eighteenth-century merchants—and particularly large-scale *négociants*—had come to depend greatly on negotiable instruments, and as was common knowledge, these were traded at a discount. Why would Sedaine, who sought to valorize modern-day commerce—and, indeed, embraced the negotiable instrument as its epitome—thus depict such an improbable use of a bill of exchange? One possible answer is that he was not himself a merchant and thus did not understand how such instruments function. But given the prevalent use of negotiable instruments, this explanation seems highly unlikely. To recognize that bills of exchange were traded at a discount required no special expertise. More persuasive, in my view, is that there were certain features of the growing trade in negotiable instruments (like the practice of discounting) that were troubling to contemporaries—even to those who, like Sedaine and other playwrights of his ilk, embraced an Enlightenment ideal of commercial progress. The portrait of the negotiable instrument that appears in *Le philosophe sans le savoir* (and other *drames* much like it) is thus, in some respects, a reflection of the anxieties to which negotiable instruments gave rise—and not only among merchants.

What were these anxieties? As argued below, a review of arbiters' reports and legal briefs filed with the Parisian Merchant Court suggests that negotiable instruments raised the specter of three developments—anonymity, bad faith, and usury—which ran counter to the goals and values that had traditionally shaped commercial practice and law. To the extent that bills of exchange and notes were employed within traditional credit transactions—as a means of making payment on book debt and where the negotiability of such instruments was not at issue—the court seems to have had little difficulty resolving the resultant disputes. It simply employed its traditional method of sending the parties before an arbiter, whose foremost task was to promote reconciliation and who focused on assessing each party's moral character.[78] But while these types of cases fit easily within traditional merchant culture, disputes concerning bills of exchange and notes *that had been negotiated* posed significant new challenges.

It is often argued that the bill of exchange represented the antithesis of modern-day, anonymous capitalism, since the market value of a given bill was measured by the reputation of its various endorsers.[79] But while, as compared with present-day credit mechanisms, the eighteenth-century bill of exchange was a highly personal instrument, contemporaries did not, of course, view their world from the perspective of centuries to come. And as compared with the modes of extending credit that had been common prior to the emergence of the negotiable bill of exchange—most importantly, nonnegotiable paper and book debt—the bill of exchange was strikingly impersonal.

Because an instrument could be endorsed multiple times before falling due, a large number of people could be held liable for it, even though many might be complete strangers to each other. The establishment of the bourse in Paris and elsewhere, as well as the growth in banking, resulted in the ready availability of brokering services, which made it that much more probable that an instrument's endorsers would not know one another. Furthermore, to the extent that people used negotiable instruments for investment purposes—and, in particular, to speculate—their attitudes to profit-making differed from those that had traditionally animated commercial activity. Short-term profit, for example, became a realistic option. This was in sharp contrast to the traditional commercial undertaking, in which the limited ability to predict demand and the limited availability of suppliers led merchants to place long-term relationships above short-term gain. As evidenced by the arbiters' reports discussed below, contemporary merchants were greatly concerned that negotiability might undermine the personal relationships underlying traditional commercial practice and replace these with a more anonymous market.

Unfortunately, the nature of the archival sources on which this book primarily draws—namely, the reports of arbiters to the Parisian Merchant Court—makes it difficult to assess the extent to which bills of exchange came to be negotiated between people who had no personal knowledge of one another. By the time a dispute arose over a negotiable instrument and a lawsuit was brought, the relevant parties had usually been identified, and the arbiters did not necessarily pause to discuss the nature of the relationship—or the lack thereof—between the various endorsers. Moreover, the merchant court's traditional approach to commercial adjudication was to foster and reinforce ties of friendship between merchants. Although, as discussed below, this approach was not well suited to disputes over negotiable instruments, arbiters frequently sought to apply it in this less than hospitable context. Thus, there is the distinct possibility that reports concerning disputes over negotiable instruments impose a framework of the personal where none really existed—suggesting greater personal ties between the instrument's endorsers than there actually were.

But despite these limitations, the arbiters' reports (as well as legal briefs and treatise literature) suggest that bills of exchange were often traded among people who did not know each other. Indeed, given the frequency with which instruments were negotiated, the pressure to accept as payment (or otherwise to obligate oneself on) instruments endorsed by strangers was hard to resist. The extent of this pressure is suggested by one arbiter's comment regarding a haberdasher who refused to accept two bills of exchange as payment on the ground that he did not know the drawer or the drawee and that he therefore had "an aversion for bills of exchange."[80] The arbiter concluded that this was a lie, insisting that "this discourse, in the mouth of a trader, seems to me to be a true paradox."[81] Although merchants might worry about commercial paper signed by strangers, the pressure to rely on such paper was too great to believe that this was the haberdasher's true reason for declining to do so.[82]

Negotiability raised not only the specter of anonymity, but also that of bad faith. The defining feature of negotiability is that no defenses and claims are good against the holder who acquired the instrument without knowledge of them and in exchange for value. While this doctrine protects the good-faith holder, it does so at the expense of another person of good faith — namely, the party with the legitimate defense or claim. In ignoring this legitimate defense or claim, negotiability permits the wrong done against this injured party to stand. Consider, for example, the following scenario. Someone agrees to draw a bill of exchange to the purchaser's order in return for a sum of money, which the purchaser then fails to pay. If the purchaser negotiates the bill to a good-faith purchaser for value, then this third-party purchaser can sue the drawer for payment of the bill — even though the drawer has a legitimate defense against enforcement *by the original purchaser*. Although the drawer acted in good faith and was duped, he must pay the good-faith, third-party purchaser. Of course, the drawer may sue the original purchaser for payment, but even if the court finds in his favor, the original purchaser will likely be judgment proof.

In this scenario, there is little chance that the claims of both the good-faith third-party purchaser and the good-faith drawer will be vindicated. Pursuant to the rise of negotiability, therefore, bad faith had to be accepted as inevitable — as an evil necessary to encourage the greatest possible extension of the credit network. In this way, negotiability undermined the traditional conception of merchant litigation as a conflict between parties of good and bad character, in which it was the court's task to ensure the triumph of virtue.

The final challenge posed by negotiability was the threat of usury. Historians disagree about how much force the usury prohibition continued to exercise as late as the eighteenth century.[83] On the one hand, it is clear that the definition of usury continuously evolved over the centuries in order to enable the traditional doctrine to accommodate new commercial practices.[84] While in the Middle Ages any profit on a loan was deemed usury, by the eighteenth century Church thinkers had developed a multitude of exceptions to this strict definition so as to permit such practices as insurance contracts for shipping, and deposit and exchange banking. On the other hand, even in the eighteenth century, there remained several prominent scholastics who rejected these practices as usurious.[85] Indeed, the usury prohibition was evidently deemed to be of sufficient ongoing significance that, over the course of the century, at least two hundred books were devoted to the topic.[86] Many of these continued to adhere to the hard-line, anti-usury stance adopted by the Counter-Reformation Church in its efforts to distinguish itself from Protestantism.[87]

That such Church thinkers and their arguments against usury continued to wield significant influence well into the eighteenth century is suggested by contemporary efforts to refute them, such as a treatise first published in 1756 by the head of the Chamber of Commerce of La Rochelle and entitled "Dissertation on the Legitimacy of the Interest on Money Used in Commerce."[88] As the author explained, he was moved to write this treatise by the fact that "all the laws agree in prohibiting usury, and several interpreters of these laws regard as usurious the majority of commercial practices concerning credit."[89] And while some merchants, like the author of this treatise, sought directly to resist the Church's continued battle against usury, others attempted accommodation instead. Consider, in this regard, a proposal dating from the 1760s, which is contained in the archives of the Parisian Merchant Court. Advocating the establishment in Paris of a royal pawnshop (or *mont de piété*)—an institution designed expressly as a mechanism for lending money at interest—the proposal goes to great lengths to distinguish such interest from usury. According to the author, the interest that the proposed pawnshop would charge would be "destined for the administration" of the pawnshop and thus "it is no longer possible to regard the interest that it collects as usurious."[90] Nonetheless, the proposal concluded, "since the institution . . . could be criticized," there was no question but that it was necessary to "seek approval from messieurs [the canon lawyers] of the Sorbonne."[91]

As with this proposal for a royal pawnshop, which was eventually established in 1777,[92] ways were often found to reason around the official usury prohibition. But it would, nonetheless, be a mistake to dismiss the prohibition as irrelevant. As Emma Rothschild has argued, as late as the final decades of the Old Regime "the merchant contemplating lending money in France was surrounded by . . . [theological] distinctions" concerning usury.[93] The fact in itself that it continued to be necessary to engage with such distinctions between what was and was not usury shaped contemporary values and assumptions, such that, even if a particular practice were ultimately deemed legitimate, it was nonetheless likely to generate lingering distrust and distaste. Moreover, as Turgot insightfully suggested in his *Mémoire sur les prêts d'argent,* the disjunction between the formal usury prohibition and the reality that "most commercial activity . . . runs on money borrowed without alienating capital" led to the "debasement [of merchants] in public opinion."[94]

In addition, it bears emphasis that it was not always possible to reason around the usury prohibition. Whether the charging of interest would be deemed usurious depended in no small part on which institution was responsible for making the determination. As Turgot observed, "the merchant courts allow the stipulation of interest without alienation of capital, while the ordinary courts condemn it."[95] And given the rampant jurisdictional conflict that pervaded the Old Regime, merchants could never be sure that they would be subject to the exclusive jurisdiction of merchant courts and thus largely immune to charges of usury. Moreover, while Turgot was clearly correct that the merchant courts were much less likely than the ordinary ones to condemn a practice as usurious, they too exhibited concern about usury.

Such concern was readily apparent, for example, in a 1778 lawsuit between the *associés* of the Tax Farm of Brittany.[96] The Parisian Merchant Court appointed three arbiters, two of whom were financiers. Citing merchant custom, these financiers held that it was not unlawful usury for the tax farm to pay investors 6 percent interest. As argued by Fossard du Mesnil, a director of the General Farm, "There would be no *sociétés* of finance if interest on capital invested was not guaranteed. . . . [N]o individual would loan his money without a profit."[97] In contrast, the third arbiter—Jacques Heury de Froger chevalier seigneur d'Igneaucourt, a lawyer and member of the Parisian bar—insisted that merchant custom must yield to the well-established civil law prohibition of usury: "In vain, the company invokes the usage of interest on capital in commerce, in enterprises, in finance, in instruments, even those sold on the bourse, on which brokers [*agents de change*] take interest. . . . When the parties want this, there is nothing to say: but, when there is a dispute, and this dispute is taken to the courts, where the law decides judgments, the usages invoked by or for the company are of no relevance: they cannot weaken the laws, and these to the contrary destroy usages, which always derive only from abuse . . . : it is even part of a universal jurisprudence that whenever one . . . liquidates some amount of money in such a way that there is involved interest without the alienation of principal, as soon as this is known in court, it will be proscribed by the courts."[98]

While the majority of arbiters found that no usury had been committed, the fact that such a debate could occur within the Parisian Merchant Court at this late date is indicative of the extent to which the usury prohibition continued to exert real force. And because the official penalties for usury remained quite severe—including banishment and condemnation to galley slavery—the risk of conviction, while likely small, was quite worrisome.[99]

The extent to which a usury conviction remained of concern to late-eighteenth-century French merchants is perhaps best revealed by the *cause célèbre* that inspired Turgot to write his *Mémoire* concerning interest.[100] The scandal arose when a number of traders in Angoulême, seeking to earn a quick profit, drafted negotiable notes to one another, which they each endorsed (thereby making themselves liable) in an effort to increase the notes' marketability. Although no value whatsoever had been given in exchange for any of the notes, the members of what Turgot referred to as the "cabal" succeeded in using them to make payments or borrow money. When the notes fell due and were not paid, the payees sued the endorsers — namely, the schemers who had fabricated and endorsed these valueless notes. The conniving endorsers responded by "threatening to . . . denounce [the payees] to the police [*à la justice*] as having demanded usurious interest."[101] Since many of the payees were thus persuaded to reach a settlement — a result which, to Turgot's horror, "served only . . . to multiply the number of claimants" — the threat of a usury conviction apparently exerted real force.[102]

As suggested by this *cause célèbre,* commercial paper was particularly prone to be viewed with suspicion as a potential object of usury. For example, the commercial jurist Toubeau wrote of bills of exchange in the late seventeenth century that "the exchange [*le change*] that is tolerated for the benefit and maintenance of commerce would become the tyrant and executioner of commerce, and would smother rather than nourish it, if one did not curb abuses of exchange, and if one did not prevent usury in exchange, which, being a type of traffic without labor . . . is also a road to idleness, entirely opposed to commerce."[103] As the practices of negotiability and discounting emerged during the late seventeenth and eighteenth centuries, longstanding concerns about the usurious nature of bills of exchange and notes were exacerbated. Thus, a half century after Toubeau cast suspicion on bills of exchange as potential instruments of usury, the anonymous author of a treatise on commercial litigation concluded that interest earned on negotiable notes was, though common practice, a form of usury, whose justification "in these unfortunate times" he left "for discussion among those who lend and the directors of their consciences [*directeurs de leurs consciences*]."[104] Likewise, in the late eighteenth century, the *Encyclopédie méthodique*'s tome on "Commerce" distinguished between "licit" and "illicit" uses of bills of exchange based on whether these were usurious.[105] It was legitimate for a banker or merchant to draw a bill to someone's order when this "trade in money . . . is done with honor and faithfulness."[106] However, the *Encyclopédie* explained, "there is another sort of trade in money that is prohibited by divine and human laws; this is the usurious trade in money, such that without alienating the capital, one lends at high interest."[107] Similarly, it was acceptable for someone to endorse a bill to another "without loss"[108] — namely, in return for the bill's full face value. But to sell the bill for an amount below face value, "at half and three-quarters loss, sometimes more"—in other words, to negotiate it at a discount—was an "illicit trade in paper that is called . . . *agiotage*."[109] Distrust of the usurious nature of bills of exchange was, in sum, a deep-rooted feature of French commercial culture, which the rise of such practices as negotiability and discounting served only to reinforce.

Responding to the Challenges Raised by Negotiability

By examining the seemingly dry, doctrinal disputes over negotiable instruments contained in the arbiters' reports to the Parisian Merchant Court, it is possible to explore the challenges posed by negotiable instruments and the ways that merchants responded to them. This examination reveals that, even though such practices as negotiability and discounting were by the end of the eighteenth century common, well-established features of French commercial life, they continued to generate a great deal of resistance. Right until the Revolution—and likely well beyond—modern commercial practices and doctrinal developments continued to coexist with and confront traditional commercial norms.

NEGOTIABILITY AND DISCOUNTING

Although both merchants and nonmerchants regularly negotiated bills of exchange and notes, they often exhibited a marked discomfort with the basic principles of negotiability. The ongoing concern that negotiability bred anonymity and bad faith is readily apparent, for example, in the case of *Richard v. Desnon*, decided in 1783.[110] Richard, who appears to have held a position in the king's library, asked the Parisian Merchant Court to reconsider a decision condemning him to pay 800 livres for two notes that he had drawn. According to Richard, he had written these notes to the order of Delavallée, with the understanding that Delavallée would have them discounted on his behalf, presumably in exchange for a fee. Delavallée endorsed the notes to Jouan,[111] who was to sell them at a discount and give the money thereby obtained to Delavallée.[112] Jouan was acquainted with a man named Desnon, to whom he offered to sell the notes. Desnon agreed to purchase the notes at a discount of 6 percent, but only on the condition that someone other than Jouan would endorse the notes to him. Since Jouan was known to have serious financial problems, his signature was of little value, and moreover, Desnon did not want to be associated with someone of such ill repute. Accordingly, Desnon said that he would purchase the notes only if his friend, a musician named Noel, signed in Jouan's place, so that it would seem that Desnon had purchased the notes from Noel. Jouan apparently agreed.[113]

Pursuant to this agreement, Noel endorsed the notes and gave them to Desnon, who, in turn, paid Jouan for their discounted value. Jouan, however, gave Delavallée only 144 livres in cash. He gave Delavallée the remainder in notes which he drew and which he then failed to pay when they fell due. Delavallée, in turn, gave both the cash and the notes to Richard.[114] When the two notes originally drawn by Richard fell due and Desnon demanded payment, Richard refused. Desnon then sued Richard, Delavallée, and Noel for payment, and the court held the defendants jointly liable. In requesting that the court reconsider its judgment, Richard argued that, even though he had subscribed the notes, he should not have to pay Desnon, their holder, because he had received in exchange only 144 livres in cash and the notes drawn by Jouan, which were never paid.

The arbiter reporting on Richard's request for reconsideration concluded that the court must affirm the judgment against him, because the holder of a negotiable instrument is always entitled to payment, provided that he gave value for the instrument and took it in good faith. According to the arbiter, Desnon, the holder, clearly gave value: "[Desnon] furnished value of some kind, he is the holder of the notes, and although this value, except for 144 livres in cash, did not make its way to M. Richard, who subscribed the notes, . . . M. Richard is nonetheless obligated to pay them."[115] In addition, Desnon claimed to have purchased the notes in good faith, stating that he had agreed to purchase the notes only "after having gathered information about M. Richard" and having thereby determined that the notes were fully enforceable.[116] Relying on these basic principles of negotiability, the arbiter decided that Richard was obligated to pay Desnon the value of the notes.

But while the arbiter knew that the doctrine of negotiability necessitated a decision for Desnon, he was not entirely comfortable with this result. Requiring Richard to pay Desnon, he suggested, would reward bad faith, rather than good. Should the court really find in Desnon's favor, given his questionable dealings with Noel and Jouan? As the arbiter noted, "everything points to the shadiness of the negotiation arranged by M. Desnon, which brought Noel in, while it was with Jouan that he really dealt."[117] Furthermore, to find in Desnon's favor was essentially to ignore the plight of Richard, who received only a small fraction of the value of the notes he subscribed, and would require Richard to undertake a new lawsuit against "those who abused his confidence."[118] Accordingly, a judgment for Desnon, though clearly correct under basic principles of negotiability, seemed to represent the triumph of bad faith over good.

The arbiter also appears to have been concerned by the specter of anonymity—by the fact that, once Richard endorsed the notes and gave them to

Delavallée, they escaped his control. Richard had drawn the notes to Delavallée's order on the understanding that Delavallée himself would serve as a broker. He had no expectation that the notes would pass through so many hands, including those of a person (Jouan) whose signature never even appeared on the notes. Pitying Richard's predicament, the arbiter berated Desnon for failing to deal directly with Richard: "He [Desnon] told us that he had inquired about M. Richard by speaking to people at the king's library, but if he had spoken with M. Richard, he would have known that M. Richard entered these two notes into commerce only in order to profit by selling them at a discount, and he would have dealt directly with him."[119] In the arbiter's view, it was deeply disturbing that Richard could so easily lose control over the notes once he entered them into the stream of commerce—that the needs and desires of people who did not all know one another could so easily overwhelm individual plans and expectations.

In an effort to uphold the principle of negotiability, while at the same time recognizing the injustice of Richard's loss, the arbiter suggested that the judge and consuls grant him a delay of one year in which to pay the debt: "Given the shadiness that is perceivable in the negotiation undertaken by M. Desnon and the fact that M. Richard effectively received only 144 livres and two notes from Jouan . . . which were not paid, we believe we must propose to you that you accord him a delay of one year."[120] But while this resolution assuaged suffering in this particular case, it failed to address the underlying dangers of bad faith and anonymity to which negotiability lent itself.

Moreover, negotiability and the associated practice of discounting raised fears not only of bad faith and anonymity but also of usury. Such anxieties about usury were at times couched in the language of *lésion*—a doctrine that, as we have seen, was applied far more broadly in eighteenth-century France than scholars have assumed. Just as merchant court arbiters revised the price term in sales contracts, so too, in deciding disputes concerning bills of exchange, they willingly imposed their own discount rate on the grounds that an unlawful *lésion* had occurred. Indeed, unlike the just price of a particular item of merchandise, which could be quite difficult to determine, the value of a negotiable instrument appeared on its face. Accordingly, the practice of discounting instruments, which was explicitly designed to procure the seller less than face value, might seem to be particularly susceptible to charges of *lésion.*

Anxiety about usury clearly lurks behind the arbiter's report in *Boullan v. Michel,* a case heard in 1785, in which the arbiter concluded that a bill of exchange had been sold at too great a discount.[121] Joseph Boullan, a Parisian *bourgeois,* possessed a bill of exchange for 700 livres, drawn to his order. Desperate for cash, Boullan entrusted the bill to Michel, an *ancien* of the tapestry guild, with the understanding that Michel would either purchase it himself or negotiate it to another. Somehow a decision was made that Michel would use the bill of exchange to purchase merchandise, which he would sell, in order to give the proceeds to Boullan.[122] With Boullan's written authorization to sell "the most advantageously that could be done,"[123] Michel sold the merchandise for approximately 327 livres. Deducting 25 livres as his fee, Michel then gave Boullan 302 livres.

Boullan promptly filed suit in the Parisian Merchant Court, arguing that he had not received fair value for the bill of exchange. While admitting that the bill of exchange had been sold "at a very low price [*à vil prix*]," Michel claimed that Boullan was responsible because he "had showed too much eagerness."[124] According to Michel, he had notified Boullan of the price prior to the sale, and Boullan had consented to it because he "claimed to be pressed for money."[125] Without addressing Michel's assertion that Boullan had consented to the price, the arbiter concluded that it was unjustly low — so low, in other words, that the issue of consent was irrelevant. "To lose three-sevenths," he explained, "is too much."[126] There had been, in other words, a *lésion* of the value of the bill, since it was sold for less than half the just price. Accordingly, the arbiter recommended that the court order Michel to pay 100 livres as an indemnity. Why he chose this particular sum for the indemnity is not clear. Presumably, however, one factor in his decision was that Boullan would thereby receive a total of 402 livres. Unlike the 302 livres that Boullan had previously received, this amount was more than half the just price — the bill's face value of 700 livres — and thus cured the *lésion*.

BLANK ENDORSEMENTS

Blank endorsements greatly facilitated the ability of Old Regime merchants and nonmerchants alike to negotiate bills of exchange and notes at a discount. Like the principle of negotiability itself and other subsidiary practices that facilitated the extension of credit, the blank endorsement was widely employed and came to be recognized as legitimate over the course of the eighteenth century. But legitimacy was not immediate, as many feared that the blank endorsement, while making it easier to obtain credit, also promoted anonymity, bad faith, and usury.

The Commercial Ordinance of 1673 established four requirements for negotiating a bill of exchange: the endorser's signature, the date of the endorsement, the name of the endorsee, and a statement of the value that the endorsee gave to the endorser in return for the bill.[127] As commentators on the ordinance suggested, these requirements were intended, in large part, to prevent blank endorsement, which was considered an abuse.[128] Blank endorsement occurred when the endorser signed his name on the back of the bill without complying with the three other requirements for negotiation. Pursuant to the ordinance, bills of exchange negotiated in blank would remain the property of the endorser, such that, if he defaulted, they could be seized by his creditors.[129]

The advantage of the blank endorsement was that it greatly facilitated discounting. The holder of a bill who hoped to receive payment before it fell due could entrust it to a broker, who would then sell it at a discount. Since the holder had no way of knowing whom the broker would find to purchase the bill, when the broker would find this person, or the exact amount and form of payment that the broker would negotiate, the holder signed only his name. But while blank endorsements thus facilitated discounting, they also promoted market anonymity by greatly increasing the number of people to whom a negotiable instrument might be negotiated. The holder of a bill who endorsed it in blank and entrusted it to a broker to have it discounted was not limited to seeking potential purchasers among his acquaintances. This meant that he had a better chance of selling the instrument at a good price, but it also meant that he was likely to know less about the potential purchasers. Likewise, the potential purchaser was not likely to know very much about the seller or about previous endorsers of the instrument. Any of these unknown individuals might be on the brink of financial collapse and his cosigners would be none the wiser.

Those who traded in negotiable instruments took every precaution to avoid the dangers of anonymity, seeking to gain as much information as possible about all who endorsed an instrument. According to one arbiter, it was impossible to negotiate an instrument without being known and recognized as having good credit: "To buy money when one lacks it [by selling an instrument], it is necessary that one be known and accredited in the market, or that a friend, motivated by trust and personal affection, supplies with his capital the credit that you have still not had the time to merit."[130] In reality, however, as a growing number of negotiable instruments began to circulate, many of them endorsed in blank, it became impractical for people to take only those instruments signed by those whom they knew and trusted. Indeed, even when information was sought, it was not always available.

Consider, for example, what happened to a Parisian stonecutter named Mouquin, who was considering whether to accept two bills of exchange as payment.[131] The bills had been drawn in Besançon and their beneficiary had negotiated them to Martin, a jewelry maker. Martin endorsed the bills in blank and then used them to purchase goods from Mouquin's agent, a Parisian haberdasher named Barrié. Before accepting the bills as payment, Barrié gave Mouquin a few days to ask his contacts whether they thought the various people obligated on the bill were creditworthy. According to the arbiter appointed to resolve the resulting lawsuit between Mouquin and Barrié, it was unclear whether Mouquin undertook a sufficiently extensive investigation and what, if any, information he received. But ultimately, for whatever reason, Barrié accepted the bills as payment. Approximately five months before the bills were to fall due, however, Mouquin received a letter "by which he was informed that no one in Besançon knows M. Rouvillac, the drawer of these two bills of exchange."[132] In the end, it had simply proven too difficult or costly for Mouquin to gain accurate information in Paris about a man from Besançon, of whom he had never heard.

Instruments negotiated through blank endorsements were not only particularly subject to the dangers posed by anonymity but also especially likely to encourage bad faith. A negotiable instrument that had been endorsed in blank could easily fall into the hands of someone of unknown or dubious credit, who failed to give proper value in exchange for it. Even more worrisome, it might come into the possession of a thief, who either stole it from the holder or appropriated it once it had been misplaced. This malfeasant could then fill in the blank to his own order. The instrument itself would appear no different than if a broker had sold it at a discount to a buyer who had then filled in his own name. Alternatively, the thief might be the broker himself who, entrusted with an instrument that had been endorsed in blank, could not resist the temptation to make out the order to his own name. This is exactly the sort of broker encountered by several unfortunate merchants in the case of *Amiot v. Rimbault.*[133]

The case arose when LeBon, a Parisian jewelry merchant, and LaPierre, a Parisian art dealer, decided to entrust two negotiable instruments endorsed in blank to Gauvain, who promised to negotiate them on their behalf. According to Gauvain, he knew a paper merchant, named Rimbault, who offered "to have them discounted."[134] Gauvain, however, was Rimbault's debtor. As a result, Gauvain, LeBon, and LaPierre all feared that Rimbault would appropriate these instruments for himself "by means of the blank endorsements that were on the back."[135] For this reason, they decided to conceal Gauvain's involvement by having LeBon's neighbor, a man named Amiot, deliver the instruments to Rimbault. Upon receiving the instruments, Rimbault told Amiot that he would negotiate them by the end of the day and that he would give him the proceeds that evening. Yet, exactly as feared, Rimbault decided to keep the instruments, filling them out to his own order.

Perhaps most disturbing of all was the possibility that, by means of blank endorsements, negotiable instruments might be fraudulently manufactured from whole cloth. According to Desbois Dumont, she was the victim of precisely such a scheme.[136] Dumont was the defendant in a lawsuit brought by Clair, who argued that he was the holder of three bills of exchange drafted to his order by a woman named Varin. According to Clair, Dumont was liable as a drawee who had signed her acceptance to pay. Dumont, in turn, insisted that nothing could be further from the truth.

According to Dumont, she and a surgeon by the name of Cottereau had lived together for three years and were, as the arbiter euphemistically observed, "friends with one another."[137] At the end of this period, Cottereau decided to leave and offered to sell Dumont their furniture for 1,625 livres. Dumont agreed, paying Cottereau, in part, with *mandats* or orders—namely, nonnegotiable letters directing an agent to make payment. Critically, Dumont signed these *mandats* in blank—that is, without identifying the person entitled to receive payment. According to Dumont, when her agent ceased making payments on the *mandats*, Cottereau "through bad faith . . . managed to make bills of exchange from my blank endorsement [*ma signature en blanc*]."[138] Looking for an "illicit way" to be paid what Dumont still owed him, he then used Varin—yet another young woman apparently under his sway—to negotiate the fake bills to the poor dupe, Clair.[139] The money that Varin obtained then presumably entered directly into Cottereau's pocket. Fortunately, for Dumont's sake, however, the arbiter discovered Cottereau's fraud. Observing that "good faith and the truth must be the foundation" of bills of exchange, the arbiter insisted to the judge and consuls that "from the moment that you perceive in them the least bit of fraud, you [must] declare them null."[140] Accordingly, he concluded, the three bills of exchange should be declared null and void, and Clair's suit against Dumont should be dismissed—though Clair was, of course, free to file suit against Cottereau.

A more subtle form of theft facilitated by blank endorsements was that perpetrated by the merchant who acquired the negotiable instrument through fair means but then became insolvent. During the ten-day period before a merchant went bankrupt, he was no longer permitted to sell his property, to entrust it to a confidant, or to give it away.[141] The purpose of this preference law was to ensure that the bankrupt's property, including all negotiable instruments, would be fairly distributed among his creditors. If the bankrupt owned an instrument that had been endorsed in blank, however, he could avoid the ten-day rule by filling in the blank to a friend's order, such that the instrument would appear to belong to the friend. Upon receiving payment on the instrument, the friend would then give the money to the bankrupt. Alternatively, the bankrupt might endorse the instrument to one of his creditors, thereby giving this creditor more than his fair share of the bankrupt's remaining possessions. In either case, the bankrupt would falsely date the endorsement to a period before the ten days preceding his bankruptcy, so that the endorsement would be respected.

That the Commercial Ordinance of 1673 prohibited blank endorsements in itself indicates that the practice must have been fairly well established, since otherwise there would have been no interest in preventing it. In the early years of the ordinance's enactment, however, the Parisian Merchant Court seems to have made a genuine effort to enforce the prohibition. Take, for example, the case of *Favin v. Stollay* decided in 1678.[142] Vincent Favin, a Parisian merchant, endorsed a bill of exchange to Benjamin Saichaze, who then endorsed it in blank to the widow Stollay in Hamburg. When the drawee failed to pay the bill, Stollay sued Favin as one of the bill's endorsers. Favin countersued, arguing not only that he was not responsible for paying the bill but that it actually belonged to him. Because Saichaze had endorsed the bill in blank, claimed Favin, it never became Stollay's property, and instead, pursuant to the ordinance, remained Saichaze's. According to Favin, however, the fact that Saichaze had never paid Favin for the bill meant that it actually belonged to Favin. Relying on the ordinance, the court adopted Favin's argument—despite evidence offered by Stollay that she had paid Saichaze for the bill and that the requirement to make the bill to her order was therefore merely a formality.[143]

A century later, attitudes toward blank endorsements had changed significantly. As one commentator observed in 1767, "Bills of exchange are negotiated on all exchanges by means of the owner's blank endorsement, . . . even in France, where the law proscribed blank endorsements."[144] In line with this shift in attitudes, arbiters appointed by the Parisian Merchant Court regularly examined disputes in which bills of exchange had been negotiated through blank endorsements without concluding that these endorsements failed to transfer a property interest in the bills.[145] Thus, for example, in the case of *Laurens v. Ginisty,* decided in 1769, the arbiter held that the failure to date an endorsement—and thus to observe the rule against blank endorsements—did not negate the holder's right to payment, as long as it could be shown that "value was furnished before the time limit prescribed for cases of insolvency."[146] Indeed, he observed, the formal rule against blank endorsement "is observed by us only when there is a suspicion of connivance"—namely, when there was some concrete reason to conclude that the blank endorsement had been used as a means of violating bankruptcy preference law.

Nonetheless, even though blank endorsements were accepted as legitimate, they continued to raise lingering concerns. Thus, for example, in a lawsuit filed in 1767, the arbiter recommended that the court enforce payment of two notes, which had been endorsed in blank—not by the original maker but by a subsequent endorser.[147] In so holding, however, the arbiter expressed great concern. The provisions of the Commercial Ordinance of 1673 prohibiting blank endorsements were designed, he explained, to "preserve for creditors the instruments found in the hands of a bankrupt [*banqueroutier*], in the period close to his insolvency, by preventing him from transferring them by means of sham or backdated endorsements."[148] Accordingly, he observed, "it is dangerous to depart from the terms of the ordinance in order to deem valid the endorsements on the back of notes; this is to deprive you, messieurs, of the surest means of discovering sham or backdated endorsements."[149] But while there was reason to suspect that the notes at issue in this case may in fact have been falsely dated for illicit purposes, this could not be proven. Moreover, the arbiter determined that the maker of the notes, Rouillon, had drafted them to the order of Sannegond, in such a way as to suggest falsely that they were in payment of a debt that he owed Sannegond. In reality, however, Rouillon and Sannegond had engaged in this transaction as part of a complex scheme secretly to provide money to a third party. Since there was no clear evidence that preference law had been violated, and since Rouillon and Sannegond had acted deceptively, the arbiter concluded that they ought to be held liable on the notes. This, however, would mean recognizing the property interest of those who had obtained the notes by means of blank endorsements—a conclusion that the arbiter presented as inevitable, but highly undesirable.

ACCOMMODATION PAPER

Another practice associated with the rise of negotiability and thus deemed suspect was the use of accommodation paper. An accommodation bill or note is an instrument that a person signs, thereby incurring liability, solely for the purpose of accommodating the instrument's holder. The accommodation party, as the signer is called, receives no payment for signing and, though liable on the instrument, is not expected to pay it when it falls due. The idea is simply that, by signing, the accommodation party becomes a surety, thereby making it easier for the holder to negotiate the instrument.

For example, when a business association established in August 1777 to undertake mining and ironworks in Burgundy attempted to raise capital, it sought the assistance of an acquaintance—a lawyer named Renard, who practiced before the *Parlement* of Paris.[150] In particular, the association asked Renard "to endorse notes totaling 132,000 livres that it wished to place on the market."[151] With Renard's signature, the association succeeded in negotiating the notes. Ultimately, however, when the notes fell due, the association failed to pay, and "Renard was sued for payment as an endorser . . . [and] he was obliged to pay."[152]

Though accommodation parties served to make the extension of credit *more* secure, accommodation paper—however widely employed—remained of doubtful legitimacy in eighteenth-century France. Distrust of accommodation paper is evident, for example, in the arbiters' reports regarding *Vadaux v. Pleyard.* This complicated dispute concerned ten notes which Garand, a jeweler, had subscribed to the order of Vadaux, an engraver. When Garand died, Vadaux sued his widow and her new husband, Pleyard, claiming that Garand owed him money for engravings he had done. The Pleyards replied that the value of the ten notes should be deducted from the amount Vadaux claimed, because Garand had written these notes to Vadaux's order as payment for Vadaux's work. According to Vadaux, however, the notes were simply accommodation paper, which he had endorsed so that they could be more easily discounted on behalf of Garand, who needed money. Because he signed as an accommodation party, Vadaux claimed he never received any payment on the notes, and the Pleyards must not be permitted to deduct the value of the notes from their debt to him.

While as discussed in a previous chapter, the various arbiters reporting on this case based their recommendations largely on guild loyalties, much can be gleaned from their reports about contemporary attitudes to accommodation paper. For example, after observing that "M. Vadaux has admitted before the judges that . . . [the notes] were drawn only for the purpose of making money available to M. Garand by helping improve his credit," the arbiters who decided for the Pleyards claimed that "accommodation paper [*billets de plaisir*]" is "that which the honor of commerce repudiates."[153] Even more damaging to Vadaux's credibility, they continued, and thus "prejudicial to his claims," was his admission that "he is in the habit of employing this means with several merchants."[154] Thus, even if Vadaux was to be believed that the notes were accommodation paper (for which he therefore received no payment), he had no right to recover.

To the extent that bills of exchange and notes are viewed as instruments of credit, accommodation paper would seem to be highly desirable, since it increases the likelihood that the holder will be paid. This was not, however, the perspective of the arbiters deciding *Vadaux v. Pleyard.* Although they did not make explicit why they viewed accommodation paper as dishonorable, their concern seems to have been that it was fraudulent or in bad faith: "[Vadaux] did not give value for these notes, even though it appears that he did, . . . he discounted them by means of his endorsement, . . . he immediately returned the cash he received to M. Garand."[155] Because the notes were drawn to Vadaux's order, it falsely appeared that Vadaux had received them as part of a sales transaction—as payment, in other words, for engravings that he had done. To the arbiter, it was therefore clear that accommodation paper entailed deceitfulness and that, for this reason, it reeked of bad faith.[156] Moreover, as James Steven Rogers has suggested in his analysis of eighteenth-century England, contemporaries widely associated the deceit implicit in accommodation paper—namely, the fact that it was drafted so as to appear that it arose from a sales transaction—with the possibility of widespread financial collapse. In the view of many, it was only "real paper"—instruments that had been created as part of actual sales transactions, rather than falsely made to appear as such—that was likely to be paid when due. Accommodation paper, in contrast, was thought to lack a solid commercial foundation and thus to be prone to being dishonored. Since accommodation paper appeared no different from real paper, and thus was likely to be negotiated extensively, there was widespread fear—probably shared by the arbiters deciding *Vadaux v. Pleyard*—that the use of such paper would lead to a chain of lawsuits and insolvencies.[157]

FORGED SIGNATURES

As trade in negotiable instruments expanded over the course of the eighteenth century, so too did the fear of forged signatures. Merchant courts were generally deemed to lack the power to verify signatures and otherwise assess the validity of evidence—as these were matters that touched on fraud and were thus criminal in nature.[158] Nonetheless, according to one commercial jurist, those "ordinary judges who claim that the judge and consuls lack jurisdiction to verify writings" were mistaken, and it was essential that the merchant courts be recognized to possess such jurisdiction.[159] Not surprisingly, the Parisian Merchant Court fully agreed, and thus regularly undertook to verify signatures. Numerous arbiters' reports address the question whether a signature that appears on a negotiable instrument is indeed that of the person whose name was signed. Those assigned to serve as arbiters in such cases were often members of the *Bureau académique d'écriture,* founded by Louis XVI. After evaluating other documents that were indisputably signed by the person whose signature was in question, these experts offered their opinion regarding the signature's authenticity.[160]

Forgery presented the prospect of anonymity and bad faith run amok and, in so doing, raised some terribly difficult questions. To what extent were the drawee and the endorsers of a negotiable instrument responsible for recognizing and ensuring the validity of one another's signatures? If a signature on a bill of exchange or note turned out to be false, could the debtor who had obligated himself without knowledge of this fact thereby escape his obligation? And if the debtor paid someone claiming falsely to own the instrument, only to discover subsequently that another person proved to be the rightful holder, would he have to pay a second time? Given the growing number of instruments in circulation, a certain number of false signatures was inevitable. If endorsers could escape liability simply by pointing to the invalidity of a signature on the back of an instrument, credit would quickly dry up because few would be willing to assume the risk of a forged signature. At the same time, holding the endorser liable despite the fact that a signature had been forged was equivalent to accepting the inevitability of forgery. It was a surrender to bad faith.

Over the course of the eighteenth century, jurisprudence decided in favor of credit over traditional conceptions of virtue.[161] As long as negotiable instruments continued to be extensively traded, it would be impossible for people to recognize all the signatures they contained. For this reason, people who traded in negotiable instruments were deemed to assume the risk of mistaken or forged identities that such trade necessarily entailed. For example, the person who accepted an instrument as payment and later discovered that those liable on it were not who they seemed could not thereby withdraw his acceptance. Likewise, those liable on an instrument were not expected to ensure the validity of the holder's claim, and thus were not required to pay the true holder after having mistakenly paid a false claimant.

Although the rule requiring assumption of risk was fairly well established by the end of the century, there was much discomfort with the fact that it seemed to accept as inevitable (and thus in a sense to legitimate) bad-faith behavior. Such discomfort is exemplified by *Charlot v. Duvigier,* a dispute that arose over a bill of exchange which St. Aulair agreed to accept and pay on behalf of his creditor, a *chevalier* by the name of Charlot.[162] The bill was drawn to Charlot's order by a drawer who appeared to be named Perrein. In fact, however, Charlot had drawn the bill himself and signed it Perrein, the name of his valet, in order to make it appear that Perrein was the drawer. Presumably, Charlot made use of Perrein's name in this manner because it was technically impossible to draw a bill to one's own order. As the arbiter noted, Charlot and St. Aulair "made use of this signature [i.e., Perrein's] only in order to cloak the bill of exchange with all its formalities."[163]

After creating the bill, Charlot gave a copy of it, which had already been accepted by St. Aulair, to a musketeer named Duvigier as partial payment on a debt. When Duvigier realized that Charlot had forged Perrein's signature, he filed suit, arguing that Charlot had acted in bad faith by forging Perrein's signature and demanding that Charlot pay him the value of the bill. The arbiter decided for Charlot, holding that Duvigier saw the signatures on the bill and that it was his responsibility, before allowing Charlot to sign it over to him, to determine who Perrein and St. Aulair were and if he wanted to deal with them: "It was for him to inquire about them before taking possession of the aforementioned bill of exchange."[164]

By deciding for Charlot, the arbiter affirmed the increasingly recognized principle that those who purchase negotiable instruments assume the risk of forged signatures and mistaken identities. Nonetheless, the arbiter expressed some hesitation. While Duvigier's refusal to take responsibility for his failure to investigate was less than honorable, Charlot had after all committed forgery: "According to my limited understanding, messieurs, good faith does not closely follow these two characters."[165] A decision in favor of Charlot was consistent with the evolving doctrine, but it was anything but easy.

Overcoming Resistance to Negotiability

DOCTRINAL CONFUSION

Legal thinking, which self-consciously seeks to ground itself in precedent or tradition, is in certain senses a fundamentally conservative enterprise. This was particularly true of the early-modern world, where change was traditionally viewed with suspicion and the king's goal in promoting justice was long understood to be preservation of the established order.[166] Accordingly, the eighteenth-century Parisian Merchant Court was discomfited by the rise of negotiability and associated practices, in part because it did not know how these meshed with the established legal tradition. The attempt to harmonize new practices with old legal doctrine, in short, gave rise to much confusion among those who employed negotiable instruments, as well as the arbiters who heard their disputes.

For example, in *Mogier v. Ollier,* decided around 1762, the arbiter was evidently confused about the basic principle of negotiability—namely, the right of the good-faith purchaser for value to hold everyone who signed the instrument liable.[167] The dispute arose when the defendant, the widow Ollier, drew a note for 269 livres to the order of a woman named Morillierre. Morillierre, in turn, endorsed the note to the plaintiff, Mogier. When the note fell due and Ollier failed to pay, Mogier sued her, demanding payment. In her defense, Ollier claimed that she did not have to pay Mogier because she had never received payment from the original payee, Morillierre. Mogier, in turn, argued that he had paid Morillierre for the note and that at the time he did so he did not know that she had failed to pay Ollier—and thus did not know that Ollier had a legitimate defense against enforcement. Mogier, in other words, insisted that he was a good-faith holder who had purchased the note for value and that, for this reason, he was entitled to payment.

Had the arbiter understood the basic principle of negotiability, he would have recognized that all he had to do was establish the truth of Mogier's claim that he was a good-faith holder for value. Instead, however, he took the testimony of Morillierre, seeking to determine whether Ollier, the maker of the note, really had a legitimate defense against Morillierre, the original payee. Morillierre denied Ollier's charge that she had not paid for the note, claiming that she had given Ollier both cash and other negotiable instruments in exchange for it.

After much hesitation, the arbiter ultimately found for Mogier, but the grounds on which he did so are far from clear. At one moment, he appears to have recognized the irrelevance of whether the maker has a defense against the original payee, querying, "But can these [arguments] prevent payment of a note to the person who is its holder?"[168] At the next moment, however, he observed that Ollier and her witnesses "cannot deny that Morillierre furnished value," and he therefore concluded that Morillierre had paid Ollier for the note.[169] Thus, it is not apparent whether the arbiter found for Mogier on the grounds of negotiability or on those of contract. Too uncertain to rest his decision on the basis of negotiability alone, the arbiter also relied on Ollier's failure to establish her contract defense—namely, that she had not received payment from Morillierre.

It was not only the arbiters but also the parties who came before them who sometimes failed to comprehend the basic elements of negotiability. Take, for example, *Duplessis v. Gobert,* a dispute that arose when Foulon Duplessis agreed to sell some merchandise to the *chevalier* de Jennessierre in return for two bills of exchange worth 800 livres each.[170] Upon receiving the bills of exchange, Duplessis made a written promise, or *reconnaissance,* to deliver to de Jennessierre 406 livres worth of tapestries or cloth within the month. De Jennessierre endorsed this *reconnaissance* and gave it to Gobert, a master tailor, presumably as a means of paying a debt.

In a lawsuit brought by Duplessis against Gobert, charging Gobert with failing to deliver goods he had purchased, Gobert claimed that his delivery obligation was excused by Duplessis' failure to honor his own obligation to deliver 406 livres worth of tapestries or cloth to de Jennessierre. According to Gobert, he had acquired the right to delivery of these tapestries or cloth because de Jennessierre had endorsed the *reconnaissance* and given it to him. As the arbiter rightly concluded, however, the *reconnaissance* of which Gobert was the "holder" was not "a negotiable instrument."[171] Thus, Duplessis' obligation, as recorded in the *reconnaissance,* was to de Jennessierre alone, and de Jennessierre's right could not be transferred to Gobert through de Jennessierre's mere signature. That Gobert could raise this defense, however—and that he and de Jennessierre actually attempted to negotiate what was in essence a receipt—suggests that the doctrine and practice of negotiability remained a confusing innovation to some.

Even jurists of the time—at least those of the traditional civil-law sort—

sometimes exhibited a marked lack of clarity regarding basic principles of negotiability. Consider, for example, the work of Pothier, who was perhaps the age's most noted and influential jurist. In his 1773 treatise on negotiable instruments, entitled *Traité du contrat de change,* Pothier applied the traditional — and by then long outdated — model of the bill of exchange as contract of exchange.[172] Both the drawer and drawee, he argued, as well as the drawer and giver of value, are linked by contractual bonds. Moreover, he claimed, the relationship between the endorser and endorsee is also one of contract — a contract that happens to be accompanied by an assignment.[173] In so asserting, Pothier characterized the defining act of negotiability — namely, negotiation of the instrument via the endorsement — as nothing more than an assignment of contract. As a result, he failed to acknowledge the key feature of negotiability, which is that a good-faith endorsee can have rights greater than those of the endorser.

Pothier's depiction of the bill of exchange as a series of contracts derived from his attempt to make negotiable instruments consistent with longstanding legal doctrine — in particular, with traditional civil-law rules of contract. In addition, however, by characterizing the bill of exchange as a contract of exchange, he was able to distinguish it from a loan and thereby eschew any hint of usury. Whereas the contract of exchange benefits both parties, each of whom needs a certain amount of money in a different place and time from the other, a loan benefits only one of the parties. Accordingly, he concluded, profit earned on the buying and selling of bills of exchange does not consist of risk-free interest on loans, which would be usury, but is simply the result of unpredictable fluctuations in exchange rates.[174]

That Pothier, the man whose treatises provided the foundation — and, indeed, much of the text — of the Napoleonic Civil Code, could refuse as late as 1773 to accept negotiability on its own terms highlights the resistance it had to overcome. Pothier's effort to force negotiability into traditional contract-law doctrine was, however, doomed. It was simply a stopgap. To conceptualize the negotiable instrument as a contract required too great a strain in reasoning to withstand the test of time. Another approach to making negotiability palatable had to be found.

REINFORCING MORALITY AND COMMUNITY

Rather than attempting to make it consistent with longstanding legal doctrine, another approach to negotiability was instead to emphasize its compatibility with the values underlying traditional commercial culture. Thus, a major theme running throughout the arbiters' reports is the centrality of good faith in the negotiation of commercial paper. While good faith is the foundation of all commerce, these reports suggest, it is particularly important in cases involving negotiable instruments. As one arbiter noted of bills of exchange, "with these instruments [*titres*] (the most sacred that we have) good faith and truth must be the foundation."[175]

Arbiters attempted in various ways to reinforce ideals of morality and community against the dangers posed by negotiable instruments. Consider, for example, the arbiter's recommended decision in *Renault v. Poullain.*[176] Renault, a merchant from Beauvais, had for many years deposited money with Poullain, a Parisian merchant, paying for items that he purchased for his business with bills of exchange that he drew on Poullain. Although Poullain claimed that he had accepted and paid all the bills drawn on him, Renault decided at one point, for reasons that are not clear, that he wanted Poullain to give him the discharged bills as evidence of payment. When Poullain refused, Renault sued him.

The arbiter observed that, as a matter of law, Poullain should be permitted to keep the discharged bills proving that payment had been made. It was Poullain, as the drawee, who was the bill's primary debtor[177] and thus the most deserving of the protection afforded by possession of the (supposedly) discharged bills. Nonetheless, the arbiter acknowledged, it was reasonable for Renault to worry that, after drawing the bills and entering them into the stream of commerce, he lost all control over them, and that he might ultimately be held liable should Poullain not pay and prove incapable of doing so. While acknowledging the reasonableness of Renault's concerns, however, the arbiter also berated him for his failure to have faith in his colleague of many years. Since Renault had deposited so much money with Poullain, Renault more than anyone had reason to trust Poullain's word: "Renault . . . should be fully reassured because he knew better than anyone else M. Poullain's character and manner of thinking."[178] Ultimately, the arbiter sought to establish by fiat the friendship and trust that was so clearly lacking between the parties. According to the arbiter, Poullain must be allowed to keep the discharged bills, but the court should also order him to do everything possible to help Renault should Renault be sued by a holder claiming not to have been paid.

Mouquin v. Barrié, considered above, is another case in which an arbiter attempted to restore the trust and friendship jeopardized by negotiability. Barrié, a Parisian haberdasher, purchased goods from Mouquin, a Parisian stonecutter, over the course of several years and occasionally served as Mouquin's sales agent. The good relationship that they had developed was suddenly destroyed, however, by the uncertainty surrounding two bills of exchange that Barrié, serving as Mouquin's agent, accepted as payment for goods sold. After the decision was made to accept the bills, Mouquin received a letter from a colleague in Besançon informing him that no one there had ever heard of the bills' drawer, a man named Rouvillac, who claimed to be from Besançon. Fearful that he would never be paid, Mouquin sued Barrié, demanding full payment of the two bills.

The arbiter concluded that, because the bills had not yet fallen due—and thus might in fact be paid—Mouquin's claim had to be dismissed. Furthermore, it was Mouquin's responsibility, before accepting the bills as payment, to determine whether they were sound by investigating the people who had signed them: "It is difficult to excuse him, he was given the time to make inquiries."[179] Nonetheless, the arbiter was sympathetic to Mouquin's plight. Mouquin had, for whatever reason, failed to gain sufficient information about the bills' drawer. Since Barrié had played a role in accepting these potentially shoddy bills as payment, the arbiter concluded that the fairest solution would be for the two men to divide equally any loss that might arise: "I would have hoped that . . . in case these instruments are not paid the parties would agree each to bear half this loss."[180] The arbiter's hope was that by convincing the parties to split any resulting loss he would be able to restore the friendship and trust that had been destroyed by negotiability and the anonymity it promoted. As he explained, "I made the ultimate effort to get them to reconcile."[181] Unlike the arbiter in *Renault v. Poullain,* however, this arbiter was unwilling to command friendship where it no longer existed—perhaps, though we will never know, because he believed that, in the long run, it was the establishment of fixed, ex ante rules governing rights and liabilities that would best enable merchants to predict the consequences of their actions and thus to form stable, long-lasting relationships. As a result, when he failed to convince Barrié and Mouquin to share in any loss, he simply recommended that the court dismiss Mouquin's claim.

DEVELOPING THE IDEAL OF COMMERCE AS A SOCIAL GOOD

While in individual cases arbiters attempted to address the dangers posed by negotiability by reinforcing traditional commercial values of morality and community, this was but a piecemeal solution. Negotiable instruments were commercially viable precisely because they afforded the good-faith holder who had not been paid a cause of action against all prior endorsers. This protection afforded the holder, however, necessarily entailed a concomitant risk for the endorsers. The endorser of an instrument could not know or control who would later come into possession of it. Yet, if these later possessors (and the drawee) failed to pay the instrument, he might have to pay in their stead. And any effort to reduce the risk for those who had endorsed the instrument necessarily limited the recourse of the good-faith holder and thereby hindered the circulation of credit. As in *Renault v. Poullain* and *Barrié v. Mouquin,* it was possible retroactively to order individuals who had signed a particular instrument to divide the burden of risk in a particular manner. But this was no global solution to the problems posed by negotiability.

The global solution ultimately adopted by eighteenth-century merchants was, first, to acknowledge the inevitability of a trade-off between protecting the endorsers of negotiable instruments against risk and facilitating the circulation of credit; and second, to embrace credit as the more important end. The challenges posed by negotiability to traditional commercial culture were not to be resisted, but rather accepted as the inevitable, if unfortunate, side effects of otherwise highly desirable practices. Merchants were able to accept the dangers of negotiability in this manner because they adopted a new conception of commerce as the credit-fueled, private exchange engaged in by individuals across the social order, which in aggregate inured to the benefit of society as a whole. They adopted, in other words, precisely that view of commerce to which they were also led, as we have seen, by reason of status interests and jurisdictional conflict.

Implicit in the new view of commerce that merchants brought to bear in analyzing disputes concerning negotiable instruments was a new understanding of the function of the merchant court. Rather than repressing inappropriate conduct in each instance where it appeared—an approach that characterized the court's decisions in run-of-the-mill contract and partnership disputes—arbiters sought to engage in a utility calculus. The relevant question, in other words, was no longer whether a particular individual's conduct was bad, but instead whether the costs of that conduct in aggregate—undertaken by individuals across society—were sufficiently great to outweigh counterbalancing considerations. Moreover, costs were now to be measured not in traditional moralistic terms—that is, in view of any jeopardy posed to communal harmony and virtue—but instead, quite explicitly in terms of economic effects, and in particular effects on the availability of credit. This is not to suggest that, as an objective matter, negotiability was necessarily a net economic gain. Indeed, modern-day commercial law scholars generally agree that the question of who is best suited to bear the risk of property loss is a complex question, requiring extensive (and often inconclusive) cost-benefit analysis.[182] The point is, instead, that eighteenth-century merchants began themselves to undertake such an analysis and that they came to conclude that the benefits of negotiability clearly outweighed the costs.

Arbiters and parties appearing before the Parisian Merchant Court repeatedly justified discomfiting practices associated with negotiability by means of such a utility calculus. Consider, for example, an expert opinion written on behalf of the defendants in *Prevôt v. Delarue et Compagnie*[183]—a case that raised the question of who should be liable when a note was stolen and payment mistakenly made to the thief. The lawsuit arose when Hardouin drew a note to the order of Prevôt. Someone who assumed the name Marillan stole the note from Prevôt and sent it to a group of Parisian bankers, Delarue et compagnie, asking them to present it to Hardouin for payment when it fell due. Although the bankers did not know Marillan, they did as he requested and Hardouin paid. When Prevôt discovered the theft, he sued both the bankers and Hardouin, demanding to be reimbursed for the note's value.

A group of merchant-notables engaged to write a *consultation* in defense of the bankers argued that the bankers had already paid the note and should not have to pay a second time. Holding the bankers liable, they claimed, would "disturb commerce, rendering the negotiation of bills of exchange and negotiable notes absolutely impracticable."[184] In particular, such a holding would establish the precedent that bankers who are delegated by a negotiable instrument's holder to obtain its payment must verify the validity of every endorsement, since only by so doing could they establish that they had not acted negligently. The problem with such a precedent, explained the authors, is that instruments drawn for a substantial amount are often endorsed up to fifty or sixty times before falling due, requiring the attachment of additional pieces of paper in order to provide space for all the signatures. In such cases, verification of every signature would be costly beyond imagination. Indeed, the authors suggested: "Verification will often be impossible. How many bills of exchange are received in commerce which carry endorsements made by persons whom one does not know, of whom one has not even heard people speak? How does one verify them? Where does one find documents with which to compare the signatures of people of whom one knows neither their status [*qualité*], nor their residence, nor perhaps their existence?"[185] Given these difficulties, a verification rule would hinder the negotiation of commercial paper and thereby destroy the circulation of credit, which was the lifeblood of commerce: "Must one then seek documents for comparison from all the countries of the universe in order to verify all these signatures? One might just as well renounce forever all negotiation by bills and notes, and as a result commerce, which cannot subsist without this assistance, as establish that it is permissible to require the verification of all the signatures constituting endorsements."[186]

Critically, the authors of the *consultation* were fully aware that rejecting a verification requirement entailed accepting the inevitability that individuals would continue to steal instruments and forge signatures. In some cases, the victims of such theft would have acted negligently and would therefore be rightfully made to bear the loss, but in many others, the nonnegligent would suffer. And while the rightful holder might sue the thief, the chances of finding the thief—and one capable of paying—were minimal. Nonetheless, the authors concluded, the loss suffered by the rightful, nonnegligent holder whose negotiable instrument has been stolen was "a misfortune that falls on an individual, whose sacrifice is necessary [*dû*] for the public good, which would suffer infinitely more, if in order to prevent this particular accident, a usage was established that would be so prejudicial to it."[187] In their view, in short, the cost-benefit analysis was clear.

Blank endorsements could likewise be justified by means of a utility calculus aimed at promoting the social good of commerce and credit. In 1774, the judge and consuls of the Merchant Court of Chartres sent a letter to the Parisian Merchant Court, inquiring whether pursuant to the Commercial Ordinance of 1673 the endorser's signature and a date were sufficient to transfer the property interest in a negotiable note, or whether instead such a note remained the property of the endorser.[188] The Parisian judge and consuls replied that the provision of the ordinance establishing four requirements for endorsing a bill of exchange—and thereby transferring a property interest in it—had been interpreted to apply to notes as well. Thus, technically, the mere signing and dating of a note did not constitute an endorsement. However, this technicality had no bearing, they suggested, on the real question raised by their colleagues' inquiry, which was to determine which methods and techniques were of "indispensable necessity in the daily practice [*l'usage journalier*] of commerce."[189] And here, there was every indication that the blank endorsement of notes was vital to commercial well-being: "Although this usage of negotiating by means of mere blank endorsements seems to be abrogated by Arts. 23 and 25 of title 5 of the Ordinance of 1673, nonetheless, it has always continued to be practiced and is practiced daily, the ease and freedom necessary for negotiation having rendered it indispensable, such that Arts. 23 and 25 of the ordinance are not applicable according to jurisprudential usage except in cases of fraud and sham acquisition."[190] Merchants, in short, regularly ignored the language of the ordinance, and such disregard for the letter of the law was legitimated by social utility—by the crucial role that blank endorsements played in facilitating the negotiation of commercial paper, and thus the circulation of credit.

Merchants employed a similar valorization of the social utility of commerce and credit to justify abandoning the rule of different places. This longstanding rule provided that a bill of exchange had to be drawn in a different place from the one where it was to be paid.[191] If a bill were drawn in and on the same place, there would be no currency exchange—and this in turn would highlight the bill's potential to facilitate a risk-free and thus usurious loan. Accordingly, the rule of different places was necessary to preserve the fiction that bills of exchange did not function to extend credit at interest.

By the seventeenth century, the rule of different places appears to have been so well established, and thus so self-evident, that it did not occur to the drafters of the Commercial Ordinance of 1673 to identify it as a technical requirement for bill formation.[192] But the rise of negotiability and the related practice of discounting undermined the rule by enabling people easily to purchase instruments from others in the same place by means of mere endorsement. Thus, while in the late seventeenth century Jacques Savary, the author of the Commercial Ordinance of 1673, wrote that the breaking of the rule was an " 'abuse very prejudicial to the public,' "[193] attitudes had clearly changed by the end of the following century. As suggested by the 1773 case of *Guerin v. LaConté*, the key to this change in attitude was a new conception of the social utility of credit as the driving force of commercial exchange.[194]

The plaintiff in *Guerin* was the holder of a bill of exchange for 450 livres drawn on and accepted by the defendant, which the defendant then refused to pay when it fell due. According to the defendant, he was not obligated on the bill because it was drawn in Paris, to be paid in Paris, and thus violated the rule of different places. The arbiter agreed that the bill violated the rule and that, pursuant to traditional doctrine, it should therefore be deemed at most a nonnegotiable acknowledgment of debt: "The truth is . . . that often such instruments have been regarded as not being bills of exchange, . . . [and] they have been reduced to having value only as an acknowledgment of some debt or other."[195] After setting forth this traditional approach, however, the arbiter rejected it, arguing that the court should treat the writing as the parties intended — namely, as a bill of exchange.

According to the arbiter, the rule of different places served only to hinder the extension of credit. To the extent that faithless debtors seeking to escape liability could point to violations of the rule as grounds for invalidating a bill of exchange, the rule had the perverse effect of making it more difficult and costly for the rightful creditor to collect: "What disorder in commerce . . . if all transactions of this type could long after their completion be submitted to such an examination, and if all those who contract such bills of exchange were permitted to avoid having to pay them when they fall due by means of similar objections."[196] Moreover, the arbiter asserted, the majority of bills of exchange currently in circulation violated the rule of different places. As a result, the possibility that strict enforcement of the rule would undermine the interests of creditors and discourage further negotiation of bills of exchange was not slim, but significant: "It is clear that of all those [bills of exchange] that are used in commerce, the majority are thus conceived, and without this source, commerce as well as finance would have difficulty finding the necessary capital; without this manner of operating, merchants would lack many occasions for negotiating usefully."[197] Accordingly, the social utility of readily available credit necessitated the violation of the long-established rule of different places.

Yet another practice associated with negotiability—that of drawees accepting a bill of exchange for payment and thereafter reneging—came to be legitimated by the embrace of commerce and credit as social goods, whose promotion rightly merited the sacrifice of other dearly held values. Before the rise of negotiability, the drawer of a bill of exchange typically drew the instrument either on a debtor or on an agent to whom he then sent money (called a *provision*) with which to pay. Accordingly, the holder could be relatively certain that when he asked the drawee to accept the instrument for payment, the drawee would do so. But with the rise of negotiability and the emergence of modern banking, it became increasingly easy for drawers to draw bills of exchange on merchants and bankers who were neither their debtors nor their agents.[198] In such cases, the drawee might refuse to pay the holder of the bill, as long as he had not accepted a *provision* from the drawer with which to do so. As a result, negotiability undermined holders' confidence that when they presented a bill to the drawee, the drawee would pay.

For this reason, drawers or endorsers who wished to increase the chances of negotiating a bill often sent a copy of it to the drawee long before it fell due, asking the drawee to sign his acceptance. By accepting the bill, the drawee made himself its primary debtor, regardless of whether the drawer sent him a *provision* before its due date.[199] At times, however, drawees would promise to accept the bill and then in the last minute refuse to do so. Or they would sign their acceptance and then, before returning the bill to the holder, change their minds and cross it out.[200] How was the merchant court to address such apparent bad faith?

In reporting on the case of *Brentani Cunaroli v. Grand,* the arbiter weighed such bad-faith behavior against the costs of prohibiting it and decided that the availability of credit, and thus commercial well-being, necessitated accepting some bad faith as inevitable.[201] Brentani and Cunaroli, Viennese bankers, sued Grand, a Parisian banker, for payment of five bills of exchange that they had drawn on him. The dispute arose when, on August 30, 1783, the plaintiffs wrote the defendant a letter explaining that they had drawn these bills on him and asking him to sign his acceptance on a copy of the bill that they were enclosing.[202] In addition, they requested that the defendant pay the bills when they fell due with money drawn from an account that Véguelin, Scherb, and Company had with him. On September 11, the defendant wrote back as follows: "I took note of the bills you drew on me . . . in order to accept them."[203] A few days later, the defendant discovered that Véguelin, Scherb, and Company had become insolvent. On September 18, he wrote the plaintiffs, notifying them of this discovery and of his decision not to accept the bills for payment. Given this insolvency, the defendant explained, he would accept the bills only if the plaintiffs sent him a written authorization to pay them with money from their account, as well as a *provision* before the bills fell due. Arguing that the defendant had broken his promise to accept the bills, the plaintiffs sued for payment.

The arbiter concluded that the court should find for the defendant, even though he had failed to honor his word, and thus acted in bad faith. Many bills of exchange, the arbiter reasoned, were drawn on people who did not owe the drawer money. In many such cases, it could be assumed that the drawee had promised just before or after the bill was drawn that he would accept and pay it. Circumstances, however, often changed between the time the drawee made this promise and the time the bill fell due. Drawees would thus be willing to accept bills for payment only if they had the freedom to renege on their promises, and even to cross out an acceptance that they had signed. For this reason, the defendant's statement that he "took note of the bills . . . in order to accept them" must be recognized as "terms of convention and simple formula which clearly indicate the current disposition of the writer to accept or pay a bill of exchange, but which do not impose on him the necessity to do so; . . . this disposition can change from one moment to the next, and . . . it is irrevocably fixed only by acceptance; . . . these are only words whose effect is always subordinated to the integrity of the drawer's account, or of that of the person for whom one draws, and sometimes even to circumstances and opinion, as when the payer believes he has something to fear; because one scarcely ever accepts on behalf of a man about whom one has doubts, and even less for a man who is insolvent, even though one has promised to do so!"[204] To interpret the defendant's words as a binding obligation to accept and pay the bills would permit drawees to suffer such serious economic harm that the extension of credit through bills of exchange would be seriously endangered. Accordingly, the social utility of commerce demanded that, at least on occasion, merchants be permitted to break their promises with impunity.

The Red-Ink Case and the Triumph of Commerce

A desperate young woman prostitutes herself for a bill of exchange drawn in blood, and the merchant court orders the man who corrupted her virtue to marry her. This, in short, is Bedos' Red-Ink Case — the story of how a bill of exchange corrupted (sexual) commerce, and of how the merchant court managed to restore virtue.

By linking the once virtuous woman's downfall to a bill of exchange, Bedos suggested that such bills were responsible for a profound crisis in virtue. In particular, the bill of exchange threatened to commercialize the most sacred of human relationships; and, if it could commercialize the sexual union, then no relationship was beyond its reach. Virtue, however, was easily saved by the merchant court, which simply enforced the values of traditional commercial culture through its longstanding, equitable approach. As recounted by Bedos, the merchant court judge employed the sentimental legal reasoning so characteristic of traditional commercial jurisprudence. By questioning the parties, the judge unfolded a narrative of virtue succumbing to vice—of a chaste woman driven by poverty to sell her body to a lust-ridden man. Given this narrative structure, there was only one outcome that might result in justice, or the triumph of virtue. The man who took the woman's virtue had to restore it, and to this end the judge ordered him to marry her. Swayed by the court's moral force, the parties complied.

In reality, however, as this chapter has described, the Parisian Merchant Court was no longer capable by the end of the eighteenth century of so easily reconciling virtue and commerce. Indeed, in contrast to the Red-Ink Case, most cases concerning negotiable instruments that came before the court did not present such easy choices between virtue and vice. One of the most perplexing features of the rise of negotiability was precisely that protecting the interests of the holder in good faith required accepting the inevitability of—and thus implicitly sanctioning—prior acts of bad faith. As a result, cases involving negotiable instruments did not lend themselves so readily to sentimental legal reasoning. Arbiters in the Parisian Merchant Court were able to reconcile themselves to the bad faith entailed in negotiability only by positing the social good of commerce as an end worthy of sacrificing traditional conceptions of virtue.

It bears emphasis, however, that by thus embracing commerce as a social good, merchants did not reject virtue tout court, but rather sought to reconfigure it. Merchant virtue was traditionally conceived as inhering in the personal relationships that bound together merchant brothers and that ensured that none would promote his own self-interest at the expense of others. But in seeking to reconcile the rise of negotiability with their longstanding pursuit of virtue, eighteenth-century merchants came to view the latter as inhering less in personal loyalty to particular fellow merchants and more in an impersonal commitment to the increasingly anonymous structures and processes of a credit-driven market. This is not, of course, to suggest that the element of the personal simply disappeared from commercial life. The small-scale, relational contract disputes that served as the foundation of traditional merchant court practice and procedure did not change notably over the course of the century. And the court continued to resolve these disputes through its longstanding, virtue-oriented methods for testing moral character and promoting fraternal harmony.[205]

But while longstanding conceptions of virtue did not vanish, they did make way for a new and very different conception in which the well-being of commerce as an abstract process came to replace the well-being of particular, flesh-and-blood merchants.[206] With commerce thus reconceived as the credit-based exchange activities necessary for a society of interdependent persons to survive and thrive, it was possible to accept the notion (so central to the principle of negotiability) that individuals of good faith might have to suffer for the greater good of commerce itself. Crucially, however, what justified such suffering was precisely the fact that commerce as a social function was understood to be key to public welfare and thus a form of virtuous, other-serving *bienfaisance*. Accordingly, much like the contemporary authors of political-economic texts recently studied by John Shovlin,[207] the eighteenth-century merchants responsible for constructing the new commercial and legal practices surrounding negotiability never understood themselves to be embracing the kind of naked self-interest that they had so long eschewed.

Although the merchants associated with the Parisian Merchant Court did not simply abandon virtue, their efforts to legitimate negotiability by appealing to a new conception of commerce as a social good served significantly to transform merchant court practice and procedure. To begin with, this new conception greatly elevated the importance of fixed, universally applicable legal rules. In order for negotiable instruments to serve as a secure and widely available source of credit, it was essential that those who employed them knew their exact rights and liabilities. Most fundamentally, they had to be certain that the holder in good faith would always be entitled to payment. Such legal certainty, however, required that merchant courts consistently apply a set of fixed rules to all cases raising the same legal issue, regardless of how the parties or circumstances differed from case to case. Applying rules in this manner ran counter to the equitable, case-specific approach that traditionally characterized merchant court adjudication and that was a defining feature of sentimental legal reasoning. As concerns disputes over negotiable instruments, sentimental legal reasoning gave way to values of uniformity and predictability, as embodied both in the Commercial Ordinance of 1673—or as many called it, *Le Code marchand*—and in the court's judge-made law.

Codification constrains judicial discretion by requiring judges to apply a set of fixed rules to all cases raising the same legal issue, regardless of factual differences. For precisely this reason, negotiable instruments, whose effectiveness hinged on the application of fixed legal rules, were one of the central topics addressed by the ordinance, or Merchant Code. In contrast, the ordinance was silent regarding matters of contract—namely, the types of transaction that gave rise to disputes most conducive to the merchant court's traditional, equitable approach. And while, as described above, arbiters willingly disregarded provisions of the ordinance that commercial practice had rendered obsolete, their analysis in cases involving negotiable instruments generally (though by no means always) adhered closely to the applicable legal rule—whether drawn from the ordinance or from superseding case law.

In undermining sentimental legal reasoning, the rule-based adjudicatory style so crucial to cases concerning negotiable instruments also undermined the merchant court's self-conception as a voice of the merchant community, whose task it was to implement the values implicit in the common, lived experience of that community. Whereas the merchant court and its arbiters had traditionally relied on past experience and common sense, the rise of negotiability required them to consult the commercial ordinance, as well as a growing number of legal publications addressing the law of negotiable instruments and its distinctive, often nonintuitive rules. Such publications included treatises and manuals that addressed the subject of negotiable instruments comprehensively, as well as the many articles on particular aspects of negotiability that filled the pages of contemporary newspapers.[208] The new focus on clear, predictable rules, in other words, gave rise to specialization.

Given these pressures toward specialization, it is not surprising to discover that parish priests—the embodiment of the court's community-based, nonspecialized adjudicatory style—were seldom selected to serve as arbiters in disputes relating to negotiable instruments.[209] Unfortunately, arbiters in such cases rarely identified their professions. Presumably, many were *négociants* or bankers who were familiar with the rules of negotiability as a result of their commercial endeavors.[210] Others claimed to be lawyers.[211] The most striking shared characteristic of these arbiters, however, was that the merchant court often called on them repeatedly to resolve negotiability-related disputes.[212] While arbiters selected to decide contract disputes might also be called on repeatedly, this was generally because they were leaders of the guild implicated in the dispute, or priests of the parish whose resident was party to the dispute—and thus, in both cases, because of their status within the community. In contrast, in disputes involving negotiable instruments, the arbiters who served repeatedly usually did not bother to identify their professions. They thus seem to have been chosen not because of their status per se, but because of the specialized knowledge that they had acquired in part through repeatedly adjudicating cases involving negotiable instruments.

But while the rise of negotiability and associated practices led to a narrowing in the body of applicable law and in the range of people authorized to apply it, these developments greatly expanded the category of defendants subject to merchant court jurisdiction. Precisely the same forces that led the merchant court in such cases to cease viewing itself as the voice of the merchant community impelled it to seek jurisdiction over defendants who were not considered merchants—including, notably, the many noblemen who continued to eschew overt association with base commercial matters. The expanded nature of merchant court jurisdiction in lawsuits concerning negotiable instruments was already evident in the Commercial Ordinance of 1673, which as noted above, conferred on merchant courts exclusive jurisdiction over disputes concerning bills of exchange "between all persons"—and not just between "*négociants* and merchants."[213] As argued by the jurist Bornier, this provision of the ordinance recognized that negotiable instruments were being employed by nonmerchants in ever growing numbers: "The use of bills of exchange was introduced in the beginning only among merchants, for the convenience of commerce, so that they could transport their money from one place to another. . . . [F]inally, this use extended to other people of different ranks [*condition*] and professions."[214]

As we shall see, the extent of merchant court jurisdiction over nonmerchants, and especially nobles, was a topic of great debate between traditional, university-trained, civil-law jurists of the Old Regime and commercial jurists, many of whom were also merchants.[215] Because the ordinance so clearly expressed an intent that merchant court jurisdiction extend to all people who employed bills of exchange, the focus of this debate tended to be on the ordinance's more ambiguous language concerning exchange notes. Nonetheless, for civil-law jurists like Guyot, who were reluctant to abandon the status of the litigant as a fundamental requirement for merchant court jurisdiction, the ordinance's provision concerning bills of exchange remained deeply troubling. Indeed, Guyot reconciled himself to it only by arguing that, in most cases, at least some of an instrument's endorsers were merchants: "Although today the use [of bills of exchange] has extended to individuals who are not merchants, it is nevertheless a type of commercial negotiation that is done principally through the mediation of merchants."[216]

But despite Guyot's efforts to suggest that negotiable instruments were not undermining the personal basis of merchant court jurisdiction, the reality was that in the years after the ordinance was enacted, the number of people, including noblemen, who used negotiable instruments continued only to increase—thus forcing a reconceptualization of the foundations of merchant court jurisdiction. As merchants began to view negotiable instruments and the credit they facilitated as the lifeblood of a national economy constituted by all society's members, including merchants and nonmerchants alike, so too they came to identify the subject matter of commerce, rather than the person of the merchant, as the basis of merchant court jurisdiction.

For all these reasons, the Red-Ink Case is perhaps better read for the anxieties that it depicts than for the solution that it propounds. Bedos presented the case as evidence that the merchant court could confront and contain the dangers of negotiability through its traditional, equitable, and sentimental adjudicatory style. Indeed, the judge in the Red-Ink Case expressly declined to resolve the case by applying the relevant legal rule. He rejected the plaintiff's argument that the bill of exchange complied with the commercial ordinance on the ground that it did not comply with "the ordinance of modesty."[217] However, it was precisely the dangers that Bedos sought to contain—dangers of anonymity and bad faith—that undermined the feasibility of the court's longstanding equitable approach and encouraged a new emphasis on legal rules.

That the Red-Ink Case captured late eighteenth-century anxieties and aspirations rather than the reality of contemporary jurisprudence is suggested by the way the Parisian Merchant Court resolved its own version of the case in 1773. Like the Red-Ink Case, *Tellier v. Beycheirat* was a dispute over a negotiable instrument, rooted in a story of sexual seduction and the loss of virtue.[218] The case concerned a note for 168 livres that Beycheirat had written to the order of a demoiselle Trouvain, who then endorsed it to Tellier. When the note fell due, Beycheirat refused to pay, and Tellier sued. In his defense, Beycheirat argued that he should not have to pay the note because he had never received value for it from Trouvain. According to Beycheirat, he had employed Trouvain in his wig-making workshop beginning in May 1772. About six months later, Beycheirat claimed, she told him that he was the father of her unborn child, and that, unless he drew this note to her order, she would reveal all to his fiancée. As the arbiter reported, Beycheirat explained: "That he was astonished one day to receive a summons to appear before the Commissioner Desormeaux at the Place Maubert! That as soon as he was there who did he find! Mademoiselle Trouvain! That after a thousand bitter reproaches concerning the state of crisis in which she found herself, *as a result of the illicit commerce that he had had with her,* she forced him in the presence of the commissioner to make out to her a note for 168 livres. Otherwise she was going to enter an objection to his future marriage! That he, Beycheirat, in order to avoid all dispute, and fearing that the relatives of his future wife would be informed, blindly signed the note in question with the phrase, for value received in the form of cash."[219]

By 1773, notes were fully negotiable, and thus Beycheirat's defense that he had not received value from Trouvain was clearly invalid as against Tellier. The person obligated on a negotiable instrument cannot deny payment to a good-faith purchaser for value, who like Tellier, bought the note without ever suspecting that its maker had a defense against enforcement. In addition, as was also true of the instrument in the Red-Ink Case, this note could not be challenged on the grounds that it was improperly drawn. As the arbiter observed, "the note is in good form."[220] Nonetheless, in spite of its evident flaws, the arbiter allowed Beycheirat's defense. Perhaps he did so because he concluded that Beycheirat had signed under duress, but he never developed this position clearly. Likely aware of the irregularity of his decision, the arbiter did not recommend that the court excuse Beycheirat from the entire debt, but instead that it order him to pay Tellier only half the amount of the note. Tellier, he concluded, could sue Trouvain for the other half.

The arbiter permitted Beycheirat's legally impermissible defense because the moral weight of the narrative led him to do so. Without determining the truth of Trouvain's claim that she and Beycheirat were lovers, the arbiter apparently concluded that, either way, Beycheirat had been tricked. He was either the dupe of a blatant lie, or a well-meaning man who, lured by a dangerous seductress, succumbed to temptation. Trouvain, in contrast, was a manipulative whore, who lacking gratitude for Beycheirat's decision to employ her, had the audacity to threaten him and endanger his chances of marrying a respectable woman. In the arbiter's view, it was simply wrong for Beycheirat to have to pay Trouvain, and for this reason he should not be required to do so.

Tellier v. Beycheirat, however, proved to be one of those relatively few cases where the judge and consuls decided to reject the arbiter's recommendation. The official report on the court's decision states clearly that "without regard to [the arbiter's] report the defendant [will be] condemned to the aforementioned sum of 168 livres with interest, on penalty of imprisonment."[221] Unfortunately, as was always the case, this report offered no account of the court's reasoning. The obvious explanation, however, for the court's decision to ignore the arbiter's report was that it did not believe that Beycheirat's mental anguish rose to the level of duress—and that, more importantly, by the time the case was heard in 1773, the principle of negotiability had been firmly established. This meant that, legally speaking, Beycheirat had no defense against paying the note he had made. The law of negotiable instruments, in other words, led the court to reject the kind of moralistic reasoning that the arbiter had employed. Commerce as a social good triumphed over traditional conceptions of virtue.

6

Launching a National Campaign: The Administrative Monarchy and the Demands of le Commerce

*All commercial marketplaces [*places de commerce*] experience the positive influence [of the merchant courts]; they demand their preservation; and there never will be a court that costs the nation less, where justice is meted out with greater speed or the subtleties of chicanery are so little known.*

—Paul Nairac, deputy of the Constituent Assembly, May 27, 1790

The Parisian Merchant Court and its members were not alone among Old Regime merchants in coming to view commerce as the credit-based exchange necessary to sustain the social order, rather than a status function associated with particular corporate entities. In the fall of 1788, merchant courts and chambers of commerce across France united to demand representation of *le commerce* in the newly called Estates General. Drawing on a conception of commerce as that set of exchange relationships enabling society to function and prosper, they argued that it was vital to national well-being that commercial expertise inform government policy. This, in turn, necessitated that representatives of *le commerce*—a vast corporate entity consisting of all who engaged in this key social function—be admitted to the Estates General and given a voice in governing the nation.

How did this happen? How did the sixty-seven merchant courts in existence at the end of the Old Regime,[1] each with its own particular, local interests, come to see themselves as together constituting a unified *corps,* capable of, interested in, and entitled to a role in national governance? And what precisely was this *corps* of *le commerce?* How could it appeal to a new conception of commerce as a function sustaining an interdependent social order—and thus not limited to particular corporate entities—while at the same time presenting itself as a *corps?* The story of how Old Regime merchants were led to join together in 1788 in this meta-*corps* of commerce, and the implications of their choice to do so must be traced back to the late seventeenth century, when the monarchy greatly increased its efforts to administer commerce and thereby augment taxable wealth. It was as an unintended consequence of the monarchy's efforts thus to empower itself that *le commerce* was called into being.

The Monarchy's Program for Administering Commerce

According to Michel Antoine, the late seventeenth and eighteenth centuries witnessed the transformation of the Old Regime monarchy from a judicial to an administrative state.[2] The traditional, judicial conception of sovereignty, enunciated by such theorists as Bodin and Loyseau, was that it functioned to maintain the status quo—a divinely instituted, hierarchical social order—by preventing incursions on the longstanding rights and privileges of the corporate entities constituting that order. Beginning in the late seventeenth century, as the monarchy sought to replace venal officeholders with a growing bureaucracy of salaried officials, this judicial, stasis-oriented conception of sovereignty started to erode. In its place, argued Antoine, there arose a new view that the sovereign's function was to administer the various activities and processes, such as trade, manufacturing, agriculture, finance, and transportation that together sustained the social order. Unlike the judicial state, which sought to preserve the status quo, this new, administrative state was oriented toward change, aiming constantly to improve those activities and processes under its administration.

While Antoine is clearly correct that the Old Regime monarchy became increasingly interventionist, and thus focused on promoting change rather than preserving the status quo, the forms of change that it promoted did not all imply the demise of the traditional corporatist order. The monarchy did seek to develop a centralized bureaucracy of salaried officials, which would be more responsive to royal commands than the entrenched, venal office-holding elite and which, in promoting uniform, national policy, would willingly sidestep traditional patronage relationships and override corporate privileges. But at the same time, as David Bien and others have shown, the monarchy also fostered the development and expansion of the corporatist order, by creating, selling, and reselling numerous venal offices—in no small part as an indirect means of obtaining much-needed credit.[3] Thus, the institutions of privilege, corporatism, and patronage did not simply disappear in the eighteenth century, but instead continued to exist alongside newer practices of equality, individuation, and bureaucratic routine.

Launched during the second half of the seventeenth century, the monarchy's campaign to reform the administration of commerce emerged as part of a broader, mercantilist program for building a commercial empire and embodied the Old Regime's contrasting corporatist and centralizing impulses. Like its rivals, the French monarchy had come to believe that state supremacy hinged first and foremost on the acquisition of economic riches (and particularly precious metals). Such wealth was essential for sustaining the population, for enabling the displays of grandeur that served to reinforce royal claims to absolute power, and perhaps most importantly, for subsidizing the costs of war. Toward this end, the monarchy committed itself to a series of policies aimed at promoting the intersecting goals of protectionism and imperialism. Among these policies were its imposition of high tariffs on imports and its subsidization of domestic (especially luxury) manufacturers and colonial trade.[4]

As part and parcel of these efforts to build a commercial empire, the monarchy pursued three goals aimed at fundamentally restructuring its approach to the administration of commerce: (1) promoting the guild system, (2) developing a uniform body of commercial law, and (3) centralizing the formulation of commercial policy. In promoting the guild system, the monarchy fortified the corporatist foundations of the social order, and thus the relations of patronage and privilege underlying it. In contrast, in developing a uniform commercial law and in centralizing the formulation of commercial policy, it established norms and practices of bureaucratic routine and equality that undermined patronage and privilege. It was from the coexistence of these two very different corporatist and centralizing tendencies—and the institutions and practices associated with each—that the campaign to obtain representation in the Estates General for a meta-*corps* of commerce eventually emerged in the fall of 1788.

PROMOTING THE GUILD SYSTEM

As we have seen, the monarchy launched a very successful program in March 1673 to promote its first goal—namely, ensuring that manufacturing and trade would occur primarily within guilds operating under its control. This goal stemmed, in part, from fiscal concerns. By selling offices in corporate entities like guilds, the monarchy, which regularly defaulted on its loans, was able, in essence, to borrow indirectly at a far better rate than it could do so directly. Would-be masters served as intermediaries, borrowing money to purchase masterships—and thus passing on these funds to the monarchy—at competitive rates. In exchange for this sum, the monarchy agreed to pay the master *gages,* an annual payment calculated as a percentage of the capital invested, and thus, at core, an interest on the loan.[5] In addition to such fiscal considerations, however, the monarchy had reasons of commercial policy for initially promoting the guild structure. Guilds were thought to be essential tools for regulating competition and thereby ensuring that goods would be produced in accordance with the highest quality standards, such that they would be competitive in a growing international market.[6]

The monarchy's initial success in promoting guilds was a development that it would later come to rue. In the second half of the eighteenth century, as the Physiocrats' calls for laissez-faire became increasingly insistent and persuasive and the great commercial success of the Dutch and especially the English increasingly hard to ignore, the monarchy began to doubt the virtues of corporatism.[7] Doubt turned into outright antagonism when in February 1776 Comptroller General Turgot issued an edict outlawing the guilds, as part of a concerted program to liberalize French trade.[8] But by that time, and in no small part through the efforts of the administrative monarchy itself, corporate entities, including the guilds, had become a deeply entrenched feature of the social order. Accordingly, Turgot's edict gave rise to a vocal opposition, not only from the guilds but also from the *Parlement* of Paris, which had come to identify itself as the defender of corporate liberties against the monarchy's despotic program of administrative reform.[9] Noting that its leaders were "themselves members of the principal *corps* included in . . . [Turgot's] proscription,"[10] the Parisian Merchant Court joined its voice to that of the mounting opposition.

Unable to hold firm, the monarchy quickly reversed itself, restoring the guilds six months later in an edict of August 1776.[11] While the number of guilds was greatly reduced, and various changes were implemented to expand guild membership—including, opening most guilds to women and lowering entry fees[12]—the reinstituted guilds remained in place until the Revolution. Lasting even beyond the general abolition of corporate privilege on the night of August 4, 1789, they were outlawed only in the Allarde Law of March 1791.[13] In sum, as a number of historians have recently emphasized, corporatism was far from dead at the end of the Old Regime, and the monarchy itself bore significant responsibility for its continued strength.[14]

DEVELOPING A UNIFORM BODY OF COMMERCIAL LAW

As with its goal of promoting the guild system, the monarchy proved very successful in achieving its second goal—establishing a uniform body of commercial law. In March 1673, in the very same month that the monarchy issued an edict requiring merchants and artisans to join guilds, it enacted a commercial ordinance establishing a uniform body of commercial law for all of France.[15] Henceforth, to the extent that the ordinance addressed a relevant legal issue, merchant courts were required to apply it, rather than to draw from the hodgepodge of sources, including case-specific equitable determinations, on which they had previously relied.[16]

Given the timing of its issuance, as well as the fact that it was largely the work of Jacques Savary[17] — a successful merchant who had begun his career as a master in the Parisian haberdashers' guild[18] — the ordinance, not surprisingly, undertook extensive regulation of the structure and operation of the guilds.[19] Nonetheless, the conceptual underpinnings of the ordinance were quite distinct from those of the March 1673 edict regarding guilds. Whereas the edict sought to promote guild formation, and by implication, a corporatist social order, the commercial ordinance focused primarily on individual merchants. Its goal was to ensure that all merchants across France would be equally subject to the same rules and regulations in the conduct of their professional lives. Toward this end, it sought to regulate guilds, as one among a number of institutions and practices — including business associations and negotiable instruments — with which individual merchants engaged.

To achieve a truly uniform system of commercial law, however, uniform legal doctrine was insufficient. A uniform system of enforcement was also required. Accordingly, the commercial ordinance declared that all merchant courts across the country were to have the same structure, follow the same procedure, and apply the same law. The ordinance embraced a two-pronged method for standardizing the merchant courts. First, all legislation that the monarchy had ever issued regarding any merchant court was henceforth to be applied to all others. Second, the Parisian Merchant Court was to serve as a model. In the words of the ordinance, "We declare common to all merchant courts, the edict establishing a merchant court in our good city of Paris . . . and all other edicts and declarations concerning merchant courts registered in our *parlements*."[20]

To declare retrospectively that the approximately forty merchant courts established in France between the mid-sixteenth and late-seventeenth centuries[21] were henceforth to be alike was, it would seem, wishful thinking. These courts were formed at different times, under different pieces of legislation, and had since developed their own distinctive customs and practices. Moreover, to handle the growing amount of commercial litigation that followed from the expansion of commerce, the monarchy increased the number of merchant courts by over 50 percent over the course of the eighteenth century.[22] Remarkably, however, the monarchy's demand that all merchant courts become alike came to be implemented, as merchants increasingly embraced the idea and value of uniformity.

The Parisian Merchant Court and its sister courts throughout France enthusiastically pursued the task of establishing a uniform body of commercial law and procedure, with the Parisian Merchant Court serving as a model for all the others. Merchant courts from across the country regularly sent letters to their Parisian counterpart inquiring about the procedural rules and substantive law that it applied, to which the Parisian judges appear to have responded promptly and at length. The provincial merchant courts inquired about a great range of topics, such as whether the Parisian Merchant Court would approve a change in their judicial attire;[23] whether the Parisian Merchant Court was obligated to pay various kinds of taxes, and if so, whether it collected these from the litigants or from the lawyers who pled before it;[24] and whether the Parisian Merchant Court believed that certain provisions of the commercial ordinance concerning bills of exchange should be interpreted as applying to promissory notes.[25]

Over time, as provincial merchant courts grew accustomed to modeling themselves on their Parisian counterpart and to contacting it when they were unsure of the law, they and the Parisian Merchant Court came to recognize common interests. Accordingly, they began to exchange letters seeking to garner and provide much-needed support on behalf of these interests, which included, perhaps most importantly, interests in status disputes and jurisdictional conflicts. In this way the monarchy achieved much success in its goal of developing a uniform commercial law, but this success came at the unanticipated price of creating a powerful lobbying group that was willing and ready to make demands from and against the monarchy that had (unintentionally) called it into being.

Consider, for example, the series of letters exchanged between the merchant courts of Auxerre and Paris in April 1774 regarding a status dispute. On April 16, the judge and consuls of Auxerre wrote to their "dear colleagues [*chers confrères*]" in Paris, explaining that "it is only too just that we communicate to one another everything that might concern innovation in all the [merchant] courts of the kingdom."[26] The "innovation" which so concerned the judge and consuls of Auxerre was the demand of a former merchant court judge, who had acquired noble status by purchasing the office of *secrétaire du roi*,[27] to precede all non-noble members of the court in public ceremonies. Having begun their letter by referring to the importance of sharing information relevant to their common interests, the judge and consuls also ended on this note, observing that "this pretension is something that might become common to all the [merchant] courts of the kingdom, and . . . we must not tolerate any incursion on our rights."[28]

Agreeing that the relative rank of non-noble merchants was an important shared interest, the Parisian judge and consuls wrote a lengthy response, setting forth the procedure followed by their own court. According to the judge and consuls, several members of the court [*compagnie*] had acquired noble status, as *secrétaires du roi* or otherwise, but rank within the court was based exclusively on seniority—namely, the date on which an individual was first elected judge or consul. In their view, the Merchant Court of Auxerre was obligated to adopt this same, seniority-based procedure for determining rank because the monarchy had directed that the Merchant Court of Paris serve as a model for other merchant courts: "Almost all merchant courts, and yours in particular, were established on the model of ours and to follow our procedures, laws, usages; one can therefore say that the usage of Paris concerning questions of precedence and that serves as law there, can and must be applied concerning the same questions that arise in your court."[29]

Moreover, the Parisian Merchant Court continued, the monarchy had expressly decided the question of the relative precedence of noble and non-noble merchants in two separate edicts concerning the merchant courts of Lille and Valenciennes.[30] These edicts were applicable to the Merchant Court of Auxerre, as to all others, because the Commercial Ordinance of 1673 provided that all merchant courts were to follow the same law and procedure: "It is a principle of law as applied in the merchant courts [*droit consulaire*] that a matter decided in one merchant court applies to all others, because all must have the same procedures and because article 1 of title 12 of the Ordinance of 1673 so provides."[31]

Having offered their "*confrères*" in Auxerre as much legal ammunition as they could muster, the Parisian judge and consuls concluded by observing that, if the troublesome *secrétaire du roi* failed to desist in his unjust demands and went so far as to seek "a decision from some higher authority [*une décision supérieure*]," they wished to be included in any proceedings that followed.[32] The Parisian Merchant Court, in other words, was willing and eager not only to advise its fellow merchant court on commonalities in their law and procedure, but also to join it in actively defending and lobbying for their shared interests.

CENTRALIZING THE FORMULATION OF COMMERCIAL POLICY

It was to the *Bureau du Commerce*, created by the monarchy to pursue its third goal—centralizing the formulation of commercial policy—that merchant courts usually turned to advocate their common interests. Created by a decree of June 29, 1700, the *Bureau* was an advisory body without any decision-making authority, from which the king and his ministers regularly sought assistance in developing commercial policy. Initially entitled the *Conseil de Commerce,* until its name was changed in 1722,[33] the *Bureau* was reconfigured several times over the course of the century, but it remained in existence in substantially the same form until it was abolished by the Constituent Assembly on September 27, 1791.[34] It consisted of a few high-level ministers, including the comptroller general, several members of the King's Council (*conseillers d'État*), six intendants for commerce, and thirteen[35] merchant deputies from cities throughout France.[36]

The merchant deputies were elected annually by the guilds and *négociants* of the cities they represented.[37] In the case of Paris, which was granted two merchant deputies, responsibility for the election did not fall directly on the city's guilds and *négociants,* but instead on the Parisian Merchant Court[38] — a procedure that highlighted and reinforced the court's role as the voice of Paris's merchant community. Not surprisingly, given the important role played by the Parisian Merchant Court in the election of deputies to the *Bureau du Commerce,* one of the two deputies chosen was often a current or former judge or consul.[39]

To assist the *Bureau* and its merchant deputies, the monarchy also created a network of chambers of commerce in commercial cities throughout France.[40] These were intended to serve as a link between the centralizing state and the population it administered, facilitating the ability of the *Bureau* to obtain vital information from local merchant communities and to implement commercial policy.[41] Because judges of the regional merchant courts frequently served on the local chamber of commerce, the institutional boundary between merchant court and chamber of commerce was often quite porous. In Paris, however, the extraordinary power wielded by the city's merchant court was such that no chamber of commerce was ever established prior to the Revolution.[42]

Through such mechanisms as the merchant deputies and chambers of commerce, the monarchy sought to ensure access to merchants across the country and the information they possessed. But as David Kammerling Smith has shown, the establishment of the *Bureau* had the inadvertent consequence of involving merchants, manufacturers, and artisans not only in providing information but also in forming policy. As the *Bureau* developed routine administrative procedures for handling the matters that came before it — procedures both for transmitting materials among its own personnel in Paris and for seeking information from and providing directions to the intendants and inspectors of manufacturing in the provinces — an organized, predictable administrative system emerged. The predictability of this system enabled individuals and groups outside traditional patronage networks to observe the operations of government and bring pressure to bear directly on policymakers. As a result, manufacturers, guilds, masters, and non-guild artisans began to petition the *Bureau,* seeking royal intervention in their local affairs—often with the assistance of the merchant deputies whom they had elected.[43]

Like these other merchants and merchant *corps* discussed by Kammerling Smith, merchant courts also discovered that the establishment of the *Bureau du Commerce* provided a centralized administrative forum to which they could turn to advocate their interests. And since the merchant deputies who reviewed their petitions regularly sided with them,[44] the *Bureau,* they soon realized, was quite a favorable forum. Individual merchant courts petitioned the *Bureau* to request numerous kinds of assistance, which—since the *Bureau* itself lacked decision-making authority—ultimately required action by the King's Council. For example, merchant courts petitioned the *Bureau* to request that the King's Council quash an unfavorable jurisdictional ruling entered by the local *Parlement;*[45] that it authorize the imposition by the court of a tax on local merchants;[46] that it permit the current judge and consuls to extend their term since there were not enough Catholic merchants available to serve;[47] and that, as described below, it find in the court's favor in status disputes and authorize new forms of jurisdiction. As merchant courts came to view commercial law and courts as uniform, they often cited in their petitions to the *Bureau* favorable rulings and decrees concerning other merchant courts—thus contributing further to the development of legal uniformity as norm and practice.

Sometime around midcentury, the practice of merchant courts corresponding with one another regarding common interests came to intersect with that of individual merchant courts petitioning the *Bureau du Commerce.* As a result, merchant courts began jointly petitioning the *Bureau* on behalf of common interests. The first major lobbying campaign of this kind, discussed below, appears to have arisen in 1759, in response to a royal declaration of that year that sought to limit the geographic scope of merchant court jurisdiction. Extant records suggest that no other such extensive, coordinated lobbying campaign occurred again until the calling of the Estates General in 1788.

But while campaigns of this kind seem to have been rare, merchant courts continued throughout the eighteenth century to correspond with one another and to petition the *Bureau du Commerce,* individually or in small numbers, regarding matters of common interest. The common interests that thus galvanized merchant courts into action concerned either status disputes or jurisdictional conflicts—interests that were traditionally matters of privilege. Accordingly, the merchant courts that advocated these common interests did not view themselves as in any way challenging the corporatist foundations of the social order. Nonetheless, through this process of mutual correspondence, individual petitioning, and ultimately joint petitioning, merchant courts gradually came to see themselves as constituting a unified entity that transcended traditional corporate and geographic divides. In advocating their common interests, they largely cast aside a corporatist idiom of privilege, staking their claims instead on a functionalist discourse of commerce that emphasized social utility rather than corporate prerogatives. Significantly, however, the corporatist idiom was never fully abandoned. The persistence of this idiom—itself a consequence of the monarchy's great, and ultimately much regretted, success in promoting corporatism—would prove critical when the Estates General was called in 1788, and the question of how to represent the social order before the king was raised for a final, decisive time.

Status Disputes

Status disputes were a pervasive feature of Old Regime society, from which merchant courts were in no way immune. In the traditional Old Regime conception of the Great Chain of Being, the social order consisted of numerous corporate entities arranged in hierarchical order, with the king—as God's representative on earth—at the pinnacle. It was the king's function to maintain order by overseeing the entire structure and, like a good father, recognizing and rewarding merit. Those, such as the nobility, who occupied the upper tiers of the social order were deemed to have merited the privileges accorded them by virtue of the service they provided the king, historically in battle.

Even as the structure of state and society evolved in the late seventeenth and eighteenth centuries—leading many noblemen to serve in judicial or administrative capacities, rather than military ones, and giving rise to a growing bureaucracy that included many in the Third Estate—it remained common belief that it was in the king's gaze that merit was established and, through the according of privilege, rewarded.[48] Indeed, it was precisely because the king oversaw the social order in this fashion that he (and he alone) was empowered formally to establish corporate entities by providing charter provisions, and most importantly, selling offices. In return for the sums expended to purchase these offices, buyers received a variety of privileges, which served as formal recognition and recompense for meritorious service. These included the right to collect certain fees, tax exemptions, and the authority to precede those of lower status in communal assemblies. Because the corporate entities constituting the social order were deemed to be hierarchically ordered—and because various kinds of privilege were associated with this hierarchy—corporate entities in the Old Regime regularly vied with one another to achieve supremacy. Moreover, since it was in the eyes of the king that this hierarchy was ultimately established, corporate entities sought to resolve these status disputes by appealing for judgment to the king and his council.

Like other corporate entities, merchant courts were involved in numerous conflicts regarding their relative status in the social hierarchy. Individually (and on occasion with one or two others), they petitioned the *Bureau du Commerce* and its generally sympathetic merchant deputies to seek rulings from the King's Council that would find in their favor in these status disputes, and thereby definitively establish their superior merit. These status disputes—of which there were two main types—typically developed in the context of the processionals that accompanied such communal events as meetings of the municipal government or church ceremonies, where it was necessary to determine the order in which representatives of the various corporate entities participating would march. The first type of status dispute arose between merchant courts and other nearby entities—usually, the local solicitors' *corps,* the notaries' *corps,* and ordinary, nonmerchant courts.[49] The second type of dispute arose between those merchants and merchant court judges who had received noble status, frequently through purchase of an office, and those who had not.

While it is tempting for the modern-day reader to dismiss such status disputes as petty affairs, it would be a mistake to do so. Ceremonial display was one of the primary ways that power was legitimated, contested, and reaffirmed within the highly status-conscious society of the Old Regime.[50] Thus, for those contemporaries who participated in processionals, the question of precedence (namely, the order in which people would march) was serious business—so serious, in fact, that it merited extensive and costly litigation. Accordingly, the status disputes in which the merchant courts engaged often wended their way through several jurisdictions over the course of many years before finally making it to the *Bureau du Commerce* and then the King's Council for ultimate resolution.

Such disputes were of their essence corporatist in nature since they concerned the question of the relative merit of corporate entities and how to establish this in the eyes of the king. Thus, to some extent, resolution of these disputes necessarily turned on the question of how to define the corporate entities whose status was in question. This was no easy matter, since the Old Regime—a corporatist social order, which took the group rather than the individual as the constitutive unit of society—was replete with different types of corporate entities. *Corps* in the formal, legal sense were officially established by the monarchy through the selling of offices and the provision of corporate charters. Once established, such a *corps* possessed a single legal personality that enabled it to pursue legal action or undertake debt in its own name, thereby binding all current and future members.

Guilds were the institutions that were the most commonly recognized as constituting *corps* in this formal sense.[51] But there were other such *corps*, including the many different entities that exercised judicial and/or administrative powers within the Old Regime, such as municipal governments. As explained by the *Dictionnaire universel de commerce*, the term "*corps*" designates "the several persons who compose or form a jurisdiction or association [*compagnie*]."[52] While the term "*corps*" was used to identify many kinds of judicial and administrative entities, it was usually not employed in relation to royal courts of general jurisdiction, and in particular the *parlements*. The notion of a *corps* implied a degree of subservience to royal power and was thus inconsistent with the *parlements*' increasingly autonomous self-conception. Moreover, because guilds were widely viewed as the prototype of the *corps*, royal courts likely sought to eschew a term that was associated with individuals of relatively low standing.[53] Nonetheless, since royal courts were formally constituted by the monarchy, consisted of venal officeholders, disciplined their members, and undertook unified action, they operated as formally constituted *corps* in all but name.

In addition to those institutions that were formally established as *corps* (regardless of whether they embraced the term), there were a number of entities in the Old Regime that were not so constituted but which nonetheless had various corporate characteristics. Thus, for example, as David Bell has shown, the Parisian barristers' association staunchly resisted key aspects of formal corporate status—including the practice of venal office-holding and the bestowal of royal letters patent establishing it as an entity. At the same time, much like a *corps*, the association was tremendously successful in disciplining its members and thus in pursuing unified action.[54]

The merchant courts were among those institutions that came within this second, more informal category of corporate entity. On the one hand, merchant courts functioned in many respects like formally established royal *corps* —a fact that is hardly surprising, given that the judge and consuls were themselves guild leaders and therefore intimately familiar with the corporatist system. Thus, merchant courts were established through royal legislation, and they possessed one of the defining features of corporate identity: a single legal personality. On the other hand, unlike members of official royal *corps*, such as guild masters, a merchant court's judge and consuls did not actually own offices purchased from the crown and were instead elected for brief terms by the town's merchant community.

The elusive nature of the merchant courts' corporate identity led to some confusion when they were involved in status disputes about precisely whose honor was being challenged—that of the judge and consuls alone, or that of the entire merchant community that had elected them. At times, merchant courts petitioning the *Bureau du Commerce* regarding status disputes focused on defending the merit (and the attendant privileges) of the judge and consuls. They argued that, since the merchant courts had been officially established as royal courts, the judge and consuls possessed the corporate status of royal judges, which was superior to that of their adversaries. This strategy, however, was risky, since merchant court judges did not, in fact, own their offices, and thus it was far from clear that they possessed formal corporate status as royal judges. Moreover, as the case of the Parisian Merchant Court suggests, merchant courts had come to identify themselves as the voice of the merchant community, taking great pride in their summary procedure and commitment to dispute resolution, which they took to be representative of a distinctive sort of merchant virtue. The temptation was thus enormous for merchant courts to deploy the status disputes in which they became involved as a means of defending the beleaguered honor of merchants in general, and not just that of the judge and consuls. To do so, many merchant courts abandoned a formal conception of themselves as royally established *corps* and embraced instead a more informal and implicitly democratic corporate identity, which took the merchant community—defined by its common participation in commerce—rather than the king, as its constitutive force.

The strategy of appealing to a formal conception of the merchant courts' corporate identity, as well as this strategy's limits, is evident in the approximately decade-long status dispute that took place between the Merchant Court of Angers and the town's *corps* of notaries between 1726 and 1736.[55] The dispute began when the municipal government of Angers convened a town assembly on February 19, 1726, for the purpose of electing those who would serve as officers in the upcoming government. Among those invited to attend this assembly as electors were two notaries and two merchant court judges. Since the order of the processional that would convene this assembly was based on status, the question arose whether the notaries or the judges were of higher rank and thus entitled to precedence.

According to the Merchant Court of Angers, the two merchant court judges were entitled to precede the notaries—and thus to stand directly behind the royal judges of the local court of general jurisdiction (the *sénéchaussée et présidial*)—because they possessed the status of royal judges: "Messieurs the notaries are misplaced in disputing the prerogative of the merchant court judges, given the antiquity of the merchant court's establishment and the dignity granted to royal judges, as expressly stated in the royal letters patent [establishing them in office]."[56] In the view of the merchant court, those who were now and had previously served as merchant court judges together constituted a *corps*—or as they expressed it, "*compagnie*"—of royal judges, which by virtue of its meritorious service to the king was entitled to recognition greater than that bestowed on the *corps* of notaries.[57]

But as the judge and consuls were soon to learn, it was risky to place so much emphasis on this formal conception of merchant courts' corporate identity. According to the notaries, the merchant court judges were not royal judges, and in fact did not even constitute a *corps*. The judge and consuls, they argued, "imagined that it sufficed to have been established by the edict of November 1563 to be able to call themselves royal judges," but "they ignore the distinction that must be drawn between an edict creating royal offices and an edict establishing for the benefit of commerce arbiter-judges to adjudicate its disputes; it is the resolution of these disputes and not the creation of a judge and consuls that is the [edict's] purpose."[58] The king, in other words, had never established the merchant court as a corporate entity, with the judge and consuls as venal officeholders, confirmed in and owning their positions as royal judges and possessing official documents of title that served as proof and ensured transmissibility to their heirs. Instead, the judge and consul were mere merchants, elected by their fellow merchants to serve on a purely temporary basis: "It is not from the king that they receive their appointment, but from the *corps* of commerce. Their election is their title [of ownership]; they have no other."[59]

Indeed, the notaries mockingly observed, the only claim that the judge and consuls had to the status of royal judges was "the right that they have to wear inside the walls of their court a short robe, which they call the consular robe" — a right which they inanely believed "establishes them as magistrates . . . [thus] persuad[ing] themselves that once their year in office has passed, they retain the dignity [associated with it]."[60] Having thus voiced this anxiety about the confusion of status markers — an anxiety common to the age — the notaries proceeded to assure themselves that their readers in the *Bureau du Commerce* and the King's Council would be able to distinguish between true merit, acquired by virtue of owning an office within an official royal *corps*, and the mere appearance of merit, acquired by those who owned only the vain, outer trappings of status: "There are grounds to presume that the vanity of these merchants decorated [with the honor of] a temporary position will never prevail against the royal notaries' title [of ownership] and possession [of their offices]."[61]

The notaries then concluded that, since the merchant court judges were not true royal judges, they had not been invited to the assembly in this capacity, but instead as deputies of the merchant community as a whole. And as between merchants and notaries, argued the latter, it was not remotely imaginable that one might "put in parallel the mechanical functions of the merchant with those of the royal notaries."[62] Here, the notaries proceeded to recite all the traditional arguments for why commerce was a "vile profession" in which "one thinks only of profit."[63] It was the notaries who merited greater privilege since it was they who, rather than focusing on their own self-interest, served the state by practicing a profession that required them to be "very honest," "useful to the public," and replete with "talents and feelings."[64]

Since the judge and consuls had based their claim to precedence on their status as royal judges, they never engaged with the notaries on the question of whether the profession of the notary or that of the merchant was more meritorious and thus worthy of greater privilege. Instead, the merchant court simply insisted that its judges were entitled to precedence by virtue of their position as royal judges. In this, it had the firm support of the merchant deputies of the *Bureau du Commerce,* who agreed that the matter was decided by the fact that the merchant court judges were royal judges, and therefore concluded that the "claim of the notaries . . . seemed . . . absurd."[65]

There were other occasions when arguments for precedence based on merchant court judges' formal corporate status as royal judges proved effective.[66] Yet, there was also significant truth to the assertion of the notaries of Angers that, since the judge and consuls were not venal officeholders, they could not rightfully demand the privilege of precedence by appeal to their formal corporate identity. Moreover, by resting their claim to precedence entirely on their corporate status as royal judges, the judge and consuls had permitted the notaries' arguments about the vileness of merchant character to go unchallenged. Well aware that any claim they might have to status as incorporated royal courts was on shaky grounds, and deeply concerned with defending merchant honor, some merchant courts asserted their merit (and thus their demand for precedence) by adopting a different strategy.

These courts emphasized that, while they had been initially established by the monarchy, it was the local merchant community, rather than the king, that selected the judge and consuls. This, in turn, suggested that the corporate entity whose status merchant courts had to defend was not a small, royally appointed *corps* of judge and consuls, but a larger and seemingly naturally arising one, consisting of the many merchants who annually elected the judge and consuls from among themselves. By thus appealing to a broad conception of their corporate membership as encompassing the merchant community as a whole—of which they were simply the representatives—these merchant courts were able to champion the status not simply of the judge and consuls but of all merchants within the jurisdiction. But in order to do so, they had to abandon the language of corporate privilege.

Consider, for example, the approach adopted in 1705 by the Merchant

Court of Toulouse in a status dispute with the city's *corps* of solicitors.[67] The dispute erupted on May 24, when in an assembly of the owners of a local mill, two solicitors, named Revel and Duverger, "refused to cede precedence" to Dutout, a former consul of the merchant court. According to Revel and Duverger, their status as solicitors before the *Parlement* entitled them to precede all merchants, except for those few who had served as *capitouls* — the officers who headed Toulouse's municipal government. Deeply distressed that "the solicitors undertake similar actions to the detriment of commerce and merchants every day," and convinced that these "must not be tolerated any longer," the Merchant Court of Toulouse decided to champion Dutout's cause and petitioned the *Bureau du Commerce* to intercede on its behalf with the King's Council.[68]

As its reference to "commerce" and "merchants" suggests, the Merchant Court of Toulouse framed the issue not in terms of the privileges owed to the judge and consuls, but instead more broadly in terms of the status of all merchants. As it explained, the question with which it presented the *Bureau* was that of "the precedence [to be established] between merchants and solicitors."[69] Citing a number of earlier decrees issued by the King's Council, regarding not only Toulouse but also Bordeaux and Poitiers,[70] the court insisted that "the goal of the council has always been to establish perfect equality between merchants and solicitors."[71] In practice, this meant that, as among those merchants and solicitors who had served as officers in the municipal government or as judges in the merchant court, the order in which these individuals would march in all "public and particular assemblies" would be determined by "the order and date of their election to these posts."[72] Likewise, among those merchants and solicitors who had not served in these positions, their rank would be fixed by "the length of their practice of the professions of merchant and solicitor."[73]

According to the merchant court, while the council had repeatedly recognized and sought to enforce perfect equality between merchants and solicitors, the latter consistently chose to ignore the council's rulings: "Although the solicitors of Toulouse should feel honored by this equality between their profession and that of the merchants, which is as ancient, as necessary to the state, and as honorable, nevertheless these solicitors affect at every moment to give public signs of their contempt for commerce and for those who make it their profession, and they endeavor to trouble the order that the council established between them and the merchants."[74] By thus demanding precedence and respect on behalf of all Toulouse merchants, the Merchant Court of Toulouse implied that these merchants constituted a large corporate entity, of which they were the leaders — a *corps* whose existence did not hinge on royal declaration or decree but on the nature of the "ancient" and "necessary" commercial activities its members performed.

The Merchant Court of Bordeaux adopted a similar strategy when it petitioned the *Bureau du Commerce* in 1722 to intervene in a status dispute that was taking place within the merchant community.[75] According to the court, the dispute arose because various *négociants* of Bordeaux had begun claiming, based on "titles of nobility" [*lettres de noblesse*] that the crown had recently bestowed on them, the right to "precede in the assemblies of the municipal government and the bourse all other bourgeois and *négociants* with greater seniority than they and who on this basis had always preceded them."[76] In support of their claim, these *négociants* pointed to a royal edict of December 1701, which sought to encourage noblemen to undertake wholesale commerce by providing that those who chose to do so would not jeopardize their noble status. In particular, the *négociants* cited the edict's second article, which stated that noblemen who undertook wholesale commerce would continue to precede all other *négociants* in communal assemblies.

The demands of these newly ennobled *négociants* infuriated the ordinary, non-noble merchants of Bordeaux. Long accustomed to the traditional disdain in which merchants were held, they, like other Old Regime merchants, had managed to carve out a niche for themselves—within such institutions as the merchant court and guilds—in which they applied their own, distinctively mercantile metric of virtue and honor. Now the newly ennobled *négociants* were undermining these safe-havens, forcing the broader society's reverence for noble honor—and concomitant disdain for merchants—directly into merchant assemblies. Claiming to speak for the merchant community as a whole, the Merchant Court of Bordeaux sought to prevent what it perceived as an inversion of long-established merchant norms of merit, by lobbying the *Bureau du Commerce* to intervene and persuade the King's Council to issue a decree rejecting the recently ennobled *négociants'* claim to superior rank.

While the arguments made by the merchant court have, unfortunately, not been preserved, those of the *Bureau*'s merchant deputies, who (as was so often the case) sided largely with the court, provide a good indication of what these likely were. The deputies concluded that while "nobles by descent, by office, or otherwise" could precede non-noble *négociants* in the many assemblies that took place outside merchant institutions, "this prerogative must not apply in assemblies of the guilds or associations of *négociants,* in which each individual must take and maintain the rank associated with his seniority."[77]

The claim of the newly ennobled *négociants,* argued the deputies, was clearly contrary to the monarchy's primary goal in enacting the edict of December 1701, which was to persuade noblemen that commerce is an honorable endeavor and that they therefore had nothing to lose—and indeed everything to gain—by undertaking it. Because the goal of the edict was thus to honor commerce, it made no sense to interpret it as entitling someone who had been a merchant for five years to precede someone who had been a merchant for thirty, simply because the former happened to acquire noble status. As the deputies explained: "If the edict of December 1701, issued to favor and honor commerce, could support the claim of the ennobled *négociants* from Bordeaux, one could say with reason that this edict, in honoring these *négociants,* dishonored . . . those to whom it denied precedence, to the prejudice of their seniority."[78] Thus, like the Merchant Court of Toulouse in its status dispute with the solicitors, the judge and consuls of Bordeaux (or their supporters in the *Bureau du Commerce*) claimed to speak for the entire, local merchant community, which they identified as a large corporate entity, established not by any formal royal grant of corporate status and privilege, but instead by virtue of the commercial activities its members performed.

Unsure about how best to define their own corporate identity and eager to defend merchant character, eighteenth-century merchant courts that engaged in status disputes hesitated between claiming formal corporate status—as official royal *corps*—and asserting a very different, more informal corporate identity. Pursuant to this informal corporate identity, merchant courts did not owe their existence to royal fiat. Instead, each merchant court was simply a representative of a much larger corporate entity, consisting in some vague, undefined way of the local merchant community as a whole. The local merchant community, in turn, was clearly not established as a formal royal *corps* and was, instead, bound together by its members' common participation in the activity of commerce. But what precisely was this activity of "commerce" to which the merchant courts alluded and which, they suggested, served as the glue binding together the merchant community? It was in the context of a different set of disputes—namely, those over jurisdiction—that merchant courts would have occasion to develop a more complete theory of commerce as the private, credit-based exchange enabling society to survive and thrive.

Jurisdictional Conflict

As Lauren Benton has argued, the study of "jurisdictional politics"—or disputes over the nature and extent of the power with which legal entities are endowed—is vital for understanding how social groups construct the cultural boundaries by means of which they define themselves and legitimate claims to power.[79] While Benton's work focuses on the colonial context, jurisdictional politics were, as she herself observes, a pervasive feature of early-modern

European states as well. Thus, in the world of Old Regime France, where there were numerous courts operating pursuant to overlapping authorities, conflict between them was rampant. In the case of the merchant courts, the jurisdictional politics resulting from such conflict served as a key site for the reconceptualization of the nature of commerce and its place in the social order.

Like status disputes, jurisdictional conflicts were in a certain sense conflicts over privilege. Indeed, there was a long tradition of viewing jurisdiction as a form of privilege, in two distinct but interrelated ways. First, jurisdiction—in the sense of power to require the appearance of certain defendants and to adjudicate rights in certain kinds of property—was a privilege belonging to the court. The right to judge was a longstanding attribute of royal sovereignty. According to the sixteenth-century jurist Claude de Seyssel, the king "is chosen by divine Providence . . . primarily to maintain and do Justice."[80] Accordingly, when courts exercised jurisdiction, this was (at least in theory) as a special privilege accorded by the king. Second, jurisdiction—as a right to appear before particular courts and not others—was a privilege belonging to the litigants. As Montesquieu opined, "One of the privileges least burdensome to society . . . is that of being allowed to plead before one tribunal rather than another."[81]

Like other courts, merchant courts traditionally claimed jurisdiction as a matter of privilege.[82] When the first merchant courts were officially established by the monarchy in the mid-sixteenth century,[83] they were generally understood to be courts of and for merchants and hence, in common parlance, were designated the "judges of merchants." These were, in other words, specialized merchant-run institutions, endowed with the privilege of applying the law of merchants for merchant litigants engaged in mercantile transactions—and before whom such merchants had the privilege of appearing. This in turn reflected the prevailing view of the early-modern French social order as a fixed hierarchy of corporate entities, each of which possessed distinctive privileges, or its own private laws. The edict of November 1563, which established a merchant court in Paris, neatly captured this conception of merchant court jurisdiction, by providing simply that the court would adjudicate "suits and differences . . . between merchants concerning merchandise only."[84] Likewise, the Commercial Ordinance of 1673, which established the law to be applied in the merchant courts, was commonly, though unofficially, termed *Le Code marchand*—literally a body of law particular to merchants.[85]

Over the course of the seventeenth and eighteenth centuries, however, it became increasingly difficult for merchant courts to frame jurisdictional claims in the traditional language of corporate privilege. As commerce expanded, its importance not only for the economic well-being of French men and women but also for the fiscal health and geopolitical position of the monarchy became increasingly apparent to all. This in turn suggested that merchant courts' jurisdictional claims were not simply matters of merchant privilege, and therefore of concern to merchants alone. Moreover, many of those participating in commercial activities were no longer merchants as traditionally conceived (primarily guild members), and in fact included noblemen—long defined by their supposedly innate antipathy to such base endeavors as commerce. As the monarchy gradually permitted noblemen to engage in various kinds of commerce without jeopardizing their titles,[86] many took advantage of this new freedom, particularly by investing in commercial associations. In addition, increasing numbers of people from all walks of life came to rely on negotiable instruments as a means of making payments, obtaining credit, and engaging in financial speculation.[87] Any claim to exercise jurisdiction over such nonmerchant litigants could not easily be presented as one of merchant privilege. Accordingly, in making jurisdictional claims—and, in particular, claims to bankruptcy jurisdiction and to expand the geographic scope of their jurisdiction—merchant courts abandoned the traditional corporatist idiom of privilege. In its place, they turned instead to a functionalist discourse that emphasized the utility of commerce, now conceived as the private, credit-based exchange sustaining the social order.

BANKRUPTCY JURISDICTION

Any examination of bankruptcy in the Old Regime must start from the distinction between a *faillite,* or innocent insolvency, and a *banqueroute,* or criminal bankruptcy. Dating back to royal legislation of the sixteenth century, and reinforced by the Commercial Ordinance of 1673,[88] this distinction turned largely on an assessment of the debtor's intent, and in particular on whether he was deemed to be of good or bad faith. If the debtor had done his best to conduct business in a responsible manner—as attested by the fact that he had not overextended himself and that he had made every effort to pay creditors—then he was deemed a *failli* and could escape debtors' prison by turning his remaining assets over to the court, which would in turn arrange for their distribution among creditors.[89] In contrast, if the debtor had undertaken extremely risky investments, and even more damaging, had sought to defraud his creditors, then he was a *banqueroutier,* subject to criminal punishment—usually in the form of forced labor and shame sanctions.[90] As the commercial jurist Masson explained, "*Faillite* is the disorder of a *négociant*'s business, caused by setbacks that render him insolvent . . . when he presents himself honestly before his creditors, explains his misfortune, [and] asks them for time or for remission [of the debt]."[91] In contrast, "The *banqueroute* of a *négociant* is a fraud to enrich himself by falsifying losses, by claiming more creditors than he has, by misappropriating part of his assets in order to give to his creditors only those which are the least liquid, and when he has succeeded in reaching an agreement with them, regaining an establishment that is more luxurious than ever with money that he stole from them; or if they do not agree to the transaction, leaving the country with their money."[92]

Although the Commercial Ordinance of 1673 extensively regulated *faillites* and *banqueroutes* and required merchants undergoing either to deposit their accounting books with the local merchant court, it said nothing about which courts would have jurisdiction over such matters.[93] Not surprisingly, this led to extensive jurisdictional conflict between merchant courts and ordinary courts—conflict that persisted throughout the eighteenth century, without either side achieving clear victory. Such conflict was temporarily halted on June 10, 1715, when the monarchy issued a declaration providing that merchant courts would have jurisdiction over *faillites,* as well as all civil proceedings stemming from *banqueroutes,* for a nine-month period, running from April 1, 1715, though January 1, 1716.[94] Criminal proceedings intended to adjudicate the guilt of *banqueroutiers* were to remain with the ordinary royal courts—though the monarchy sought to limit the number of these proceedings by such measures as requiring creditors to agree to them.[95] After issuing this declaration, the monarchy repeatedly extended it for brief periods of six months to one year, the final such declaration appearing on August 5, 1732, and running through September 1, 1733.[96]

The driving force behind the issuance of the 1715 declaration appears to have been the economic crisis (and concomitant bankruptcies) that followed from the lengthy and costly wars to which Louis XIV committed France in the final decades of his reign—the War of the League of Augsburg (1688–97) and the War of the Spanish Succession (1702–13). Citing the fact that merchant courts relied on summary procedure and low fees—an argument that, as discussed below, merchant courts themselves advanced in favor of their claim to bankruptcy jurisdiction—the monarchy concluded that these courts would be better able than ordinary courts to stem the tide of bankruptcies. Accordingly, it decided to grant them bankruptcy jurisdiction until the crisis was staved. Since the economic difficulties experienced during this period were further exacerbated by the Mississippi Bubble of 1720, the monarchy repeatedly extended the 1715 declaration in the years that followed.[97]

As of the final extension issued in 1732, however, the monarchy determined that the economic situation had improved and ceased ordering further extensions. Although merchant courts and chambers of commerce throughout France repeatedly petitioned the *Bureau du Commerce* for legislation conveying bankruptcy jurisdiction to the merchant courts on a permanent basis, such legislation did not appear until the French Revolution, when *faillites* were entrusted to the newly established *tribunaux de commerce.*[98] Nonetheless, while a wholesale grant of bankruptcy jurisdiction would have to await the Revolution, many individual merchant courts managed in the years after 1732 to obtain royal legislation granting them bankruptcy jurisdiction — or at least certain aspects thereof — on a temporary basis.[99] And even when such legislation granted only partial jurisdiction, courts often claimed (and acted as if) it entitled them to bankruptcy jurisdiction in its entirety. Consider, for example, a royal declaration of September 13, 1739, which empowered merchant courts simply to verify the debts claimed by creditors in cases of *faillite.*[100] Despite the fact that this jurisdictional grant was clearly limited in nature, the commercial jurist and former merchant court judge Masson cited it as evidence that "jurisdiction over *faillites* is again attributed to the merchant courts."[101]

Merchant courts petitioning for jurisdiction over *faillites* and *banqueroutes* could not, for a number of reasons, easily frame their claims in the traditional corporatist idiom, as a demand for merchant privilege. First, existing law placed no limit on the types of persons eligible to pursue *faillite* or subject to *banqueroute.*[102] The bursting of the Mississippi Bubble in 1720, and the chain of bankruptcies that ensued — some among nonmerchants — made it abundantly clear that to exercise bankruptcy jurisdiction was to exercise jurisdiction over nonmerchants.[103] Thus, to the extent that merchant courts claimed bankruptcy jurisdiction in such cases, they were claiming authority to adjudicate disputes involving some, such as noblemen, who were not merchants in the traditional sense.

Second, as the Mississippi Bubble once again served to illustrate, bankruptcies — even among merchants — had effects that clearly extended beyond the confines of the merchant community and its traditional merchant *corps.* In a society that was increasingly dependent on credit — where even noblemen required credit to purchase the venal offices and lordly attire by which they identified themselves as a supposedly noncommercial elite — a single bankruptcy could destabilize countless creditors, thereby generating a wave of bankruptcies. This too made it very difficult for merchant courts to claim bankruptcy jurisdiction as a form of merchant privilege, and thus presumably of interest to merchants alone.

In petitioning for bankruptcy jurisdiction, merchant courts therefore abandoned the corporatist idiom, demanding jurisdiction not as a grant of privilege but instead on grounds of social utility. It was because merchant courts were better than ordinary courts at facilitating commerce, the petitioners argued —

and, in particular, at rescuing it from the demise that bankruptcies threatened —that they, and not the ordinary courts, were entitled to exercise bankruptcy jurisdiction. Like the Parisian Merchant Court in its jurisdictional conflict with the municipal government, the petitioners claimed that commerce was a network of private, freely entered exchange relationships, all of which depended on credit. It was credit that enabled the production and purchasing of goods—by merchants and nonmerchants alike—and thereby fueled the economy. But precisely because credit was so vital and omnipresent, the failure of one individual to meet his obligations could cause countless others to default as well. Moreover, to the extent that merchants feared such a chain of bankruptcies, they would become reluctant to extend credit, which would in turn deter production and exchange and thus lead to further bankruptcies.

Along these lines, the Merchant Court of Poitiers petitioned the *Bureau du Commerce* for bankruptcy jurisdiction in 1762 by asserting that only merchant court jurisdiction could ensure merchant confidence and that such "confidence . . . [is] the soul of commerce, in that it produces the credit without which commerce languishes."[104] Likewise, the Chamber of Commerce of Lille argued in 1773 that it was entitled to bankruptcy jurisdiction because, should there be a diminution in merchants' "confidence and their credit," the result would be "that the products of our agriculture and manufacturing no longer sell as quickly, that traffic in our commodities necessarily becomes limited, that lenders no longer open their tills with the same ease to hard-working borrowers, that money no longer circulates as rapidly, and finally that commerce finds itself plunged into a state of inertia."[105] Asserting that "confidence . . . [is] [t]he prime mover of commerce," the Merchant Court of Lille made almost the identical argument in 1776, observing that, without confidence, "the fear that most merchants will have of losing all the money owed to them will necessarily hinder the progress [of commerce]; . . . that as a result of this fear, the circulation of currency and of negotiable instruments will necessarily be restricted; that in general the products of our agriculture and our manufacturing will no longer sell as quickly; finally that commerce will be completely plunged into a state of languor and inertia."[106]

According to the petitioners, the key to avoiding a disastrous economic collapse was to adjudicate bankruptcies in a manner that would ensure that creditors received sufficient funds to avoid having to declare bankruptcy themselves. This in turn required preserving as much as possible of the debtor's resources. For two reasons, they argued, it was the merchant courts, rather than the ordinary courts, that were in the best position to achieve this goal, and thereby restore the networks of credit sustaining the economy.

First, because of the simplicity of the procedure employed by merchant courts, they spent less time and money than ordinary courts in adjudicating a bankruptcy. This meant that more resources remained for creditors. Writing in 1779, the Merchant Court of Tours argued that in ordinary royal courts, as compared with merchant courts, "[one] finds . . . obstacles and formalities which, in hindering the goal of limiting the fees charged during the disaster of bankruptcies, harm the general welfare. . . . [The ordinary courts employ] an incredible panoply of ruinous procedure, which absorbs the most liquid of capital [*denier*] and takes away from the unhappy creditor the little hope that he has."[107] Similarly, the Merchant Court of Poitiers observed, "as a result of the points of law and subtleties . . . of ordinary judges, [*négociants* and manufacturers] see the assets of bankrupts consumed in judicial fees and . . . after a long and painful discussion lose all the money owed them, whereas they would have retrieved a portion, if their natural judges, whose services are free, had exclusive jurisdiction over bankruptcies."[108]

A second reason given by the merchant courts and their supporters for why they should adjudicate bankruptcies was that, because they were run by merchants, they were in a better position to detect fraud and thereby distinguish criminal *banqueroutes* from mere *faillites*. As explained by the merchant deputies of the *Bureau du Commerce* in a 1718 memorandum summarizing the demands for bankruptcy jurisdiction made by numerous merchant courts, merchants were better able to detect fraud "because *négociants* know those among themselves who can be suspected of this fault; . . . [moreover,] because these frauds can be undertaken only by altering the various accounting books of the bankrupt and also of his creditors, one must have been a *négociant,* and a very experienced one at that, in order to make these kinds of discoveries."[109] The distinctive capacity of merchant courts to detect fraud would ensure that individuals engaging in it would be found—and the money they unlawfully converted thereby recovered for creditors—while also protecting the unfortunate individual of good faith from unjustified attacks on his reputation and pocketbook. By thus recovering funds for creditors and bolstering the reputation of the innocent, the merchant courts would in turn preserve the viability of credit networks and thereby sustain the vital social function of commerce.

GEOGRAPHIC SCOPE OF JURISDICTION

While merchant courts communicated with one another and petitioned the *Bureau du Commerce* (individually or in small numbers) regarding status disputes and bankruptcy jurisdiction, it was another type of jurisdictional conflict—a conflict over the geographic scope of merchant court jurisdiction—that galvanized them into undertaking their first truly organized, concerted lobbying campaign. In this campaign, as in their petitions for bankruptcy jurisdiction, merchant courts drew heavily on the conception of commerce as a network of private exchange relationships sustained by credit. Here, however, they not only abandoned the corporatist idiom but, indeed, outright rejected it.

The conflict between ordinary and merchant courts concerning the geographic scope of merchant court jurisdiction emerged at least as far back as February 1703,[110] when the *Parlement* of Paris issued a judgment vacating a decision of the Merchant Court of Compiègne on the grounds that it had acted beyond its jurisdiction, which according to the *Parlement* was limited to the bailiwick in which it sat.[111] Several royal edicts issued in 1710 held, to the contrary, that merchant court jurisdiction was not limited in this manner.[112] Nonetheless, these edicts failed to deter the ordinary, nonmerchant courts from their efforts to counter what they perceived as the illegitimate jurisdictional ambitions of their merchant court rivals.[113]

For reasons that are, unfortunately unclear, this ongoing dispute came to a head once again in 1756, leading the comptroller general to seek another royal resolution. On January 31, 1756, he wrote to intendants throughout France explaining that the monarchy was concerned by ongoing jurisdictional conflicts between merchant and ordinary, nonmerchant courts. The ordinary courts claimed that a merchant court had jurisdiction only if the defendant resided within the bailiwick in which the court was located. In contrast, the merchant courts claimed that the merchant court closest to the defendant's place of residence had jurisdiction, whether or not that place of residence was within the bailiwick in which the court was located.[114]

Before issuing a ruling that would settle this dispute once and for all, the comptroller general asked the intendants to offer their views as to the proper bounds of merchant court jurisdiction.[115] All but two of the intendants advised the monarchy that the jurisdiction of the merchant courts should not be limited to the bailiwicks in which they sat.[116] This was also the view of the merchant deputies of the *Bureau du Commerce*, who were about to present their report when the monarchy—without first consulting with the *Bureau*—issued the Declaration of April 7, 1759.[117]

Contrary to the opinion of the intendants and the deputies, the declaration provided that merchant court jurisdiction extended only to those defendants residing in the bailiwick where the court was located.[118] If the defendant lived in a bailiwick that lacked a merchant court, the plaintiff could not sue in the nearest merchant court, but would instead have recourse only to the ordinary courts of the defendant's bailiwick.[119] Pursuant to the declaration, these ordinary courts were required to apply commercial procedure and law as established in the Procedure Ordinance of 1667 and the Commercial Ordinance of 1673.

Infuriated by this limitation on their jurisdiction and by the failure to solicit the views of the *Bureau*'s merchant deputies, merchant courts throughout France joined together to petition the monarchy for the declaration's repeal. Although this campaign appears to have begun at the grassroots level, the Parisian Merchant Court, the *six corps de Paris,* and the merchant deputies of the *Bureau du Commerce* soon took responsibility for leading it. Merchant courts—as well as chambers of commerce—sent petitions for repeal to the comptroller general in his capacity as head of the *Bureau du Commerce.* As explained by the *Bureau*'s merchant deputies in a report recommending repeal, "merchants [*le commerce*]" decided "that it was necessary to protest against this declaration," and "all the requests and petitions were sent to the *Bureau du Commerce.*"[120] As a result, the deputies gained access to and control over the petitions,[121] which they then gave to the Parisian Merchant Court and the *six corps* in order to assist them in publishing a book advocating repeal. Published in 1766 by the "printer of the Merchant Court [of Paris]," the book begins with the separate and joint petitions of the Parisian Merchant Court and the *six corps de Paris*—all three penned by the same lawyer.[122] These are followed by lengthy summaries of the petitions for repeal that had been drafted by provincial merchant courts and chambers of commerce and that the merchant deputies had given to the Parisian Merchant Court and *six corps.*

That the Parisian Merchant Court, the *six corps,* and the *Bureau*'s merchant deputies would unite to lead the campaign for repeal is hardly surprising given the strong institutional ties binding them together—ties so strong that the same individual might be at various times a leading member of the *six corps,* a judge or consul in the Parisian Merchant Court, and one of Paris's two deputies to the *Bureau.*[123] Moreover, the campaign for repeal marked the coming to fruition—and intersection—of the developments described above. First, as a result of the ongoing correspondence between the provincial merchant courts and the Parisian Merchant Court, the latter had emerged as the leader of a group of courts that had come to perceive their interests as unified. Second, individual merchant courts had grown accustomed to petitioning the *Bureau* (and its frequently supportive merchant deputies) on behalf of these common interests.

The convergence of these developments enabled the Parisian Merchant Court and the *Bureau*'s merchant deputies to spearhead a campaign for repeal of the Declaration of 1759 that, while never attaining its ultimate goal, was able to sustain merchant interest and support until the Revolution.[124] For example, in his legal dictionary, published in 1786, the jurist Denisart observed that "merchants [*le commerce*] hope, by means of representations that they do not cease to bring to the foot of the throne, to obtain the revocation [of the declaration]."[125] Likewise, many of the *cahiers* submitted by the Third

Estate in 1788 regarding the calling of the Estates General demanded the establishment of merchant courts whose jurisdiction would not be limited to the bailiwicks in which they sat.[126]

In the 1759 campaign, as in merchant courts' petitions for bankruptcy jurisdiction, the petitioners argued[127] for merchant court jurisdiction, not on the basis of corporate privilege but instead on utilitarian grounds — and, in particular, by reference to the merchant courts' capacity to facilitate commerce.[128] Relying on a conception of "public utility" grounded in a natural-law theory of government and society that reads as if penned by — and indeed plagiarizes from — Burlamaqui, the Parisian Merchant Court and the *six corps* rejected the traditional Old Regime conception of law as those principles dating to time immemorial that underlie an ideal, unchanging social order. Instead, they embraced Burlamaqui's definition of law as that set of rules that promote happiness, the true end of human existence: "Since the ultimate end of man is happiness; and . . . since man can attain happiness only through reason, it follows that one must understand by the term law [*Droit*] only that which reason approves as a sure means of attaining happiness."[129]

Because happiness is a changeable rather than fixed state of being, the petitioners argued, law designed to promote happiness was law that sought change and thus differed radically from the traditional, stasis-oriented conception of law. By implication, any argument for or against the Declaration of 1759 based on whether it restored the traditional order was irrelevant. The only valid basis for evaluating the declaration was whether it furthered happiness, or public utility: "It suffices to consider whether [the declaration] satisfies the necessary end and intention of the legislator, that is to say, public utility."[130]

Having established that the legitimacy of the declaration hinged on its capacity to promote happiness, the Parisian Merchant Court and *six corps* then claimed that it failed to do so. In support of this claim, they mustered two sets of arguments, both of which drew on a conception of commerce as the credit-based private exchange sustaining the social order. The first set concerned the effects the declaration would have on merchants' ability to bring suit and thus on their willingness to take risk and extend credit. The second, more surprising set of arguments proposed a reading of history in which the declaration was made incompatible with the forces that had given rise to modernity.

The petitioners' first set of arguments for why the Declaration of 1759 detracts from happiness were premised on the following assumptions: happiness consists of prosperity, prosperity is created by commerce, commerce flourishes only if credit is easily available, and easily available credit hinges on merchant courts having exclusive jurisdiction over commercial disputes. In the petitioners' words, "no more merchant courts, no more credit; no more credit, no more commerce."[131] According to the petitioners, the declaration would greatly hinder the extension of credit for a number of reasons. First, it would force many merchants to sue in ordinary, nonmerchant courts, whose judges did not have the knowledge and experience to decide cases according to the dictates of commercial law and custom. As a result, certainty in the outcome of lawsuits would be severely diminished, and many judgments rendered would defy the standards of good faith and equity that were the hallmark of commercial jurisprudence. Second, merchants would have to file suit in many more courts than before, which would greatly increase the costs of litigation. Whereas a merchant had previously been able to bring several suits against different defendants in one merchant court, he would now have to sue each defendant in the court of his place of residence. Given these shortcomings, many merchants might prefer not to sue. To the extent that they hesitated to sue defaulting debtors, they were less likely to make potentially risky extensions of credit.

The dangers to credit were particularly great, argued the petitioners, given how dependent French society was becoming on negotiable instruments. When the drawee of a bill of exchange or the maker of a promissory note refused to pay, the holder in due course was entitled to collect from any and all endorsers. Seeking to make best use of this right, the holder who wanted to ensure payment would prefer to sue not one but all of the endorsers. But if the holder had to sue each endorser in a different court, his ability to bring suit against all, and thus to force payment, would be greatly diminished. To the extent that enforcing payment proved difficult or impossible, people would stop accepting negotiable instruments, and this increasingly important source of credit would dry up: "Having once suffered these inconveniences, the trader will cease extending credit, and since there is no commerce without credit, your subjects will find themselves forced to abandon it, rather than run the risks to which the new law exposes them."[132] In contrast, in the years prior to the enactment of the Declaration of 1759, "the facility that merchants had of suing several debtors in the same day, [and] the speed with which they obtained a judgment against them, stimulated them to extend credit more easily and to procure by this means abundance in commerce."[133]

In addition to discussing these concrete ways in which the declaration would hinder prosperity, or happiness, the Parisian Merchant Court and the *six corps* also advanced a rather sophisticated theoretical argument based on a reading of history that, like their definition of law, was grounded in natural-law jurisprudence. They began by distinguishing between two stages of social development. Society, they argued, is "as useful as it is natural to men."[134] It arises without any initial contract or agreement, but rather from men's recognition that they must join together to further their common needs. Later, as men begin to struggle with one another in pursuit of their individual interests, this state of total equality gives way to civil and political society—a form of social organization in which a sovereign authority is invested with the power to resolve all disputes. Because the sovereign requires assistance in maintaining the peace, he establishes judges to prosecute violent assaults and to enforce property rights: "The original judges were established to remedy, first, assaults [occurring] in civil society, and next, the disputes born of the natural division of inheritances and possessions."[135] Each of these first or original judges is assigned a specific territory in which he has jurisdiction over the persons and property of the residents. As different groups of people develop their own local customs, the sovereign appoints more of these original judges in order to ensure that each territory has its own judge capable of enforcing local customs: "The variety of laws, uses, customs, and privileges particular to each region required that these original tribunals be multiplied, and that each one of these be confided with a certain expanse of terrain, in which it was to maintain tranquillity by enforcing the particular laws and usages."[136]

Once this original judicial framework is fully established, the petitioners argued, the sovereign can turn his attention to matters other than maintaining the peace. In particular, the sovereign can now concern himself with actively promoting the welfare of society, by attending to the "common needs of this body politic."[137] Just as he appointed an original set of judges to resolve disputes between individuals, so too he appoints a new set of judges to administer to society's common needs: "The security of travelers, the preservation of state property, navigation, the administration of the rivers and the forests, the assessment of public taxes, currency, finally COMMERCE; each requires an administration along the lines of that established for the interests of private individuals [*Particuliers*]."[138]

Unlike the original judges, who were concerned with preventing disturbances of the peace—and thus with maintaining the status quo—these new judges are assigned the task of actively promoting prosperity, and thus change. And whereas the original, peace-maintaining laws were infinitely varied, since they arose as the customs unique to particular peoples and territories, the new, prosperity-promoting laws are universal in scope. The law of commerce, for example, is designed to advance an interest common to all society and thus does not vary across different regions of France. The merchant courts, explained the petitioners, "are created only to judge the same thing, which is governed by the same law, throughout the entire expanse of the kingdom, and is not subject to any custom or local law."[139] Because of the vast extent of commercial activity, the sovereign establishes many merchant courts, each of which has exclusive jurisdiction over commercial matters within its territory. Initially, however, there was "a single tribunal that had the entire kingdom within its jurisdiction."[140] Thus, all merchant courts are united by a shared history and by the fact that they apply the same, unified body of law.

While each merchant court, like each original, or "ordinary" court, has jurisdiction only within prescribed geographic limits, the nature of the jurisdiction it exercises within its territory differs significantly from that exercised by an ordinary court within its territory. The merchant court has jurisdiction over all commercial matters within its territory, whereas the ordinary court has jurisdiction over all people within its territory: "Merchant courts are courts whose competence is *ratione materiae et non ratione personarum:* commerce is their attribution, and not persons."[141] The Declaration of 1759 interfered with this historically determined jurisdictional order by limiting the jurisdiction of the merchant court to the people within its territory, such that it would have the power to adjudicate a commercial dispute within its territory only if the defendant also happened to reside there. Because the merchant courts' subject-matter-based jurisdiction followed from the nature of commerce—from the fact that it was a universal activity, not confined by local custom—and because happiness required the promotion of commerce, any interference with the jurisdiction of the merchant courts necessarily detracted from the pursuit of happiness and, in so doing, ran counter to the direction of history.

In thus arguing that merchant court jurisdiction was based on the subject matter of commerce, rather than the merchant status of the defendant, the petitioners echoed arguments made by commercial jurists in the context of another ongoing debate regarding merchant court jurisdiction—namely, whether merchant courts had jurisdiction over such nonmerchants as noblemen. The increased involvement of nonmerchants, and particularly noblemen, in commercial activity gave rise to a heated debate in the late seventeenth and eighteenth centuries between commercial jurists (who were usually also merchants) and ordinary, university-trained, civil-law jurists regarding whether merchant court jurisdiction extended to nonmerchants.[142] Since merchant courts had the power to imprison those who failed to pay their debts, the stakes of this debate were quite high. Indeed, even such advocates of commerce as the editors of the monthly newspaper *Journal de Commerce* expressed shock at the fact that the Parisian Merchant Court imprisoned such noble elites as a duke, the lieutenant general of the king's army, and the magistrates of the *Parlement* of Paris for failing to pay money owed on bills of exchange.[143] Such imprisonments were, in its view, an "ignominious scandal."[144]

Seeking to protect the jurisdiction of the ordinary courts with which they were associated and to shield noblemen from the affront to their dignity implicit in being subject to merchant court jurisdiction (and thus perhaps to debtors' prison),[145] the ordinary jurists argued that merchant court jurisdiction was based on the merchant status of the litigants and that it therefore did not extend to nonmerchants.[146] In contrast, the commercial jurists attempted to expand merchant court jurisdiction and to defend the honorable status of their profession. Accordingly, they asserted that merchant court jurisdiction was based on the commercial subject matter of the dispute, and not the merchant status of the litigants. Thus, for example, Toubeau argued in 1682 that merchant courts "must hear . . . disputes about merchandise, even if the two parties are not merchants, and involving any person that might be, when commerce is at issue."[147] Likewise, almost a century later, the commercial jurist Rogue asserted that all nonmerchants who engaged in commercial activity, no matter their status and no matter how transitory the activity, were subject to merchant court jurisdiction: "Whoever by his occupation [*état*] is not a merchant and does a fleeting traffic is subject to the jurisdiction of the merchant court."[148]

In thus seeking to expand merchant court jurisdiction to encompass all manner of defendants, Old Regime commercial jurists proved quite successful, leading the contemporary commentator and playwright Louis-Sébastien Mercier to observe of the Parisian Merchant Court that its "judges and consuls order *arrest* [*prise de corps*] for nonpayment of bills of exchange, without regard to *status distinctions* [*sans distinction de personne*]."[149] It was, in part, to these arguments, successfully deployed by commercial jurists advocating merchant court jurisdiction over noblemen, that the Parisian Merchant Court and the *six corps* turned in petitioning for repeal of the Declaration of 1759. As this suggests, there was a radical implication to the petitioners' insistence that merchant court jurisdiction was based on the subject matter of commerce, rather than the merchant status of the litigants. In so insisting, the petitioners implied that merchant court jurisdiction must be determined on the basis of purely functionalist, utilitarian considerations, rather than corporate privilege. Privilege, in short, was no longer a legitimate basis for claiming power.

But while these merchant petitioners were happy to eradicate noblemen's claims to privilege, they had no intention of eliminating their own. Indeed, in the fall of 1788, shortly before corporatism collapsed for good, merchant courts and chambers of commerce across France launched a massive campaign for *corporate* representation at the Estates General. In the process, this final group of petitioners soon discovered that its predecessors had miscalculated. By arguing that merchant court jurisdiction was based on the social function of commerce, rather than merchant status—that commerce, the activity, was distinct from the people who performed it—the Parisian Merchant Court, the *six corps*, and the provincial merchant courts supporting them had helped lay the groundwork for the subsequent demise of the corporatist social order, including ultimately the abolition of the guilds and the nationalization of the merchant courts.

The Estates General and Beyond

On the verge of bankruptcy, the monarchy finally acceded to widespread demand and agreed in the summer of 1788 to call the Estates General. That July, it invited all interested parties to submit recommendations regarding the form the Estates General should take.[150] And in the fall, in response to the monarchy's call, merchant courts and chambers of commerce throughout France united in a second major campaign, publishing petitions that *le commerce* be permitted to send its own representatives to sit as a distinct group within the Third Estate. In thus arguing for representation of *le commerce*—a kind of meta-*corps* encompassing all merchants—these petitioners demanded the granting of formal legal status and recognition to an entity that they themselves had called into being through their previous efforts to lobby together on behalf of common interests. But in seeking formal legal status, French merchant courts and chambers of commerce were forced to confront a question that they had thus far managed to dodge—namely, what exactly was the entity on behalf of which they claimed to speak?

In petitioning the *Bureau du Commerce* regarding status disputes, individual merchant courts had identified the local merchant community as a corporate entity bound together by common participation in commerce—an entity whose interests each court claimed to represent. This somewhat vague assertion left two questions unanswered—one concerning the meaning of commerce and the other the nature of the merchant community's corporate identity. While merchant courts had had occasion in their petitions regarding jurisdictional conflict to elaborate more fully on their conception of commerce, they had never had to grapple more directly with the question of the merchant community's corporate identity. Indeed, there was no need to do so. The social order of the Old Regime was traditionally conceived as an agglomeration of corporate entities, only some of which, as described above, were understood to be *corps* in the formal, legal sense. Accordingly, the notion that a local merchant community was itself a kind of informal *corps*, represented by the local merchant court, was not necessarily incongruent with prevailing social understandings.

But through their developing practice of petitioning the *Bureau du Com-*

merce on behalf of common interests—and especially their joint campaign for repeal of the Declaration of 1759—merchant courts and chambers of commerce across France had come to view the *corps* of *le commerce* as nationwide, rather than local. With the calling of the Estates General—itself a kind of vast processional in which the many entities constituting the social order had to represent themselves before the king—merchant courts and chambers of commerce suddenly found themselves engaged in what was in essence a massive, nationwide status dispute, the scale of which they had never before encountered. Seeking to give voice to the nationwide *corps* that they claimed to represent, merchant courts and chambers of commerce argued that the glue holding this *corps* together was commerce, as they themselves had come to understand it—namely, a necessary function of an interdependent social order. In this way, fusing both corporatist and functionalist accounts of the nature of commerce, merchant courts and chambers of commerce joined together in a final lobbying campaign, the likes of which had occurred only once before—in response to the royal Declaration of 1759. Speaking on behalf of all French merchants, whom, they claimed, together constituted a giant national *corps* of *le commerce,* they demanded representation at the Estates General.

Galvanized into action by an initial petition distributed by the Merchant Court of Nantes,[151] provincial merchant courts and chambers of commerce worked furiously to demand representation. They sent numerous unsolicited letters to the Parisian Merchant Court, enclosing petitions that they had addressed to the monarchy and requesting that the Parisian judge and consuls join in their campaign. The Picardy Chamber of Commerce, for example, asked the Parisian judge and consuls "to join your representations to ours, so as to obtain from his majesty's justice a guarantee that *le commerce* is heard in the National Assembly."[152] Moreover, many of the letters sent to the Parisian Merchant Court refer to the various efforts of merchant courts throughout France to persuade fellow merchants to seek special representatives. For example, the judges of the Merchant Court of Beauvais expressed their gratitude to those "commercial cities of the kingdom . . . that have kindly sought to inform us . . . of their petitions."[153] Likewise, the Merchant Court of Auxerre explained that it was sending its petition to all merchant courts as a way of notifying them "that they are invited to take the same actions and to make common cause."[154]

Throughout their correspondence regarding this campaign for representation, merchant courts and chambers of commerce constantly referred to the entity on behalf of which they sought representation as *le commerce*—a giant merchant *corps* encompassing all the merchant communities of France. For example, in a letter to the Parisian Merchant Court, the judges of the Merchant Court of Arles suggested that if the monarchy granted their request for representatives to the Third Estate, these representatives ought to meet separately as a distinct *corps:* "We believe that it is appropriate to ask in addition that the deputies of commerce be permitted to assemble together outside the meetings of the Estates General, so as to deliberate among themselves concerning the actions to take and the proposals to make for the prosperity of commerce."[155] Likewise, the Merchant Court of Auxerre declared that "the interest of commerce [*l'intérêt du Commerce*] naturally must lead it to form but one *corps* and to have but one representative."[156] And according to the Chamber of Commerce of Picardy, *le commerce* was entitled to representation because "it constitutes at this moment a very large *corps,* which work and need have caused to develop the most wide-ranging knowledge about the true principles of administration and political interests."[157] In like manner, the Merchant Court of Calais demanded representation for *le commerce* by arguing that much had changed since the days that "this *corps,* just born, had . . . only a very slight influence on the political system."[158]

But if *le commerce* was a *corps,* it was also a basic function of society—one that, as merchant courts had argued in their petitions regarding bankruptcy jurisdiction and in their campaign to repeal the Declaration of 1759, could be undertaken regardless of corporate status. Accordingly, merchant courts—even while demanding corporate representation—did so not on the grounds of some corporate privilege granted by the king, but because they possessed specialized knowledge that would be of particular use to the monarchy in its efforts to administer commerce. And just as the Parisian Merchant Court and the *six corps* had based their arguments for repeal of the Declaration of 1759 on a historical analysis of changes in the structure of commerce and the state, so too did the petitioners in 1788.

The petitioners turned, in particular, to a set of historically grounded arguments about the relationship between commerce and the state that had become widely known as a result of the ongoing debate over the abbé Coyer's *La noblesse commerçante* (published in 1756),[159] but with which merchants had, in fact, been familiar for much longer. In the first major, comprehensive treatise on French commercial law, published in 1682, Jean Toubeau, himself a merchant, anticipated by more than half a century Coyer's famous portrait of the *noblesse commerçante*—an achievement for which he has received almost no recognition.[160] According to Toubeau, the laws and mores that prohibited noblemen from engaging in commerce developed during a feudal era that had long since passed, in which the state's survival depended on the nobility's wholehearted military service to the king. Such military service, however, was no longer required in the new commercial age that had arisen. Indeed, what was needed was a new set of laws and mores that would encourage the nobility to participate in commerce and thereby ensure the production and transfer of wealth across the social order. As Toubeau explained, "Old ordinances that prohibited noblemen from undertaking commerce were enacted in a time in which all the forces of the nobility were necessary to drive out enemies from the state . . . ; but now that the nobility is employed more in searching for its enemies outside the state than in driving them out . . . such great transformations in the state of our mores and affairs would be more than sufficient to introduce also some change in our laws."[161]

Because the feudal age had passed, Toubeau claimed, noblemen at present had no purpose or goal through whose pursuit they might seek to distinguish themselves. Indeed, they had literally nothing to do. As he observed, "To convince oneself easily [that noblemen should engage in commerce], it is necessary first to imagine what gentlemen who have nothing to do are like."[162] Because "idleness cannot reside in great souls, gentlemen must not stay in their castles, just like rats, . . . nor at court, languid and dull, behaving like children who run after butterflies."[163] Given that the traditional paths to honor were now closed to the nobleman, "his status, which seems to constitute his entire glory, is a hindrance that opposes his happiness and his fortune, and that closes to him all the avenues that the laws open to commoners."[164] It was therefore time for noblemen to abandon their ancient prejudice against commerce.

According to Toubeau, noblemen could engage in commerce without derogation of their noble status, because commercial activity was a perfectly honorable endeavor. In so arguing, Toubeau drew on an image of the merchant that paralleled some of the views expressed in the early-seventeenth-century political-economic writings of such authors as Jean Eon and Antoine de Montchrestien,[165] but which was fully developed and popularized by Toubeau's highly influential contemporary (and fellow merchant) Jacques Savary, the primary author of the Commercial Ordinance of 1673. Savary offered a comprehensive portrait of the merchant in his 1675 publication *Le parfait négociant* (fig. 4)—a book that was reissued in numerous editions throughout the late seventeenth and eighteenth centuries and that appeared in translation across much of Europe.[166] Seeking to reverse the longstanding Christian conception of those who pursue wealth as the embodiment of such cardinal sins as avarice and sloth, Savary argued that the "natural disposition" of the perfect trader bore no resemblance to this negative stereotype. Indeed, he argued, the perfect trader was characterized, first, by imagination, because this was the trait that enabled traders "to invent new materials . . . ; to be subtle and prompt to respond with natural arguments when flaws are found; to know how to write well, to know arithmetic, and the other things necessary for the mercantile profession."[167] Second, the perfect trader was "strong and robust," because only an individual so constituted could "resist all the fatigues that are encountered in doing commerce."[168] Finally, the perfect trader had a "good look" because "most people would prefer to do business and deal with a good-looking man, since he always renders himself more agreeable than another who does not have the same external advantage."[169]

Taking Savary's line of reasoning one step further, Toubeau argued that the perfect trader exhibited so many virtues and talents that he could easily be a nobleman. In fact, according to Toubeau, commerce required just as much heroism, and was thus just as worthy of honor, as military service: "Commerce . . . is a worthy enterprise for a gallant, because noblemen cannot maintain that they are more determined and brave than merchants."[170] For example, in maritime commerce "one does not have only men to fight but sometimes also the four elements together, which is the greatest test to which a man's resolution can be put."[171] Likewise, as Toubeau demanded in a particularly effusive piece of prose, "Can anything more determined and hardy be seen . . . than that which our illustrious merchants have undertaken and executed in the discovery of the new world? Is there anything more advantageous than these enterprises, since without them we would be deprived of the most beautiful things that we have? Can the nobility deny that to undertake such a great purpose it is necessary to be determined, to have a lofty soul; that to succeed in this purpose, it is necessary to have a lot of courage and to be above [fear of] the greatest perils? Would these great actions be unworthy of a gentleman, who prides himself on his bravery, generosity, hardiness, and heart?"[172] Indeed, those who possessed the qualities necessary to triumph on the battlefield were also likely to succeed in commerce, because "great voyages should be regarded more as conquests than as something mercenary."[173]

In 1756, more than a half-century after Toubeau's treatise was first issued, the abbé Coyer published *La noblesse commerçante* (fig. 5), a book that spawned an entire literature arguing for and against its claims. As John Shovlin has suggested, the debate surrounding Coyer's publication was a key moment in the development of a "political economy of virtue"—a widespread (though far from unified) discourse that emerged during the second half of the eighteenth century and that, particularly in the wake of France's losses in the Seven Years' War, sought in economic development of various kinds a program for the nation's patriotic regeneration.[174] But while Coyer's efforts may well have been spurred by a patriotic anxiety about national degeneration distinctive to the period in which he wrote, much of his analysis would have seemed entirely familiar to Toubeau. Like Toubeau before him, Coyer pleaded

Fig. 4 *The Perfect Trader* [*Négociant*] (Frontispiece to Jacques Savary, *Le parfait négociant*, 1675. Courtesy of Bibliothèque nationale de France/Archives Charmet/Bridgeman Art Library.)

for the nobility to abandon its longstanding prejudice against mercantile activity and to embrace the merchant life as fully compatible with traditional noble virtues. According to Coyer, noblemen resisted becoming merchants because they mistakenly believed that commerce was incompatible with honor. Pursuant to the pro-noble (as opposed to pro-royal) model of Old Regime government, most influentially articulated by Montesquieu, the genius of the French monarchy was that it trusted in a noble elite, motivated by the pursuit of honor to serve as a bulwark against despotism.[175] Noblemen, however, were denied the right to engage in commercial activity for fear that their pursuit of honor, and thus devotion to serving the state, would be overwhelmed by the self-interested pursuit of wealth. As Coyer noted: "Those among us who allow themselves to be frightened by the idea of a *noblesse commerçante* focus with M. de Montesquieu on the principle of monarchies, namely honor . . . . [a] principle that is destroyed (they say) by a completely opposite principle that is found in commerce, namely interest."[176] For this reason, Coyer bemoaned, "one would like . . . to distance monarchies [from commerce], as from a deceptive region that with beautiful appearances would devour its inhabitants, the nobility above all."[177]

Coyer, however, rejected this traditional, Montesquieuian model of government in which commerce was deemed incompatible with honor. Like Toubeau, he argued that in the feudal era the nobility had served the state and thereby attained honor by engaging in military battle, but that the modern era was an age of commerce in which military conquest itself was becoming increasingly dependent on successful commercial competition: "It is true that commerce loves peace . . . but as soon as war becomes necessary, it sustains it by finances, of which it is the principle source, and by the shipowners that emerge from its breast."[178] In this new commercial age, claimed Coyer, it was primarily through commercial activity, rather than military battle, that the nobility could serve the state and gain honor. And while commercial activity might not entail quite the same heroism and glory as military action, it too required such honorable traits as duty, intelligence, and strength. As Coyer explained, the *noblesse commerçante* "would content itself with this other, less brilliant honor that consists of the knowledge of needs, the perfection of the arts, application, economy, probity, public credit, enterprises that are peaceful but useful to the family and the state."[179]

In demanding representatives of *le commerce* at the Estates General, merchant courts and chambers of commerce claimed, like both Toubeau and Coyer, that the traditional view of the merchant as devoted to private gain rather than the public good was the product of a military-feudal social order that no longer existed. As the judges of the Merchant Court of Arles explained

Fig. 5 *What purpose does this vain heap of useless glory serve?* (Frontispiece to Gabriel François Coyer, *La noblesse commerçante*, 1756. Courtesy of Stanford University Libraries.)

in their petition, France had been a "military state" concerned only with the "glory of arms" until Colbert discovered commerce, thereby generating the resources that enabled France to attain its current preeminence.[180] As commerce flourished, it replaced land as the source of value. Indeed, it was only by means of commerce that France, like England, would be able to transform itself from a subsistence economy to one in which an agricultural surplus was available for trade: "It is commerce alone that procures the sale and increases the value of foodstuffs, and by this means stimulates emulation and multiplies the number of farmers."[181]

Along similar lines, the Merchant Court of Beauvais observed that France was initially a military state governed by "feudal law."[182] At that time, the king consulted only the nobility in making governance decisions because the nobility alone had the responsibility to bear arms. As the clergy acquired the right to own fiefs, the monarchy came to consult with it as well, but the vast majority of the population remained serfs and "did not form a *corps* within the state."[183] With time, the monarchy permitted the Third Estate to participate in "general assemblies," but allowed it no real power.[184] Subsequently, however, France grew strong through the expansion of commerce, for which the Third Estate was solely responsible. Because commerce had become so critical to the survival of the state, concluded the merchant courts of Arles and Beauvais, the monarchy had a significant interest in hearing the views of those who practiced it, and merchant courts and chambers of commerce should therefore be permitted to send representatives to the Estates General.

Other petitions argued, once again like both Toubeau and Coyer, that because commerce was now the lifeblood of the state, merchants could no longer be denigrated as narrowly self-interested, but instead had to be recognized as public-serving and hence honorable. According to the Chamber of Commerce of Guienne, "The trader is no longer what he once was: avidity is no longer the quality that distinguishes him, nor extreme ignorance his endowment. He seeks in study some relaxation from his work; he has applied himself to knowing the political administration of commerce; he knows how to distinguish the gain of the state from that of the individual."[185] Because of the merchant's new, expansive character, he was perfectly suited to serve on the Estates General and to advise the monarchy: "He will tell you, Sir, what is the amount of liberty that suits him, the treaties that bother him, the regulations that obstruct him, the encouragement that he requires and that which is useless to him."[186]

Similarly, the Merchant Court of Brioude insisted that "the Third Estate has risen to the level of the general and disinterested sentiments of the clergy and the nobility, with which it has often shared the glory and the work."[187] Members of the Third Estate, and particularly merchants, had acquired this public-serving nature traditionally associated with the higher estates because they had no choice but to do so. While those belonging to the First and Second Estates retained their honor, even as they ceased to perform any socially useful function, the merchant had to work for a living and in the process contributed greatly to the state's well-being: "Excluded from all military grades by innovations contrary to the public good, suited to destroying emulation and stifling talent, without hope of obtaining any success in the Church, whose rights and dignities should be less a favor accorded to birth than a reward for piety, science, mores, and virtue, there is nothing more that remains to him but to confine himself to deploying his industry."[188] Precisely because the Third Estate, and merchants especially, were so necessary for and devoted to the national welfare, they were worthy of having their own representatives at the Estates General.

In thus insisting that merchants actively sought to promote the national interest, the petitioners echoed much of the political-economic discourse of the period, which claimed that merchants, like noblemen, were spurred patriotically to pursue activities beneficial to the nation by a laudable desire to gain honor and esteem.[189] Indeed, the petitioners' arguments drew on a growing body of popular literature, extending well beyond the genre of political economy, in which the merchant, and in particular the elite *négociant,* was portrayed as the embodiment of the enlightenment ideal of *bienfaisance*—namely, an inclination to promote the well-being of others. During the latter half of the eighteenth century, an array of publications by merchants and nonmerchants alike, ranging from plays to newspaper articles, depicted the *négociant* as someone worthy of great honor and status by virtue of his involvement in commercial activity. Through such activity, the *négociant* facilitated the creation and transfer of wealth, thus benefiting not only himself but all members of society. As explained by the *négociant* Aurelly, the main character in Beaumarchais' 1770 *drame Les deux amis, ou le négociant de Lyon,* the correct measure of "merit" is "the utility of our virtues and our talents in serving others," and here the *négociant* easily measured up to such traditional elites as the noble warrior.[190] Similarly, in August 1761 the *Journal de Commerce* declared that since "commerce necessarily serv[es] public utility,"[191] it is of all "profession[s] [*états*] . . . the one . . . that presents the most opportunities to demonstrate *bienfaisance.*"[192]

Drawing on the idea that commerce was a source of *bienfaisance,* the petitioners developed a conception of commerce as a function that sustains the modern, as opposed to feudal, social order—and which is therefore not restricted to certain merchant *corps.* But they then deployed this conception for the purpose of obtaining corporate representation.[193] In thus transcending local interests and demanding representation as a national corporate entity, the merchant courts call to mind other judicial institutions of the Old Regime which, during the second half of the eighteenth century, similarly united in common cause—including, in particular, the *parlements* (and their "*union des classes*")[194] and the *bureaux des finances.* Like the merchant courts, both the *parlements* and the *bureaux des finances* were distinct corporate entities with particularist interests which, largely as a result of the monarchy's own regulatory efforts, came to view themselves as national bodies.

There were, however, important differences in the paths to unification taken by these three sets of institutions. Because of their unique power and position in the Old Regime social and political order, the *parlements* that began joining together in the 1750s did not demand representation before a national representative body, but instead claimed to be such a national body—one that stood in the shoes of the absent Estates General. In contrast, the *bureaux des finances,* just like the merchant courts, united at the end of the Old Regime to demand corporate representation at the Estates General.[195] This parallel between how the *bureaux des finances* and the merchant courts came to identify themselves as national *corps* confirms recent research concerning the monarchy's role in its own demise. In particular, it confirms research suggesting that the tensions generated by the monarchy's continued promotion of corporatism, on the one hand, and its efforts to centralize and rationalize, on the other, contributed significantly to its eventual collapse.[196] But despite the obvious parallels, there were also great differences in the paths to demanding national representation taken by the *bureaux des finances,* on the one hand, and the merchant courts, on the other—differences that highlight the unique (and unintended) role of the merchant courts in facilitating the ultimate triumph of a modern conception of commerce.

As Gail Bossenga has shown, the *bureaux des finances,* like many other corporate entities in the Old Regime, progressively lost their judicial and administrative powers over the course of the seventeenth and eighteenth centuries. As the monarchy increasingly sold privilege-bearing offices within the *bureaux des finances,* it transformed these institutions of government into mere investment properties and transferred real authority to its growing bureaucracy of intendants. In the final decades of the Old Regime, as part of its effort to promote a rational tax policy, the monarchy then attempted to eliminate the privileges that it had sold to those holding office within the *bureaux des finances,* and ultimately to abolish these offices entirely. This was the final straw. Already resentful of their loss of power vis-à-vis the intendants, the *bureaux des finances* rose up to defend their property interests against the threat of royal despotism. But in order to justify their privileges, officeholders within the *bureaux des finances* needed to claim that they served a useful social function—and since they had long been stripped of any real judicial and administrative powers, this was a particularly difficult claim to make. Unsuccessful in their effort to obtain representation at the Estates General, the *bureaux des finances* were soon thereafter abolished.[197]

The merchant courts, in contrast, were not corporate entities in the formal, legal sense, since their officers—the judge and consuls—did not own offices purchased from the crown. Moreover, these courts—in part, precisely because they were not true corporations—did not experience a decline in their powers over the course of the seventeenth and eighteenth centuries. Indeed, if anything, they proved remarkably adept at expanding their powers vis-à-vis other institutions. In this sense, they are comparable to the Parisian barristers' association studied by David Bell, which likewise managed to deploy its lack of formal corporate status—and in particular the fact that its members were not venal officeholders—as a means of gaining significant independence from the crown. Whether by ignoring the letter of the law and permitting blank endorsements, or by expanding their jurisdiction to extend to bankruptcies and to nonmerchant, noble defendants, the Old Regime merchant courts remained vigorous institutions, exercising a great deal of authority, independent of direct royal control.

As argued throughout this book, one of the key means by which the merchant courts thus solidified their power—both in developing new commercial doctrine and in expanding their jurisdiction—was by appealing to a new conception of commerce as a necessary and natural social function. Accordingly, when in 1788 the merchant courts united to petition the monarchy for representation at the Estates General, it was to this conception of commerce—one that they had long and successfully elaborated—that they turned. And while, as described below, the merchant courts ultimately failed to obtain representation as a national *corps* of commerce, they did manage to survive the Revolution. This was no mean feat, given that all other judicial institutions of the Old Regime, including the *bureaux des finances,* were abolished. The *juridictions consulaires* were renamed and reconceived as courts of commerce, rather than of merchants, but structurally they were largely unchanged. Their remarkable endurance is testimony to the extraordinary power of the new conception of commerce that they themselves helped to develop and propagate during the Old Regime—and under whose banner they managed to survive into the next.[198]

But this takes us ahead of our story. As of the fall of 1788, merchant courts and chambers of commerce drew on their self-conception as a nationwide *corps* of commerce to demand representation at the newly called Estates General. While this demand was, in many ways, but the fruition of earlier developments, the second Assembly of Notables, which convened in October 1788 to determine the form that the Estates General would take,[199] viewed the matter from a different perspective. For both the traditionalists (who wanted the Estates General to meet as it had last, in 1614) and the supporters of the Third Estate (who rejected any plan that would call for divisions within the Third Estate), the notion that *le commerce* would be formally recognized as a distinct *corps* within the social order was unacceptable.[200] Accordingly, the notables rejected the merchant courts' demand for corporate representation. And shortly thereafter, as the Third Estate assumed the title of National Assembly, the notion that any corporatist entity might stand between the individual citizen and his elected representatives became so inconceivable that the demand for representation of a nationwide *corps* of *le commerce* was not to be heard again.

But while merchant courts and the merchants that they claimed to represent were denied official recognition as a corporate entity of *le commerce,* they were nonetheless long accustomed to viewing themselves as such. It thus came as an enormous surprise when the revolutionaries—relying on arguments about the nature of commerce as a social function that they themselves had played a key role in developing—decided to nationalize the merchant courts and their property. Indeed, nationalization was particularly shocking since the revolutionaries, who were otherwise universally hostile to the judicial institutions of the Old Regime, were generally quite enthusiastic about the merchant courts.

On May 27, 1790, the Constituent Assembly discussed whether to maintain a separate set of courts to try "matters of commerce" and decided to do so.[201] Those advocating this proposal pointed to the virtues of the Old Regime merchant courts, and in particular to the ways in which these courts had somehow remarkably avoided the corruption of the old order. As one deputy intoned, "The merchant courts . . . resisted contagion by example."[202] Indeed, he exhorted his colleagues, "If it had been possible to organize all the courts of the kingdom on such simple foundations, if the judges of the superior courts had had the same zeal, the same disinterestedness, and the same lack of power to abuse their authority, you would certainly not have had to reconstitute the judicial branch."[203] The merchant courts were so admirable, he suggested, because they emerged as republican, democratic institutions before their time. Their judges, he claimed, "had no other interest than being just, no other ambition than serving their fatherland and meriting the esteem of their fellow citizens."[204] In so arguing, the deputy rehearsed the classical litany of merchant court features—but now presented these features as evidence of republican, rather than merchant virtue. Underlying this argument from republican virtue was the now prevailing view that commerce was a necessary social function, such that the merchant courts—as institutions seeking to facilitate commercial activity—were by definition patriotic entities, working for the benefit of all citizens, rather than for that of merchants alone. Accordingly, the deputy concluded, "similar courts would have to be instituted if they did not already exist."[205]

Notably, to the extent that certain deputies opposed maintaining a separate system of courts for commercial matters, their grounds for doing so were not that they fundamentally disagreed with this portrait of the Old Regime merchant courts as proto-republican bastions of virtue. They simply rejected, as a matter of principle, the possibility of establishing any courts of limited jurisdiction. Only a single trial court of general jurisdiction, competent to hear all cases, including commercial ones, would be able, they believed, to prevent the reemergence of the jurisdictional confusion that characterized the Old Regime and to establish definitively the constitutional principle of equality before the law. To allow particular persons or disputes to appear before special courts, not open to all, was to risk the reemergence of corporatism. As one deputy argued, it would be a big mistake to "depart from the beautiful unity that you have always tried to maintain in your constitution."[206] In so insisting, however, this deputy fully agreed that there was much to admire in—and, indeed, replicate from—the Old Regime merchant courts. Thus, he observed, "the method of [using] arbiters is beautiful, great, and too neglected" and should be employed by the ordinary courts when deciding commercial matters.[207]

Ultimately, the voices advocating the maintenance of a separate system of courts for "matters of commerce" won the day. Having come to believe that "commerce is the source of public abundance and private wealth, . . . [which] encourages agriculture, . . . makes the arts flourish, . . . [and] makes destructive prejudices disappear," the deputies concluded that no other institution would be better able to promote commerce—now expressly conceived as a function necessary for society to survive and flourish.[208] Thus, several months later, on August 16, 1790, the Constituent Assembly enacted a decree providing for the establishment of a *tribunal de commerce* in every city where the departmental government so requested.[209] Shortly, thereafter, on January 27, 1791, a *tribunal de commerce* was created in Paris.[210] Aside from its new name, the Merchant Court of Paris appeared to be little changed. It would still have five presiding officers, but all would now be called judges.[211] As in the past, judges were to be elected indirectly, with the merchant community voting for electors and the electors choosing the judges. But whereas in the past an arbitrarily determined number of electors had been chosen from among the leading guilds, electors were now to be selected through a more democratic process.

The merchants in each of Paris's forty-eight sections were entitled to select a certain number of electors based on the number of merchants voting in that section.[212] And rather than hailing from particular guilds, these electors were to be local "*négociants,* bankers, manufacturers, and factory owners."[213] Thus, while the Allarde Law of March 1791, which abolished the guilds, was yet to be enacted, the Assembly sought to distance the court from its roots in the guild system.[214]

The new Parisian *tribunal de commerce* and its sister courts across the country survived the upheavals of the Revolution. Napoleon's *Code de Commerce,* enacted in 1807, confirmed that the *tribunaux de commerce* would be preserved, their lay merchant judges to be chosen by electors who were to be selected from "traders, directors of corporations [*sociétés anonymes*], finance and industrial companies, and stock brokers," as well as ship captains and masters of coasting vessels.[215] Thus, aside from its severance from the now defunct guild system, the Parisian *tribunal de commerce,* as it emerged in the early nineteenth century, did not differ much from its Old Regime predecessor. The judges continued to send large numbers of cases to arbiters for resolution, and the substantive and procedural law of the court was little changed.[216] As scholars have observed, the *Code de Commerce* of 1807 essentially codified the law as inherited from before the Revolution.[217] The merchant court would therefore appear to be but another manifestation of Tocqueville's famous observation of the Revolution: old wine in new bottles.[218]

But bottles can be important. The renaming of the merchant court—the transformation of *les juges des marchands,* the name by which the court had been popularly known, into *le tribunal de commerce*—was intended to bring about more than a change in name. It was intended to transform the court from a court of merchants into a court of commercial transactions. The court was to become one among many public institutions designed to serve the interests of the nation as an (abstract) whole, rather than a representative and facilitator of merchant interests. It was to promote the interests of *le commerce* as a social function, rather than *le commerce* as a *corps* of merchants. Indeed, it was precisely because the revolutionaries wanted to ensure that commerce was henceforth recognized as a necessary social function, rather than an activity associated with a particular corporate entity, that some were opposed to maintaining a separate system of commercial courts. For like reasons, the Constituent Assembly decreed on March 24, 1791, that appeals from the *tribunaux de commerce* must be heard by courts of general jurisdiction.[219] In the words of deputy Le Chapelier, this was necessary "to avoid the commercial courts' establishing among themselves the foundations of a distinct corporate entity [*corporation particulière*]."[220] And in a further effort to ensure that commercial courts not be permitted to form a *corporation particulière*—and, of course, as of April 1792, to fund the growing war effort—the Assembly decided to nationalize commercial-court property.

Early in 1791, the revolutionary government directed the Parisian Merchant Court to provide it with a list of all the court's property, so that this could be nationalized.[221] Shocked and upset, the former judges and consuls, organized in the *compagnie des anciens,* selected three former judges and one former consul to draft a response. Their argument was very simple: "All the properties attached to the Parisian *tribunal de commerce* belong to the merchants of Paris; the nation did not contribute anything to them."[222] When the French monarchy first established the Parisian Merchant Court in 1563, they reasoned, it did not provide the merchants with a courthouse, but instead ordered merchants to tax themselves for this purpose. Merchants complied and eventually succeeded in building their own courthouse, which for centuries was operated by merchants on their own behalf. While the Revolution had created a new *tribunal de commerce* in place of the old *juridiction consulaire,* it differed only in that the electors who selected the judges were no longer chosen on the basis of guild membership but rather the location of their residence within Paris. Put simply, the judges and consul concluded, "These properties [of the *tribunal de commerce*] are commerce's own properties, which have never been national, and the property owners . . . continue to own them and are their natural administrators."[223]

This reasoning still made sense in May 1776 when the Parisian Merchant Court—eager to maintain its existence despite Turgot's abolition of the guilds in February—successfully thwarted a proposal that it be merged with the municipal government by arguing that its officers fulfilled their duties "with the amiability that they owe to their fellow *négociants.*"[224] As an institution devoted to promoting the interests and reinforcing the structure of the merchant community, the merchant court rightly belonged to this community. But in 1791, this was a losing argument. By this time, commerce—in no small part through the efforts of merchants themselves—had come to be conceived as the set of activities necessary to sustain the social organism, rather than the function of a particular status group. In this new world, merchants were to run the court and appear before it, but it was to be a court that adjudicated commercial transactions, rather than a court of merchants. As a court of commercial transactions, it could belong only to the nation—to the people as a whole whom commercial activity sustained, rather than to that particular subset that engaged in the profession of commerce. Thus, in April 1792, just a year after it raised its short-lived resistance, the *compagnie des anciens* relinquished any claim to the property of the *tribunal de commerce*. Shortly thereafter, having lost both its ties to the guilds and its property, the *compagnie,* which was at the heart of the ancient court, ceased to exist.[225] On December 24, 1793 (4 nivôse, an II), the National Convention declared that all *tribunaux de commerce* were to suffer the same fate as that of Paris: "The property . . . belonging . . . to the former merchant courts is part of the national property."[226] Henceforth, the *tribunaux de commerce* were relieved of all other administration than that of justice, and the burden of financing the courts' operation was to fall on the various departmental governments—and thus on the tax-paying citizenry as a whole.[227]

Conclusion

While 1791 is the endpoint of this book, it is not, of course, the end of the story. The rise of the *tribunal de commerce* marked the triumph of what I have called the modern conception of commerce, and with it, the demise of legally enshrined corporatism. But these developments did not lead, as scholars once believed, to the total suppression of institutions of civil society in nineteenth-century France. As a number of historians have recently shown, the nineteenth century witnessed something of a resurgence of the language of corporatism.[1] By appealing to this language, entities such as trade unions and professional associations justified their right to exist and asserted their interests vis-à-vis other groups and against the state. Indeed, according to Claire Lemercier, the Parisian *tribunal de commerce* itself played a crucial role in legitimating the reemergence of corporatist forms—and, in particular, the development of powerful employers' unions, or *syndicats*—by regularly employing these nascent organizations to serve as arbiters and thus, like the guilds before them, to help resolve disputes.[2]

To argue that the rise of the *tribunal de commerce* marked the triumph of a new conception of commerce is thus not to claim that the role of group interests in commercial and political life simply disappeared after 1791. Similarly, it is not to assert that those engaged in commercial activity came to embrace an ethic of unbounded self-interest that led them entirely to dispense with questions of virtue.[3] To the contrary, a central claim of this book has been that the eighteenth-century merchants who ultimately opted in favor of the defining modern practice of negotiability were able to do so only because they reconceived of commerce as a necessary social function and thus as a kind of reconfigured, depersonalized virtue. Moreover, through to the very end of the Old Regime (and likely well beyond), the Parisian Merchant Court continued to resolve small-scale, relational contract disputes by means of its highly personal, tried-and-true methods for restoring harmony and thereby resuscitating virtue as traditionally understood. But while there were some important continuities between the Old Regime and the new, the differences were nonetheless profound. In the years after the Revolution, group interests were reasserted and economic virtue remained a concern, but the grounds on which such interests could be legitimately advanced and the ways in which virtue was imagined were significantly transformed. The developments traced in this book, in short, marked a revolution in commerce—a series of profound, interrelated transformations in both commercial practice and conceptions of commerce, which in turn provoked a significant reconfiguration of the social order, the relationship between state and society, and the foundations of governance.

Merchants themselves played a key (though largely unintended) role in fomenting this revolution. Over the course of the eighteenth century (and especially the latter half), the merchant courts of Old Regime France, and in particular that of Paris, came to develop new ways of thinking and talking about commerce. This new discourse of commerce suggests an important change in the ideas and values of those ordinary but important people who actually engaged in commerce—and a small but significant percentage of whom would ultimately serve in the National Assembly.[4] At the same time, this new discourse did more than simply mark a conceptual transformation; it also contributed to important shifts in real-world institutions and practices.

Why did the new discourse of commerce arise? And how did it contribute to actual social change? A key answer to both these questions lies in the law. The realm of the law—understood broadly as that set of discourses and institutions responsible for elaborating and enforcing the norms that structure civil society and the state—serves as a locus for the (socially legitimate) resolution of conflicting interests and values. And in so doing, it necessarily bridges discourse and practice.

Law and legal institutions (ranging from courts to administrative agencies to juristic practices) operate through discourse—through language that prescribes a normative ordering of the social condition and that can, as we have seen, derive from a wide variety of sources, including not only legal but also religious, political, and economic thought. But legal institutions are also charged with implementing this discourse, and thereby promoting real-world change. Accordingly, as this book has recounted, Old Regime judges, jurists, royal administrators, and ordinary litigants all struggled to deploy legal discourse and institutions to translate their differing visions of the social order into reality. And the legal system provided a framework (however imperfect) for determining whose visions would ultimately triumph and whose would fail. Thus, for example, through legal battles, merchant court judges, jurists, and litigants who sought to expand merchant court jurisdiction succeeded to a remarkable extent in countering the demands of their ordinary, civil-law counterparts—though with consequences that they had not fully anticipated.

Legal institutions and practices do more, however, than simply implement discourse; they also serve as an important agent of discursive, or conceptual, change. Because legal actors are charged with the daily, unremitting task of creating, transforming, and enforcing the rules that undergird social institutions—ranging from the family to the business association to the state—they are regularly forced to confront the question of social change. And confronted with such change, they have no choice but to evaluate its merits, since they must decide whether to continue to implement preexisting law, or whether instead to transform the law in accordance with changing social practices. As we have seen, for example, changes in how eighteenth-century French men and women used bills of exchange impelled a wide range of legal actors to question the legitimacy of these new practices and, in the process, to start thinking and talking about social and commercial relations in new ways. Thus, as mediated by the law, changing social practices can give rise to important shifts in discourse.

The key importance of law and legal institutions in engendering new patterns of discourse and, in turn, in remaking social institutions is implicit—though insufficiently acknowledged—in the recent and very thought-provoking studies that have been undertaken of such legal institutions and practices as marriage and the family, taxation, and the Parisian bar.[5] Indeed, it is no accident that so many historians struggling with the question of how to proceed after "the linguistic turn"—and, in particular, how best to explain the link between changing modes of discourse and changing social practices—have chosen to focus on the law and legal institutions. This trend follows from the fact that the law is *the* conduit between discourse and practice. It is, in other words, a set of socially sanctioned institutions and practices for debating and then implementing (differing) conceptions of the social good. To recognize the centrality of the law in processes of social ordering and change is thus to augment and refine the revisionist understanding of the Old Regime and the Revolution by treating transformations in political culture as part of a broader story about changes in legal discourses, practices, and institutions. Indeed, it bears emphasis that, starting with the Third Estate's decision to declare itself the National Assembly and extending to, inter alia, its abolition of corporatism and remaking of the legislative and judicial branches of government, the French Revolution itself was, in a fundamental sense, a revolution in law and legal institutions. And while this book has confined itself to but one component of this broad set of legal transformations—namely, those associated with commerce in the Old Regime—it is clear that, even within this relatively narrow frame, legal institutions and practices contributed to fundamental changes in both discourse and social practice.

As we have seen, merchant courts (along with the chambers of commerce with which they were associated) were impelled to develop and deploy a new discourse of commerce in several different contexts, each of which was at core a legal one. These included electoral struggles, status disputes, and jurisdictional conflicts (all of which were the object of extensive administrative action and litigation), and the adjudication of commercial litigation (concerning in particular negotiable instruments). And while long ignored in the scholarly literature, this new discourse of commerce extended to important and widespread segments of the French population in the decades before the Revolution. The electoral struggles in which the Parisian Merchant Court engaged involved all of Paris's leading guilds, and the arguments deployed—often printed as pamphlets for public distribution—likely reached an even broader segment of the Parisian community. Moreover, in the joint campaigns that they undertook on behalf of their jurisdictional and status-related interests, merchant courts petitioned upward to the central *Bureau du Commerce* (itself staffed by both merchant deputies and high-level ministers) and outward to fellow merchants in commercial towns throughout France, among whose numbers were included the country's leading bankers and *négociants*.

Likewise, in developing new doctrine regarding negotiable instruments, the Parisian Merchant Court established ways of thinking about commerce and commercial practices that reached the many litigants and other interested merchants who regularly appeared before it. Indeed, because the court's adjudicatory process drew so extensively on community networks, the court's thinking about commerce did more than simply reach large numbers of people. It was itself the product of what was in essence a large-scale communal discussion. Moreover, since merchant courts across the country sought to model themselves on that of Paris and, toward this end, regularly solicited its legal advice (including as concerns negotiable instruments), there is good reason to suspect that the Parisian Merchant Court's thinking about commerce in this doctrinal context extended even beyond its jurisdiction.

Fundamental transformations in commercial practice—and in particular in the law governing negotiable instruments—were made possible in part because merchants chose to embrace a new conception of commerce as a vital social function. While such practices as discounting, blank endorsements, and the demise of the rule of different places arose independently of the discourse that would ultimately come to justify them, this discourse served to legitimate them and thereby ensure their survival in the face of contrary and competing practices and values. That these practices did survive—and that negotiable paper thus came to be so widely used—was, in turn, a development that had profound consequences for French society. It was the ready availability of such paper (and of the short-term credit that it afforded) that helped to fuel the tremendous expansion in domestic and foreign trade, and in industrial and agricultural production, that occurred during the eighteenth century. Moreover, negotiable paper, ranging from bills of exchange to the shares of those *sociétés de capitaux* that undertook large-scale (often transatlantic) commerce, gave rise to the speculative boom that consumed Paris and its bourse in the 1780s. Likewise, negotiable paper facilitated the emergence of a consumer-oriented economy, driven in part by mass advertising and making available to ever larger numbers of people the items once reserved for a small elite.

As recent historians have increasingly come to recognize, the results of these developments were profound. Not only did they point the way toward a fundamental reconfiguration of the French economy, but in so doing they also suggested a concomitant reshaping of social and political relations. As contemporary critics of luxury complained, a world in which commercial capital had become so fundamentally important was a world without order. In this new commercial world, the low-born could aspire to noble status through the purchase of a venal office, an estate, or at least the accoutrements of aristocratic living, and entire fortunes could be made to rise or fall on the basis of mere, seemingly insubstantial paper. As a result, the material displays of status, by means of which social and political power had long been symbolically represented in the Old Regime, ceased to have a clear, fixed meaning, and contemporaries struggled to identify a new foundation for order in a world that had seemingly lost its moorings. Particularly troubling was the fact that those who seemed best able to navigate within this apparent disorder were the financiers to whom the monarchy increasingly turned for capital. Deploying speculative techniques that were grounded in the new practices of negotiability developed by the merchants studied in this book, such financiers earned vast profits for themselves, while at the same time exerting a powerful stranglehold on the monarchy. In this way, they were able to exercise an influence on royal policy that struck many contemporaries as profoundly illegitimate, giving rise to a deep public animosity that would eventually play an important role in undermining the Old Regime.[6]

Merchant courts thus contributed to transformations not only in commercial practice but also in social and political relations. Likewise, they helped to provoke the emergence of a new relationship between state and society. Through the deployment of a new discourse of commerce, the Parisian Merchant Court and its sister courts throughout France valorized commercial activity as a necessary function of society that naturally tended toward the social good, thus implicitly obviating any need for guild and police regulation. In this way, they helped to develop a modern, functionalist conception of commerce—one that was readily available and comprehensible to larger sections of the French populace than was the discourse of the Physiocrats and other elite (or even middling) theorists. As a result, Old Regime merchants unwittingly worked to undermine some of the key conceptual foundations of the corporatist order, including the notion that private exchange necessarily constitutes a public hazard, and that group interests could and should be the primary focus of state regulation and law.

Moreover, through their electoral and jurisdictional battles, the merchant courts undermined corporatism not only on a conceptual level but also on an institutional one. For example, it was the Parisian Merchant Court, as part of its ongoing electoral struggles and status conflicts, that first identified itself as an entity distinct from the guilds—one designed to promote the interests of commerce as a whole, rather than those of particular corporate entities. And it was to precisely this conception of the court that the Constituent Assembly would later turn, when in January 1791—shortly before abolishing the guilds—it declared that the judges of the Parisian *tribunal de commerce* were to be selected from among elite merchant individuals, rather than from particular guilds. Given the extent to which the leading Parisian guilds had long deployed the court as a power base, it seems likely that the decision thus to restructure the court's electoral foundations played some part in sealing the guilds' ultimate fate. In this sense, the abolition of the guilds, which occurred about one month later, can be traced, however indirectly, to the arguments previously deployed by the Parisian Merchant Court.

Likely more important in undermining corporatism was the way that the Parisian Merchant Court laid claim to jurisdiction over goods transported into Paris through the ports, and that all merchant courts demanded jurisdiction over bankruptcies, defendants residing beyond the bailiwicks in which they were located, and nonmerchants. These jurisdictional claims implied a shift in the basis of merchant court jurisdiction from personal to real—from jurisdiction over those possessing the status of merchant to (at least in part) jurisdiction over the subject matter of commerce. Given that the Old Regime was premised on privilege—on the idea that particular types of persons ought to be governed by their own particular laws—this was no small shift. Its clear implication was that corporate status had ceased to be an appropriate basis for legal regulation and that the law was instead to treat all individuals alike. From here to the abolition of corporatism—including the elimination of the entire judicial system (but for the merchant courts), the nationalization of merchant court property, and the destruction of the guilds—was but a relatively short step.

Finally, it was, in part, the new ways that merchants came to think and talk about commerce—and in particular their new recognition that commerce was so vital to national well-being—that caused them to rise up in 1788 and demand political power. As economically productive members of society, they argued, they were entitled to a voice in governing the nation. And while their demand for representation in the Estates General was ultimately denied, their reasoning was shortly thereafter embraced by the Third Estate as a whole, when it decided to declare itself the National Assembly.

A key conceptual shift that led the Third Estate to make this radical move was the revolutionaries' embrace of what Keith Baker has called a "social theory of representation."[7] This theory, whose roots lay in the writings of the Physiocrats, among others, was developed by Sieyès in his highly popular political tract *Qu'est-ce que le tiers état?*—a tract setting forth the revolutionary plan of action that the Third Estate came to follow. Pursuant to the social theory of representation, society consisted not of hierarchically arranged corporate entities, but instead of individuals bound together through the division of labor, such that individual productivity ought to serve as a key foundation of citizenship. In joining together to demand representation at the Estates General, merchant courts and chambers of commerce sought representation as a corporate entity, rather than—as Sieyès would soon advocate—representation of the individual as a citizen of the nation. Nonetheless, the merchants' call for representation anticipated a key aspect of the theory of representation that Sieyès would popularize—namely, that those who participate in a highly productive and necessary social function are entitled to representation and thus to a share in the exercise of political power. By uniting to demand representation in the fall of 1788, merchant courts and chambers of commerce thus helped to lay the conceptual groundwork for the remarkable triumph of Sieyès's proposal a few months later.

The merchants who played such an important role in developing a conception of commerce that would ultimately be deployed to dismantle corporatism (and thus to remake the social and political order) were themselves, it bears emphasis, guild leaders. Although recent scholarship concerning eighteenth-century guilds has provided an important corrective to the once prevailing view that these were defunct institutions, whose demise was all but inevitable, this effort to steer clear of teleology has led historians to avoid exploring the ways in which merchants themselves contributed to the collapse of corporatism. This book's examination of a set of merchant institutions and discourses that historians have largely ignored, however, reveals that guild merchants themselves—in their capacity as merchant court judges, rather than guild leaders—did indeed contribute significantly to corporatism's demise. But they did so without in any way seeking to undermine their guild-based privileges. For this reason, they were able to utilize the new discourse of commerce in the contexts that I have described, while at the same time continuing to defend their guild privileges well into the Revolution. This suggests that the paradigm shift implicit in the reconceptualization of commerce from a legally enshrined marker of status to a natural and necessary function of society was possible, in part, precisely because contemporaries—or at least those key contemporaries who actually engaged in commercial activity—did not, in fact, experience it as such. From their perspective, they were simply operating within an established legal framework, deploying available discourses and institutions as best they could to promote their immediate interests.

What then were the interests that impelled merchant courts to embrace a new conception of commerce as the credit-fueled private exchange necessary to sustain society? Key among these were interests in expanding their jurisdiction and in enhancing their status vis-à-vis other corporate entities within the social order—interests that they understood to be claims of privilege. Such fundamentally corporatist interests were, as historians have increasingly come to recognize, alive and well in France through to the very end of the Old Regime—embraced not only by a supposedly reactionary noble elite but even by those, like merchants, who were once thought to be at the forefront of a bourgeois revolution. This book's demonstration that merchant court judges—themselves guild leaders—long continued to advance their corporatist claims to privilege thus complements recent work showing that guild members remained deeply loyal to the guild system.

But by changing the legal framework within which such corporatist interests could be advanced, the monarchy itself helped to create the dynamic whereby merchants' efforts to promote their corporatist interests ultimately contributed to the demise of corporatism. Through its program of administrative reform and rationalization—and in particular the establishment of a uniform body of commercial law and courts, and of the central *Bureau du Commerce*—the monarchy created a powerful set of tools whereby merchants were able to advance their interests against other competing entities and then, ultimately, against the monarchy itself. Thus, while the monarchy embraced administrative centralization as a means of augmenting its own tax base, and therefore power, the unintended consequences of its actions were to facilitate its own demise.

Indeed, as revisionists have argued, the key to the Revolution lay in the monarchy's own contradictory impulses—and, in particular, in its continued commitment to corporatism, on the one hand, and its efforts to advance policies of centralization and rationalization, on the other. Operating under the pressure of these contradictory impulses, many different groups within the Old Regime ultimately concluded that the status quo had become untenable. But unlike the corporate entities that others have studied, the merchant courts examined in this book did not turn against the monarchy in anger and frustration. To the contrary, these courts—precisely because they were not corporate entities in the formal sense—grew increasingly powerful and self-satisfied over the course of the century. It was based on a conviction of their own importance rather than of their impotence that—under the banner of commercial modernity—they ultimately demanded a voice in governance in the fall of 1788. Accordingly, unlike the guilds on which they were based, and unlike all other judicial institutions of the Old Regime, the merchant courts were able to negotiate the transition to a modern, individualist, rather than corporatist social order. In this sense, Marx was quite right to suggest that the Revolution marked the triumph of a liberal economic order—though he mistook the causation.

As revisionists have amply demonstrated, there was no radical shift in modes of production during the eighteenth century and thus no clear set of uniform, bourgeois economic interests that followed from such a (nonexistent) shift.[8] Indeed, as we have seen, the merchants who developed a new conception of commerce never sought to eradicate the corporatist legal framework undergirding guild-based modes of production. But while Marx was wrong to insist on the bourgeois class origins of the Revolution, he was right to assert that economic developments played a profoundly important role in reshaping the eighteenth-century French social and political order.

The eighteenth century witnessed the rise of a new kind of credit economy, which dramatically reconfigured the means by which social practices of all kinds—including not only the commercial sales and production examined in this book, but also state institutions and endeavors, and strategies for promoting familial wealth[9]—were financed and thereby enabled. The importance of new modes of credit is implicit in much of the recent literature on eighteenth-century French political economy, including works discussing the consumer revolution and the growing power of financiers.[10] But changing consumer practices and the speculative activities of financiers were themselves developments that ultimately hinged on—and, in turn, served to promote—the new availability of extensive and increasingly anonymous forms of credit. For this reason, a complete account of the rise of new modes of credit would require an in-depth exploration of a number of developments far exceeding the scope of these pages, including, perhaps most importantly, methods of state finance.[11] But while this book has focused on only a subset of the issues surrounding credit in Old Regime France, these alone suggest the profound importance of changing credit practices in helping to reconfigure both civil society and the state.

To argue for the significance of changing practices of credit in the remaking of eighteenth-century society, and thus in the rise of modernity, is emphatically not to deny that discourse plays a crucial role in processes of social change. The revisionist lesson that discourse must be taken seriously—that it, indeed, acts as a crucial motor of social change—has led to many new insights concerning key historical developments, and promises to continue to do so. Discourse is not, however, the only motor of change. As indicated by the shift in approaches to credit explored in this book, economic developments must also be given their due. Neither modes of discourse nor economic developments, in short, can or do operate independently of the other, and to ask which comes first is to confront something like the perennial problem of the chicken and the egg.

As suggested by the model of law and legal institutions with which I began this concluding chapter, modes of discourse and social practices (including economic developments) constantly inform and shape one another, and we should study them accordingly. By taking discourse seriously, we avoid the teleological reasoning that tends to follow from an exclusive focus on economic developments and that denies a meaningful place to human agency in accounting for historical change. But by recognizing that economic developments exert their own pressure, we also identify a key factor that impels reconceptualization of the social condition, and thus, significant discursive transformation. Accordingly, as we have seen, the new credit practices that arose in the eighteenth century provoked a series of crises—commercial, moral, and religious—that a wide range of people, including Church thinkers and literary figures, struggled to address. At the same time, it was ultimately by means of legal discourses and processes that these crises were resolved—and because of the choices made by various legal actors, resolved in such a way that the new credit practices were able to take root and flourish, thus laying the groundwork for a set of fundamental commercial, social, and political transformations, only some of which are described in this book.

This brings us, finally, to the standard narrative of the law merchant. As this narrative extends across many centuries and geographic borders, any conclusions about its validity that can be drawn from the activities of the eighteenth-century Parisian Merchant Court are necessarily limited in scope. But despite this limitation, such conclusions are based on actual archival evidence, and thus fill an important gap in a body of literature that has tended to be highly speculative in nature. Accordingly, they bear serious consideration. Moreover, given the extent to which those advancing the standard narrative of the law merchant have been motivated by presentist concerns—with promoting a transnational order for commercial dispute-resolution and with helping developing countries achieve greater economic prosperity—the possibility that this narrative is flawed suggests reason for particular concern. To the extent, in other words, that bad history will (or has) formed the basis for modern-day policy-making, the need to correct this history is all the more urgent.

So what are the conclusions about the standard narrative suggested by the history of the Parisian Merchant Court? They are, in short, that, while aspects of the standard narrative are certainly correct, many are quite misleading. True to the standard narrative, the eighteenth-century merchants studied in this book did employ the merchant courts to promote interests that they felt were inadequately served by the ordinary, civil-law courts—including interests in fast and inexpensive dispute resolution and, ultimately, in legal doctrine that would promote a rapid and secure credit market. And while it is impossible to draw a clear distinction between the private and public spheres in the early-modern period, merchant courts did indeed rely significantly on what we today would think of as private, community-based mechanisms for both adjudication and enforcement.

At the same time, however, this history of the Parisian Merchant Court supplements and confirms many of the suspicions of those scholars who have recently challenged the standard narrative. The law applied by the court does not easily fit the standard narrative's description of "the law merchant" as a single, coherent body of law.[12] It was, instead, a hodgepodge of rules, practices, and sensibilities, many of which were developed on a case-by-case basis. Even merchant custom (in the sense of clear default rules)—that hobbyhorse of the standard narrative and of modern commercial-law scholars alike—was largely absent from the court's adjudicatory toolbox. Moreover, contrary to the standard narrative, it cannot be said that the law merchant persisted as a purely private ordering encapsulated within (but somehow fundamentally unchanged by) early-modern codifications. The monarchy played an important part in developing the law applied by the merchant court. So too did the university-trained civil-law jurists, who worked in the tradition of the *ius commune* or that of the *coutumes,* and who generally had little sympathy for the merchant courts and their commercial-jurist allies. Moreover, royal bailiffs and prisons played a crucial (though never sufficient) role in enforcing the merchant court's judgments.

Most importantly, the history of the Parisian Merchant Court indicates that the merchant interests that the court sought to promote were far more complex and diverse than what the standard narrative would suggest. According to this narrative, merchants were interested, first and foremost, in facilitating economic growth. In reality, however, it is clear that, while this was an important interest, merchants also had distinct interests in achieving substantive fairness. In pursuit of these other interests, the court at times rewrote contract terms and canceled debt—and it did so with apparently little concern for any effect this might have on merchants' capacity to predict the consequences of their actions and thus on market confidence. While it may well be that the court understood itself in such cases to be reinforcing the communal institutions and values that were so vital to a market traditionally dependent on relational contracting, its desire to promote charity (and other manifestations of merchant virtue) cannot be reduced solely to such economic concerns.

There is, finally, yet another, perhaps even more fundamental, sense in which the standard narrative of the law merchant has misconstrued the nature of the interests that the Parisian Merchant Court sought to advance. The standard narrative is concerned with elaborating the evolution of modern commercial law—and, as deployed by some of its proponents, with legitimating the birth of a new transnational commercial order and promoting economic prosperity in the developing world. Because of this presentist orientation, proponents of the standard narrative have anachronistically assumed that merchant courts were judicial institutions in the modern sense—devoted to the resolution of private disputes between individual litigants. As was the case with so many judicial institutions of the Old Regime, however, the Parisian Merchant Court was always much more than simply a court in this narrow sense. Like the guilds from which it emerged, the merchant court was also an administrative or regulatory body. Moreover, as the eighteenth-century progressed, and the court joined with its sister courts and chambers of commerce to petition the *Bureau du Commerce,* it also came to serve as a political institution, seeking to promote the common interests of its members and, ultimately, to demand a voice in governance. To focus exclusively on the fact that the court helped to develop and implement "the law merchant" is thus to ignore key aspects of its role—aspects that were important in shaping not only its sense of identity but also the social, economic, and political life of the Old Regime.

Appendix

Table 1 All Arbiters' Reports from Box AP $D^6B^6/15$: Percentage Distribution of Known Types of Dispute[1]

Type of Dispute	Number	Percentage Represented
Bankruptcy	2	0.7%
Business Association	25	8.2%
Cash Loan	3	1.0%
Employment	35	11.4%
Negotiable Instruments	64	20.9%
Payment of Agent	7	2.3%
Sales of Goods and Services	170	55.6%

1. Because a single case sometimes involved more than one type of dispute (for example, both "Sales" and "Negotiable Instruments"), the total number of disputes included in this table is greater than the actual number of arbiters' reports.

Table 2 All Arbiters' Reports from Box AP D⁶B⁶/15: Percentage Distribution of Known Arbiters' Professions[1]

Percentage Represented	Profession(s)
Less than 1%	army; builder; carpenter (*menuisier*); cartwright; caster; engraver; fruit seller; goldsmith; grain merchant; hatter; mason; owner of a royal factory; painter; solicitor; surveyor; tapestry merchant; wigmaker
1% up to 2%	architect; blacksmith; book seller; examiner at the *Châtelet*; grocer; handwriting expert; notary
2% up to 3%	wine seller
3% up to 4%	(none)
4% up to 5%	(none)
5% up to 6%	(none)
6% up to 7%	royal administrator
7% up to 8%	barrister; unidentified merchant
8% up to 9%	saddler
9% up to 10%	(none)
10% up to 11%	(none)
11% up to 12%	priest
12% up to 28%	(none)
28% up to 29%	guild leaders

1. In cases decided by guild leaders, I have identified the relevant profession of the arbiters as a single instance of "guild leaders," rather than multiple instances of the particular trade practiced by that guild. Percentages were then computed relative to the total number of arbiters in all cases, rather than the total number of cases. As there are relatively few cases with more than one arbiter, the resulting distribution remains an accurate portrayal of the types of arbiters that typically assisted the court.

Table 3 All Arbiters' Reports from Box AP $D^6B^6/15$: Percentage Distribution of Known Plaintiffs' Professions[1]

Percentage Represented	Profession(s)
Less than 1%	agent; army officer; assembled creditors; baker; banker; book seller; bookkeeper; brewer; button merchant; carrier; caster; cloth merchant; clothing seller; coach driver; cooper; day laborer; director of royal glassworks; draper; engraver; fruit seller; gardener; gilder; goldsmith; hairdresser; gun merchant; innkeeper; locksmith; maker of paper for dyeing; marble merchant; mason; miller; notary; oats seller; paver; pork merchant; priest; quarrier; renter of coaches; roofer; ropemaker; royal administrator; saltpeter maker; seller of moldings; silk merchant; soap maker; starch merchant; stationer; surveyor; tapestry merchant; tax farmer; tithe collector; unloader
1% up to 2%	builder; carpenter (*charpentier*); cattle merchant; chambermaid; cobbler; farmer; horse merchant; iron merchant; lumber merchant; nonmerchant consumer; painter; plasterer; saddler; stone cutter; watchmaker; wigmaker; worker
2% up to 3%	barrister; blacksmith; butcher; grocer; heirs
3% up to 4%	carpenter (*menuisier*); cartwright
4% up to 5%	flour seller; haberdasher; wine seller
5% up to 6%	négociant
6% up to 7%	business association; unidentified merchant

1. Percentages have been computed relative to the total number of plaintiffs in all cases, rather than the total number of cases. As there are relatively few cases with more than one plaintiff, the resulting distribution remains an accurate portrayal of the types of plaintiffs that typically appeared before the court. In addition, in cases in which plaintiffs sued as a husband and wife pair, I treat them as a single litigant, identifying the profession as that of the husband, unless the wife was a *marchande publique* and filed suit in that capacity.

Table 4 All Arbiters' Reports from Box AP $D^6B^6/15$: Percentage Distribution of Known Defendants' Professions[1]

Percentage Represented	Profession(s)
Less than 1%	art dealer; assembled creditors; banker; blacksmith; book seller; bookkeeper; brewer; broker; button merchant; carpenter (*charpentier*); caster; caterer; cattle merchant; cloth merchant; coalman; cobbler; cutler; draper; embroiderer; farmer; fruit seller; gardener; gilder; heirs; hosier; iron merchant; laundress; linen maid; livestock farmer; machinist; *marchand forain*; merchant of paper for furniture; miller; owner of mail-coach service; plumber; pork merchant; quarrier; roofer; seamstress; seller of mattresses to French and Swiss regiments; stagehand; tax farmer; water carrier; wine grower; writer
1% up to 2%	carrier; cartwright; clothing seller; flour seller; lumber merchant; painter; plasterer; tailor; tanner; tapestry merchant; wigmaker
2% up to 3%	builder; carpenter (*menuisier*); goldsmith; grocer; haberdasher; horse merchant; innkeeper; mason; renter of coaches; watchmaker
3% up to 4%	business association; butcher; locksmith
4% up to 5%	*négociant*; saddler
5% up to 6%	baker; wine seller
6% up to 7%	(none)
7% up to 8%	unidentified merchant

1. Percentages have been computed relative to the total number of defendants in all cases, rather than the total number of cases. As there are relatively few cases with more than one defendant, the resulting distribution remains an accurate portrayal of the types of defendants that typically appeared before the court. In addition, in cases in which defendants were sued as a husband and wife pair, I treat them as a single litigant, identifying the profession as that of the husband, unless the wife was a *marchande publique* and was sued in that capacity.

Table 5 All Arbiters' Reports from Box AP D⁶B⁶/15 by Known Location of Arbiter

Distance from Paris (in miles from Paris Center)	Percentage Represented	Name(s) of Town(s)
In Paris	85.6%	Paris
Less than 5	2.2%	Vaugirard (now Paris); Vincennes
5 up to 10	2.2%	Chatou; Meudon; Saint-Brice[-sous-Forêt]; Saint-Denis
10 up to 15	3.3%	Longjumeau; Marly-le-Roi; Poissy; Saint-Germain-en-Laye
15 up to 20	1.7%	Arpajon; Luzarches; Pontoise
20 up to 25	1.7%	Beaumont[-sur-Oise]
25 up to 30	0.6%	Fontenay[-Trésigny]
30 up to 40	0.0%	(none)
40 up to 50	0.0%	(none)
50 up to 100	1.1%	Orléans
100 up to 150	1.1%	Bourges; Lille
150 up to 200	0.6%	Pontmain
200 up to 300	0.0%	(none)
Outside of France	0.0%	(none)

Table 6 All Arbiters' Reports from Box AP $D^6B^6/15$ by Known Location of Plaintiff

Distance from Paris (in miles from Paris Center)	Percentage Represented	Name(s) of Town(s)
In Paris	56.2%	Paris
Less than 5	4.6%	Châtillon; Montrouge; Vaugirard (now Paris); Vincennes
5 up to 10	6.9%	Chatou; Créteil; Meudon; Nogent[-sur-Marne]; Saint-Brice[-sous-Forêt]; Saint-Denis; Saint-Maur[-des-Fossés]
10 up to 15	3.1%	Longjumeau; Saint-Germain-en-Laye; Versailles
15 up to 20	0.8%	Villeneuve
20 up to 25	4.6%	Beaumarchais; Dammartin; Gouvieux; Mezières; Saint-Benoît
25 up to 30	0.8%	Meaux
30 up to 40	0.8%	Clermont
40 up to 50	1.5%	Beauvais; Voigny
50 up to 100	10.8%	Amiens; Broglie; Charleville; Essarts; Gacé; L'aigle; Loché; Montdidier; Orléans; Rouen; Échauffour
100 up to 150	3.8%	Abbeville; Fontenay[-sur-Vègre]; Pouilly-sur-Loire; [La] Baroche[-Gondouin/-sous-Lucé]
150 up to 200	2.3%	Chemillé; Metz; Mornay
200 up to 300	3.1%	Besançon; Mâcon; Nantes; Saint-Quirin
Outside of France	0.8%	Vienna (Austria)

Table 7 All Arbiters' Reports from Box AP D⁶B⁶/15 by Known Location of Defendant

Distance from Paris (in miles from Paris Center)	Percentage Represented	Name(s) of Town(s)
In Paris	59.1%	Paris
Less than 5	9.8%	Arcueil; Bagneux; Charenton[-le-pont]; Neuilly[-sur-Seine]; Passy (now Paris); Vaugirard (now Paris); Vincennes
5 up to 10	13.6%	Champigny[-sur-Marne]; Chaville; Créteil; Houilles; Meudon; Nanterre; Nogent[-sur-Marne]; Pierrefitte[-sur-Seine]; Saint-Cloud; Saint-Denis; Sceaux; Stains; Vitry[-sur-Seine]
10 up to 15	6.8%	Brunoy; Chauvry; Mainville; Saint-Germain-en-Laye; Versailles; [Cormeilles/Fontenay-en-]Parisis
15 up to 20	1.5%	Arpajon; Conflans-Sainte-Honorine
20 up to 25	3.0%	Beaumont[-sur-Oise]; Plailly; [Le] Plessis-aux-Bois
25 up to 30	0.8%	Marles[-en-Brie]
30 up to 40	0.0%	(none)
40 up to 50	0.8%	Beauvais
50 up to 100	1.5%	Gacé; Échauffour
100 up to 150	0.0%	(none)
150 up to 200	0.0%	(none)
200 up to 300	2.3%	Courtille; Crève Cœur; Ruffec
Outside of France	0.8%	Ostende (Belgium)

Table 8 Percentage Distribution of Unknown Items in Tables Concerning All Arbiters' Reports from Box AP D⁶B⁶/15

Table	Percent Unknown
Table 1: Types of Dispute	8.0%
Table 2: Arbiters' Professions	62.6%
Table 3: Plaintiffs' Professions	20.8%
Table 4: Defendants' Professions	20.9%
Table 5: Arbiters' Locations	41.2%
Table 6: Plaintiffs' Locations	57.7%
Table 7: Defendants' Locations	56.3%

Notes

Citations are given in full on first mention in each chapter; however, for a bibliography, please visit http://yalepress.yale.edu/yupbooks/book.asp?isbn=9780300113978 or http://www.law.stanford.edu/sourcematerials/kessler_revolution. Unless otherwise noted, all translations are my own. The following abbreviations have been used: AP, Archives de Paris; AN, Archives nationales.

Introduction

1. Isser Woloch, *The New Regime: Transformations of the French Civic Order, 1789–1820s* (New York: W. W. Norton, 1994), 297–354.

2. A number of scholars have noted the remarkable fact that the merchant courts, unlike all others, managed to survive the Revolution. Jean-Pierre Royer, *Histoire de la justice en France: De la monarchie absolue à la république* (Paris: Presses Universitaires de France, 1995), 277–78; Jean-Claude Farcy, *L'histoire de la justice française de la Révolution à nos jours: Trois décennies de recherches* (Paris: Presses Universitaires de France, 2001), 190; Ana Maria Falconi et al., "Le contrôle social du monde des affaires: Une étude institutionelle," *L'année sociologique* 55 (2005): 451–83; Jacqueline-Lucienne Lafon, "L'arbitre près la juridiction consulaire de Paris au XVIIIe siècle," *Revue historique de droit français et étranger* 51 (1973): 269–70. To my knowledge, however, the only work exploring the reasons for the merchant courts' survival is an article by Jean Hilaire. Jean Hilaire, "La Révolution et les juridictions consulaires," in *Une Autre justice: Contributions à l'histoire de la justice sous la Révolution française,* ed. Robert Badinter (Paris: Fayard, 1989), 243–66.

3. Session of 27 May 1790, *Archives Parlementaires de 1787 à 1860: Recueil complet des débats législatifs et politiques des chambres françaises: 1. série* (Paris: Libraire administrative de P. Dupont, 1879), 15:685 (deputy Paul Nairac).

4. Ibid.

5. Ibid.

6. Ibid.

7. See, for example, Emmanuel Lazega and Lise Mounier, "Interlocking Judges: On Joint Exogenous and Self-Governance of Markets," *Research in the Sociology of Organizations* 20 (2003): 267–96; Antoine Gaudino, *La mafia des tribunaux de commerce* (Paris: A. Michel, 1998).

8. Keith Michael Baker, *Inventing the French Revolution* (Cambridge: Cambridge University Press, 1990); François Furet, *Penser la Révolution française,* new ed. (Paris: Gallimard, 1983).

9. Gail Bossenga, *The Politics of Privilege: Old Regime and Revolution in Lille* (Cambridge: Cambridge University Press, 1991); Michael Kwass, *Privilege and the Politics of Taxation in Eighteenth-Century France: Liberté, Égalité, Fiscalité* (Cambridge: Cambridge University Press, 2000); John Shovlin, *The Political Economy of Virtue: Luxury, Patriotism, and the Origins of the French Revolution* (Ithaca, N.Y.: Cornell University Press, 2006); Michael Kwass, "Consumption and the World of Ideas: Consumer Revolution and the Moral Economy of the Marquis de Mirabeau," *Eighteenth-Century Studies* 37 (2004): 187–213; John Shovlin, "Toward a Reinterpretation of Revolutionary Antinobilism: The Political Economy of Honor in the Old Regime," *Journal of Modern History* 72 (March 2000): 35–66; Jay M. Smith, "Social Categories, the Language of Patriotism, and the Origins of the French Revolution: The Debate over *noblesse commerçante,*" *Journal of Modern History* 72 (June 2000): 339–74.

10. Rondo Cameron and Charles E. Freedman, "French Economic Growth: A Radical Revision," *Social Science History* 7 (Winter 1983): 3–30; Don R. Leet and John A. Shaw, "French Economic Stagnation, 1700–1960: Old Economic History Revisited," *Journal of Interdisciplinary History* 8 (Winter 1978): 531–44.

11. Paul Butel, *L'économie française au XVIII*[e] *siècle* (Paris: SEDES, 1993), 62; Sarah Maza, "Luxury, Morality and Social Change: Why There Was No Middle-Class Consciousness in Prerevolutionary France," *Journal of Modern History* 69 (June 1997): 213 (stating that the French population grew from 20 to 27 million during the eighteenth century).

12. Butel, *L'économie française,* 142–45.

13. Ibid., 116–17.

14. Clare Haru Crowston, *Fabricating Women: The Seamstresses of Old Regime France, 1675–1791* (Durham, N.C.: Duke University Press, 2001), 12, 23–24; Daniel Roche, *The People of Paris: An Essay in Popular Culture in the Eighteenth Century,* trans. Marie Evans and Gwynne Lewis (Leamington Spa, U.K.: Berg, 1987), 160–94; Colin Jones, "The Great Chain of Buying: Medical Advertisement, the Bourgeois Public Sphere, and the Origins of the French Revolution," *American Historical Review* 101 (February 1996): 13–40; Maza, "Luxury," 215.

15. Bossenga, *Politics of Privilege;* Kwass, *Privilege.*

16. See, for example, Elizabeth Fox-Genovese, *The Origins of Physiocracy: Economic*

Revolution and Social Order in Eighteenth-Century France (Ithaca, N.Y.: Cornell University Press, 1976); Henry C. Clark, *Compass of Society: Commerce and Absolutism in Old-Regime France* (Lanham, Md.: Lexington Books, 2007); Shovlin, *Political Economy;* John Shovlin, "The Cultural Politics of Luxury in Eighteenth-Century France," *French Historical Studies* 23 (2000): 577–606; Kwass, "Consumption."

17. Michael Sonenscher, *Work and Wages: Natural Law, Politics and the Eighteenth-Century French Trades* (Cambridge: Cambridge University Press, 1989); Steven L. Kaplan, "La lutte pour le contrôle du marché du travail à Paris au XVIIIe siècle," *Revue d'histoire moderne et contemporaine* 36 (July–September 1989): 361–412; Steven Laurence Kaplan, "Social Classification and Representation in the Corporate World of Eighteenth-Century France: Turgot's 'Carnival,'" in *Work in France: Representations, Meaning, Organization, and Practice*, ed. Steven Laurence Kaplan and Cynthia J. Koepp (Ithaca, N.Y.: Cornell University Press, 1986), 176–228; Crowston, *Fabricating Women.* See also Simona Cerutti's work on the guilds of Turin. Simona Cerutti, *La ville et les métiers: Naissance d'un langage corporatif (Turin, 17e–18e siècle)* (Paris: École des hautes études en sciences sociales, 1990).

18. Claire Lemercier, *Un si discret pouvoir: Aux origines de la chambre de commerce de Paris, 1803–1853* (Paris: Découverte, 2003); France Bouchardeau, *Histoire de la chambre de commerce de Valence* (Grenoble: Université des sciences sociales de Grenoble, 1981); *Histoire de la chambre de commerce et d'industrie de Bordeaux*, ed. Paul Butel (Bordeaux: Chambre de Commerce et d'Industrie de Bordeaux, 1988); David Kammerling Smith, "Structuring Politics in Early Eighteenth-Century France: The Political Innovations of the French Council of Commerce," *Journal of Modern History* 74 (September 2002): 490–537; David Kammerling Smith, "'*Au Bien du Commerce*': Economic Discourse and Visions of Society in France" (Ph.D. diss., University of Pennsylvania, 1995); Harold T. Parker, *An Administrative Bureau during the Old Regime: The Bureau of Commerce and Its Relation to French Industry from May 1781 to November 1783* (Newark, Del.: University of Delaware Press, 1993).

19. David D. Bien, "Offices, Corps, and a System of State Credit: The Uses of Privilege under the Ancien Régime," in *The Political Culture of the Old Regime*, vol. 1, *The French Revolution and the Creation of Modern Political Culture*, ed. Keith Michael Baker (Oxford: Pergamon Press, 1990), 89–114; Bossenga, *Politics of Privilege.*

20. *Dictionnaire de l'Académie française,* s.v. "Commerce" (Paris: Chez la veuve de Jean Baptiste Coignard, 1694), 1:214.

21. *Dictionnaire de l'Académie française,* 5th ed., s.v. "Commerce" (Paris: Chez J. J. Smits et compagnie, 1798), 1:268.

22. Gail Bossenga, "Protecting Merchants: Guilds and Commercial Capitalism in Eighteenth-Century France," *French Historical Studies* 15 (Autumn 1988): 693–703; Kaplan, "Social Classification."

23. Carolyn Sargentson, *Merchants and Luxury Markets: The Marchands Merciers of Eighteenth-Century Paris* (London: Victoria and Albert Museum, 1996), xi (discussing estimated annual incomes in France from 1726 to 1790).

24. Crowston, *Fabricating Women,* 280 (discussing prices of offices within the *six corps* as of 1691).

25. Leon E. Trakman, *The Law Merchant: The Evolution of Commercial Law* (Lit-

tleton, Colo.: Fred B. Rothman, 1983); Harold J. Berman, *Law and Revolution: The Formation of the Western Legal Tradition* (Cambridge: Harvard University Press, 1983), 333–56; Bruce L. Benson, "The Spontaneous Evolution of Commercial Law," *Southern Economic Journal* 55 (January 1989): 644–61.

26. James Steven Rogers, *The Early History of the Law of Bills and Notes: A Study of the Origins of Anglo-American Commercial Law* (Cambridge: Cambridge University Press, 1995); Mary Elizabeth Basile et al., ed., *Lex Mercatoria and Legal Pluralism: A Late Thirteenth-Century Treatise and Its Afterlife* (Cambridge, Mass.: Ames Foundation, 1998); Charles Donahue Jr., "Medieval and Early Modern Lex Mercatoria: An Attempt at the Probatio Diabolica," *Chicago Journal of International Law* 5 (Summer 2004): 21–7; J. H. Baker, "The Law Merchant and the Common Law before 1700," *Cambridge Law Journal* 38 (November 1979): 295–322; Albrecht Cordes, "À la recherche d'une lex mercatoria au moyen âge," in *Stadt und Recht in Mittelalter* (Göttingen: Vandenhoeck and Ruprecht, 2003), 117–32; Emily Kadens, "Order within Law, Variety within Custom: The Character of the Medieval Merchant Law," *Chicago Journal of International Law* 5 (Summer 2004): 39–65.

27. Henri Lévy-Bruhl, *L'endossement des lettres de change en France aux XVIIe et XVIIIe siècles* (Paris: A. Rousseau, 1930); Henri Lévy-Bruhl, *Histoire juridique des sociétés de commerce en France aux XVIIe et XVIIIe siècles* (Paris: Domat-Montchrestien, 1938); Henri Lévy-Bruhl, *Histoire de la lettre de change en France aux XVIIe et XVIIIe siècles* (Paris: Recueil Sirey, 1933); Jean Hilaire, *Introduction historique au droit commercial* (Paris: Presses Universitaires de France, 1986); Raymond de Roover, *L'évolution de la lettre de change: XIVe–XVIIIe siècles* (Paris: A. Colin, 1953).

28. John P. Dawson, *The Oracles of the Law* (Ann Arbor: University of Michigan Press, 1968), 374–431; John H. Merryman, *The Civil Law Tradition: An Introduction to the Legal Systems of Western Europe and Latin America,* 2d ed. (Stanford: Stanford University Press, 1985), 14–47.

29. G. Denière, *La juridiction consulaire de Paris, 1563–1792: Sa création, ses luttes, son administration intérieure, ses usages et ses mœurs* (Paris: Henri Plon, 1872); Georges Leclerc, *La juridiction consulaire de Paris pendant la Révolution* (Paris: Plon, 1909). Leclerc's book, moreover, focuses primarily on the Revolution, rather than the Old Regime.

30. Steven Laurence Kaplan, *Provisioning Paris: Merchants and Millers in the Grain and Flour Trade during the Eighteenth Century* (Ithaca, N.Y.: Cornell University Press, 1984); Steven Laurence Kaplan, *The Bakers of Paris and the Bread Question, 1700–1775* (Durham, N.C.: Duke University Press, 1996); Thomas Manley Luckett, "Credit and Commercial Society in France, 1740–1789" (Ph.D. diss., Princeton University, 1992).

31. Lafon, "L'arbitre."

32. Félix Gaiffe, *Le drame en France au XVIIIe siècle* (Paris: A. Colin, 1910); Sarah Maza, *Private Lives and Public Affairs: The Causes Célèbres of Prerevolutionary France* (Berkeley: University of California Press, 1993), 61–63; Philip T. Hoffman, Gilles Postel-Vinay, and Jean-Laurent Rosenthal, *Priceless Markets: The Political Economy of Credit in Paris, 1660–1870* (Chicago: University of Chicago Press, 2000); Fox-Genovese, *Origins of Physiocracy.*

Chapter 1. Situating the Court: Institutional Structure, Jurisdictional Conflict, and the Rise of a New Conception of Commerce

Epigraph. "Réponse à lettre sur les contraintes par corps," *Journal de Commerce* (Brussels), December 1760, 47.

1. *Observations des juge et consuls des marchands de Paris sur l'éxtinction des corps et communautés* (n.d.), AP D^1B^6/37 (5659).

2. William H. Sewell Jr., *Work and Revolution in France: The Language of Labor from the Old Regime to 1848* (Cambridge: Cambridge University Press, 1980), 19–25.

3. Jean Antoine le Vachet, *L'artisan chrestien, ou la vie du bon Henry, maistre cordonnier, à Paris* (Paris: Chez Guillaume Desprez, 1670), 173.

4. Henry C. Clark, "Commerce, the Virtues, and the Public Sphere in Early Seventeenth-Century France," *French Historical Studies* 21, no. 3 (Summer 1998): 427.

5. Ibid., 420.

6. Steven Kaplan, "Réflexions sur la police du monde du travail, 1700–1815," *Revue Historique* 261 (1979): 17–77; Sewell, *Work and Revolution,* 16–61.

7. Alan Williams, *The Police of Paris, 1718–1789* (Baton Rouge: Louisiana State University Press, 1979), 19.

8. Ibid., 24.

9. Ibid., 18–19.

10. Ibid., 25.

11. Ibid., 25.

12. Ibid., 38.

13. Ibid., 28–30.

14. Ibid., 166; *Édit du roy du mois de décembre 1678, portant suppression des corps de métiers, communautez, maitrises et jurandes des faux-bourgs de Paris* (Saint Germain en Laye: December 1678), 1, AN F^{12}781/B (2?).

15. *Édit portant suppression,* 2, AN F^{12}781/B (2?).

16. Alain Thillay, *Le faubourg Saint-Antoine et ses 'faux ouvriers'* (Mayenne: Champ Vallon, 2002), 96.

17. *Édit portant suppression,* 1, AN F^{12}781/B (2?).

18. The monarchy reestablished these courts on a piecemeal basis between April 1674 (just two months after it issued the edict banning them) and 1678. Williams, *Police of Paris,* 167.

19. Ibid., 117; David Garrioch, *The Formation of the Parisian Bourgeoisie, 1690–1830* (Cambridge: Harvard University Press, 1996), 271; *Requête des six corps des marchands tendante a ce que nul ne puisse s'établir dans les lieux priviligiez* (n.d.), AN F^{12}781/D (3).

20. David D. Bien, "Offices, Corps, and a System of State Credit: The Uses of Privilege under the Ancien Régime," in *The Political Culture of the Old Regime,* vol. 1, *The French Revolution and the Creation of Modern Political Culture,* ed. Keith Michael Baker (Oxford: Pergamon Press, 1990), 90–94.

21. *Édit du Roy pour l'établissement des arts et métiers en communauté* (March 23, 1673) (Paris: Frederic Leonard, 1673), AN F^{12}781/B (10); Clare Haru Crowston, *Fabricating Women: The Seamstresses of Old Regime France, 1675–1791* (Durham, N.C.: Duke University Press, 2001), 187–89.

22. *Édit pour l'établissement,* 5, AN F¹²781/B (10).

23. *Arrest du Conseil d'état du roy, qui ordonne que par les lieutenans generaux des bailliages et sénéchaussées, premiers juges des justices du royaume, il sera envoyé au Conseil des états de toutes les communautés, corps et jurandes établies* (Paris, 17 June 1673), AN F¹²781/B (1).

24. Emile Coornaert, *Les Corporations en France avant 1789,* 2d ed. (Paris: Éditions Ouvrières, 1968), 121. The monarchy first attempted to promote the guild system by issuing edicts in 1581 and 1597, which ordered the establishment of guilds throughout the kingdom. These, however, seem to have been largely ignored.

25. Williams, *Police of Paris,* 118.

26. *Arret du conseil d'état du roy, qui ordonne que toutes personnes, qui ont ou prétendent avoir dans la ville et fauxbourgs de Paris des droits de justice ou de police, des privilèges ou affranchissements de maitrises* (28 November 1716) (Paris: L'imprimerie Royale, 1716), 1–2, AN F¹²781/B (9?).

27. Ibid., 2.

28. Ibid.

29. Ibid., 2–3.

30. The edict was reissued in January 1717, August 1717, July 1725, March 1727, and March 1734. *Arret du conseil d'état du roy, qui ordonne que toutes personnes, qui ont ou prétendent avoir dans la ville et fauxbourgs de Paris des droits de justice ou de police, des privilèges ou affranchissements de maitrises* (2 January 1717) (Paris: L'imprimerie Royale, 1717), AN F¹²781/B (9?); *Arret du conseil d'état du roy qui enjoint a tous priviligiez de la ville et fauxbourgs de Paris, ou soy prétendants tells* (9 August 1717) (Paris: L'imprimerie Royale, 1717), AN F¹²781/B (9?); *Arret du conseil d'état du roy concernant les priviligiés de la ville et fauxbourgs de Paris* (28 July 1725) (Paris: L'imprimerie Royale, 1725), AN F¹²781/B (9?); *Arret du conseil d'état du roy concernant les priviligiés de la ville et fauxbourgs de Paris* (11 March 1727) (Paris: L'imprimerie Royale, 1727), AN F¹²781/B (9?); *Arret du conseil d'état du roy qui renvoye pardevant les sieurs commissaires du Bureau des Peages, l'examen des titres* (16 March 1734) (Paris: L'imprimerie Royale, 1734), AN F¹²781/B (9?).

31. *Requête des six corps,* AN F¹²781/D (3).

32. Ibid.

33. Sewell, *Work and Revolution,* 29.

34. Coornaert, *Corporations en France,* 185; William M. Reddy, *The Rise of Market Culture: The Textile Trade and French Society, 1750–1900* (Cambridge: Cambridge University Press, 1984), 34–38.

35. Sewell, *Work and Revolution,* 29.

36. Michael Sonenscher, *Work and Wages: Natural Law, Politics and the Eighteenth-Century French Trades* (Cambridge: Cambridge University Press, 1989), 110.

37. Sewell, *Work and Revolution,* 40, 48.

38. Ibid., 121–24.

39. Steven L. Kaplan, "La lutte pour le contrôle du marché du travail à Paris au XVIIIᵉ siècle," *Revue d'histoire moderne et contemporaine* 36 (July–September 1989): 361–412.

40. Sonenscher, *Work and Wages,* 104; M. Marion, *Dictionnaire des institutions de la*

France aux XVIIe et XVIIIe siècles, s.v. "six grands corps de marchands" (Paris: A. et J. Picard, 1993), 152.

41. Sewell, *Work and Revolution,* 32–36; Cynthia Maria Truant, *The Rites of Labor: Brotherhoods of Compagnonnage in Old and New Regime France* (Ithaca, N.Y.: Cornell University Press, 1994).

42. Historians have offered varied accounts of the precise interrelationship between confraternities and guilds. Abel Poitrineau, *Ils travaillaient la France: Métiers et mentalités du XVIe au XIXe siècles* (Paris: Armand Colin, 1992), 59; Sewell, *Work and Revolution,* 33; Coornaert, *Corporations en France,* 224; Sonenscher, *Work and Wages,* 79–80.

43. Coornaert, *Corporations en France,* 223.

44. By the eighteenth century, most traditional confraternities catered exclusively to masters. Journeymen, however, formed either their own (local, trade-based) confraternities or (nationwide, multi-trade) *compagnonnages,* both of which—like the masters' confraternities—infused daily commercial life with religious ritual and belief. Sewell, *Work and Revolution,* 51–52.

45. Ibid., 34; Coornaert, *Corporations en France,* 223; Poitrineau, *Ils travaillaient la France,* 61.

46. Roger Chartier, *The Cultural Origins of the French Revolution,* trans. Lydia G. Cochrane (Durham, N.C.: Duke University Press, 1991), 106–8. It bears emphasis, however, that the Enlightenment's own view of the eighteenth century as a fundamentally anti-Christian age—a view that was adopted largely without challenge by succeeding generations of historians—has recently come under sustained criticism. Marisa Linton, *The Politics of Virtue in Enlightenment France* (Hampshire, England: Palgrave, 2001), 179–84; Dale K. Van Kley, *The Religious Origins of the French Revolution: From Calvin to the Civil Constitution, 1560–1791* (New Haven: Yale University Press, 1996).

47. Jacques-Louis Ménétra, *Journal of My Life,* trans. Arthur Goldhammer (New York: Columbia University Press, 1986). Ménétra appears to have composed his autobiography intermittently between 1764 and 1803. Daniel Roche, introduction to Ménétra, *Journal of My Life,* 7–8. That he wrote portions of it after the Revolution—and thus at a time of pervasive anticlerical sentiment—raises the possibility that his description of his earlier, prerevolutionary attitudes was colored by later, postrevolutionary anticlericalism.

48. According to Ménétra, each member of the association contributed twelve and a half *sols* to fund the processional, which he described at length. At the conclusion of the ceremony, he contentedly observed, "the abbess [of Baumont] in her princess's garb . . . said to me I am very satisfied with the blessed bread I have just received and with the compliment of my little glazier." Ménétra, *Journal of My Life,* 37.

49. Priests, he insisted, are "hypocrites who take advantage of the people's credulity" and are moved by "fanaticism and superstition." Ibid., 19.

50. *Mémoire pour les maîtres et gardes en charge du corps des marchands merciers de la ville et fauxbourgs de Paris* (Paris: L'imprimerie de J. Chardon, 1761), 21, AP D^1B^6/36 (5583).

51. Ibid., 21.

52. Steven Laurence Kaplan, "Social Classification and Representation in the Corpo-

rate World of Eighteenth-Century France: Turgot's 'Carnival,'" in *Work in France: Representations, Meaning, Organization, and Practice,* ed. Steven Laurence Kaplan and Cynthia J. Koepp (Ithaca, N.Y.: Cornell University Press, 1986), 181–93.

53. *Réflexions des maitres serruriers de Paris sur la destruction annoncée de leur jurande et communauté* (n.d.), AP D1B6/37 (5660).

54. See discussion in chapter 2.

55. Kaplan, "Social Classification," 181; Crowston, *Fabricating Women,* 6–7.

56. Charles Carrière, *Négociants marseillais au XVIIIe siècle: Contribution à l'étude des économies maritimes* (Marseille: Institut Historique de Provence, 1973), 1:239–50.

57. Romuald Szramkiewicz, *Histoire du droit des affaires* (Paris: Montchrestien, 1989), 91.

58. Ibid., 241; Sonenscher, *Work and Wages,* 64. Some of these merchants and artisans formed trades groups that, while not formally constituted as legal *corps,* tended to be structured much like the official *métiers jurés.*

59. Garrioch, *Formation,* 117.

60. Steven Laurence Kaplan, *Bakers of Paris and the Bread Question, 1700–1775* (Durham, N.C.: Duke University Press, 1996), 187, 572; Jacques Revel, "Les corps et communautés," in *The Political Culture of the Old Regime,* vol. 1, *The French Revolution and the Creation of Modern Political Culture,* ed. Keith Michael Baker (Oxford: Pergamon Press, 1990), 241.

61. Sonenscher, *Work and Wages,* 132–33.

62. Ibid., 148.

63. Kaplan, "Lutte."

64. See the discussion later in this chapter of the electoral conflict between the *six corps* and the wine sellers' and printers' guilds.

65. See the discussion later in this chapter of the jurisdictional conflict between the Parisian Merchant Court and the municipal government, which reflected, in part, an ongoing struggle between the Parisian luxury merchants (including the *six corps*) and the water-based merchants who sold items of basic necessity.

66. Louis-Sébastien Mercier, *Tableau de Paris,* new ed. (Amsterdam, 1782; repr., Geneva: Slatkine Reprints, 1979), 2:26–27.

67. [Couchot], *Le praticien des juges et consuls; ou, Traité de commerce de terre et de mer* (Paris: Prault père, 1742), 246.

68. G. Denière, *La juridiction consulaire de Paris, 1563–1792: Sa création, ses luttes, son administration intérieure, ses usages et ses mœurs* (Paris: Henri Plon, 1872), 43, 67–68. See also the discussion of the court's electoral procedure in the next section of this chapter.

69. Examples of the contemporary practice of referring to the merchant court's judges as the *juge et consuls des marchands* include: "Ordonnance civile touchant la réformation de la justice," tit. 16 ("De la forme de procéder par-devant les juge et consuls des marchands"), in *Code Louis* (Milano: Giuffrè, 1996), 1:23; *Observations des juge et consuls des marchands de Paris sur l'éxtinction des corps et communautés,* AP D1B6/37 (5659); *Mémoire des ouvrages de sculpture faits pour la juridiction royalle des juge et Consuls des Marchands à Paris* (n.d., around March 1747), AP D1B6/7 (791); and *Arrest de la Cour de Parlement, pour les juge et consuls, contre le prevost de Paris, son Lieutenant civil et officiers du Chastellet* (Paris: Chez Jean Bessin, 1634), 4, AP D1B6/25 (4949).

70. Denière, *Juridiction consulaire,* 167.

71. "Édit qui crée la juridiction consulaire des juges et consuls de Paris et règle leur competence," arts. 14–16 (Paris, November 1563), in François André Isambert, Athanase-Jean-Léger Jourdan, and Decrusy, *Recueil général des anciennes lois françaises, depuis l'an 420, jusqu'à la révolution de 1789* (Paris: Belin-Leprieur, 1829), 14:153–58; [Couchot], *Praticien,* xv; Denière, *Juridiction consulaire,* 7; Georges Leclerc, *La juridiction consulaire de Paris pendant la Révolution* (Paris: Plon, 1909), 2–3.

72. Denière, *Juridiction consulaire,* 75–78.

73. Ibid., 167; Leclerc, *Juridiction consulaire,* 3–4.

74. Denière, *Juridiction consulaire,* 90. On Tuesdays, Thursdays, and Saturdays, the court deliberated those cases that had already been heard. Sunday was, of course, a holiday. Ibid., 92.

75. Ibid., 167–70, 175–82; Leclerc, *Juridiction consulaire,* 3–5, 26–29.

76. The arbiters are discussed at length in chapter 2. The court also received assistance from *conseillers,* who numbered about forty to fifty and served rotating one-week sessions in groups of five or six. They were generally young, inexperienced merchants, who were given simple but time-consuming tasks, such as accountings. [Couchot], *Praticien,* 275, 277; Denière, *Juridiction consulaire,* 79–80; Leclerc, *Juridiction consulaire,* 59–60; Philibert-Joseph Masson, *Instruction sur les affaires contentieuses des négociants, la manière de les prévenir, ou de les suivre dans les tribunaux* (Paris: Chez LeClerc, 1786), vii, 365.

77. See discussion in chapter 2.

78. "Ordonnance civile touchant la réformation de la justice," tit. 16, arts. 1–2, in *Code Louis,* 1:23; Jean Baptiste Denisart, Jean-Baptiste-François Bayard, and Armand-Gaston Camus, *Collection de décisions nouvelles et de notions relatives à la jurisprudence,* 8th ed., s.v. "Consuls des Marchands" (Paris: Chez la veuve Desaint, 1786), 5:391.

79. Denière, *Juridiction consulaire,* 107–12; Leclerc, *Juridiction consulaire,* 164–67; Jean Hilaire, "La Révolution et les juridictions consulaires," in *Une Autre justice: Contributions à l'histoire de la justice sous la Révolution française,* ed. Robert Badinter (Paris: Fayard, 1989), 249.

80. See, for example, Heury Lepitre, Arbiter's Report in Paupe v. Bertin, 18 July 1785, AP D^{6}B^{6}/17 (4); Pinchauf, Arbiter's Report in le comte de Colincour v. Bequet, 1 July 1785, AP D^{6}B^{6}/17 (369); Pinchauf, Arbiter's Report in Augustin Menard v. Ricard cadet, 12 July 1785, D^{6}B^{6}/17 (221); Collients, Arbiter's Report in Bienchi v. Chaffenere, 7 February 1783, D^{6}B^{6}/15 (237).

81. Denisart, Bayard, and Camus, *Collection de décisions,* 8th ed., s.v. "Consuls des Marchands," 5:391–95; Pierre Jean Jacques Guillaume Guyot, *Répertoire universel et raisonné de jurisprudence civile, criminelle, canonique et bénéficiale,* s.v. "Consul" (Paris: Chez Panckoucke, 1777), 15:151–52; [Couchot], *Praticien,* 274–75. Technically, of course, as the commercial jurist, Toubeau argued, the *agréés* were not lawyers, since Old Regime lawyers belonged either to the order of barristers or the corporation of solicitors, and the *agréés* belonged to neither. Jean Toubeau, *Les institutes du droit consulaire ou les elemens de la jurisprudence des marchands* (Bourges, 1700), 1:218. Nonetheless, the use of *agréés* in the merchant court clearly violated the spirit, if not the letter, of the law.

82. A significant marker of the prominence of commercial lawyers in eighteenth-century France is that Joseph-Philippe Gorneau — who had spent much of his career as an

agréé in the Parisian Merchant Court—was chosen as one of the main jurists responsible for drafting the *Code de Commerce* in 1807, and as co-author of its foreword. Denière, *Juridiction consulaire,* 124; Leclerc, *Juridiction consulaire,* 167–68 and n. 1; Hilaire, "La Révolution," 249 n. 21.

83. Mercier, *Tableau de Paris,* 12:166.

84. Chartier, *Cultural Origins,* 188–90.

85. Toubeau, *Institutes du droit consulaire,* 1:215–16.

86. [Couchot], *Praticien,* x.

87. As argued in chapter 5, the new conception of commerce that merchants came to embrace can be understood as a reconfiguration of virtue. There was, however, a world of difference between virtue as traditionally conceived (personal devotion to fellow guild members) and as reconfigured (devotion to the largely impersonal structures and processes of a wealth-producing, and thus public-serving, market).

88. "Édit qui crée la juridiction consulaire," art. 2, in Isambert, Jourdan, and Decrusy, *Recueil général,* 14:154; [Couchot], *Praticien,* xi–xii. The Edict of 1563 established a somewhat different procedure for the election of the first judge and consuls. "Édit qui crée la juridiction consulaire," art. 1, in Isambert, Jourdan, and Decrusy, *Recueil general,* 14:153–54; [Couchot], *Praticien,* xi.

89. This was the composition of the *six corps de Paris* until February 1776, when the guilds were briefly abolished. When the guilds were reestablished in August, the monarchy reconstituted the *six corps* as follows: the drapers and haberdashers; the grocers; the hosiers, furriers, and hatters; the goldsmiths, goldbeaters, and gold drawers; the fabric and gauze makers and cloth and ribbon makers; and the wine sellers. Denière, *Juridiction consulaire,* 50.

90. Electoral conflict appears initially to have emerged on January 14, 1689, when the King's Council ordered that at least one of the Parisian Merchant Court's judicial officers must be a member of the grocers' guild. Since the five other guilds constituting the *six corps,* as well as the wine sellers' guild, objected vehemently, the monarchy ultimately withdrew its order and peace was temporarily restored. Babille, *Mémoire pour les Juges et Consuls de Paris, au sujet de deux Requêtes présentées par la Communauté des Libraires et par les Marchands de Vin* (Paris: P. G. Le Mercier, 1756), 6, AP D^1B^6/36 (5619); *Discours Tenu Par Monsieur le Prevot des marchands a l'hotel de Ville* (2 May 1776), 13–14, AP D^1B^6/25 (4969).

91. A report written by the deputies of the *Bureau du Commerce* indicates that, while the furriers originally joined the hosiers and goldsmiths in petitioning for a restructuring of the merchant court, they later withdrew from the petition. *Sur les mémoires des corps de la bonneterie et orfeverie de Paris à l'effet de faire augmenter le nombre des Consuls* (1 June 1725), AN F^{12}696.

92. Ibid.

93. Although the parties to this pamphlet war did not at this early date refer to *l'opinion public,* each claimed to speak for *le public* and denounced the other as having falsely usurped the public mantle. For example, according to the petitioners, "the . . . leading guilds make the public speak or remain quiet as best suits their views." *Sur les mémoires des corps,* AN F^{12}696.

94. Keith Michael Baker, *Inventing the French Revolution* (Cambridge: Cambridge

University Press, 1990), 185–90; David A. Bell, *Lawyers and Citizens: The Making of a Political Elite in Old Regime France* (Oxford: Oxford University Press, 1994), 10–15.

95. *Réponse aux objections faites contre le mémoire concernant le consulat de Paris* (Paris: l'Imprimerie d'André Knapen, n.d.), 3, AP D^1B^6/36 (5611).

96. Ibid., 4.

97. Ibid., 8.

98. Ibid., 20.

99. *Réponse des deux derniers corps des marchands de Paris au nouveau mémoire des quatre premiers, touchant le consulat de cette ville* (Paris: André Knappen, n.d. [perhaps 1725]), 6, AN F^{12}793 (15).

100. Ibid., 3.

101. Ibid., 2.

102. *Mémoire pour les Syndics de la Librairie, et les Gardes de la Marchandise de Vins, Demandeurs* (N.p.: Jacques Vincent, n.d. [around 1727]), 1, AP D^1B^6/36 (5618).

103. Ibid., 4.

104. Ibid., 2.

105. Ibid., 8.

106. Ibid., 8.

107. Ibid., 2.

108. Ibid., 8.

109. Babille, *Mémoire pour les Juges et Consuls,* 8, AP D^1B^6/36 (5619).

110. Ibid., 8–9; Denière, *Juridiction consulaire,* 53–55.

111. Babille, *Mémoire pour les Juges et Consuls,* 10, AP D^1B^6/36 (5619); *Mémoire pour les six corps des Marchands de Paris contre les Marchands de Vin de la meme Ville* (n.d.), AP D^1B^6/36 (5621).

112. *Mémoire des ouvrages,* AP D^1B^6/7 (791).

113. Ibid.

114. Ibid.

115. Ibid.

116. *Mémoire pour les six corps,* AP D^1B^6/36 (5621).

117. Babille, *Mémoire pour les Juges et Consuls,* 4, AP D^1B^6/36 (5619).

118. Ibid.

119. Ibid.

120. This is not to suggest that arguments that elections be based on individual merit were unique to the merchant court. Such arguments also became commonplace within guilds and were associated with the nascent democratic movement described above. Nor is this to suggest that conceptions of merit in the Old Regime were necessarily anticorporatist. As Jay M. Smith has shown, notions of merit were integral to the construction of noble identity in the Old Regime. Jay M. Smith, *The Culture of Merit: Nobility, Royal Service, and the Making of Absolute Monarchy in France, 1600–1789* (Ann Arbor: University of Michigan Press, 1996). The point is simply that, in the case of the Parisian Merchant Court, the emergence of such merit-based arguments marked the rise of a new conception of the court as an entity distinct from the guilds and the corporatist system that they sustained.

121. Babille, *Mémoire pour les Juges et Consuls,* 4–5, AP D^1B^6/36 (5619).

122. *Mémoire pour les six corps,* AP D[1]B[6]/36 (5621).

123. Ibid.

124. Babille, *Mémoire pour les Juges et Consuls,* 1, AP D[1]B[6]/36 (5619).

125. *Mémoire pour les six corps,* AP D[1]B[6]/36 (5621).

126. Marion, *Dictionnaire des institutions,* s.v. "Bailli" and "Bailliages, Sénéchaussées," 31–33.

127. Ibid., s.v. "Présidiaux," 449–50; François Olivier-Martin, *Histoire du droit français des origines à la Révolution* (Paris: Éditions Domat Montchrestien, 1951), 555–56.

128. Marion, *Dictionnaire des institutions,* s.v. "Châtelet," 88–89.

129. Szramkiewicz, *Droit des affaires,* 183–85.

130. Masson, *Affaires contentieuses,* 83, 326–27; Marion, *Dictionnaire des institutions,* s.v. "Amiral, Grand-Amiral" and "Amirauté de France," 17–18.

131. Masson, *Affaires contentieuses,* 437–38.

132. Jean Baptiste Denisart, *Collection de décisions nouvelles et de notions relatives à la jurisprudence actuelle,* s.v. "Hôtel-de-Ville de Paris" (Paris: Chez Savoy, 1764), 2:279; Denière, *Juridiction consulaire,* 8–9; Steven Laurence Kaplan, *Provisioning Paris: Merchants and Millers in the Grain and Flour Trade during the Eighteenth Century* (Ithaca, N.Y.: Cornell University Press, 1984), 36–37.

133. Williams, *Police of Paris,* 171–73. Moreover, while it remained a great honor to serve as one of the municipal government's primary officers—namely, the *prévôt des marchands* and the four *échevins,* who worked under him—the electoral process was such that the king had substantial control over who was appointed. Ibid., 171–72.

134. Ibid., 172–73; Gilbert de Voisins, Paillet des Brunieres, and Martin d'Arras, *Mémoire pour les juge et consuls de la ville de Paris, sur leur intervention* (Paris: P. Emery, n.d.), 52–53, AP D[1]B[6]/25 (4953).

135. As was typical of the Old Regime, jurisdictional conflict continued to simmer despite the monarchy's efforts to end it—in part because water and land were integrally connected through such practices as the sale of goods in shops located on quays and bridges. Williams, *Police of Paris,* 172–73.

136. Denisart, *Collection de décisions,* 1764 ed., s.v. "Hôtel-de-Ville de Paris," 2:281.

137. As explained by Masson, "The policing of the ports . . . entails jurisdiction over the sales and deals that take place there, in order to ensure the execution of the police ordinances concerning the ports and . . . in order thus to prevent the monopolizing and retaining of merchandise at a port for purposes of rendering such merchandise rare at another port." Masson, *Affaires contentieuses,* 425.

138. "Ordonnance du commerce" (Versailles, March 1673), in Isambert, Jourdan, and Decrusy, *Recueil general,* 19:92–107.

139. See chapter 5 for an in-depth discussion of negotiable instruments.

140. As discussed in chapter 6, the merchant court also deployed its claim to exclusive jurisdiction over negotiable instruments to make other jurisdictional demands—notably, to demand jurisdiction over noblemen. See also Amalia D. Kessler, "A 'Question of Name': Merchant-Court Jurisdiction and the Origins of the *Noblesse Commerçante,*" in *A Vast and Useful Art: The Gustave Gimon Collection on French Political Economy,* ed. Mary Jane Parrine (Stanford: Stanford University Libraries, 2004), 49–65 (also on-line at http://www-sul.stanford.edu/depts/hasrg/frnit/gimon_papers.html).

141. Allart, *Mémoire signifié pour Pierre Duclos, marchand brasseur à Paris, appellant* (Paris: Montalant, 1736), 1–2, AP D^1B^6/25 (4952).

142. Ibid., 2.

143. Ibid.

144. Ibid.

145. Ibid.

146. Denisart, *Collection de décisions*, 1764 ed., s.v. "Hôtel-de-Ville de Paris," 2:280; Masson, *Affaires contentieuses*, 428; Hecquard, *Mémoire sommaire pour les juge et consuls de Paris contre messieurs les prevost des marchands et echevins de la même ville* (Paris: A. Boudet, 1752), 1, AP D^1B^6/25 (4955); Tascher, *Nouveau mémoire sur l'objet du réglement annoncé par l'arrêt du conseil du 18 décembre 1758, pour les prevôt des marchands et échevins de la ville de Paris contre les juge et consuls de la même Ville* (Paris: P. G. Le Mercier, 1759), 20, AP D^1B^6/25(4958).

147. Denisart, *Collection de décisions*, 1764 ed., s.v. "Hôtel-de-Ville de Paris," 2:280; Tascher, *Nouveau mémoire*, 20, AP D^1B^6/25(4958).

148. Goulleau, *Mémoire pour les six corps des marchands et négocians de la ville de Paris contre les sieurs prévôt des marchands et échevins de la même ville* (Paris: P. Al. Le Prieur, 1767), 1, AP D^1B^6/25 (4962); Gillet and Mercier, *Mémoire à consulter et consultation, pour les marchands et commerçans de la riviere et des ports, fournissant la provision de Paris; les voituriers et les fermiers des coches par eau* (Paris: Chardon, 1767), 1, AP D^1B^6/25 (4963).

149. Masson, *Affaires contentieuses*, 424–29.

150. Old Regime jurists cited this litigation as an event of great significance. For example, in his famous jurisprudential dictionary, Jean Baptiste Denisart discusses at some length—in his entry concerning the municipal government—the decrees issued by the *Parlement* of Paris deciding de Villamay's lawsuit. Denisart, *Collection de décisions*, 1764 ed., s.v. "Hôtel-de-Ville de Paris," 2:279–80. Likewise, Masson's litigation manual for merchants contains a chapter on the municipal government, which focuses almost exclusively on the jurisdictional conflict initiated by de Villamay's lawsuit. Masson, *Affaires contentieuses*, 424–29. See also [Couchot], *Praticien*, 268–74.

151. Tension between the merchant court and the municipal government continued to simmer through the very end of the Old Regime. For example, in the litigation manual that Masson, a former merchant court judge, published in 1786, he acknowledged the *Parlement*'s decree in the municipal government's favor, but made every effort to limit its applicable scope. Accordingly, he insisted that this decree did not deprive the Parisian Merchant Court of jurisdiction over bills of exchange since "jurisdiction over [disputes concerning these instruments when employed by] all sorts of persons is granted to the merchant court judges." Masson, *Affaires contentieuses*, 429.

152. As the core elements of the merchant court's argument remain the same throughout the lengthy litigation, I discuss the argument as a unitary whole, rather than addressing in chronological order each of the legal briefs in which it is set forth.

153. *Observations des juge et consuls de Paris, relatives au réglement que le roi s'est réservé de faire entre le bureau de la ville et la jurisdiction consulaire* (Paris: De l'imprimerie de Le Breton, premier imprimeur ordinaire du Roi, 1767), 6, AP D^1B^6/25 (4961).

154. Voisins, Brunieres, and d'Arras, *Mémoire pour les juge et consuls,* 52, AP D^{1}B^6/25 (4953).

155. *Observations des juge et consuls,* 10, AP D^{1}B^6/25 (4961).

156. Ibid., 18.

157. Ibid.

158. Ibid.

159. De Chancourt, *Précis pour les juge et consuls de Paris contre les prevôt des marchands et échevins de la même ville* (Paris: Antoine Boudet, 1759), 9–10, AP D^{1}B^6/25 (4957). Moreover, the merchant court concluded, to the extent that the credit represented by the negotiable instrument rendered a novation, then as a conceptual matter, so too did other forms of credit extended from seller to buyer—including such traditional forms as book debt. Ibid., 10.

160. Ibid., 9–10.

161. Ibid., 9.

162. Ibid., 10.

163. Ibid.

164. *Observations des juge et consuls, relatives au réglement,* 7, AP D^{1}B^6/25 (4961).

165. Ibid.

166. Goulleau, *Mémoire pour les six corps,* 18, AP D^{1}B^6/25 (4962).

167. Ibid., 19.

168. *Observations des juge et consuls, relatives au réglement,* 6, AP D^{1}B^6/25 (4961).

169. Ibid.

170. De Chancourt, *Précis pour les juge et consuls,* 9, AP D^{1}B^6/25 (4957).

171. Ibid.

172. In so arguing, the court recognized that an ordinance of December 1672 "confirmed the jurisdiction of the officers of the municipal government over the sale and display" of many of these same goods—such as wheat and lumber. Voisins, Brunieres, and d'Arras, *Mémoire pour les juge et consuls,* 48, AP D^{1}B^6/25 (4953). According to the court, however, this ordinance—like the Commercial Ordinance of 1673—simply confirmed that "the officers of the municipal government have jurisdiction over the sale and display of such merchandise, when the dispute that arises between buyer and seller concerns a police matter . . . but . . . when the police matter has ceased, jurisdiction over the differences that may arise from these same sales, and in particular, over payment, *cum res abiit in creditum,* . . . will belong to the merchant court." Ibid.

173. *Observations des juge et consuls, relatives au réglement,* 3, AP D^{1}B^6/25 (4961).

174. De Chancourt, *Précis pour les juge et consuls,* 7, AP D^{1}B^6/25 (4957). Furthermore, litigants before the merchant court had no "need of the services of lawyers, nor of solicitors"—though, in practice, they often chose to employ them. Hecquard, *Mémoire sommaire,* 3, AP D^{1}B^6/25 (4955). And, in contrast to the rule applicable in most courts, including the municipal government, litigants in the merchant court were permitted to establish the existence of an enforceable contract through "testimony of witnesses," rather than exclusively through written evidence—and even when the disputed contract was for a "sum[] greater than 100 livres." Ibid. For a further discussion of the merchant court's distinctive approach to contract litigation, see chapter 2.

175. De Chancourt, *Précis pour les juge et consuls,* 8, AP D^{1}B^6/25 (4957).

176. [Couchot], *Praticien,* 361. See also Masson, *Affaires contentieuses,* 328, 368–69.

177. Denisart, *Collection de décisions,* 1764 ed., s.v. "Hôtel-de-Ville de Paris," 2:281.

178. Olivier-Martin, *Histoire du droit français,* 553–56; Marion, *Dictionnaire des institutions,* s.v. "Gens du roi," 258.

179. *Avis des deputés du commerce sur la contestation entre les juge et consuls d'Angers et les notaires de la même ville* (13 April 1736), AN F^{12}792 (6).

180. *Observations des juge et consuls, relatives au réglement,* 4, AP D^1B^6/25 (4961).

181. Ibid., 1.

182. Elizabeth Fox-Genovese, *The Origins of Physiocracy: Economic Revolution and Social Order in Eighteenth-Century France* (Ithaca, N.Y.: Cornell University Press, 1976), 134.

183. Tascher, *Nouveau mémoire,* 25, AP D^1B^6/25(4958).

184. Ibid., 25–26.

185. Ibid., 26.

186. Tascher, *État sommaire des preuves parlesquelles les prévôt des marchands et échevins de la ville de Paris, justifient le droit ancien et actuel qu'ils ont de juger les contestations entre marchands et autres* (Paris: P. G. Le Mercier, 1759), 18–19, AP D^1B^6/25(4959).

187. Tascher, *Nouveau mémoire,* 26, AP D^1B^6/25(4958).

188. Ibid., 27.

189. Ibid., 28–30.

190. Ibid., 33.

191. Ibid., 34.

192. Ibid.

193. Ibid.

194. Ibid., 31.

195. Ibid., 32.

196. Ibid.

197. Ibid.

198. Ibid.

Chapter 2. The Court's Self-Conception as a Bastion of Virtue: Relational Contracting and a Community-Based Approach to Procedure

Epigraph. [Couchot], *Le praticien des juges et consuls; ou, Traité de commerce de terre et de mer* (Paris: Prault père, 1742), x.

1. Ian R. Macneil, *The New Social Contract: An Inquiry into Modern Contractual Relations* (New Haven: Yale University Press, 1980); Stewart Macaulay, "Non-Contractual Relations in Business: A Preliminary Study," *American Sociological Review* 28 (1963): 55–67; Robert Dore, *Taking Japan Seriously: A Confucian Perspectve on Leading Economic Issues* (London: Athlone Press, 1987), 169–82.

2. Philip T. Hoffman, Gilles Postel-Vinay, and Jean-Laurent Rosenthal, *Priceless Markets: The Political Economy of Credit in Paris, 1660–1870* (Chicago: University of Chicago Press, 2000). See also Philip T. Hoffman, Giles Postel-Vinay, and Jean-Laurent Rosenthal, "Information and Economic History: How the Credit Market in Old Regime

Paris Forces Us to Rethink the Transition to Capitalism," *American Historical Review* 104, no. 1 (February 1999): 69–94.

3. Michael Sonenscher, *Work and Wages: Natural Law, Politics and the Eighteenth-Century French Trades* (Cambridge: Cambridge University Press, 1989), 132–39, 191–92.

4. See, for example, Hés, Arbiter's Report in Bas v. Grapin, 24 August 1785, AP D^{6}B^6/17 (n.a.).

5. See, for example, Abouselle, Arbiter's Report in Guerard v. LaCroix, 30 June 1785, AP D^{6}B^6/17 (559).

6. See, for example, Evignon, Arbiter's Report in Devaux v. Hayet, 30 May 1785, AP D^{6}B^6/17 (440).

7. Steven Laurence Kaplan, *The Bakers of Paris and the Bread Question, 1700–1775* (Durham, N.C.: Duke University Press, 1996), 375–79.

8. Sonenscher, *Work and Wages,* 23.

9. Ibid., 27.

10. For purposes of stylistic simplicity, and because most merchant-artisans were men, I use the masculine pronoun throughout the book. It bears emphasis, however, that as discussed in chapter 4, there were women's guilds. See also Clare Haru Crowston, *Fabricating Women: The Seamstresses of Old Regime France, 1675–1791* (Durham, N.C.: Duke University Press, 2001). Moreover, as revealed by many of the arbiters' reports discussed in this book, merchants' wives (and widows) often played a vital role in the family business.

11. "Ordonnance civile touchant la réformation de la justice," tit. 20, art. 2, in *Code Louis* (Milano: Giuffrè, 1996), 1:29–30; Jean Toubeau, *Les institutes du droit consulaire ou les elemens de la jurisprudence des marchands* (Bourges, 1700), 2:37. Akin to the parol evidence rule of the Anglo-American tradition, Article 2 provided that in the ordinary, non-merchant courts, a notarized document or privately signed writing was required to prove contracts exceeding 100 livres.

12. Toubeau, *Institutes du droit consulaire,* 2:5.

13. Pierre Jean Jacques Guillaume Guyot, *Répertoire universel et raisonné de jurisprudence civile, criminelle, canonique et bénéficiale,* s.v. "Consul" (Paris: Chez Panckoucke, 1777), 15:124–25.

14. Modern-day merchants, like their eighteenth-century counterparts, often view efforts to draft detailed contract provisions addressing all possible contingencies as likely to erode the bonds of trust conducive to a mutually beneficial, long-term relationship. Thus, even today, the written contract often does not embody the full agreement, which instead evolves gradually through the course of dealing and subsequent renegotiations. Macaulay, "Non-Contractual Relations," 58–59, 64–65.

15. That extensive reliance on book debt (and the relational contracting it facilitated) were integrally linked to the interdependent nature of communal life in the early-modern world is suggested by the striking parallels between Old Regime France and contemporary colonial America and England. According to Bruce Mann, for example, book debt was widely used in eighteenth-century Connecticut because debtors and creditors "might also be neighbors, relatives, fellow church members" and thus "did not, indeed could not, limit their relations to single transactions." Bruce H. Mann, *Neighbors and Strangers:*

Law and Community in Early Connecticut (Chapel Hill: University of North Carolina Press, 1987), 18. Likewise, Craig Muldrew argues that in early-modern England "credit could be extended for often very long periods as a means of forming social bonds to secure repeated custom" and "given the ubiquity of such actions, . . . mutual interdependence . . . was stressed and formed a much more comprehensive means of social interpretation than the private desire for profit." Craig Muldrew, *The Economy of Obligation: The Culture of Credit and Social Relations in Early Modern England* (Houndmills, Eng.: Palgrave, 1998), 124.

16. David Garrioch, *Neighborhood and Community in Paris, 1740–1790* (Cambridge: Cambridge University Press, 1986), 62; Sonenscher, *Work and Wages,* 124.

17. Sonenscher, *Work and Wages,* 124.

18. Carolyn Sargentson, *Merchants and Luxury Markets: The Marchands Merciers of Eighteenth-Century Paris* (London: Victoria and Albert Museum, 1996), 26.

19. Garrioch, *Neighborhood and Community,* 63.

20. Sargentson, *Merchants and Luxury Markets,* 26; Steven Laurence Kaplan, *Provisioning Paris: Merchants and Millers in the Grain and Flour Trade during the Eighteenth Century* (Ithaca, N.Y.: Cornell University Press, 1984), 321–25.

21. David Garrioch, *The Formation of the Parisian Bourgeoisie, 1690–1830* (Cambridge: Harvard University Press, 1996), 101.

22. Ibid., 133–35.

23. Garrioch, *Neighborhood and Community,* 99–100.

24. Emile Coornaert, *Les corporations en France avant 1789,* 2d ed. (Paris: Éditions Ouvrières, 1968), 267.

25. Garrioch, *Neighborhood and Community,* 24–27.

26. Ibid., 20–23.

27. Ibid., 162–63.

28. *Mémoire pour demoiselle Chotart, veuve Prud'homme, demandresse, contre le sieur Aubin, deffendeur* (Paris: P. A. Paulus-du-Mesnil, n.d. [approx. late 1720s]), 2, AP D^1B^6/32 (5254).

29. Garrioch, *Neighborhood and Community,* 38–39; Sonenscher, *Work and Wages,* 135.

30. Garrioch, *Neighborhood and Community,* 53.

31. Ibid., 45–46.

32. "Ordonnance civile touchant la réformation de la justice," tit. 16, art. 11, in *Code Louis,* 1:24.

33. Ibid., tit. 16, art. 1, in *Code Louis,* 1:23.

34. For a discussion of the decline of the jury in France and its replacement by the judge-centered canonist inquest, see John P. Dawson, *A History of Lay Judges* (Cambridge: Harvard University Press, 1960), 39–94.

35. [Couchot], *Praticien,* 246–47.

36. G. Denière, *La juridiction consulaire de Paris, 1563–1792: Sa création, ses luttes, son administration intérieure, ses usages et ses mœurs* (Paris: Henri Plon, 1872), 91–92.

37. [Couchot], *Praticien,* 93, 275–76. The *huissiers* of the merchant court, supported by the commercial jurists, claimed the exclusive right to serve the summons following the defendant's *initial* failure to appear. Ibid., 275; Philibert-Joseph Masson, *Instruction sur*

les affaires contentieuses des négociants, la manière de les prévenir, ou de les suivre dans les tribunaux (Paris: Chez LeClerc, 1786), 330.

38. [Couchot], *Praticien,* 423–25; Kaplan, *Bakers of Paris,* 397 and n. 60; Romuald Szramkiewicz, *Histoire du droit des affaires* (Paris: Montchrestien, 1989), 148.

39. "Édit portant création de dix officiers-gardes du commerce, et réglement pour les contraintes par corps pour dettes civiles dans Paris," in François André Isambert, Athanase-Jean-Léger Jourdan, and Decrusy, *Recueil général des anciennes lois françaises, depuis l'an 420, jusqu'à la révolution de 1789* (Paris: Belin-Leprieur, 1829), 22:551–54.

40. Thomas Manley Luckett, "Credit and Commercial Society in France, 1740–1789" (Ph.D. diss., Princeton University, 1992), 110–11; Kaplan, *Bakers of Paris,* 397 and n. 60.

41. Alan Williams, *The Police of Paris, 1718–1789* (Baton Rouge: Louisiana State University Press, 1979), 91; Kaplan, *Bakers of Paris,* 397 and n. 60.

42. "Édit portant création de dix officiers-gardes," in Isambert, Jourdan, and Decrusy, *Recueil general.*

43. Williams, *Police of Paris,* 91. As these were not venal offices, the monarchy had no direct financial incentive for increasing their number. Ibid.

44. Luckett, "Credit," 105–06.

45. Ibid., 113–14.

46. The Civil Procedure Ordinance of 1667 provided for the entry of default judgments. "Ordonnance civile touchant la réformation de la justice," tit. 16, arts. 5–6, in *Code Louis,* 1:23.

47. This estimate is based on (1) a rough count of the court's decisions, which were recorded in chronological order and grouped according to the day of decision (*Registres des sentences,* AP D^{2}B^{6}), and (2) records preserved by the court for all the cases filed on Monday, January 5, 1784 (AP D^{7}B^{6}/1691).

48. *Encyclopédie méthodique: Commerce,* s.v. "Consulat" (Paris: Chez Panckoucke, 1783), 1:720.

49. Session of 27 May 1790, *Archives Parlementaires de 1787 à 1860: Recueil complet des débats législatifs et politiques des chambres françaises: 1. série* (Paris: Libraire administrative de P. Dupont, 1879), 15:687 (deputy Leclerc) and 688 (deputy Démeunier).

50. [Couchot], *Praticien,* 277; *Encyclopédie méthodique: Commerce,* s.v. "Consulat," 1:720.

51. On January 5, 1784, a total of 223 of the 350 cases appear to have been resolved by means of default judgments. AP D^{7}B^{6}/1691.

52. Masson, *Affaires contentieuses,* viii.

53. [Couchot], *Praticien,* 283.

54. Reports from 1762 through 1767 are contained in a single box (AP D^{6}B^{6}/7), and the box containing reports from 1771 to 1773 appears to be missing all reports from 1772 (AP D^{6}B^{6}/9).

55. AP D^{6}B^{6}/21.

56. The only scholars who have examined the arbiters' reports in any depth are Jacqueline-Lucienne Lafon and Thomas Manley Luckett. Jacqueline-Lucienne Lafon, "L'arbitre près la juridiction consulaire de Paris au XVIIIe siècle," *Revue historique de droit français et étranger* 51 (1973): 217-70; Luckett, "Credit."

57. Tables presenting various features of the arbiters' reports contained in Box AP D^6B^6/15 can be found in the appendix.

58. Records of the court's judgments are contained in *Registres des sentences,* AP D^2B^6.

59. Szramkiewicz, *Droit des affaires,* 142–44.

60. "Édit portant que tous différens entre marchands pour fait de leur commerce, les demandes de partage et les comptes de tutelle et administration seront renvoyés à des arbitres" (Fontainbleau, August 1560), in Isambert, Jourdan, and Decrusy, *Recueil general,* 14:51–52.

61. "Édit qui crée la juridiction consulaire des juges et consuls de Paris et règle leur competence" (Paris, November 1563), in Isambert, Jourdan, and Decrusy, *Recueil general,* 14:153–58.

62. "Ordonnance du commerce," tit. 4, art. 9, in Isambert, Jourdan, and Decrusy, *Recueil general,* 19:97; Philippe Bornier, *Conferences des ordonnances de Louis XIV* (Paris: Chez les associés choisis par ordre de sa Majesté, 1760), 2:388.

63. "Ordonnance civile touchant la réformation de la justice," tit. 16, art. 3, in *Code Louis,* 1:23.

64. The court archives appear to contain no documents relating to the appointment of arbiters.

65. Leclerc, Arbiter's Report in Picol et fils, négociants v. Bonveyron, Posnel et compagnie, 12 July 1783, AP D^6B^6/14 (103).

66. Arthur Engelmann and Robert Wyness Millar, *A History of Continental Civil Procedure* (Boston: Little Brown, 1927), 723; M. Marion, *Dictionnaire des institutions de la France aux XVIIe et XVIIIe siècles,* s.v. "Commissaires" (Paris: A. et J. Picard, 1993), 120.

67. See, for example, Bourderelle, Arbiter's Report in Piel v. Grand, n.d. (around October 1783), AP D^6B^6/15 (41); Chesseigneur, Arbiter's Report in Ballin v. Lebrienne, 7 February 1783, AP D^6B^6/15 (88).

68. Delavoigniere, Arbiter's Report in Louis François Dufour v. Lequint et sa femme, 14 September 1784, AP D^6B^6/15 (70).

69. The court does not seem to have ratified or enforced the compromise reached through arbitration. As discussed in chapter 4, ratification was required only in the special case of the arbitration of partnership disputes. Henri Lévy-Bruhl, *Histoire juridique des sociétés de commerce en France aux XVIIe et XVIIIe siècles* (Paris: Domat-Montchrestien, 1938), 275.

70. Numerous arbiters' reports begin with the almost identical refrain, "You asked me to try to reconcile the parties and, if I could not, to send you my report." See, for example, LeBenarc, Arbiter's Report in Barré v. Chalons, 29 December 1785, AP D^6B^6/17 (359); Salong, Arbiter's Report in Aie v. Delamotte, 7 September 1785, AP D^6B^6/17 (95?); Rousseau, Arbiter's Report in Florentin v. Grelet, 16 August 1785, AP D^6B^6/17 (n.a.); Timothin, Arbiter's Report in Le Serteur et Guérin, associés v. Texier, 18 December 1783, AP D^6B^6/15 (112); Heury Lepitre, Arbiter's Report in Paupe v. Bertin, 18 July 1785, AP D^6B^6/17 (4)

71. Reinhard Zimmermann, *The Law of Obligations: Roman Foundations of the Civilian Tradition* (Oxford: Clarendon Press, 1996), 528–30.

72. See, for example, Robert M. Rodman, *Commercial Arbitration with Forms* (St.

Paul, Minn.: West Publishing Co., 1984), 1–6; Mariano P. Marcos, "Concept, Legal Basis and Scope of Commercial Arbitration," in *Commercial Arbitration: Proceedings of the Symposium on Commercial Arbitration, 1981,* ed. Juliana R. Ricalde (Quezon City: U.P. Law Center, 1983), 8.

73. Toubeau, *Institutes du droit consulaire,* 1:85.

74. Vignon, Arbiter's Report in Renard v. Roëttieos de la Tour, 30 August 1784, AP $D^6B^6/15$ (182). See also Pontoin fils, Arbiter's Report in Camus v. Boyer, 16 October 1783, AP $D^6B^6/15$ (161).

75. Report, Renard v. Roëttieos de la Tour, AP $D^6B^6/15$ (182).

76. Renou, Arbiter's Report in Hamond v. de Saint Ligier, 3 December 1785, AP $D^6B^6/17$ (n.a.).

77. Ibid.

78. Ibid.

79. Gillet and Mercier, *Mémoire à consulter et consultation, pour les marchands et commerçans de la riviere et des ports, fournissant la provision de Paris; les voituriers et les fermiers des coches par eau* (Paris: Chardon, 1767), 9 n. b, AP $D^1B^6/25$ (4963).

80. See table 8 in the appendix.

81. See table 2 in the appendix.

82. The two book-length authorities describing the institutional structure of the Parisian Merchant Court, as well as more general accounts of Old Regime commercial law, discuss arbitration only briefly and do not mention that priests served as arbiters. Denière, *Juridiction consulaire,* 79–80; Georges Leclerc, *La juridiction consulaire de Paris pendant la Révolution* (Paris: Plon, 1909), 59–60, 400–405; Jean Hilaire, *Introduction historique au droit commercial* (Paris: Presses Universitaires de France, 1986), 74; Szramkiewicz, *Droit des affaires,* 143. Other works recognize that priests were often selected as arbiters but fail to explore the meaning and significance of this fact. Paul Dupieux, "Les attributions de la juridiction consulaire de Paris (1563–1792): L'arbitrage entre associés, commerçants patrons et ouvriers au XVIIIe siècle," *Bibliothèque de l'école des chartes* 95 (1934): 124; Lafon, "L'arbitre," 220 and n. 18; Luckett, "Credit," 76.

83. Masson, *Affaires contentieuses,* 350. That priests served as arbiters in the merchant court is particularly surprising since, according to Jean-Baptise Denisart, one of the era's most influential jurists, "clergy may not be arbiters." Jean-Baptiste Denisart, *Collection de décisions nouvelles et de notions relatives à la jurisprudence actuelle,* s.v. "arbitrage, arbitres" (Paris: Chez la veuve Desaint, 1771), 1:146. Denisart, however, was an expert on the learned law and thus had little familiarity with the distinctive practices of the merchant court. In contrast, Masson, who acknowledged that priests regularly served as merchant court arbiters, was a practicing merchant, who spent two years as a judge in the Parisian Merchant Court. Masson, *Affaires contentieuses,* iii. That the merchant courts were apparently willing to ignore the learned-law rule against priests serving as arbiters may be a further reflection of the importance they placed on incorporating Christian norms and practices into merchant court adjudication.

84. Session of 27 May 1790, *Archives Parlementaires,* 15:686 (deputy Leclerc). As Leclerc had himself been a merchant court judge, he had particular reason to know whereof he spoke. Jean Hilaire, "La Révolution et les juridictions consulaires," in *Une Autre justice: Contributions à l'histoire de la justice sous la Révolution française,* ed. Robert Badinter (Paris: Fayard, 1989), 247.

85. Gillet and Mercier, *Mémoire à consulter,* 9 n. b, AP D^{1}B^6/25 (4963).

86. In the box of arbiters' reports that I systematically reviewed, 13 of the 108 reports in which the arbiters identified themselves were written by parish priests. Of these thirteen reports, only one seems to have been written by a priest from Paris. Garan, Arbiter's Report in Legy v. Lucas, 25 May 1784, AP D^{6}B^6/15 (n.a.).

87. Lilloud, Arbiter's Report in Darmais v. Martin, 29 April 1786, AP D^{6}B^6/17 (96).

88. Garrioch, *Neighborhood and Community,* 155–56; John McManners, *Church and Society in Eighteenth-Century France,* ed. Henry and Owen Chadwick (Oxford: Clarendon Press, 1998), 1:358–83; Timothy Tackett, *Priest and Parish in Eighteenth-Century France: A Social and Political Study of the Curés in a Diocese of Dauphiné, 1750–1791* (Princeton: Princeton University Press, 1977), 166–69.

89. Garrioch, *Neighborhood and Community,* 156–57.

90. Pachal, Arbiter's Report in Réal v. Hellan, 24 November 1784, AP D^{6}B^6/15 (204).

91. F. Regnault, Arbiter's Report in Jolle v. Moreau et sa femme, 5 September 1741, AP D^{6}B^6/5 (n.a.). In addition to relying on his assessment of the plaintiff's moral character, the arbiter-priest in this case based his decision on the defendants' repeated failure to appear when summoned. The default itself seems to have served as a presumption of bad faith.

92. Folio, Arbiter's Report in Gatines v. Girard, 31 January 1784, AP D^{6}B^6/15 (189).

93. Ibid.

94. A. Jean, Arbiter's Report in Viennos v. Launoy, 29 July 1747, AP D^{6}B^6/5 (n.a.).

95. Ibid.

96. McManners, *Church and Society,* 1:358–83; Tackett, *Priest and Parish,* 166–69.

97. Adrien Bailié, Arbiter's Report in Meusnier v. Meusnier, 26 May 1785, AP D^{6}B^6/17 (194).

98. Ibid.

99. Ibid.

100. Déyeux, Arbiter's Report in Dorozin dit Flamant v. Sarget, 7 April 1784, AP D^{6}B^6/15 (526).

101. Ibid.

102. Ibid.

103. Ibid.

104. See table 2 in the appendix.

105. See the discussion in chapter 3.

106. Panniers, Le Cours, and Hellant, Arbiters' Report in Manjard v. Chopard, 4 December 1783, AP D^{6}B^6/15 (128).

107. Ibid.

108. Santilly, Arbiter's Report in Hanblin v. Tinfouin père, n.d. (around August 1784), AP D^{6}B^6/15 (n.a.).

109. Ibid.

110. Ibid.

111. Froton, Arbiter's Report in Bayard v. Botté, 6 May 1785, AP D^{6}B^6/17 (322).

112. Ibid.

113. "Ordonnance civile touchant la réformation de la justice," tit. 16, art. 7, in *Code Louis,* 1:23.

114. Dunquetis, Arbiter's Report in Herbelle v. Ferret, 3 March 1785, AP D^{6}B^6/17 (194).

115. Lapin, Arbiter's Report in Jean Marchand v. Collinet, 4 April 1786, AP D^6B^6/17 (163).

116. Masson, *Affaires contentieuses,* 145.

117. Report, Herbelle v. Ferret, AP D^6B^6/17 (194).

118. Ibid.

119. Ibid.

120. Charles Naris, Arbiter's Report in Gossé v. Derient, 12 December 1783, AP D^6B^6/15 (48).

121. Ibid.

122. Ibid.

123. Ibid.

124. Ibid.

125. Ibid.

126. Ibid.

127. Ibid.

128. Ibid.

129. Ibid.

130. Ibid.

131. Ibid.

132. "Ordonnance du commerce," tit. 3, art. 1, in Isambert, Jourdan, and Decrusy, *Recueil general,* 19:95; Bornier, *Conferences des ordonnances,* 1760 ed., 2:375.

133. For a discussion of the various kinds of accounting books kept by early-modern merchants, see Bornier, *Conferences des ordonnances,* 1760 ed., 2:375; "Suite de l'essai sur l'education du négociant," in *Journal de Commerce* (Brussels), April 1762, 41–46; and [Couchot], *Praticien,* 49–50.

134. Bornier warned that "merchants must be very careful not to write anything in the *grand livre* that was not first written in the *livre-journal,*" because otherwise the accuracy of their books could be challenged. Bornier, *Conferences des ordonnances,* 1760 ed., 2:378.

135. Because notaries retained copies of the contracts that they signed and sealed, it was far riskier to tamper with such contracts than with ones that had been privately signed. However, as discussed earlier in this chapter, Old Regime merchants tended not to rely extensively on notarized contracts.

136. "Ordonnance du commerce," tit. 3, art. 5, in Isambert, Jourdan, and Decrusy, *Recueil general,* 19:95; Bornier, *Conferences des ordonnances,* 1760 ed., 2:377.

137. Bornier, for example, stated that if a debtor presented accounting books in his defense, and the creditor failed to offer his own books into evidence, merchant courts would find for the debtor, even if the creditor's claim was based on a signed writing. Bornier, *Conferences des ordonnances,* 1760 ed., 2:380.

138. Ibid., 2:378.

139. Magunes, Arbiter's Report in Colon v. De Sainte Beuve, 18 June 1785, AP D^6B^6/17 (222).

140. Ibid.

141. Ibid.

142. Toubeau, *Institutes du droit consulaire,* 2:69 (paraphrasing Bornier, *Conferences des ordonnances,* 1760 ed., 2:377).

143. Leclerc, Arbiter's Report in Gornier et Dardrieu v. Chandon, 19 October 1784, AP D6B6/15 (n.a.).

144. Ibid.

145. Ibid.

146. Toubeau, *Institutes du droit consulaire,* 1:29.

147. The decisory oath is officially still an element of French procedure today, but it is deferred to one litigant at the request of the other, rather than as practiced in the merchant court, upon the judge's unilateral decision. Moreover, it is very rarely used, since the litigant "will usually consider it unhelpful to call upon the good faith of his adversary." Henri and Léon Mazeaud, Jean Mazeaud, and François Chabas, *Leçons de droit civil,* 11th ed. (Paris: Montchrestien, 1996), 591. See also Guy Raymond, *Droit Civil* (Paris: Litec, 1993), 67.

148. Toubeau, *Institutes du droit consulaire,* 1:249.

149. For a discussion of the history of the decisory oath in the Roman and canon-law traditions, see R. H. Helmholz, *The Spirit of Classical Canon Law* (Athens, Ga.: University of Georgia Press, 1996), 156–57; Anne Lefebvre-Teillard, *Les officialités à la veille du Concile de Trente* (Paris: Libraire Générale de Droit et de Jurisprudence, 1973), 56–57.

150. For a general discussion of standards of proof in the Roman-canon system, see Michael R. T. Macnair, *The Law of Proof in Early Modern Equity* (Berlin: Duncker and Humblot, 1999), 93–94, 249.

151. François Bourjon, *Le droit commun de la France et la coutume de Paris* (Paris: Chez Grangé, 1770), 2:412.

152. Ibid.

153. Rogue suggested that the merchant courts applied the Roman-canon law rule requiring a public writing or two witness to form a full proof. Rogue, *Jurisprudence consulaire et instruction des négociants* (Angers: Chez A. J. Jahyer, 1773), 1:70.

154. Toubeau, *Institutes du droit consulaire,* 1:128–29. This view of the accounting book as a distinctive kind of written proof may also have been, in part, a heritage of Roman law—in particular, the contract *litteris*. Though little is now known about this contract, it appears to have been an obligation to pay a sum of money arising from the creditor's recording of the debt in his accounting book. Barry Nicholas, *An Introduction to Roman Law* (Oxford: Clarendon Press, 1962), 196; Zimmermann, *Law of Obligations,* 32 n. 178.

155. Guyot, *Répertoire universel,* s.v. "Consul," 15:126.

156. Rogue, *Jurisprudence consulaire,* 1:99.

157. Toubeau, *Institutes du droit consulaire,* 1:29.

158. Ibid.

159. Le Roulx de la Ville, Arbiter's Report in Blaincourt v. Dubois et Dubuisson, entrepreneurs, 29 November 1773, AP D6B6/9 (n.a.).

160. Vancquetin, Arbiter's Report in Chapuy v. d'Hauteville, 10 October 1765, AP D6B6/7 (n.a.).

161. Ibid. (paraphrasing and almost quoting Philibert-Joseph Masson), *Instruction des négociants: tirée des ordonnances, édits, déclarations, arrêts, et des usages reçus* (Blois, 1748), 110).

162. L. Houssel, Arbiter's Report in Desbordes v. Desbordes, 23 September 1762, AP D6B6/7 (n.a.).

163. Ibid.

164. See generally Peter Brooks, *The Melodramatic Imagination: Balzac, Henry James, Melodrama, and the Mode of Excess* (New York: Columbia University Press, 1985).

165. Dupeigne, Arbiter's Report in Compagnie adjudicataires des bois du Parc de Meudon v. Castel, 22 September 1784, AP $D^6B^6/15$ (192).

166. Ibid.

167. Ibid.

168. Ibid.

169. Ibid.

170. Ibid.

171. Report, Blaincourt v. Dubois et Dubuisson, entrepreneurs, AP $D^6B^6/9$ (n.a.).

172. Ibid.

173. Ibid.

174. Sarah Maza, *Private Lives and Public Affairs: The Causes Célèbres of Prerevolutionary France* (Berkeley: University of California Press, 1993); David A. Bell, *Lawyers and Citizens: The Making of a Political Elite in Old Regime France* (Oxford: Oxford University Press, 1994).

175. James Q. Whitman, "From Cause Célèbre to Revolution," *Yale Journal of Law and the Humanities* 7 (Summer 1995): 467–70. In support of this argument, Whitman cites a report of a case argued in 1616, which adopts the same melodramatic tone as the trial briefs discussed by Maza and Bell. To Whitman's example, many others could be added. See, for example, the pleadings on behalf of the Ordre de la Sainte Trinité and Catherine de Rambouillet filed with the *Parlement* of Paris in the mid-seventeenth century. Olivier Patru, *Œuvres diverses de M. Patru, de l'academie française, contenant ses plaidoyers, harangues, lettres, et vies de quelques-uns de ses amis,* 4th ed. (Paris: Chez la veuve Clouzier, 1732), 1:15–31, 87–108.

176. Louis-Sébastien Mercier, *Tableau de Paris,* new ed. (Amsterdam, 1782; repr., Geneva: Slatkine Reprints, 1979), 2:26–27.

Chapter 3. An Equity-Oriented View of Contract: The Court's Resolution of Disputes Concerning Sales, Employment, and Marriage

Epigraph. Jean Toubeau, *Les institutes du droit consulaire ou les elemens de la jurisprudence des marchands* (Bourges, 1700), 2:6.

1. Business associations can, of course, be viewed as a contractual arrangement. Nonetheless, I examine them separately in chapter 4—both for the sake of clarity and because such associations have traditionally been deemed a distinct legal category.

2. Charles Donahue Jr., "Medieval and Early Modern Lex Mercatoria: An Attempt at the Probatio Diabolica," *Chicago Journal of International Law* 5 (Summer 2004): 22.

3. Bruce L. Benson, "The Spontaneous Evolution of Commercial Law," *Southern Economic Journal* 55 (January 1989): 647.

4. J. H. Baker, "The Law Merchant and the Common Law before 1700," *Cambridge Law Journal* 38 (November 1979): 295.

5. Leon E. Trakman, *The Law Merchant: The Evolution of Commercial Law* (Littleton, Colo.: Fred B. Rothman, 1983), 18 (emphasis deleted).

6. Harold J. Berman, *Law and Revolution: The Formation of the Western Legal Tradition* (Cambridge: Harvard University Press, 1983), 349; Benson, "Spontaneous Evolution," 650–51.

7. Benson, "Spontaneous Evolution," 649.

8. See the helpful overview of the standard account (including its reliance on Goldschmidt and Mitchell) in Emily Kadens, "Order within Law, Variety within Custom: The Character of the Medieval Merchant Law," *Chicago Journal of International Law* 5 (Summer 2004): 39–41 and n. 4.

9. Trakman, *Law Merchant,* 14.

10. A superb overview of this history (and the extent to which it has been ideologically driven) can be found in Mary Elizabeth Basile et al., ed., *Lex Mercatoria and Legal Pluralism: A Late Thirteenth-Century Treatise and Its Afterlife* (Cambridge, Mass.: Ames Foundation, 1998), 123–78.

11. Trakman, *Law Merchant;* Albrecht Cordes, "À la recherche d'une lex mercatoria au moyen âge," in *Stadt und Recht in Mittelalter* (Göttingen: Vandenhoeck and Ruprecht, 2003), 119 and n. 8 (discussing this trend).

12. See, for example, Douglass C. North, *Institutions, Institutional Change, and Economic Performance* (Cambridge: Cambridge University Press, 1990), 125–30.

13. Avner Greif, *Institutions and the Path to the Modern Economy: Lessons from Medieval Trade* (Cambridge: Cambridge University Press, 2006), 314–15.

14. Cordes, "À la recherche," 128–29.

15. Benson, "Spontaneous Evolution," 653.

16. Trakman, *Law Merchant,* 25.

17. Note, however, that a few authors have argued that Roman law influenced the development of the law merchant. See the useful summary in J. H. Baker, "Law Merchant," 295 and n. 4; Benson, "Spontaneous Evolution," 647.

18. R. H. Helmholz, *The Spirit of Classical Canon Law* (Athens, Ga.: University of Georgia Press, 1996), 157, 163; Anne Lefebvre-Teillard, *Les officialités à la veille du Concile de Trente* (Paris: Libraire Générale de Droit et de Jurisprudence, 1973), 56–57; Berman, *Law and Revolution,* 245–50.

19. The question of whether modern-day French judges make law has been a subject of significant dispute among American comparative law scholars. John P. Dawson, *The Oracles of the Law* (Ann Arbor: University of Michigan Press, 1968), 374–431; John H. Merryman, *The Civil Law Tradition: An Introduction to the Legal Systems of Western Europe and Latin America,* 2d ed. (Stanford: Stanford University Press, 1985), 14–47; Mitchel de S.-O.-L'E. Lasser, *Judicial Deliberations: A Comparative Analysis of Judicial Transparency and Legitimacy* (Oxford: Oxford University Press, 2004), 166–202.

20. Romuald Szramkiewicz, *Histoire du droit des affaires* (Paris: Montchrestien, 1989), 147; G. Denière, *La juridiction consulaire de Paris, 1563–1792: Sa création, ses luttes, son administration intérieure, ses usages et ses mœurs* (Paris: Henri Plon, 1872), 169.

21. Philibert-Joseph Masson, *Instruction sur les affaires contentieuses des négociants, la manière de les prévenir, ou de les suivre dans les tribunaux* (Paris: Chez LeClerc, 1786), 396–97.

22. See, for example, Szramkiewicz, *Droit des affaires,* 169–70, which describes the

parlements' efforts to enforce the rule against different places. See chapter 5 for a discussion of this rule.

23. Toubeau, *Institutes du droit consulaire,* 1: "Preface."

24. Amalia D. Kessler, "Enforcing Virtue: Social Norms and Self-Interest in an Eighteenth-Century Merchant Court," *Law and History Review* 22 (Spring 2004): 106–18.

25. For a general discussion of the *ius commune,* see Manlio Bellomo, *The Common Legal Past of Europe, 1000–1800,* trans. Lydia G. Cochrane (Washington, D.C.: Catholic University of America Press, 1995).

26. Berman, *Law and Revolution,* 245–47.

27. Barry Nicholas, *An Introduction to Roman Law* (Oxford: Clarendon Press, 1962), 161–64, 171, 175–76. This is a purely descriptive account of Roman-law understandings, rather than a normative claim that courts are, in fact, well suited to assessing what constitutes good faith and to enforcing such behavior.

28. Donald R. Kelley, *The Human Measure: Social Thought in the Western Legal Tradition* (Cambridge: Harvard University Press, 1990), 215.

29. [Couchot], *Le praticien des juges et consuls; ou, Traité de commerce de terre et de mer* (Paris: Prault père, 1742), 423 (discussing the *Coutume de Paris,* arts. 176 and 177).

30. François Bourjon, *Le droit commun de la France et la coutume de Paris* (Paris: Chez Brunet, 1775): 1:463; Michel Prevost de la Jannés, *Les principes de la jurisprudence française, exposés suivant l'ordre des diverses espéces d'actions qui se pursuivent en justice* (Paris: Chez Barrois ainé, 1780), 2:222. The *action rédhibitoire* originated in the ancient Roman *actio redhibitoria,* and jurists of the *ius commune* gradually limited its applicability. That it continued to be fully applicable in cases concerning the sale of draught animals was a product of local customary law, as contained in the *Coutume de Paris,* which resisted the incursion of the *ius commune.* Reinhard Zimmermann, *The Law of Obligations: Roman Foundations of the Civilian Tradition* (Oxford: Clarendon Press, 1996), 325–26 and n. 242.

31. Eli Leroux, Arbiter's Report in Ibert v. Moreau, 24 May 1786, AP $D^{6}B^{6}$/17 (323).

32. Ibid.

33. A number of commercial-law scholars have recently suggested that merchant custom—namely, precise, clearly defined merchant practices that can (and should) be used as default rules in the absence of contractual agreement—may not, in fact, exist. See, for example, Richard Craswell, "Do Trade Customs Exist?," in *The Jurisprudential Foundations of Corporate and Commercial Law,* ed. Jody S. Kraus and Steven D. Walt (Cambridge: Cambridge University Press, 2000), 118–48; Lisa Bernstein, "The Questionable Empirical Basis of Article 2's Incorporation Strategy: A Preliminary Study," *University of Chicago Law Review* 66 (1999): 710–80.

34. Boyes, Arbiter's Report (parties unnamed), 21 December 1743, AP $D^{6}B^{6}$/5 (n.a.).

35. Ibid.

36. Craswell, "Do Trade Customs Exist?," 142 (internal quotations omitted). See also Bernstein, "Questionable Empirical Basis."

37. "Ordonnance du commerce," tit. 4 ("Des sociétés"), in François André Isambert, Athanase-Jean-Léger Jourdan, and Decrusy, *Recueil général des anciennes lois françaises, depuis l'an 420, jusqu'à la révolution de 1789* (Paris: Belin-Leprieur, 1829), 19:96–97;

ibid., tit. 5 ("Des lettres et billets de change, et promesses d'en fournir"), in Isambert, Jourdan, and Decrusy, *Recueil general*, 19:97-101; ibid., tit. 6 ("Des intérêts du change et du rechange"), in Isambert, Jourdan, and Decrusy, *Recueil general*, 19:101–02.

38. See the discussion in chapters 4 and 5.

39. See, for example, Vancquetin, Arbiter's Report in Chapuy v. d'Hauteville, 10 October 1765, AP D^{6}B^6/7 (n.a.) (citing Masson regarding the prescription period); *Mémoire pour le sieur Nicolas Joseph de la Valette*, 8, AP D^{1}B^6/32 (5269) (citing Bornier concerning the law of business associations).

40. See the discussion in chapter 6.

41. Toubeau, *Institutes du droit consulaire*, 1: "Preface."

42. Jacqueline-Lucienne Lafon, *Les députés du commerce et l'ordonnance de mars 1673: Les juridictions consulaires, principe et compétence* (Paris: Éditions Cujas, 1979), 50 n. 49.

43. See table 1 in the appendix.

44. Michael Sonenscher, *Work and Wages: Natural Law, Politics and the Eighteenth-Century French Trades* (Cambridge: Cambridge University Press, 1989), 138–39, 147–48.

45. See tables 6 and 7 in the appendix.

46. See, for example, LeClerc, Arbiter's Report in les sieurs Brentani Cunaroli v. Grand, 30 July 1784, AP D^{6}B^6/15 (n.a.) (les sieurs Brentani Cunaroli were bankers from Vienna); Doucet de Turiny, Arbiter's Report in Texada v. Detchegaray, 10 December 1785, AP D^{6}B^6/16 (181) (Texada was a banker from Madrid); J. M. S. Batbedas and Vandenyves, Arbiters' Report in Cottin l'ainé et fils, banquiers v. les sieurs Urbain Vidal et compagnie, 6 June 1777, AP D^{6}B^6/12 (n.a.) (les sieurs Urbain Vidal et compagnie were bankers from Hamburg).

47. Chibon, Arbiter's Report in Druyes de Boncourt v. Leonard de France, 29 March 1786, AP D^{6}B^6/18 (15).

48. See, for example, Cottin fils, Arbiter's Report in Destornelle v. Fournier, 9 February 1783, AP D^{6}B^6/15 (389) (suit brought by a priest against a wine seller for payment of wine that the former sold the latter). See also table 3 in the appendix.

49. See chapter 6 for a discussion of merchant court jurisdiction over nonmerchants.

50. Barry Nicholas, *The French Law of Contract*, 2d ed. (Oxford: Clarendon Press, 1992), 138.

51. Bourjon, *Droit commun*, 1775 ed., 1:460; Prevost de la Jannés, *Principes de la jurisprudence*, 2:220; Nicholas, *French Law*, 138–39; [Couchot], *Praticien*, 636, 648.

52. Prevost de la Jannés, *Principes de la jurisprudence*, 2:220.

53. Jean-Yves Grenier, *L'économie d'ancien régime: Un monde de l'échange et de l'incertitude* (Paris: Albin Michel, 1996), 63–67; Clare Haru Crowston, *Fabricating Women: The Seamstresses of Old Regime France, 1675–1791* (Durham, N.C.: Duke University Press, 2001), 159.

54. See, for example, Renné et al. (leaders of carpenters' guild [*menuisiers*]), Arbiters' Report in Lugeard et de la Rue v. Sauvage, 30 March 1783, AP D^{6}B^6/15 (241); Passard et al. (leaders of saddlers' guild), Arbiters' Report in Chemit v. Moreau, 8 January 1783, AP D^{6}B^6/15 (220); Le Cours et al. (leaders of cartwrights' guild), Arbiters' Report in Rigoulos v. Pingal, 24 December 1783, AP D^{6}B^6/15 (129); Thevek'man et al. (leaders of carpen-

ters' guild [*menuisiers*]), Arbiters' Report in Chamoinelle v. Barreau et la dame son epouse, 27 June 1784, AP D^6B^6/15 (72); Allard, Dugy, and Lelui (leaders of fruit sellers' guild), Arbiters' Report in Delaborde et sa femme v. Marial, 3 June 1784, AP D^6B^6/15 (92); Bloicet et al. (leaders of coopers' guild), Arbiters' Report in Vetter v. Manger, 28 March 1784, AP D^6B^6/15 (187); Garibon, Boussard, and Petit (leaders of carpenters' guild [*menuisiers*]), Arbiters' Report in Alexandre v. Dumont, 24 April 1784, AP D^6B^6/15 (91); Gamiel et al. (leaders of cartwrights' guild), Arbiters' Report in Chavaune v. la dame veuve Alix, 9 September 1784, AP D^6B^6/15 (1).

55. [Couchot], *Praticien,* 613. See also Masson, *Affaires contentieuses,* 366.

56. Report, Chavaune v. la dame veuve Alix, AP D^6B^6/15 (1).

57. Ibid.

58. Laudry et al., Arbiters' Report in Darnaudery v. Desgranges, 3 May 1784, AP D^6B^6/15 (14).

59. Ibid.

60. Ibid.

61. Ibid.

62. Alfred Franklin, *Les corporations ouvrières de Paris du XIIe au XVIIIe siècle: Histoire, statuts, armoiries, d'après des documents originaux ou inédits* (New York: B. Franklin, 1971), 7–8 (describing extensive violations of the button makers' monopoly privileges in the eighteenth century and the guild's failed efforts to prevent these).

63. The goldsmiths' commitment to policing their privileges is readily apparent in *Mémoire d'observations pour les six corps des marchands en général et pour les marchands orfèvres en particulier* (n.d.), AN F^{12}781/D (29?).

64. Disnematin Dozal, Arbiter's Report in Tournu v. Fabre Duborgnes, n.d. (around 14 November 1783), AP D^6B^6/15 (64).

65. Ibid.

66. Ibid.

67. De Pellagot, Arbiter's Report in Roze v. le Gagneur, 9 April 1783, AP D^6B^6/15 (91).

68. Marquis, Arbiter's Report in Montié v. Philippe, 13 January 1784, AP D^6B^6/15 (169).

69. J. C. Le Coufles, Arbiter's Report (parties unnamed), 31 August 1741, AP D^6B^6/5 (n.a.). Unfortunately, the name of the guild is illegible.

70. Ibid.

71. Marquis, Arbiter's Report in Fouches v. Edme Huguet, 8 June 1783, AP D^6B^6/15 (273).

72. Ibid.

73. Ibid.

74. Ibid.

75. [Couchot], *Praticien,* 442; John T. Noonan Jr., *The Scholastic Analysis of Usury* (Cambridge: Harvard University Press, 1957), 105–21.

76. François Jean Serebeau, Arbiter's Report in Parin et Valette, entrepreneurs v. Bernard, 17 September 1774, AP D^6B^6/10 (n.a.).

77. Ibid.

78. The *délai de grace* was a Roman-law practice adopted by the jurists of the *ius commune.* Lefebvre-Teillard, *Officialités,* 249.

79. "Ordonnance pour la réformation de la justice, faisant la continuation de celle du mois d'avril 1667" tit. 6, art. 1, in Isambert, Jourdan, and Decrusy, *Recueil general,* 19:359; Masson, *Affaires contentieuses,* 354–55.

80. Thomas Manley Luckett, "Credit and Commercial Society in France, 1740–1789" (Ph.D. diss., Princeton University, 1992), 75. See, for example, Thomas de Bon, Arbiter's Report in Noiraut v. LeComte, 24 March 1784, AP D⁶B⁶/15 (n.a.).

81. Quatremere fils ainé, Arbiter's Report in Joseph Tasslin v. marchand et veuve Masson, 3 September 1784, AP D⁶B⁶/15 (149).

82. Ibid.

83. Ibid.

84. Ibid.

85. The November 1563 edict provided that the court could order the defendant to pay interest at the rate of 8.33 percent (*denier douze*) in cases in which there was a "delay in payment." "Édit qui crée la juridiction consulaire des juges et consuls de Paris et règle leur competence," art. 11 (Paris, November 1563), in Isambert, Jourdan, and Decrusy, *Recueil general,* 14:156; [Couchot], *Praticien,* xiv. By an edict of 1665, the monarchy reduced the interest permitted to 5 percent (*denier vingt*). [Couchot], *Praticien,* 279. As the commercial jurist Masson explained, the interest charged in the merchant courts tracked the official rate permitted by the monarchy on annuities, or *rentes.* Masson, *Affaires contentieuses,* 400.

86. Pillons, Arbiter's Report in Ganal v. Rainfray, 5 November 1786, AP D⁶B⁶/18 (n.a.).

87. Ibid.

88. Duchemin, Arbiter's Report in Crapart v. Philippes, 21 May, 1784, AP D⁶B⁶/15 (n.a.).

89. Masson, *Affaires contentieuses,* 354.

90. F. M. de Villeval, Arbiter's Report in Simon v. Dubreuil, 7 September 1747, AP D⁶B⁶/5 (n.a.).

91. Ibid.

92. Adrien Bailié, Arbiter's Report in Meusnier v. Meusnier, 26 May 1785, AP D⁶B⁶/17 (194).

93. Ibid.

94. Ibid.

95. Ibid.

96. Ibid.

97. Pinchauf, Arbiter's Report in le comte de Colincour v. Bequet, 1 July 1785, AP D⁶B⁶/17 (369).

98. Many reports dealing with disputes over horse sales were written by this arbiter, who does not appear to have been sent cases concerning any other kind of merchandise. This suggests that he probably was — or had been — a horse merchant himself. See also the description in Alan Williams, *The Police of Paris, 1718–1789* (Baton Rouge: Louisiana State University Press, 1979), 135–36, of the "professional consultants" who assisted the police.

99. Report, le comte de Colincour v. Bequet, AP D⁶B⁶/17 (369).

100. Ibid.

101. Ibid.

102. Lillond, Arbiter's Report in Vasinelle v. Blin, 8 February 1783, AP D^{6}B^6/15 (54).

103. Ibid.

104. Ibid.

105. Ibid. See also Desauges, Arbiter's Report in Mertins, Desvoyen, et Guidon v. Racoir, 18 January 1784, AP D^{6}B^6/15 (10) (recommending a delay because the plaintiffs "are comfortable, and are not anxious to receive this sum," while "on the contrary . . . [the defendant] is not wealthy, he lacks everything, [has been] sick for the past two years, [and is] responsible for his family"); Pilloud, Arbiter's Report in Vasinelle v. Domard, 14 February 1785, AP D^{6}B^6/15 (34) (recommending a delay because this would be "less prejudicial to the interests of . . . [the plaintiff] than useful, and of the greatest necessity for . . . [the defendant], in that it will ensure that he retains his profession [*état*], the only resource for him, his wife, and his children"); Mang, Arbiter's Report in Noel Birbaut v. Michel David, n.d. (around June 1783), AP D^{6}B^6/15 (n.a.) (recommending a delay with no interest "given the little commerce that . . . [the defendant] is now doing").

106. In theory, the *Coutume de Paris* afforded *saisie et revendication* to any unpaid seller. Bourjon, *Droit commun*, 1775 ed., 1:460. In reality, however, the arbiters' reports reveal that the Parisian Merchant Court generally granted the remedy only when the buyer had become insolvent. This makes sense given the nature of commercial credit transactions in the Old Regime. Since credit was often extended continuously in the context of long-lasting creditor-debtor relationships, seller-creditors had little incentive to seek *saisie et revendication*, unless they had reason to believe that the buyer-debtor had become insolvent.

107. Masson, *Affaires contentieuses*, 308.

108. Peraut, Arbiter's Report in Granjaquart v. Laurent, 29 December 1785, AP D^{6}B^6/17 (n.a.). See also LeBenarc, Arbiter's Report in Barré v. Chalons, 29 December 1785, AP D^{6}B^6/17 (359).

109. Forney and Cheret, Arbiters' Report in Vadaux v. Pleyard, 21 June 1783, AP D^{6}B^6/14 (188).

110. Ibid.

111. Chevillard, Arbiter's Report in Vadaux v. Pleyard, 11 June 1783, AP D^{6}B^6/14 (188).

112. See table 3 in the appendix.

113. Sarah Maza, "Luxury, Morality and Social Change: Why There Was No Middle-Class Consciousness in Prerevolutionary France," *Journal of Modern History* 69 (June 1997): 213–15. Roche identifies this revolution as occurring over the course of the eighteenth century. Daniel Roche, *The People of Paris: An Essay in Popular Culture in the Eighteenth Century*, trans. Marie Evans and Gwynne Lewis (Leamington Spa, U.K.: Berg, 1987), 160–94. Crowston, however, has recently suggested that it may have emerged as early as the period from the 1670s through 1700. Crowston, *Fabricating Women*, 12.

114. Collients, Arbiter's Report in Bienchi v. Chaffenere, 7 February 1783, D^{6}B^6/15 (237).

115. Panier, Arbiter's Report in la veuve Samblay v. Arsandeaux, 11 July 1783, AP D^{6}B^6/15 (374).

116. Maza, "Luxury," 209–10; Steven Laurence Kaplan, *The Bakers of Paris and the Bread Question, 1700–1775* (Durham, N.C.: Duke University Press, 1996), 116–17.

117. Jean Baptiste Coignard and Pierre François Emery, Arbiters' Report in Nicolas Duval v. Alexis Xavier Mesnier, 16 September 1726, AP $D^6B^6/4$ (143).

118. Ibid.

119. Ibid.

120. D'Huminel, Arbiter's Report in Antoine le Fuesn v. Eloy, 4 July 1771, AP $D^6B^6/9$ (n.a.).

121. Ibid.

122. Ibid.

123. Ibid.

124. Ibid.

125. Ibid.

126. Ibid.

127. Ibid.

128. Cottin, Arbiter's Report in Mielle v. De Billet, 18 March 1783, AP $D^6B^6/15$ (n.a.).

129. Ibid.

130. Ibid.

131. "Conclusions," in *Contract Law Today: Anglo-French Comparisons,* ed. Donald Harris and Denis Tallon (Oxford: Clarendon Press, 1989), 385–86; Nicholas, *French Law,* 211–16.

132. Nicholas, *French Law,* 212. See also "Conclusions," *Contract Law Today,* 385–86. During the eighteenth century, the influence of natural-law thought led to some debate regarding the contract remedy that a proper respect for morality and free will required. On the one hand, specific performance seemed to follow from a natural, moral requirement that individuals be made to honor their commitments. On the other, it seemed equally self-evident that people must not be forced to act against their will. Ultimately, this concern with free will led the authors of the *Code Civil* to hold in article 1142 that "any obligation to do or not to do" is to be satisfied through money damages. Zimmermann, *Law of Obligations,* 775. With time, however, judicial decisions have greatly narrowed this requirement, such that specific performance (or "*l'exécution forcée en nature*") is now frequently available at the discretion of the court and the creditor. Laurent Aynès, *Cour de droit civil: Les obligations,* 2d ed. (Paris: Cujas, 1990), 142–43, 557–59; François Terré, Philippe Simler, and Yves Lequette, *Droit civil: Les obligations,* 5th ed. (Paris: Dalloz, 1993), 404; Denis Tallon, "Remedies: French Report," in *Contract Law Today: Anglo-French Comparisons,* ed. Donald Harris and Denis Tallon (Oxford: Clarendon Press, 1989), 283–85.

133. Toubeau, *Institutes du droit consulaire,* 2:1.

134. See table 1 in the appendix.

135. Sonenscher, *Work and Wages,* 280.

136. Ibid., 256–57.

137. See, for example, Le Buffault et al., Arbiters' Report in Grunier v. Laurens, 9 May 1786, AP $D^6B^6/17$ (n.a.); Lagoguey̆ et al., Arbiters' Report in Jacques Blossier v. Cosme Damien LeCœur, 24 September 1761, AP $D^6B^6/6$ (n.a.); Bontesore et al., Arbiters' Report in Georges v. Lalouette, 9 February 1786, AP $D^6B^6/17$ (124); Bodiot et al., Arbiters' Report in Bojard v. Miquet, 2 June 1786, AP $D^6B^6/17$ (83).

138. See the discussion of guild leaders serving as arbiters in chapter 2.

139. See, for example, Stouff, Arbiter's Report in Moullin v. Cerf, 30 January 1783, AP $D^6B^6/15$ (7).

140. Panniers, Le Cours, and Hellant, Arbiters' Report in Manjard v. Chopard, 4 December 1783, AP $D^6B^6/15$ (128).

141. Ibid.

142. Ibid.

143. Ibid.

144. Ibid.

145. Ibid.

146. See, for example, Moel et al., Arbiters' Report in Gambiez v. Person, n.d. (around June 1783), AP $D^6B^6/15$ (112); LeCache et al., Arbiters' Report in Guyot v. Buirette, 12 April 1784, AP $D^6B^6/15$ (25); Geffroy et al., Arbiters' Report in Valadon v. Feugeres, n.d. (around January 1784), AP $D^6B^6/15$ (129).

147. Steven L. Kaplan, "La Lutte pour le contrôle du marché du travail à Paris au XVIIIe siècle," *Revue d'histoire moderne et contemporaine* 36 (July–September 1989): 370; Sonenscher, *Work and Wages,* 177–78.

148. Sonenscher, *Work and Wages,* 174–209.

149. Circuin et al., Arbiters' Report in Chainboy v. Vincent Laurent, n.d. (around January 1785), AP $D^6B^6/15$ (n.a.).

150. Ibid.

151. Ibid.

152. Ibid.

153. Legres et al., Arbiters' Report in Sallier v. Lasserre, n.d. (around February 1785), AP $D^6B^6/15$ (16).

154. Ibid.

155. Quesnel et al., Arbiters' Report in Persant v. Besse, 2 December 1784, AP $D^6B^6/15$ (52).

156. Sonenscher, *Work and Wages,* 132.

157. Ibid., 137.

158. Report, Persant v. Besse, AP $D^6B^6/15$ (52).

159. Ibid.

160. Ibid.

161. Ibid.

162. Ibid.

163. Ibid.

164. Bouvien, Arbiter's Report in Duhamel v. Flamand, 4 January 1786, AP $D^6B^6/18$ (n.a.).

165. Ibid.

166. "Ordonnance du commerce," tit. 1, art. 7, in Isambert, Jourdan, and Decrusy, *Recueil general,* 19:94; Philippe Bornier, *Ordonnance de Louis XIV, sur le commerce, enrichie d'annotations et de décisions importantes* (Paris: Libraires-Associés, 1767), 22.

167. Report, Chapuy v. d'Hauteville, AP $D^6B^6/7$ (n.a.). See also Masson, *Affaires contentieuses,* 370; [Couchot], *Praticien,* 55–56.

168. Report, Duhamel v. Flamand, AP $D^6B^6/18$ (n.a.).

169. Ibid.

170. Hubers, Arbiter's Report in Noël v. Cheret, 22 August 1786, AP $D^6B^6/17$ (72).

171. See chapter 5 for a further discussion of this case and of women's capacity to enter binding contracts.

172. Report, Noël v. Cheret, AP D^{6}B^{6}/17 (72).

173. Ibid.

174. Cologne, Arbiter's Report in Jeauly v. Lemoine, 4 September 1783, AP D^{6}B^{6}/15 (188).

175. Ibid.

176. Ibid.

177. Ibid.

178. Ibid.

179. Ibid.

180. Ibid.

181. Ibid.

Chapter 4. Société *and Sociability: The Changing Structure of Business Associations and the Problem of Merchant Relations*

Epigraph. Jean Domat, *Les loix civiles dans leur ordre naturel: Le droit public, et legum delectus,* new ed. (Paris: Le Clerc, 1777), 19 (originally published in 1689).

1. Emile Coornaert, *Les corporations en France avant 1789,* 2d ed. (Paris: Éditions Ouvrières, 1968), 267; William H. Sewell Jr., *Work and Revolution in France: The Language of Labor from the Old Regime to 1848* (Cambridge: Cambridge University Press, 1980), 19.

2. [Couchot], *Le praticien des juges et consuls; ou, Traité de commerce de terre et de mer* (Paris: Prault père, 1742), 650; Clare Haru Crowston, *Fabricating Women: The Seamstresses of Old Regime France, 1675–1791* (Durham, N.C.: Duke University Press, 2001); David Garrioch, *Neighborhood and Community in Paris, 1740–1790* (Cambridge: Cambridge University Press, 1986), 113; Rogue, *Jurisprudence consulaire et instruction des négociants* (Angers: Chez A. J. Jahyer, 1773), 1:224–26.

3. Henri Lévy-Bruhl, *Histoire de la lettre de change en France aux XVIIe et XVIIIe siècles* (Paris: Recueil Sirey, 1933), 38.

4. Bareau et al., Arbiters' Report in Marechal v. Courion, 19 February 1784, AP D^{6}B^{6}/15 (299).

5. Coornaert, *Corporations en France,* 267; Garrioch, *Neighborhood and Community,* 98.

6. See, for example, André Lespagnol's description of merchant partnerships in Saint-Malo. André Lespagnol, *Messieurs de Saint-Malo, une élite négociante au temps de Louis XIV* (Rennes: Presses Universitaires de Rennes, 1997), 1:122–23.

7. Brevon, Arbiter's Report in Brice LeChauve v. Accau de Nainville, 6 March 1784, AP D^{6}B^{6}/16 (347).

8. Ibid.

9. Ibid.

10. Hubers, Arbiter's Report in Noël v. Cheret, 22 August 1786, AP D^{6}B^{6}/17 (72).

11. Romuald Szramkiewicz, *Histoire du droit des affaires* (Paris: Montchrestien, 1989), 173.

12. Sewell, *Work and Revolution,* 31.

13. Report, Noël v. Cheret, AP D^{6}B^{6}/17 (72).
14. Ibid.
15. Ibid.
16. Ibid.
17. Ibid.
18. Henri Lévy-Bruhl, *Histoire juridique des sociétés de commerce en France aux XVII*[e] *et XVIII*[e] *siècles* (Paris: Domat-Montchrestien, 1938), 135; Paul Butel, *Les négociants bordelais, l'Europe et les iles aux XVIII*[e] *siècle* (Paris: Aubier-Montaigne, 1974), 176.
19. DuFourny and S. Coiffieren fils, Arbiters' Report in Reveillé de Beauregard v. la dame Denis, 26 June 1777, AP D^{6}B^{6}/11 (n.a.).
20. Drossob, Arbiter's Report in Joseph Alexandre v. Jean Baptiste Quainville, 23 April 1783, AP D^{6}B^{6}/15 (22).
21. Ibid.
22. Guild leaders serving as arbiters proudly self-identified as such and, moreover, served in groups of at least three or four. In contrast, arbiters who resolved disputes concerning business associations usually failed to identify their professional status and worked either alone or with at most one other arbiter.
23. Timothin, Arbiter's Report in Le Serteur et Guérin, associés v. Texier, 18 December 1783, AP D^{6}B^{6}/15 (112).
24. Ibid.
25. Ibid.
26. Balons, Arbiter's Report in Baudry v. Albert, 20 December 1777, AP D^{6}B^{6}/12 (n.a.).
27. Lévy-Bruhl, *Sociétés de commerce,* 155. According to Lévy-Bruhl, such clauses became less common as the eighteenth century progressed. Ibid.
28. Cheret, Arbiter's Report in Dujardin v. Lejeune, 3 July 1784, AP D^{6}B^{6}/15 (481).
29. Ibid.
30. Ibid.
31. Ibid.
32. Ibid.
33. Ibid.
34. Ibid.
35. Ibid.
36. Ibid.
37. Jean Toubeau, *Les institutes du droit consulaire ou les elemens de la jurisprudence des marchands* (Bourges, 1700), 2:78.
38. Reinhard Zimmermann, *The Law of Obligations: Roman Foundations of the Civilian Tradition* (Oxford: Clarendon Press, 1996), 451.
39. Ibid., 452–53; Robert Joseph Pothier, *Traité du contrat de société, selon les regles tant du for de la conscience que du for extérieur* (Paris: Debure l'aîné, 1764), 30–31.
40. Zimmermann, *Law of Obligations,* 453.
41. Pothier, *Contrat de société,* 5.
42. Domat was born in 1625—just seven years before Pufendorf, who was born in 1632. Henry Loubers, *J. Domat: Philosophe et magistrat* (Montpellier: J. Martel, ainé, 1873), 51; Richard Tuck, *Natural Rights Theories: Their Origin and Development* (Cambridge: Cambridge University Press, 1979), 156.

43. Jean Domat, *Civil Law in Its Natural Order,* trans. William Strahan, ed. Luther S. Cushing (Boston: C.C. Little and J. Brown, 1850; reprint, Littleton, Colo.: Fred B. Rothman and Co., 1980), 2–3.

44. David A. Bell, *Lawyers and Citizens: The Making of a Political Elite in Old Regime France* (Oxford: Oxford University Press, 1994); Dale K. Van Kley, *The Religious Origins of the French Revolution: From Calvin to the Civil Constitution, 1560–1791* (New Haven: Yale University Press, 1996); Monique Cottret, *Jansénismes et lumières: Pour un autre XVIIIe siècle* (Paris: Albin Michel, 1998).

45. Alexander Sedgwick, *Jansenism in Seventeenth-Century France: Voices from the Wilderness* (Charlottesville, Va.: University Press of Virginia, 1977), 5–8, 47–51.

46. Cottret, *Jansénismes et lumières,* 11.

47. Sedgwick, 28–30; Anthony Levi, *French Moralists: The Theory of the Passions, 1585 to 1649* (Oxford: Clarendon Press, 1964), 225–30; Laurence Dickey, "Pride, Hypocrisy and Civility in Mandeville's Social and Historical Theory," *Critical Review* 4, no. 3 (Summer 1990): 397–98.

48. Sedgwick, *Jansenism,* 28–29.

49. Pierre Nicole, *Essais de morale,* quoted in Sedgwick, *Jansenism,* 144.

50. Sedgwick, *Jansenism,* 169; Loubers, *J. Domat,* 58–73.

51. Domat, *Civil Law,* 5.

52. Ibid., 6.

53. Ibid., 7.

54. Ibid., 33.

55. Ibid., 34.

56. Ibid., 35.

57. Ibid.

58. Ibid.

59. Ibid.

60. Ibid., 36.

61. Ibid.

62. Samuel Pufendorf, *De jure naturae et gentium libri octo, vol. 2. English,* trans. C. H. and W. A. Oldfather (New York: Oceana Publications, Inc., 1964), 1:207.

63. Ibid.

64. Ibid., 1:209.

65. Domat, *Civil Law,* 12.

66. Pufendorf, *De Jure naturae,* 1:162–63.

67. Domat, *Civil Law,* 30.

68. Pufendorf, *De jure naturae,* 1:214.

69. A century later, a lesser known (but at the time highly popular) author relied on precisely this equation of partnership with civil society to argue that the state itself was essentially a partnership writ large: "The state is a *société;* he who claims to enjoy its benefits alone renounces in the same moment the help and the protection that he had a right to expect from it. There is no one who should regret the benefits that he affords others; every person finds more in society than he contributes to it, because he finds there his security and the peaceful enjoyment of that which he possesses." John Nickolls [Plumard de Dangeul], *Remarques sur les avantages et les desavantages de la France et de la Grande Bretagne, par rapport au commerce, et aux autres sources de la puissance des*

États (Leyde, 1754), 222. For a discussion of the success Dangeul's work enjoyed in mid-eighteenth-century France, see John Shovlin, *The Political Economy of Virtue: Luxury, Patriotism, and the Origins of the French Revolution* (Ithaca, N.Y.: Cornell University Press, 2006), 45.

70. Domat, *Loix civiles,* 1:96.

71. Domat, *Civil Law,* 30.

72. Domat, *Loix civiles,* 1:96.

73. Ibid., 1:99 (footnotes omitted).

74. Pufendorf, *De jure naturae,* 1:213 (emphases added).

75. Ibid., 1:214.

76. Toubeau, *Institutes du droit consulaire,* 1:384.

77. Ibid., 1:385.

78. Ibid., 1:391.

79. Ibid., 1:392.

80. Ibid., 1:"Preface."

81. Ibid., 1:72.

82. Ibid., 2:78.

83. Ibid., 2:75.

84. This notion of merchant sociability was fundamentally at odds with Domat's Jansenist natural-law theory, according to which the pursuit of material goods and the glorification of commerce epitomized the evil of *amour-propre.* Yet it was Domat himself who, like Nicole, lay the groundwork for the subversion of his own theory, by recognizing that *amour-propre* and the commerce it promoted were valuable sources of social cohesion.

85. Toubeau, *Institutes du droit consulaire,* 1:274.

86. Ibid., 1:393.

87. Ibid., 1:394.

88. Ibid., 2:88.

89. Henry C. Clark, "Commerce, the Virtues, and the Public Sphere in Early Seventeenth-Century France," *French Historical Studies* 21, no. 3 (Summer 1998): 438–39.

90. See the discussion in chapter 6.

91. Toubeau, *Institutes du droit consulaire,* 1:296.

92. *Encyclopédie méthodique: Commerce,* s.v. "Société" (Paris: Chez Panckoucke, 1783), 3 (pt. 2): 669.

93. "Ordonnance civile touchant la réformation de la justice," tit. 20, art. 2, in *Code Louis* (Milano: Giuffrè, 1996), 1:29–30; Toubeau, *Institutes du droit consulaire,* 2:37.

94. "Ordonnance du commerce," tit. 4, art. 1, in François André Isambert, Athanase-Jean-Léger Jourdan, and Decrusy, *Recueil général des anciennes lois françaises, depuis l'an 420, jusqu'à la révolution de 1789* (Paris: Belin-Leprieur, 1829), 19:96; Philippe Bornier, *Conferences des ordonnances de Louis XIV* (Paris: Chez les associez choisis par ordre de sa Majesté, 1755), 2:465.

95. Toubeau, *Institutes du droit consulaire,* 2:37; Lévy-Bruhl, *Sociétés de commerce,* 77–78.

96. Barry Nicholas, *An Introduction to Roman Law* (Oxford: Clarendon Press, 1962), 161–62, 171, 185–87.

97. Lévy-Bruhl, *Sociétés de commerce,* 77, 141; Zimmermann, *Law of Obligations,* 468–70.

98. Zimmermann, *Law of Obligations,* 470.

99. "Ordonnance du commerce," tit. 4, art. 7, in Isambert, Jourdan, and Decrusy, *Recueil général,* 19:97; Bornier, *Conferences des ordonnances,* 1755 ed., 2:471.

100. If the town where the *société* was located lacked a merchant court, the *associés* were to register the summary with city hall, or if there were no city hall, with whichever ordinary, nonmerchant court had general jurisdiction in that region. "Ordonnance du commerce," tit. 4, art. 2, in Isambert, Jourdan, and Decrusy, *Recueil général,* 19:96; Toubeau, *Institutes du droit consulaire,* 2:92; Bornier, *Conferences des ordonnances,* 1755 ed., 2:467; Lévy-Bruhl, *Sociétés de commerce,* 182.

101. "Ordonnance du commerce," tit. 4, art. 3, in Isambert, Jourdan, and Decrusy, *Recueil général,* 19:96; Toubeau, *Institutes du droit consulaire,* 2:92; Bornier, *Conferences des ordonnances,* 1755 ed., 2:468.

102. "Ordonnance du commerce," tit. 4, art. 4, in Isambert, Jourdan, and Decrusy, *Recueil général,* 19:97; Toubeau, *Institutes du droit consulaire,* 2:92; Bornier, *Conferences des ordonnances,* 1755 ed., 2:469.

103. "Ordonnance du commerce," tit. 4, art. 2, in Isambert, Jourdan, and Decrusy, *Recueil général,* 19:96; Toubeau, *Institutes du droit consulaire,* 2:92; Bornier, *Conferences des ordonnances,* 1755 ed., 2:467.

104. François de Boutaric, *Explication de l'Ordonnance de Louis XIV Roi de France et de Navarre, concernant le commerce* (Toulouse, 1743), 25.

105. Toubeau, *Institutes du droit consulaire,* 2:92.

106. Bornier, *Conferences des ordonnances,* 1755 ed., 2:469. Bornier did, however, suggest that "in all well-regulated companies, writings establishing the company [*écrits de Compagnies*] are made, which list . . . the capital that was put into them . . . and other particularities." Ibid., 2:466.

107. Jean Hilaire, *Introduction historique au droit commercial* (Paris: Presses Universitaires de France, 1986), 205.

108. Lévy-Bruhl, *Sociétés de commerce,* 80–81.

109. Boutaric, *Explication de l'Ordonnance,* 28.

110. Pothier, *Contrat de société,* 81.

111. Daniel Jousse, *Nouveau commentaire sur les ordonnances des mois d'août 1669, et mars 1673: Ensemble sur l'Édit du mois de mars 1673 touchant les épices,* new ed. (Paris: Chez Debure l'aîné, 1761), 48.

112. Philibert-Joseph Masson, *Instruction sur les affaires contentieuses des négociants, la manière de les prévenir, ou de les suivre dans les tribunaux* (Paris: Chez LeClerc, 1786), 349–50.

113. See, for example, Morelle, Arbiter's Report in Jean Francois Bouvri v. Boileau et Regard, 4 March, 1784, AP D^{6}B^{6}/15 (n.a.). In 1768, the Marseille Chamber of Commerce observed that courts regularly disregarded the commercial ordinance's requirement that the existence of a *société* be proved only by means of a written contract. Charles Carrière, *Négociants marseillais au XVIIIe siècle: Contribution à l'étude des économies maritimes* (Marseille: Institut Historique de Provence, 1973), 2:878.

114. Report, Baudry v. Albert, AP D^{6}B^{6}/12 (n.a.).

115. Ibid.

116. Ibid.

117. Lévy-Bruhl, *Sociétés de commerce,* 76.

118. Masson, *Affaires contentieuses,* 343.

119. [Couchot], *Praticien,* 61.

120. "Édit portant que tous différens entre marchands," art. 1, in Isambert, Jourdan, and Decrusy, *Recueil général,* 14:51–52; Lévy-Bruhl, *Sociétés de commerce,* 274.

121. "Édit qui crée la juridiction consulaire des juges et consuls de Paris et règle leur competence," arts. 14–16 (Paris, November 1563), in Isambert, Jourdan, and Decrusy, *Recueil général,* 14:153–58.

122. "Ordonnance du commerce," tit. 4, art. 9, in Isambert, Jourdan, and Decrusy, *Recueil général,* 19:97; Bornier, *Conferences des ordonnances,* 1755 ed., 2:472–73.

123. Ibid.

124. Each party was to select an arbiter, and in the event that one of the arbiters died or disappeared, the parties were to identify someone to replace him. If the two arbiters failed to agree, the arbiters would choose a third person to break the tie. Moreover, should the parties fail to replace an arbiter who had died or disappeared, or should the arbiters fail to select a third to break their deadlock, the merchant court was required to do so instead. "Ordonnance du commerce," tit. 4, arts. 10–11, in Isambert, Jourdan, and Decrusy, *Recueil général,* 19:97; Bornier, *Conferences des ordonnances,* 1755 ed., 2:473.

125. "Ordonnance du commerce," tit. 4, art. 12, in Isambert, Jourdan, and Decrusy, *Recueil général,* 19:97; Bornier, *Conferences des ordonnances,* 1755 ed., 2:473.

126. "Ordonnance du commerce," tit. 4, art. 13, in Isambert, Jourdan, and Decrusy, *Recueil général,* 19:97; Bornier, *Conferences des ordonnances,* 1755 ed., 2:474.

127. [Bedos], *Le négociant patriote, contenant un tableau qui réunit les avantages du commerce, la connoissance des spéculations de chaque nation* (Amsterdam, 1779), 302.

128. Toubeau, *Institutes du droit consulaire,* 2:88.

129. See table 1 in the appendix. See also tables 3 and 4, which identify the percentage of (known) plaintiffs and defendants that were business associations.

130. De Jouy and Pinon du Coudray, *Mémoire pour le sieur Delaleu, intimé, contre les sieurs Montz, Dupin, Dangé et Conforts, intéressés dans la société en commendite pour l'exploitation de la manufacture de Galons et Rubans* (Paris: P. A. Leprieur, 1759), 4, AP D[1]B[6]/35 (5533).

131. For discussion of the *hôpital-général* of Paris, see Thomas McStay Adams, *Bureaucrats and Beggars: French Social Policy in the Age of the Enlightenment* (Oxford: Oxford University Press, 1990), 29.

132. Anne Charles Modeux de Sieur Vast and Guillaume Perier, Arbiters' Report in la dame Girard, les sieur et dame de bergeray, et Turmeau de la Morandiere v. Nicolas Francois Thoré de société avec le feu sieur Girard, 6 June 1783, AP D[6]B[6]/15 (55).

133. Folio, Arbiter's Report in Nicolas Guigeon v. Jean-Nicolas et Jacques Guigeon, 20 July 1785, AP D[6]B[6]/17 (9).

134. Lévy-Bruhl, *Sociétés de commerce,* 275.

135. [N.a.], Arbiter's Report in Catherine Giboury fille mineure emancipé v. Robert Simon dit Jannet, 30 December 1784, AP D[6]B[6]/15 (192).

136. Ibid.

137. B. Vignon, Arbiter's Report in Lemercier v. Ameslant, 12 February 1785, AP D^6B^6/15 (186 & 187).

138. Ibid.

139. Under modern French law, general partnerships are known as *sociétés en nom collectif* and limited partnerships as *sociétés en commandite simple* (to distinguish them from *sociétés en commandite par actions*). Alain Couret and Jean-Jacques Barbiéri, *Droit Commercial,* 13th ed. (Paris: Sirey, 1996), 135–44.

140. As discussed above, the classical rule of the *ius commune* was that there was no joint liability absent express agreement to this effect, but this rule was modified—indeed reversed—by merchant practice. Lévy-Bruhl, *Sociétés de commerce,* 77, 141; Zimmermann, *Law of Obligations,* 468–70.

141. Zimmermann, *Law of Obligations,* 459.

142. Boutaric, *Explication de l'Ordonnance,* 33.

143. Toubeau, *Institutes du droit consulaire,* 2:106.

144. Ibid.

145. Report, Girard, de bergeray, et Turmeau de la Morandiere v. Thoré de société avec le feu sieur Girard.

146. Ibid.

147. Ibid.

148. According to Couret and Barbiéri, for example, "the *société* [*en commandite simple*] differs from the *société en nom collectif* primarily in that [the former] contains two very different categories of *associés.* . . . The active partners are, like the *associés* in a *société en nom collectif,* held fully and jointly liable for the debts of the *société.* . . . The limited partners, in contrast, are held neither jointly nor fully for the obligations contracted by the *société.*" Couret and Barbiéri, *Droit Commercial,* 141.

149. Harold J. Berman, *Law and Revolution: The Formation of the Western Legal Tradition* (Cambridge: Harvard University Press, 1983), 349 and n. 32; Zimmermann, *Law of Obligations,* 186 and n. 200.

150. Hilaire, *Introduction historique,* 170–71.

151. As Hilaire notes, equating *commenda* with *societas* had the distinct advantage of placing the former "under the protective shadow" of a Roman device that contemporary jurists did not suspect of usury. Ibid., 173.

152. Ibid., 192–96.

153. Szramkiewicz, *Droit des affaires,* 79; Sewell, *Work and Revolution,* 21.

154. *Encyclopédie méthodique: Commerce,* s.v. "Société," 3 (pt. 2):670.

155. Toubeau, *Institutes du droit consulaire,* 2:73.

156. Ibid.

157. Ibid., 2:105–06.

158. Jousse, *Nouveau commentaire,* 41–42.

159. Toubeau, *Institutes du droit consulaire,* 2:105.

160. Boutaric, *Explication de l'Ordonnance,* 25–26. Interestingly, the *Code de Commerce* of 1807—in a provision strongly indicative of its emergence at a moment of transition—required the publication of the capital contributions made by limited partners, but not the partners' names. Lévy-Bruhl, *Sociétés de commerce,* 80–81.

161. Bornier, *Conferences des ordonnances,* 1755 ed., 2:467.

162. Some have recently questioned the importance of limited liability. See, for exam-

ple, Henry Hansmann, Reinier Kraakman, and Richard Squire, "Law and the Rise of the Firm," *Harvard Law Review* 119 (2006): 1335 (arguing that "entity shielding," or the protection of the firm's assets from the owners' personal creditors is "economically and historically more significant than limited liability," which protects the owners' personal assets from the firm's creditors); Amalia D. Kessler, "Limited Liability in Context: Lessons from the French Origins of the American Limited Partnership," *Journal of Legal Studies* 32 (2003): 511–48.

163. "Ordonnance du commerce," tit. 4, art. 7, in Isambert, Jourdan, and Decrusy, *Recueil général,* 19:97; Bornier, *Conferences des ordonnances,* 1755 ed., 2:470–71.

164. Picquel and Rimbert, Arbiters' Report in Dupont de la Hallière v. Despres, père et fils, 13 September 1784, AP D[6]B[6]/15 (12).

165. Ibid.

166. Hilaire, *Introduction historique,* 215.

167. Szramkiewicz, *Droit des affaires,* 160–63.

168. See the discussion of negotiable instruments in chapter 5.

169. Szramkiewicz, *Droit des affaires,* 163.

170. Ibid., 160–63.

171. Couret and Barbiéri, *Droit Commercial,* 177–79.

172. François Crouzet, *La grande inflation: La monnaie en France de Louis XVI à Napoleon* (Paris: Fayard, 1993), 36; Szramkiewicz, *Droit des affaires,* 163.

173. Szramkiewicz, *Droit des affaires,* 95.

174. Ibid., 160–61.

175. Ibid.

176. Louis Petit Bachaumont, *Mémoires secrets pour servir à l'histoire de la république des lettres en France depuis 1762 jusqu'à nos jours, ou journal d'un observateur* (London), 33:228 (1 December 1786), 236 (4 December 1786), 240–41 (6 December 1786), 262–64 (13 December 1786), 281 (18 December 1786), 303 (27 December 1786); 34(1789):58–61 (20 January 1787), 99–100 (31 January 1787), 140–41 (12 February 1787), 350–51 (3 April 1787), 360–61 (6 April 1787); Thomas Manley Luckett, "Credit and Commercial Society in France, 1740–1789" (Ph.D. diss., Princeton University, 1992), 210–12.

177. One arbiter's report refers to a *société anonyme,* but it employs the term in its early-modern sense and not, as in Napoleon's *Code de Commerce* of 1807, to designate a modern corporation. Grillon Deschapelles, Arbiter's Report in the la dame veuve Robert v. Joassard, 13 May 1771, AP D[6]B[6]/10 (n.a.). In the Old Regime, a *société anonyme* was what is now termed a *société en participation,* namely a brief association formed among merchants for some limited purpose, such as jointly undertaking a large and risky purchase. Because such associations were limited in duration and scope, no formal, written procedures were required under the Commercial Ordinance of 1673 to establish them, and there was little possibility for a third party to determine which merchants were involved. The anonymity afforded merchants participating in such associations caused Savary to dub them *sociétés anonymes.* Szramkiewicz, *Droit des affaires,* 158; Carrière, *Négociants marseillais,* 2:967–68; Lespagnol, *Messieurs de Saint-Malo,* 1:129.

178. Szramkiewicz, *Droit des affaires,* 161–62.

179. Delamotte and Demoret, Arbiters' Report in De lonchamps v. Porro, Duval et Mignon, n.d. (approximately 1770s), AP D[6]B[6]/9 (n.a.).

180. Ibid.

181. Lévy-Bruhl, *Sociétés de commerce,* 108, 185. Interestingly, Pothier argued that the granting of an ownership interest to "powerful people" in exchange for their *crédit* was an illegal practice—counter to both "public honesty" and "good mores"—which nullified the contract establishing the *société.* Pothier, *Contrat de société,* 7–8.

182. *Mémoire pour le sieur Delaleu,* AP D¹B⁶/35 (5533).

183. The parties appear to have disputed whether the retrocession was ever properly completed. There seems to have been full agreement, however, that the only way for de Beauvillé to sell his shares was through such a formal retrocession.

184. Lévy-Bruhl, *Sociétés de commerce,* 48.

185. De Laurent and Arnoud, Arbiters' Report in Millin de Grandmaison v. Duchesne et de Mezieres, 24 January 1762, D⁶B⁶/7 (n.a.).

186. Ibid.

187. Ibid.

188. *Mémoire pour le sieur Delaleu,* AP D¹B⁶/35 (5533).

189. Ibid., 2.

190. Unfortunately, as the legal brief does not specify how many *associés* there were, it is impossible to determine whether eight *associés* constituted a simple majority or some other proportion of the shareholders.

191. *Mémoire pour le sieur Delaleu,* 8, AP D¹B⁶/35 (5533).

192. Report, De lonchamps v. Porro, Duval et Mignon, AP D⁶B⁶/9 (n.a.).

193. Ibid.

194. It is not clear why Harvouin's involvement was deemed necessary. Perhaps he was charged with some element of the company's daily operations such that he was considered to have crucial knowledge. Alternatively, he may have insisted on this power as a condition of his agreement to purchase shares.

195. Report, De lonchamps v. Porro, Duval et Mignon, AP D⁶B⁶/9 (n.a.).

196. Ibid.

197. Ibid.

198. Ibid.

199. Ibid.

200. Ibid.

201. Ibid.

202. Ibid.

203. Ibid.

204. Ibid.

205. Ibid.

206. Ibid.

207. Ibid.

208. Ibid.

209. David D. Bien, "Old Regime Origins of Democratic Liberty," in Dale Van Kley, ed., *The French Idea of Freedom: The Old Regime and the Declaration of Rights of 1789* (Stanford: Stanford University Press, 1994),

210. Anne-Robert-Jacques Turgot, "Memorandum on Local Government," in *University of Chicago Readings in Western Civilization,* vol. 7, *The Old Regime and the French Revolution,* ed. Keith Michael Baker (Chicago: University of Chicago Press, 1987), 97–117 (made public in 1787, but written in 1775).

Chapter 5. A Crisis in Virtue: The Challenges of Negotiability and the Rise of a New Commercial Culture

Epigraph. Jacques Accarias de Sérionne, *Les intérêts des nations de l'Europe, dévelopés relativement au commerce* (Paris: Chez Desain, 1767), 3:47.

1. [Bedos], *Le négociant patriote, contenant un tableau qui réunit les avantages du commerce, la connoissance des spéculations de chaque nation* (Amsterdam, 1779).

2. Ibid., 60.

3. Ibid., 39.

4. Ibid., 80.

5. Ibid., 263.

6. Ibid., 264.

7. Ibid., 263–64.

8. Ibid., 264.

9. There were other less important kinds of negotiable instruments as well, such as exchange notes, which were used to pay for bills of exchange when the latter fell due. "Ordonnance du commerce," tit. 5, art. 27, in François André Isambert, Athanase-Jean-Léger Jourdan, and Decrusy, *Recueil général des anciennes lois françaises, depuis l'an 420, jusqu'à la révolution de 1789* (Paris: Belin-Leprieur, 1829), 19:100; François de Boutaric, *Explication de l'Ordonnance de Louis XIV Roi de France et de Navarre, concernant le commerce* (Toulouse, 1743), 64; Robert Joseph Pothier, *Traité du contrat de change, de la négociation qui se fait par la lettre de change; des billets de change, et autres billets de commerce* (Paris: Debure père, 1773), 2–3; Thomas Manley Luckett, "Credit and Commercial Society in France, 1740–1789" (Ph.D. diss., Princeton University, 1992), 12–13.

10. [Couchot], *Le praticien des juges et consuls; ou, Traité de commerce de terre et de mer* (Paris: Prault père, 1742), 626.

11. Henri Lévy-Bruhl, *Histoire de la lettre de change en France aux XVII*[e] *et XVIII*[e] *siècles* (Paris: Recueil Sirey, 1933), 103; Raymond de Roover, *L'évolution de la lettre de change: XIV*[e]*–XVIII*[e] *siècles* (Paris: A. Colin, 1953), 113.

12. Marie-Thérèse Boyer-Xambeu, Ghislain Deleplace, and Lucien Gillard, *Monnaie privée et pouvoir des princes: L'économie des relations monétaires à la Renaissance* (Paris: Éditions du CNRS, 1986), 31–32.

13. Lévy-Bruhl, *Lettre de change,* 72; Roover, *L'évolution,* 43–44; James Steven Rogers, *The Early History of the Law of Bills and Notes: A Study of the Origins of Anglo-American Commercial Law* (Cambridge: Cambridge University Press, 1995), 34.

14. Lévy-Bruhl, *Lettre de change,* 72; Roover, *L'évolution,* 46.

15. Roover, *L'évolution,* 51–53. See also Rogers, *Early History,* 41.

16. Roover, *L'évolution,* 53.

17. Ibid., 54.

18. John T. Noonan Jr., *The Scholastic Analysis of Usury* (Cambridge: Harvard University Press, 1957), 81.

19. Privity of contract is a rule permitting only those individuals who are party to a contract to sue for the enforcement of contractual rights. See the discussion of "relative effect," the French counterpart of the Anglo-American doctrine of privity, in Barry Nicholas, *The French Law of Contract,* 2d ed. (Oxford: Clarendon Press, 1992), 169.

20. The beneficiary was deemed to be in privity only with the drawee. Roover, *L'évolu-*

tion, 92. Unlike the beneficiary, the giver of value was in contractual privity with the drawer and could, therefore, sue him. Since the giver of value and the beneficiary were often associates, the beneficiary might be able to seek recourse from the drawer through the indirect means of a lawsuit brought by the giver of value. From the beneficiary's perspective, however, this approach was clearly far from ideal.

21. The structure and function of promissory notes and bills of exchange did not simply stagnate during the many centuries separating their emergence and the rise of negotiability. For example, the practice of endorsement developed at least as far back as the late Renaissance and permitted the beneficiary of the instrument, by signing it, to assign an agent the task of collecting payment from the drawee. In this way, the beneficiary could obtain payment without having to travel to the city where the drawee lived. This sort of endorsement created only an agency relationship, however, and thus must be distinguished from the kind of endorsement associated with the rise of negotiability—namely, an endorsement that actually transferred a property interest in the instrument. Throughout the eighteenth century, both types of endorsement were frequently used, a fact that led to much linguistic and legal confusion. Henri Lévy-Bruhl, *L'endossement des lettres de change en France aux XVIIe et XVIIIe siècles* (Paris: A. Rousseau, 1930), 3.

22. Roover, *L'évolution,* 117.

23. Rogers, *Early History,* 94.

24. Roover, *L'évolution,* 118.

25. Ibid., 133.

26. Charles Carrière, "Escomptait-on les lettres de change au XVIIIe siècle?," in *Banque et capitalisme commercial: La lettre de change au XVIIIe siècle,* ed. Charles Carrière et al., (Marseille: Institut Historique de Provence, 1976), 30–44. See also Françoise Bayard and Philippe Guignet, *L'économie française aux XVIe–XVIIIe siècles* (Paris: Éditions Ophrys, 1991), 54 (suggesting that discounting emerged by the beginning of the eighteenth century).

27. Paul Harsin, "Le problème de l'escompte des lettres de change en France aux XVIIe et XVIIIe siècles," *Revue internationale d'histoire de la banque* 7 (1973): 197. See also Yves Leclercq, *Histoire économique de la France: L'ancien régime, XVIIe–XVIIIe siècles* (Paris: Dalloz, 1993), 134 (suggesting that discounting emerged in the seventeenth century); Luckett, "Credit," 31 (suggesting that discounting emerged in the early seventeenth century, along with negotiability).

28. See table 1 in the appendix.

29. Thomas de Bon, Arbiter's Report in Desnos v. Fouques du Godillon, 6 September 1784, AP D6B6/16 (98).

30. Pierre Chénon, Arbiter's Report in Richard v. Desnon, 14 April 1783, AP D6B6/14 (129).

31. Ibid.

32. "Lettre sur les contraintes par corps," *Journal de Commerce* (Brussels), December 1760, 37–38.

33. "Ordonnance du commerce," tit. 12, art. 2, in Isambert, Jourdan, and Decrusy, *Recueil general,* 19:105; Philippe Bornier, *Ordonnance de Louis XIV, sur le commerce, enrichie d'annotations et de décisions importantes* (Paris: Libraires-Associés, 1767), 570.

34. "Ordonnance du commerce," tit. 12, art. 3, in Isambert, Jourdan, and Decrusy, *Recueil général,* 19:105; Bornier, *Ordonnance de Louis XIV,* 595–97.

35. "Ordonnance du commerce," tit. 12, art. 2, in Isambert, Jourdan, and Decrusy, *Recueil général,* 19:105; Bornier, *Ordonnance de Louis XIV,* 570–73; [Couchot], *Praticien,* 263.

36. Jacqueline-Lucienne Lafon, *Les députés du commerce et l'ordonnance de mars 1673: Les juridictions consulaires, principe et compétence* (Paris: Éditions Cujas, 1979), 104–8.

37. Ibid., 106–8.

38. Philibert-Joseph Masson, *Instruction sur les affaires contentieuses des négociants, la manière de les prévenir, ou de les suivre dans les tribunaux* (Paris: Chez LeClerc, 1786), 322. The *Bureau du Commerce* and its merchant deputies are discussed in chapter 6.

39. Louis-Sébastien Mercier, *Tableau de Paris,* new ed. (Amsterdam, 1782; repr., Geneva: Slatkine Reprints, 1979), 12:163.

40. For a discussion of the Mississippi Scheme and its economic consequences, see Réné Sédillot, *Histoire du franc* (Paris: Sirey, 1979), 38–46; Paul Butel, *L'économie française au XVIIIe siècle* (Paris: SEDES, 1993), 260–66; François Crouzet, *La grande inflation: La monnaie en France de Louis XVI à Napoleon* (Paris: Fayard, 1993), 36–37. For an account of the scheme's political consequences and, in particular, the role it played in giving rise to "public opinion" as a limit on the exercise of royal power, see Thomas E. Kaiser, "Money, Despotism, and Public Opinion in Early Eighteenth-Century France: John Law and the Debate on Royal Credit," *Journal of Modern History* 63, no. 1 (March 1991): 1–28.

41. At first, this unofficial exchange was based in the rue Quincampoix. But as the number of speculators grew, it was transferred to the place Vendôme, and then to the gardens of the Hôtel de Soissons. Katie Scott, *The Rococo Interior: Decoration and Social Spaces in Early Eighteenth-Century Paris* (New Haven: Yale University Press, 1995), 227.

42. This group of brokers dated back to a royal statute of 1595. A number of changes were thereafter made in the title given to these brokers and in the nature of their duties and privileges, including by the 1724 statute, which ordered the creation of sixty brokers. François Olivier-Martin, *L'organisation corporative de la France d'ancien régime* (Paris: Sirey, 1938), 277–79, 281–82; Romuald Szramkiewicz, *Histoire du droit des affaires* (Paris: Montchrestien, 1989), 99; Bayard and Guignet, *L'économie française,* 154; Jean Bouchary, *Marché des changes de Paris à la fin du XVIIIe siècle (1778–1800), avec des graphiques et le relevé des cours* (Paris: Paul Hartmann, 1937), 15.

43. Boyer-Xambeu, Deleplace, and Gillard, *Monnaie privée,* 22–32; Crouzet, *Grande inflation,* 42–45.

44. François Bertrand de Barrême, *Le grand banquier; ou, Le livre des monnoyes etrangeres reduites en monnoyes de France* (Paris: Chez Denys Thierry, 1696); Bouthillier, *Le banquier françois; ou, La pratique des lettres de change suivant l'usage des principales places de France,* 2d ed. (Paris: Chez J. Musier, 1727); Jean-Baptiste-Thomas Bléville, *Le banquier et négociant universel; ou, Traité général des changes étrangers et des arbitrages, ou viremens de place en place,* 2 vols. (Paris: Chez Pierre Prault, Charles Hochereau, et Nicolas-Bonaventure Duchesne, 1760–1761).

45. Crouzet, *Grande inflation,* 44. The total number of bankers in eighteenth-century France ranged between 500 and 1,000. Bayard and Guignet, *L'économie française,* 57;

Didier Terrier, *Histoire économique de la France d'Ancien Régime* (Paris: Hachette, 1998), 45–46.

46. Leclercq, *Histoire économique,* 147.

47. Ibid., 147–48; Crouzet, *Grande inflation,* 38. As a point of comparison, the legal interest rate cap on annuities throughout most of the period from 1665 to 1789 was 5 percent. Leclercq, *Histoire économique,* 142; Philip T. Hoffman, Gilles Postel-Vinay, and Jean-Laurent Rosenthal, *Priceless Markets: The Political Economy of Credit in Paris, 1660–1870* (Chicago: University of Chicago Press, 2000), 19; Luckett, "Credit," 32. Discount rates for private commercial paper in eighteenth-century Paris also appear to have fluctuated around 5 percent. However, as Thomas Luckett observes, from 1740 to 1770 alone there were on the order of nine to ten peaks in the Paris discount rate, some of which exceeded 10 percent, and in the fall of 1783 it peaked at over 14 percent. Luckett, "Credit," 151, 196.

48. Crouzet, *Grande inflation,* 37–42; Szramkiewicz, *Droit des affaires,* 177.

49. Crouzet, *Grande inflation,* 42.

50. Ibid., 42–44.

51. Luckett, "Credit," 47–49.

52. "Dissertation sur la premiere propriété de toutes lettres de change," *Journal de Commerce,* February 1761, 125.

53. See the lawsuits involving tax farmers discussed in chapter 4. Anne Charles Modeux de Sieur Vast and Guillaume Perier, Arbiters' Report in la dame Girard, les sieur et dame de bergeray, et Turmeau de la Morandiere v. Nicolas Francois Thoré de société avec le feu sieur Girard, 6 June 1783, AP D^{6}B^{6}/15 (55); B. Vignon, Arbiter's Report in Lemercier v. Ameslant, 12 February 1785, AP D^{6}B^{6}/15 (186 & 187).

54. Ted W. Margadant, *Urban Rivalries in the French Revolution* (Princeton: Princeton University Press, 1992), 33; Sonenscher, *Work and Wages,* 134. See also the discussion of the relationship between merchant-bankers and financiers in Leclercq, *Histoire économique,* 145.

55. Leclercq, *Histoire économique,* 132; Bayard and Guignet, *L'économie française,* 163; Terrier, *Histoire économique,* 45.

56. Terrier, *Histoire économique,* 45.

57. Sédillot, *Histoire du franc,* 30–48.

58. Crouzet, *Grande inflation,* 35.

59. Charles Carrière, *Négociants marseillais au XVIII*e *siècle: Contribution à l'étude des économies maritimes* (Marseille: Institut Historique de Provence, 1973), 2:819.

60. Ibid., 2:818–28. Foreign sellers of a few types of goods also required cash payments. Ibid.; André Lespagnol, *Messieurs de Saint-Malo, une élite négociante au temps de Louis XIV* (Rennes: Presses Universitaires de Rennes, 1997), 1:144–45. As one contemporary commentator observed, however, "almost all foreign trade is done by means of bills of exchange." Isaac Cournaud, *Notions élementaires sur la nature du commerce en général, son origine, ses progrès et son influence sur la société* (N.p., 1787), 68.

61. See, for example, Pillons, Arbiter's Report in Ganal v. Faypoux, 8 July 1786, AP D^{6}B^{6}/17 (n.a.); Magime, Arbiter's Report in Mouquin v. Barrié, 25 April 1769, AP D^{6}B^{6}/8 (n.a.); Grouvelle, Arbiter's Report in Barallier v. Zouchaz, 4 October 1786, AP D^{6}B^{6}/18 (338).

62. See, for example, Thomas de Bon, Arbiter's Report in Heurtant v. Houblin et sa femme, n.d. (around December 1785), AP D^{6}B^{6}/16 (n.a.).

63. See, for example, Report, Barallier v. Zouchaz, AP D^{6}B^{6}/18 (338); Corteblu, Arbiter's Report in Vitrouille Dechamps v. les sieur et dame Rochet, 8 October 1784, AP D^{6}B^{6}/15 (20); Saulnier, Arbiter's Report in Moulin Le bourdonné v. Tessier fils ainé, n.d. (around March 1784), AP D^{6}B^{6}/15 (346).

64. See, for example, Report in Desnos v. du Godillon, AP D^{6}B^{6}/16 (98).

65. Luckett, "Credit," 151, 196. According to contemporary jurists, the private discount rate was often higher than the (5 percent) legal rate of interest. Cournaud, *Notions élementaires,* 73–74; Philibert-Joseph Masson, *Instruction des négociants: Tirée des ordonnances, édits, déclarations, arrêts, et des usages reçus* (Blois, 1748), 156. See also Bundelin, Arbiter's Report in Daubagnac v. Sellouf et compagnie, 10 August 1784, AP D^{6}B^{6}/16 (28) (discussing the discounting of a bill of exchange at the rate of 16 percent).

66. Crouzet, *Grande inflation,* 50; Luckett, "Credit," 197–98.

67. Crouzet, *Grande inflation,* 50-51; Luckett, "Credit," 198–201.

68. Crouzet, *Grande inflation,* 50–51; Doucet de Turiny, Arbiter's Report in Parmentier v. les sieurs Roullet frères et Ranson, 25 July 1787, AP D^{6}B^{6}/18 (60).

69. Louis Petit Bachaumont, *Mémoires secrets pour servir à l'histoire de la république des lettres en France depuis 1762 jusqu'à nos jours, ou journal d'un observateur* (London), 33:262 (13 December 1786).

70. Félix Gaiffe, *Le drame en France au XVIIIe siècle* (Paris: A. Colin, 1910), 268–69. See also R. Niklaus, "The Merchant on the French Stage in the Eighteenth Century, or the Rise and Fall of an Eighteenth-Century Myth," in *Studies in the French Eighteenth Century: Presented to John Lough by Colleagues, Pupils, and Friends,* ed. D. J. Mossop, G. E. Rodmell, and D. B. Wilson (Durham, Eng.: University of Durham, 1978), 141–56.

71. Gaiffe, *Drame,* 370.

72. Introduction to Michel Sedaine, *Le philosophe sans le savoir,* ed. Robert Garapon (Paris: Société des textes français modernes, 1990), xi (originally published in 1765); H. T. Mason, "*Le philosophe sans le savoir:* An Aristocratic *Drame Bourgeois?*" *French Studies* 30 (1976): 416 (noting that, according to Diderot, two thousand people attended the premiere alone).

73. Sedaine, *Philosophe sans le savoir,* 36.

74. Pierre Augustin Caron de Beaumarchais, "Les deux amis, ou le négociant de Lyon," in *Œuvres complètes de Beaumarchais,* new ed. (Paris: Laplace, Sanchez et compagnie, 1876); Dampierre de la Salle, *Le bienfait rendu, ou le négociant,* new ed. (Paris: Chez Duchesne, 1764).

75. Sedaine, *Philosophe sans le savoir,* 101.

76. Ibid., 103.

77. Ibid., 117 (ellipsis in original).

78. See, for example, Heury Lepitre, Arbiter's Report in Paupe v. Bertin, 18 July 1785, AP D^{6}B^{6}/17 (4); Salong, Arbiter's Report in Aie v. Delamotte, 7 September 1785, AP D^{6}B^{6}/17 (95?).

79. Carrière, *Négociants marseillais,* 2:874; Leclercq, *Histoire économique,* 135–36; Luckett, "Credit," 52.

80. Report, Mouquin v. Barrié, AP D^{6}B^{6}/8 (n.a.).

81. Ibid.

82. As Rogers observes, concerning eighteenth-century England, "Merchants and others would regularly have to take bills and notes as a form of payment, since there frequently was no other available payment medium." Rogers, *Early History,* 195.

83. Compare, for example, Berman, who argues that, by the eleventh and twelfth centuries, the usury prohibition had largely ceased to affect commercial activity, with McManners and Tavenaux, who suggest that, to the contrary, it continued to affect commercial activity as late as the seventeenth and eighteenth centuries. Harold J. Berman, *Law and Revolution: The Formation of the Western Legal Tradition* (Cambridge: Harvard University Press, 1983), 337–39; John McManners, *Church and Society in Eighteenth-Century France,* ed. Henry and Owen Chadwick (Oxford: Clarendon Press, 1998), 2:263–68; René Tavenaux, *Le catholicisme dans la France classique, 1610–1715* (Paris: Sedes, 1994), 2:441–46.

84. McManners, *Church and Society,* 2:267–68; Noonan, *Scholastic Analysis of Usury,* 81, 279–80.

85. Noonan, *Scholastic Analysis of Usury,* 225–28.

86. McManners, *Church and Society,* 2:265.

87. For a discussion of how Church thinkers continued to deem usury sinful well into the eighteenth century, see ibid., 2:263–68; Tavenaux, *Catholicisme,* 2:441–45; Jean Quéniart, *Les hommes, l'église et Dieu dans la France du XVIIIe siècle* (Paris: Hachette, 1978), 167–72, 237–40.

88. "Dissertation sur la légtimité des intérêts d'argent qui ont cours dans le commerce," *Journal de Commerce,* October 1759, 88–162 (reprinting a work originally published in 1756 by J. B. Gastumeau, Sindic de la Chambre de Commerce et Secretaire Perpétuel de l'Académie de la Rochelle).

89. Ibid., 90.

90. Richard Desglaniere, *Projet concernant le rétablissement du mont de piété établi sous le regne de Louis 13, par édit du mois de fevrier 1626* (n.d., around 1765), AP $D^{1}B^{6}$/37 (5650).

91. Ibid.

92. Cheryl L. Danieri, *Credit Where Credit Is Due: The Mont-de-Piété of Paris, 1777–1851* (New York: Garland, 1991), 42–43.

93. Emma Rothschild, *Economic Sentiments: Adam Smith, Condorcet, and the Enlightenment* (Cambridge: Harvard University Press, 2001), 42.

94. Turgot, "Mémoire sur les prêts d'argent," in *Œuvres de Turgot, nouvelle édition, classée par ordre de matières, avec les notes de Dupont de Nemours* (Paris: Guillaumin, 1844), 1:114.

95. Ibid., 1:115.

96. Each of the three arbiters appointed to resolve the dispute wrote a separate report. Fossard du Mesnil, Arbiter's Report in De Brie, Marcemay, et Marechal v. MM. les intéressés dans la ferme des devoirs de Bretagne de 1773 et 1774, 21 May 1778, AP $D^{6}B^{6}$/13 (n.a.); Rougeos, Arbiter's Report in De Brie, Marcemay, et Marechal v. MM. les intéressés dans la ferme des devoirs de Bretagne, 19 June 1778, AP $D^{6}B^{6}$/13 (n.a.); d'Igneaucourt, Arbiter's Report in De Brie, Marcemay, et Marechal v. MM. les intéressés dans la ferme des devoirs de Bretagne, 20 June 1778, AP $D^{6}B^{6}$/13 (n.a.).

97. Fossard du Mesnil, Report, De Brie, Marcemay, et Marechal v. MM. les intéressés dans la ferme des devoirs de Bretagne, AP $D^{6}B^{6}$/13 (n.a.).

98. D'Igneaucourt, Report, De Brie, Marcemay, et Marechal v. MM. les intéressés dans la ferme des devoirs de Bretagne, AP D^6B^6/13 (n.a.).

99. Turgot, "Mémoire sur les prêts," 1:115.

100. Emma Rothschild, "An Alarming Commercial Crisis in Eighteenth-Century Angoulême: Sentiments in Economic History," *Economic History Review* 51 (May 1998): 268–93.

101. Turgot, "Mémoire sur les prêts," 1:109.

102. Ibid., 1:111.

103. Jean Toubeau, *Les institutes du droit consulaire ou les elemens de la jurisprudence des marchands* (Bourges, 1700), 2:186–87.

104. [Couchot], *Praticien,* 104–5. See also ibid., 155.

105. *Encyclopédie méthodique: Commerce,* s.v. "Commerce d'argent" and "Commerce en papier" (Paris: Chez Panckoucke, 1783), 1:542.

106. Ibid.

107. Ibid.

108. Ibid.

109. Ibid.

110. Report, Richard v. Desnon, AP D^6B^6/14 (129).

111. He endorsed the notes in blank—a practice discussed later in the chapter.

112. Presumably, Jouan was paid a fee for the assistance he provided.

113. Trajectory of the notes: Richard → Delavallée → Jouan/Noel → Desnon.

114. Trajectory of the cash: Desnon (800 livres cash, less discount) → Jouan (144 livres and notes) → Delavallée → Richard.

115. Report, Richard v. Desnon, AP D^6B^6/14 (129).

116. Ibid.

117. Ibid.

118. Ibid.

119. Ibid.

120. Ibid.

121. Pierre Chénon, Arbiter's Report in Boullan v. Michel, 31 October 1785, AP D^6B^6/18 (299).

122. Boullan claimed that it was Michel's decision to negotiate the bill in this indirect manner, but Michel, in contrast, insisted that "Boullan hounded him to negotiate his bill of exchange for merchandise." Ibid. Unfortunately, the arbiter never determined which party was telling the truth nor why either one might have found it advisable to negotiate the bill in this way.

123. Ibid.

124. Ibid.

125. Ibid.

126. Ibid. The arbiter seems to have made an error in calculating the amount of the *lésion.* Boullan sold the bill for 3/7 of its face value and thus lost 4/7 of this value.

127. See the discussion of "Ordonnance du commerce," tit. 5, art. 23, in Boutaric, *Explication de l'Ordonnance,* 62–63.

128. See, for example, the discussion in Masson, *Affaires contentieuses,* 192–95.

129. Ibid., 194–95 (discussing "Ordonnance du commerce," tit. 5, art. 25).

130. Doucet de Turiny, Arbiter's Report in Texada v. Detchegaray, 10 December 1785, AP D^6B^6/16 (181).

131. Report, Mouquin v. Barrié, AP D^6B^6/8 (n.a.).

132. Ibid.

133. Falluves, Arbiter's Report in Amiot v. Rimbault, 19 October 1777, AP D^6B^6/11 (n.a.).

134. Ibid.

135. Ibid.

136. Desauges, Arbiter's Report in Clair v. la demoiselle DesBois Dumont, 18 February 1783, AP D^6B^6/15 (275).

137. Ibid.

138. Ibid.

139. Ibid.

140. Ibid.

141. The Commercial Ordinance of 1673 forbade all transfers of property by the insolvent that "defrauded creditors." "Ordonnance du commerce," tit. 11, art. 4, in Isambert, Jourdan, and Decrusy, *Recueil général,* 19:104; Bornier, *Ordonnance de Louis XIV,* 466. This provision was modified by a Declaration of November 1702, which outlawed all transfers beginning at a point ten days prior to the public declaration of insolvency. Bornier, *Ordonnance de Louis XIV,* 469–72.

142. "Sentence rendue au profit de Jean Jacques Seigneuret, faisant pour les heritiers des sieur et damoiselle Stollay marchands à Hambourg, et Vincent Favin marchand à Paris," in *Recueil contenant les édits et déclarations du roy sur l'établissement et confirmation de la juridiction des consuls en la ville de paris, et autres* (Paris: Denys Thierry, 1705), 370.

143. Not surprisingly, the *Parlement* of Paris upheld the merchant court's decision in its judgment of June 23, 1678. "Arrest du parlement, rendu sur l'appel interjetté par David Stollay et consors, marchands de Hambourg," in *Recueil contenant les edits,* 373.

144. Accarias de Sérionne, *Les intérêts des nations,* 47.

145. The following arbiters' reports, for example, note that a bill of exchange was negotiated through a blank endorsement without suggesting that this was impermissible. Ravalon, Arbiter's Report in Foulon Duplessis v. Gobert, 30 August 1763, AP D^6B^6/7 (n.a.); Pierre Chénon, Arbiter's Report in Thil v. Morel de Chermoons, 3 February 1785, AP D^6B^6/16 (78); Report, Mouquin v. Barrié, AP D^6B^6/8 (n.a.).

146. Nolpeliezes, Arbiter's Report in Laurens v. Ginisty, 7 April 1769, AP D^6B^6/5 (n.a.).

147. LeClerc, Arbiter's Report in Rouillon et Sannegond v. Raffy, 9 December 1767, AP D^6B^6/8 (n.a.).

148. Ibid.

149. Ibid.

150. Vignon, Arbiter's Report in Renard v. Roëttieos de la Tour, 30 August 1784, AP D^6B^6/15 (182).

151. Ibid.

152. Ibid.

153. Forney and Cheret, Arbiters' Report in Vadaux v. Pleyard, 21 June 1783, AP D^6B^6/14 (188).

154. Ibid.

155. Ibid.

156. A telling indication of the depth of this concern with accommodation paper is that it persisted in France, long after it had disappeared in England. By around the 1830s, argues Rogers, the English came to view bills purely as instruments of credit—and thus to accept accommodation paper. Rogers, *Early History,* 245. In contrast, modern French jurists continue to express concern about *effets de complaisance*—though they have struggled to identify the precise nature of their concern. While opinion is far from unified, the majority view—and the one adopted by most French courts—is that such instruments are null because of "the illicit nature or immorality of the cause." Michel Cabrillac, *La lettre de change dans la jurisprudence* (Paris: Libraire Techniques, 1974), 136. See also Barry Nicholas's argument that "French law takes a moral stance while English law emphasizes the security of transactions and economic efficiency." Nicholas, *French Law,* 212.

157. Rogers, *Early History,* 224–33.

158. *Encyclopédie méthodique: Commerce,* s.v. "Consulat," 1:721; Szramkiewicz, *Droit des affaires,* 148; [Couchot], *Praticien,* 263, 361.

159. [Couchot], *Praticien,* 361. See also Masson, *Affaires contentieuses,* 368–69.

160. The documents used as points of comparison ranged widely. These included baptismal records, as well as other commercial paper (Aléxis-Joseph Harger and Charles Paillason, Arbiters' Report in Mathon v. Robert Pialut, n.d. [around December 1784]), AP D^6B^6/15 [359]); signed receipts (Aléxis-Joseph Harger and Charles Paillason, Arbiters' Report in Duboc v. Feugueur et Barroyer, 5 July 1786, AP D^6B^6/17 [182]); correspondence and signatures obtained from the person in question upon the arbiters' request (Aléxis-Joseph Harger and Charles Paillason, Arbiters' Report in Pregnon v. Dufour, 29 May 1786, AP D^6B^6/17 [48]).

161. Napoleon's Commercial Code of 1807, article 145, clearly established that the debtor who paid the holder of a negotiable instrument in good faith would be deemed to have acquitted his debt, even if the payee was later discovered not to be the true owner. However, if the debtor was notified that the instrument had been stolen, he was obligated to refrain from paying the person falsely claiming to be its holder. Szramkiewicz, *Droit des affaires,* 178.

162. Bazard, Arbiter's Report in le Chevalier Charlot v. Duvigier, n.d. (around December 1782), AP D^6B^6/14 (180).

163. Ibid.

164. Ibid.

165. Ibid.

166. J. G. A. Pocock, *The Machiavellian Moment: Florentine Political Thought and the Atlantic Republican Tradition* (Princeton: Princeton University Press, 1975); Nannerl O. Keohane, *Philosophy and the State in France: The Renaissance to the Enlightenment* (Princeton: Princeton University Press, 1980).

167. Ravalon, Arbiter's Report in Mogier v. la dame veuve Ollier, 15 December (no year, but appears to be 1762), AP D^6B^6/7 (n.a.).

168. Ibid.

169. Ibid.

170. Report, Duplessis v. Gobert, AP D[6]B[6]/7 (n.a.).

171. Ibid.

172. Pothier, *Contrat de change,* 2–3.

173. Ibid., 70–71.

174. Ibid., 39–42.

175. Report, Clair v. Dumont, AP D[6]B[6]/15 (275).

176. Du Caurroy, Arbiter's Report in Renault fils ainé v. Poullain, 7 March 1785, AP D[6]B[6]/17 (51).

177. In seeking payment on the bill, the holder was required to turn first to the drawee who had accepted it. Lévy-Bruhl, *L'endossement,* 28–29.

178. Report, Renault fils ainé v. Poullain, AP D[6]B[6]/17 (51).

179. Report, Mouquin v. Barrié, AP D[6]B[6]/8 (n.a.).

180. Ibid.

181. Ibid.

182. Saul Levmore, "Variety and Uniformity in the Treatment of the Good-Faith Purchaser," *Journal of Legal Studies* 16 (January 1987): 43–65; Harold R. Weinberg, "Sales Law, Economics, and the Negotiability of Goods," *Journal of Legal Studies* 9 (June 1980): 569–92.

183. Pothouin et al., *Consultation pour les sieurs de la Rue et Compagnie, banquiers à Paris, contre le sieur Prevôt, et contre le sieur Hardouin* (Paris: Chez Brunet, 1748), AP D[1]B[6]/32 (5298).

184. Ibid., 1.

185. Ibid., 6.

186. Ibid.

187. Ibid., 7.

188. Compilation of letters sent to the Parisian Merchant Court by other merchant courts and of the letters sent back in response, 1760s and 1770s, AP D[1]B[6]/44 (5940).

189. Ibid.

190. Ibid.

191. [Couchot], *Praticien,* 74, 83–84.

192. Lévy-Bruhl, *Lettre de change,* 60.

193. Jacques Savary, Parère 37, quoted in ibid., 60.

194. Thomas, Arbiter's Report in Guerin v. LaConté et d'Argent, 9 March 1773, AP D[6]B[6]/9 (n.a.).

195. Ibid.

196. Ibid.

197. Ibid.

198. As René Squarzoni suggests, the large number of bills of exchange employed in eighteenth-century France is itself evidence that the traditional method of drawing bills solely on one's agents or debtors had ceased to be common practice. Squarzoni argues that in order for bills to be employed in this traditional manner, the drawer would have to have many debtors (for example client-purchasers) who owed amounts very similar to the amounts that the drawer owed to his own creditors (for example supplier-sellers). Furthermore, these debts would all have to be due at about the same time. It is highly unlikely, Squarzoni concludes, that the eighteenth-century French trade in bills of ex-

change could have been based on this conjunction of circumstances, given the very large number of bills that were in circulation. René Squarzoni, "L'arbitrage et les négociants banquiers, 1726–1735," in *Banque et capitalisme commercial: La lettre de change au XVIII*^{e} *siècle,* ed. Charles Carrière et al. (Marseille: Institut Historique de Provence, 1976), 137.

199. Lévy-Bruhl, *Lettre de change,* 157. See also Cottin, Arbiter's Report in Bachéviliers et compagnie v. LeClerc, 8 March 1774, AP $D^{6}B^{6}$/10 (n.a.).

200. According to the arbiters in one case, "It is a principle of the trade in bills of exchange that only acceptance of the bill obliges one [namely, the drawee] to pay it." Banquet and Pache, and Vandemyrer brothers and company, Arbiters' Report in Doré fils et Aubri de la Fosse v. Bouffé et Dangirard, 12 August 1774, AP $D^{6}B^{6}$/10 (n.a.). See also the trial brief claiming that it was commercial usage—as evidenced by the opinion of, among others, Savary —to permit merchants on whom bills of exchange were drawn to decide not to accept and even to cross out an acceptance, as long as the bills remained in their hands. Thomas, *Mémoire pour Benjamin Mendes Dacosta, négociant à Londres, contre les héritiers Maure, négociants à Rouen, et le sieur Christophe Reverdun, aussi négociant à Rouen* (Paris: G. Lamesle, 1753), 2, in AP $D^{1}B^{6}$/32 (n.a.).

201. LeClerc, Arbiter's Report in les sieurs Brentani Cunaroli v. Grand, 30 July 1784, AP $D^{6}B^{6}$/15 (n.a.).

202. The practice of drawing more than one copy of a bill of exchange was common. Multiple copies helped protect the holder in case of theft or loss. Furthermore, it enabled the practice at issue in this case—namely, sending the bill to the drawee for acceptance, while at the same time enabling its continued negotiation. Lévy-Bruhl, *Lettre de change,* 57–58; Thomas, *Mémoire pour Benjamin Mendes Dacosta,* 1.

203. Report, Brentani Cunaroli v. Grand, AP $D^{6}B^{6}$/15 (n.a.).

204. Ibid.

205. As Margot Finn argues in her study of debt in England, elements of an early-modern moral economy continued to shape credit practices—particularly in the retail sector—well into the twentieth century. Margot C. Finn, *The Character of Credit: Personal Debt in English Culture, 1740–1914* (Cambridge: Cambridge University Press, 2003).

206. Bruce Mann and Craig Muldrew offer similar accounts of changing credit practices in eighteenth-century Connecticut and England. Mann argues of Connecticut that while "the expansion of the economy . . . did not mean that all commercial dealings had become faceless and impersonal," a new reliance on written credit instruments like promissory notes "aided the intrusion of market relations into areas of social life that previously had been governed by customary arrangements, communal norms, and traditional authority." Bruce H. Mann, *Neighbors and Strangers: Law and Community in Early Connecticut* (Chapel Hill: University of North Carolina Press, 1987), 39, 41. Similarly, according to Muldrew, "the ethics of religious morality remained very important in the construction of business character," but to the extent that new methods of extending credit enabled people to rely more on "structured organizations" (such as banks and companies) than on "individual tradesmen, credit could become less dependent on individual morality." Craig Muldrew, *The Economy of Obligation: The Culture of Credit and Social Relations in Early Modern England* (Houndmills, Eng.: Palgrave, 1998), 329.

207. John Shovlin, *The Political Economy of Virtue: Luxury, Patriotism, and the Origins of the French Revolution* (Ithaca, N.Y.: Cornell University Press, 2006).

208. See, for example, "Théorie et pratique des changes," *Journal de Commerce,* February 1760, 111–32; "Sur un abus introduit à Rouen dans les faillites de plusieurs obligés," February 1760, 161–67; "Considerations sur le grand nombre de débiteurs et de prisonniers pour causes civiles, qui se trouvent actuellement en Angleterre," September 1760, 137–43; "Sur les contraintes par corps," December 1760, 33–41; "Dissertation sur la premiere propriété de toutes lettres de change," February 1761, 115–41; "Observations sur la question si les lettres de change à son propre ordre, sont des lettres de change ou des mandats," March 1761, 94–105; "Suite de l'essai sur l'éducation du négociant: des changes," May 1762, 49–95.

209. Of the sixty-four cases involving negotiable instruments in the box of reports that I systematically reviewed, there were only sixteen in which arbiters identified their professions—and among these, only two were written by priests. Guinchard, Arbiter's Report in Coudrois v. Detain, n.d. (around March 1783), AP D⁶B⁶/15 (n.a.); Beaumont, Arbiter's Report in Jean Baptiste Tiphaine v. Lornier, 25 September 1784, AP D⁶B⁶/15 (279). While it is possible that priests wrote some of the remaining forty-eight reports as well, this is unlikely since priests seem generally to have proudly self-identified as such.

210. For example, members of the Cottin family—who established a prominent Parisian banking house (Jean Bouchary, *Les manieurs d'argent à Paris à la fin du XVIIIe siècle* [Paris: Libraire des sciences politiques et socials, M. Rivière et compagnie, 1943], 3:111–29)—frequently served as arbiters, but did not identify their profession. Cottin, Arbiter's Report in Bacheviliers et compagnie v. LeClerc, 8 March 1774, AP D⁶B⁶/10 (n.a.); Cottin, Arbiter's Report in Cantin v. Chiret, 2 May 1782, AP D⁶B⁶/15 (189); Cottin fils, Arbiter's Report in Pierre Ponchut v. Dolos et compagnie, 13 April 1784, AP D⁶B⁶/15 (35); Cottin fils, Arbiter's Report in Roger v. d'Auvergne fils, 13 April 1784, AP D⁶B⁶/15 (318). Similarly, there was a Parisian banker by the name of Rousseau (Bouchary, *Manieurs d'argent,* 2:127, 3:32), who regularly decided disputes involving negotiable instruments. Rousseau, Arbiter's Report in Bourgeois v. Maignon, 3 May 1783, AP D⁶B⁶/15 (42); Rousseau, Arbiter's Report in Joseph le Moine et Demoiselle Margueritte la Lance son epouse v. Nicolas Gueny, 29 March 1784, AP D⁶B⁶/15 (85); Rousseau, Arbiter's Report in Montigny v. Thirouin, 23 December 1784, AP D⁶B⁶/15 (12). See also a report penned by the banker Leroy (Bouchary, *Manieurs d'argent,* 3:32, 278). Leroy, Arbiter's Report in Thevenot v. Gobert, 10 February 1783, AP D⁶B⁶/15 (419).

211. See, for example, Belle ("avocat en Parlement, conseiller du Roy, commissaire au Châtelet de Paris"), Arbiter's Report in Verlac v. Ceref, n.d. (around May 1784), AP D⁶B⁶/15 (45); Pierre Chénon ("avocat en Parlement, conseiller du Roy, commissaire enqueteur examinateur au Châtelet de Paris"); Pierre Chénon, Arbiter's Report in Fraumont v. Garreau et DeVilleneuve, 7 March 1786; AP D⁶B⁶/17 (n.a.); Marelles Leveau ("avocat au Parlement en ville de Roy, commissaire au Châtelet de Paris"), Arbiter's Report in Delanitre Seriant v. la femme Bokain sa sœur, 29 November 1783, AP D⁶B⁶/15 (1); Jean Marsolier Serrun ("avocat en Parlement, conseiller du Roy, commissaire au Châtelet de Paris"), Arbiter's Report in Bernier v. Gergois, 27 November 1784, AP D⁶B⁶/15 (129).

212. For example, of the arbiters' reports concerning negotiable instruments in the box

of reports that I systematically reviewed, five were written by Thomas de Bon and three by Rousseau. Thomas de Bon, Arbiter's Report in Delende v. Foreson, 1 April 1784, AP D^6B^6/15 (n.a.); Thomas de Bon, Arbiter's Report in Jeanmor v. le sieur et dame de Pechuny, 9 August 1783, AP D^6B^6/15 (35); Thomas de Bon, Arbiter's Report in Simomien v. Roques, n.d. (around June 1784), AP D^6B^6/15 (n.a.); Thomas de Bon, Arbiter's Report in Dubosque v. Louis Jacques de Lasalle, n.d. (around December 1784), AP D^6B^6/15 (248); Thomas de Bon, Arbiter's Report in Joyau v. la dame veuve Debrie, 3 July 1783, AP D^6B^6/15 (209); Rousseau, Report, Bourgeois v. Maignon, AP D^6B^6/15 (42); Rousseau, Report, Joseph le Moine et Demoiselle Margueritte la Lance son epouse v. Nicolas Gueny, AP D^6B^6/15 (85); Rousseau, Report, Montigny v. Thirouin, AP D^6B^6/15 (12).

213. "Ordonnance du commerce," tit. 12, art. 2, in Isambert, Jourdan, and Decrusy, *Recueil général,* 19:105; Bornier, *Ordonnance de Louis XIV,* 570.

214. Bornier, *Ordonnance de Louis XIV,* 572.

215. See the discussion in chapter 6.

216. Pierre Jean Jacques Guillaume Guyot, *Répertoire universel et raisonné de jurisprudence civile, criminelle, canonique et bénéficiale,* s.v. "Consul" (Paris: Chez Panckoucke, 1777), 15:114.

217. [Bedos], *Négociant patriote,* 263.

218. Bochen, Arbiter's Report in Tellier v. Beycheirat, 5 January 1773, AP D^6B^6/9 (n.a.).

219. Ibid. (emphasis in original).

220. Ibid.

221. Court's decision in Tellier v. Beycheirat, 8 January 1773, AP D^2B^6/1117.

Chapter 6. Launching a National Campaign: The Administrative Monarchy and the Demands of le Commerce

Epigraph. Session of 27 May 1790, *Archives Parlementaires de 1787 à 1860: Recueil complet des débats législatifs et politiques des chambres françaises: 1. série* (Paris: Libraire administrative de P. Dupont, 1879), 15:685 (deputy Paul Nairac).

1. Romuald Szramkiewicz, *Histoire du droit des affaires* (Paris: Montchrestien, 1989), 143.

2. Michel Antoine, "La monarchie française de François Ier à Louis XVI," in *Les monarchies* (Paris: Presses Universitaires de France, 1986), 185–208.

3. David D. Bien, "Offices, Corps, and a System of State Credit: The Uses of Privilege under the Ancien Régime," in *The Political Culture of the Old Regime,* vol. 1, *The French Revolution and the Creation of Modern Political Culture,* ed. Keith Michael Baker (Oxford: Pergamon Press, 1990), 93–97; Clare Haru Crowston, *Fabricating Women: The Seamstresses of Old Regime France, 1675–1791* (Durham, N.C.: Duke University Press, 2001), 177–78.

4. Françoise Bayard and Philippe Guignet, *L'économie française aux XVIe–XVIIIe siècles* (Paris: Éditions Ophrys, 1991), 62–64.

5. Bien, "Offices," 93–97. The relatively low rate of interest charged would-be masters was due to a number of factors—not least of which was the guilds' ability to undertake corporate liability for their members' debts. Ibid., 104–7. See also Gail Bossenga's discussion of the sale of offices in the *Bureaux des Finances.* Gail Bossenga, *The Politics of*

Privilege: Old Regime and Revolution in Lille (Cambridge: Cambridge University Press, 1991), 49–50.

6. Crowston, *Fabricating Women*, 188–89.

7. Ibid., 207–8.

8. Ibid., 208–9; Steven Laurence Kaplan, "Social Classification and Representation in the Corporate World of Eighteenth-Century France: Turgot's 'Carnival,'" in *Work in France: Representations, Meaning, Organization, and Practice*, ed. Steven Laurence Kaplan and Cynthia J. Koepp (Ithaca, N.Y.: Cornell University Press, 1986), 178.

9. Jacques Revel, "Les corps et communautés," in *The Political Culture of the Old Regime*, vol. 1, *The French Revolution and the Creation of Modern Political Culture*, ed. Keith Michael Baker (Oxford: Pergamon Press, 1990), 239.

10. *Observations des juge et consuls des marchands de Paris sur l'éxtinction des corps et communautés* (n.d.), AP $D^1B^6/37$ (5659).

11. Kaplan, "Social Classification," 210.

12. Ibid., 211.

13. Abel Poitrineau, *Ils travaillaient la France: Métiers et mentalités du XVIe au XIXe siècles* (Paris: Armand Colin, 1992), 38.

14. Bossenga, *Politics of Privilege;* Gail Bossenga, "Protecting Merchants: Guilds and Commercial Capitalism in Eighteenth-Century France," *French Historical Studies* 15 (Autumn 1988): 693–703; Crowston, *Fabricating Women*. The reason why guilds survived as long as they did—and, in particular, the question of how economically outmoded they were by the end of the Old Regime—is a point of some dispute among recent historians. See, for example, Liana Vardi, "The Abolition of the Guilds during the French Revolution," *French Historical Studies* 15, no. 4 (Autumn 1988): 704–17. But there is general agreement that they continued to serve important social and political functions.

15. "Ordonnance du commerce," in François André Isambert, Athanase-Jean-Léger Jourdan, and Decrusy, *Recueil général des anciennes lois françaises, depuis l'an 420, jusqu'à la révolution de 1789* (Paris: Belin-Leprieur, 1829), 19:92–107.

16. In reality, of course, as described in previous chapters, courts did not always conform to this requirement.

17. Szramkiewicz, *Droit des affaires*, 134–35.

18. "La vie de M. Savary," in Jacques Savary, *Le parfait négociant, ou instruction générale pour ce qui regarde le commerce des marchandises de France, et de pays etrangers* (Paris, 1800), 1:xxi; Szramkiewicz, *Droit des affaires*, 134.

19. "Ordonnance du commerce," tit. 1 ("Des apprentis, négocians et marchands, tant en gros qu'en détail"), in Isambert, Jourdan, and Decrusy, *Recueil général*, 19:93–94.

20. "Ordonnance du commerce," tit. 12, art. 1, in Isambert, Jourdan, and Decrusy, *Recueil général*, 19:105; Philippe Bornier, *Ordonnance de Louis XIV, sur le commerce, enrichie d'annotations et de décisions importantes* (Paris: Libraires-Associés, 1767), 537; Szramkiewicz, *Droit des affaires*, 143.

21. Szramkiewicz, *Droit des affaires*, 143.

22. Ibid. While there were only about forty such courts at the end of the seventeenth century, there were sixty-seven in 1789. Ibid.

23. Compilation of letters sent to the Parisian Merchant Court by other merchant courts and of the letters sent back in response, 1760s and 1770s, AP $D^1B^6/44$ (5940).

24. Ibid.

25. Ibid.

26. Ibid.

27. *Secrétaires du roi* were originally responsible for signing letters and other documents issued by the monarchy through its chancelleries. By the eighteenth century, however, the position of *secrétaire du roi* had joined the long catalogue of venal offices sold by the monarchy in its desperate bid to maintain financial solvency, and those who occupied these positions ceased to have any real responsibilities. David D. Bien, "La réaction aristocratique, avant 1789: L'exemple de l'armée," trans. J. Rovert, *Annales: Économies, Sociétés, Civilisations* 29, no. 1 (January–February 1974): 44–48; M. Marion, *Dictionnaire des institutions de la France aux XVIIe et XVIIIe siècles,* s.v. "Sécretaires du roi" (Paris: A. et J. Picard, 1993), 505.

28. Compilation of letters, AP $D^1B^6/44$ (5940).

29. Ibid.

30. The edict of February 1715 provided that in ceremonies involving the Merchant Court of Lille, the former judges and consuls would precede all other merchants, and among the former judges and consuls rank would be determined based on "the length of their service [*l'ancienneté de leurs charges*]." Ibid. The edict establishing the Merchant Court of Valenciennes in January 1718 contained similar provisions, from which it followed, asserted the Parisian judge and consuls, that "it is not the distinction between noble and commoner that determines the rank of former consuls and former judges, but solely the date of their election." Ibid.

31. Ibid.

32. Ibid.

33. Historians have referred to this agency both as the *Conseil de Commerce* and as the *Bureau du Commerce*. I opt for the latter of these terms because it better reflects the agency's actual function, which as described below, was purely advisory. In the Old Regime monarchy, *conseils* were distinguished from *bureaux* by the fact that the former had decision-making authority, while the latter could only advise. David Kammerling Smith, "Structuring Politics in Early Eighteenth-Century France: The Political Innovations of the French Council of Commerce," *Journal of Modern History* 74 (September 2002): 499.

34. Pierre Bonnassieux, *Conseil de Commerce et Bureau du Commerce, 1700–1791: Inventaire analytique des Procès-Verbaux* (Paris: Imprimerie Nationale, 1900), x–xv; Jacqueline-Lucienne Lafon, *Les députés du commerce et l'ordonnance de mars 1673: Les juridictions consulaires, principe et compétence* (Paris: Éditions Cujas, 1979), 1–4.

35. Kammerling Smith, "Structuring Politics," 499, 509. A number of authors have suggested that there were only twelve deputies. See, for example, Marion, *Dictionnaire des institutions,* s.v. "Conseil de Commerce," 136–37; "Avis touchant l'établissement d'une chambre de commerce," in *Journal de Commerce* (Brussels), July 1759, 57–58. This is likely because the royal edict that established the *Conseil de Commerce* authorized eleven cities to elect deputies of commerce—with Paris entitled to elect two. "Arrêt du Conseil d'État du Roi portant établissement d'un conseil de commerce," http://www.gale.com/ModernEconomy. Shortly after the *Conseil* was established, however, the province of Languedoc petitioned for (and was granted) the right to a deputy of its own, thus bringing the total number of merchant deputies to thirteen. *Dictionnaire universel de commerce, d'histoire naturelle, et des arts et métiers,* s.v. "Conseil de Commerce"

(Paris: Chez la veuve Estienne, 1750), 1:1090; Noël Chomel, *Supplément au Dictionnaire Œconomique, considérablement augmenté par divers curieux,* s.v. "Député du Commerce" (Amsterdam: J. Covens and C. Mortier, 1740), 167.

36. A substantial portion of the *Bureau*'s work fell to the merchant deputies, who wrote reports advising their superiors on the position the *Bureau* should take—often on matters brought to its attention by merchants throughout the country. Bonnassieux, *Conseil de Commerce,* xxii. Although the deputies were supposed to serve a merely advisory role, studies suggest that their recommendations were generally embraced by decision-makers within the *Bureau.* The *Bureau*'s decisions, in turn, were often enacted into law. Thus, the merchant deputies had a significant influence on French commercial law and policy. Kammerling Smith, "Structuring Politics," 500; Lafon, *Députés du commerce,* 9–10; Harold T. Parker, *An Administrative Bureau during the Old Regime: The Bureau of Commerce and Its Relation to French Industry from May 1781 to November 1783* (Newark, Del.: University of Delaware Press, 1993), 18–21.

37. *Procés Verbaux de l'ouverture du Conseil de Commerce* (24 November 1700), 3, AN F[12]51 (1).

38. Until 1728, the court assembled the former *maîtres* and *gardes* of the *six corps de Paris,* who together with the current judge and consuls voted on the new deputies. G. Denière, *La juridiction consulaire de Paris, 1563–1792: Sa création, ses luttes, son administration intérieure, ses usages et ses mœurs* (Paris: Henri Plon, 1872), 81–82. After this date, the comptroller general directed the court to assemble electors as dictated by the Declaration of March 18, 1728, discussed in chapter 1, which concerned the election of officers to the Parisian Merchant Court. These electors, along with the current judge and consuls, then nominated six individuals, from among whom the king selected the deputies. Ibid., 82; Georges Leclerc, *La juridiction consulaire de Paris pendant la Révolution* (Paris: Plon, 1909), 85–86.

39. Denière, *Juridiction consulaire,* 70–71.

40. Colbert established the first few chambers of commerce in 1664. But it was only in 1700, around the time that the monarchy created the *Bureau du Commerce,* that it began systematically establishing chambers of commerce. Marion, *Dictionnaire des institutions,* s.v. "Chambres de commerce," 79; Szramkiewicz, *Droit des affaires,* 108–10. As the *Encyclopédie méthodique* asserted, "the establishment . . . of a royal *conseil de commerce* in 1700 was the cause of the establishment of these *chambres [de commerce]* in the principal cities of the kingdom." *Encyclopédie méthodique: Commerce,* s.v. "Chambre de Commerce" (Paris: Chez Panckoucke, 1783), 1:390.

41. Marion, *Dictionnaire des institutions,* s.v. "Chambres de commerce," 79; Szramkiewicz, *Droit des affaires,* 108–10.

42. Marion, *Dictionnaire des institutions,* s.v. "Chambres de commerce," 79; Szramkiewicz, *Droit des affaires,* 108–10.

43. Kammerling Smith, "Structuring Politics," 530.

44. That the deputies regularly sided with the merchant courts is hardly surprising, given the prominent role played by these courts in the election of the deputies. The Parisian Merchant Court played a particularly important role, since it was responsible for orchestrating the election and often supplied its own judge or consuls as deputies. However, even in towns where the deputies were elected directly by the guilds, the deep

interconnection between the guilds and the merchant court served to ensure that the deputies elected by the guilds could be trusted to represent the court's best interests.

45. See the following reports written by the *Bureau*'s merchant deputies concerning petitions that they had received from various merchant courts: *Sur la requete des juges et consuls de la ville de Lille* (10 September 1725), AN F[12]696; *Sur la requete des juge et consuls de Bezançon* (23 August 1725), AN F[12]696. See also the extensive correspondence between the merchant deputies and the Merchant Court of Montauban: Correspondence with Merchant Court of Montauban (1725–28), AN F[12]793 (10).

46. Correspondence (1725–28), AN F[12]793 (10).

47. Ibid.

48. Jay M. Smith, *The Culture of Merit: Nobility, Royal Service, and the Making of Absolute Monarchy in France, 1600–1789* (Ann Arbor: University of Michigan Press, 1996).

49. That the solicitors' *corps*, notaries' *corps*, and ordinary courts were the primary participants in status disputes with the merchant courts followed, in part, from the proximity of these entities to one another in the status hierarchy—a proximity that was, in turn, due to the overlapping nature of the functions that each served. The ordinary, nonmerchant courts posed, by definition, a threat to merchant court jurisdiction. And solicitors and notaries were figures who—because they prepared and certified the paperwork necessary to facilitate litigation and establish proof in the ordinary courts—embodied the formality, complexity, and costliness of ordinary court procedure, against which merchant courts defined themselves.

50. See, for example, Sarah Hanley, *The Lit de Justice of the Kings of France: Constitutional Ideology in Legend, Ritual, and Discourse* (Princeton: Princeton University Press, 1983); Norbert Elias, *The Court Society,* trans. Edmund Jephcott (New York: Pantheon Books, 1983).

51. See, for example, the definitions of "*corps*" contained in *Dictionnaire universel de commerce,* s.v. "Corps," 1:1178, and in Jean Baptiste Denisart, *Collection de décisions nouvelles et de notions relatives à la jurisprudence actuelle,* s.v. "Corps," (Paris: Chez Savoy, 1763), 1:615.

52. *Dictionnaire universel de commerce,* s.v. "Corps," 1:1178.

53. David A. Bell, *Lawyers and Citizens: The Making of a Political Elite in Old Regime France* (Oxford: Oxford University Press, 1994), 52–53.

54. Ibid.

55. *Avis des deputés du commerce sur la contestation entre les juge et consuls d'Angers et les notaires de la même ville* (13 April 1736), AN F[12]792 (6).

56. *Copie de premiere mémoire de corps et communauté des marchands* (12 April 1726), AN F[12]792 (6).

57. Ibid.

58. Poitevin Dulimon, *Mémoire sommaire pour les notaires royaux d'Angers contre les consuls des marchands de la meme ville, et les marchands anciens consuls* (Paris: J. Chardon, n.d.), AN F[12]792 (6).

59. Bernard et Clou, *Mémoire pour les notaires royaux de la ville d'Angers contre les juge et consuls de la meme ville, et les marchands anciens consuls* (N.p.: May 1734), 8, AN F[12]792 (6).

60. Poitevin Dulimon, *Mémoire sommaire pour les notaires,* AN F[12]792 (6).

61. Ibid.

62. Ibid.

63. Bernard et Clou, *Mémoire pour les notaires,* 8, AN F[12]792 (6).

64. Ibid., 15. Indeed, the notaries concluded, in a striking parallel to the arguments made on behalf of a *noblesse commerçante,* it was time for noblemen to recognize that there was nothing "more useful to the state than to confide in them [noblemen] duties that consist fundamentally in integrity"—namely, the duties of the notary. Ibid., 17.

65. *Avis des deputés,* AN F[12]792 (6).

66. Consider, for example, the status dispute that arose on Christmas Day in 1720 between Estienne de la Planche, a former judge of the Merchant Court of Saintes, and Perraud, a solicitor in the local presidial court, regarding which was entitled to sit in front of the other in the church service held in the cathedral of Saintes. The provincial intendant, whose opinion the *Bureau*'s merchant deputies solicited, decided in favor of la Planche and the merchant court on the grounds that "it is the status of judge to which precedence is accorded." *Les Juge Consuls de Saintes demandent qu'il plaise au Roy declarer commune avec les marchands bourgeois de la ville de Saintes les arrets du Conseil qui ont maintenu dans la preseance* (n.d.), AN F[12]794 (2).

67. *Requete pour les prieurs et consuls, corps et communautés de la bourse commune des marchands de Toulouse, concernant le range et séance* (1705?), AN F[12] 794 (6).

68. Ibid.

69. Ibid.

70. The status dispute that had arisen previously in Poitiers is discussed in *Les Négociants de Poitiers contre les Procureurs du Conseil Superieur; Lettre de M. le Controlleur General a M. l'intendant pour le consulter sur cette affaire* (1701?), AN F[12]793(18).

71. *Requete pour les prieurs et consuls,* AN F[12] 794 (6).

72. Ibid.

73. Ibid.

74. Ibid.

75. *Sur la lettre des anciens Jurats, juges et consuls de Bordeaux au sujet de la preseance dans les assemblées de leurs corps et companies* (28 December 1722), AN F[12]792 (9).

76. Ibid.

77. Ibid.

78. Ibid.

79. Lauren A. Benton, *Law and Colonial Cultures: Legal Regimes in World History, 1400–1900* (Cambridge: Cambridge University Press, 2002), 10–15.

80. Claude de Seyssel, *The Monarchy of France,* ed. Donald R. Kelley, trans. J. H. Hexter and Michael Sherman (New Haven: Yale University Press, 1981), 89.

81. Montesquieu, *The Spirit of the Laws,* trans. Anne M. Cohler, Basia C. Miller, and Harold Stone (Cambridge: Cambridge University Press, 1989), 73.

82. See, for example, the effort of the Merchant Court of Besançon to defend its jurisdiction by arguing that "one can find in the merchant courts two types of privilege, one personal and the other real." Du Portault, *Mémoire pour les juges-consuls des marchands de Besançon au sujet de la jurisdiction consulaire* (n.d.), 3, AN F[12] 792 (8).

83. Szramkiewicz, *Droit des affaires,* 142–43.

84. "Édit qui crée la juridiction consulaire des juges et consuls de Paris et règle leur competence," art. 3 (Paris, November 1563), in Isambert, Jourdan, and Decrusy, *Recueil general,* 14:154; [Couchot], *Le praticien des juges et consuls; ou, Traité de commerce de terre et de mer* (Paris: Prault père, 1742), xii; Szramkiewicz, *Droit des affaires,* 144.

85. [Couchot], *Praticien,* ix.

86. See the discussion of the various late-seventeenth- and early-eighteenth-century royal edicts permitting noblemen to engage in commerce without risk of *dérogation* in Philibert-Joseph Masson, *Instruction sur les affaires contentieuses des négociants, la manière de les prévenir, ou de les suivre dans les tribunaux* (Paris: Chez LeClerc, 1786), 120–21, and in *Mémoire pour les maîtres et gardes en charge du corps des marchands merciers de la ville et fauxbourgs de Paris* (Paris: L'imprimerie de J. Chardon, 1761), 14, AP D^1B^6/36 (5583).

87. Jean Hilaire, *Introduction historique au droit commercial* (Paris: Presses Universitaires de France, 1986), 63–64.

88. "Ordonnance du commerce," tit. 11, in Isambert, Jourdan, and Decrusy, *Recueil général,* 19:104–5.

89. This procedure, allowing for distribution of the *failli*'s assets, was known as "la cession de biens." Szramkiewicz, *Droit des affaires,* 187.

90. Ibid., 182–91.

91. Masson, *Affaires contentieuses,* 285.

92. Ibid., 285–86.

93. "Ordonnance du commerce," tit. 11 ("Des faillites et banqueroutes"), in Isambert, Jourdan, and Decrusy, *Recueil général,* 19:104–5; Szramkiewicz, *Droit des affaires,* 183; Lafon, *Députés du commerce,* 113.

94. "Déclaration du roi du 10 juin 1715, portant que les procès et differends civils pour raison des faillites et banqueroutes seront portés pardevant les juges et consuls, jusqu'au premier janvier 1716," in [Couchot], *Praticien,* 201–3; Szramkiewicz, *Droit des affaires,* 184; Lafon, *Députés du commerce,* 114.

95. "Déclaration du roi du 10 juin 1715," in [Couchot], *Praticien,* 203; "Déclaration du roi du 11 janvier 1716, concernant les faillites et banqueroutes, dont la connoissance est attribué aux juges et consuls," in ibid., 207; "Déclaration du roi du 4 octobre 1723, concernant les faillites et banqueroutes," in ibid., 221–22.

96. Szramkiewicz, *Droit des affaires,* 184; Lafon, *Députés du commerce,* 114.

97. Szramkiewicz, *Droit des affaires,* 184; Lafon, *Députés du commerce,* 114.

98. Szramkiewicz, *Droit des affaires,* 184.

99. Lafon, *Députés du commerce,* 124–30.

100. "Déclaration du roi, concernant les faillites et banqueroutes, du 13 septembre 1739," in [Couchot], *Praticien,* 244–45; Lafon, *Députés du commerce,* 127–28.

101. Masson, *Affaires contentieuses,* 323.

102. Szramkiewicz, *Droit des affaires,* 145; Claude Dupouy, *Le droit des faillites en France avant le Code de Commerce* (Paris: Libraire générale de droit et de jurisprudence, 1960), 79–83.

103. Szramkiewicz, *Droit des affaires,* 192.

104. Petition to the *Bureau* from the Merchant Court of Poitiers (31 October 1762), AN F^{12}793 (18).

105. Petition to the Chancellor from the Chamber of Commerce of Lille (11 March 1779), subsequently sent to the *Bureau,* AN F^{12}793 (5), Document A.

106. Petition to the Keeper of the Seals from the Merchant Court of Lille (12 November 1776), subsequently sent to the *Bureau,* AN F^{12}793 (5), Document F.

107. Petition to the Director-General of Finance from the Merchant Court of Tours (4 December 1779), subsequently sent to the *Bureau,* AN F^{12}794 (7).

108. Petition to the *Bureau* from the Merchant Court of Poitiers, AN F^{12}793 (18).

109. *Sur les remonstrances des juges et consuls de St. Malo, de Bourges, d'Amiens, de Clermont en Auvergne, d'Abbeville, de Caen, de Chartres, de la Rochelle, de Montpellier, de Bayonne, de Toulouse, de Montauban, de Compiegne, Dieppe, Nantes, Le Mans, Tours, Rion, Troyes, Reims, Dijon, Saulieu, Bordeaux qui demandent que S.M. veuille bien leur continuer pour toujours l'attribution des faillites à la forme de la déclaration du feu Roy 10 juin 1715 et les suivantes* (17 October 1718), AN F^{12}792 (1).

110. Noting that the effort of the ordinary judges to extend their jurisdiction "has often given rise to such disputes," the merchant deputies to the *Bureau du Commerce* suggested that the jurisdictional dispute between ordinary and merchant courts predated even the February 1703 judgment by the *Parlement* of Paris. *Mémoires et pieces au Conseil de sa Majesté, pour les jurisdictions consulaires et les chambres de commerce du royaume, concernant la déclaration du 7 avril 1759* (Paris: P. G. Le Mercier, 1766), part 3, 53–54. The pagination in *Mémoires et pieces au Conseil* is completely out of order. To assist the reader, I cite page numbers as they appear in the text and also identify in which of the book's three parts the cited material can be found.

111. *Arrêt de nosseigneurs de la cour de parlement, entre les lieutenans generaux, baillis, senechaux, provosts et juges royaux du royaume, et les juge et consuls, portant reglement pour la connoissance des affaires de leurs jurisdictions* (14 February 1703), AN F^{12}793 (15); Lafon, *Députés du commerce,* 47.

112. Lafon, *Députés du commerce,* 49. See also the October 22, 1710, letter written by procurator-general [*procureur général*] d'Aguesseau to the comptroller general expressing concern that a royal declaration of October 4, 1710, had broadened merchant court jurisdiction beyond the bounds established in the Commercial Ordinance of 1673, AN F^{12}792 (1).

113. See "Déclaration du 4 octobre 1710" and "Déclaration du 21 octobre 1710" in *Mémoires et pieces au Conseil,* part 3, 390–95. See also the discussion of this ongoing jurisdictional conflict in Lafon, *Députés du commerce,* 46–53.

114. Lafon, *Députés du commerce,* 50–51.

115. *Mémoires et pieces au Conseil,* part 2, 1–3.

116. Ibid., part 1, 177

117. Ibid., part 2, 51.

118. "Déclaration du 7 avril 1759," in *Mémoires et pieces au Conseil,* part 1, 5–8.

119. Although largely ignored by contemporary jurists, the declaration established one exception to the rule that the defendant could be sued in a merchant court only if there was such a court within the bailiwick where he resided. If the contract was formed, merchandise was delivered, or payment was to occur in a bailiwick other than where the defendant resided, the plaintiff could sue the defendant in the merchant court located in that bailiwick — assuming, of course, that there was such a merchant court. Jean-Baptiste

Denisart, Jean-Baptiste-François Bayard, and Armand-Gaston Camus, *Collection de décisions nouvelles et de notions relatives à la jurisprudence,* 8th ed., s.v. "Consuls des Marchands" (Paris: Chez la veuve Desaint, 1786), 5:359 (discussing Declaration of April 7, 1759, art. 3).

120. *Mémoires et pieces au Conseil,* part 2, 51.

121. Ibid.

122. This lawyer was Goulleau.

123. Denière, *Juridiction consulaire,* 69–71.

124. For example, the Merchant Court of Tours wrote a letter to Director-General of Finance Necker on December 4, 1779, requesting among other things repeal of the Declaration of 1759, AN F[12]794 (7). Similarly, in 1775, the Merchant Court of Montpellier published a pamphlet, which it submitted to the *Bureau*'s merchant deputies, seeking, among other things, repeal of the Declaration of 1759. *Très-humble requête des Prieur et Consuls de la Bourse des Marchands de Montpellier* (Montpellier: Augustin-François Rochard, 1775), 8, AN F[12]793(11). And an article concerning French merchant courts in the September 1762 edition of the *Journal de Commerce* devoted itself largely to calling for the repeal of the Declaration of 1759. "Jurisdictions consulaire," in *Journal de Commerce,* September 1762, 123–29.

125. Denisart, Bayard, and Camus, *Collection de décisions,* 8th ed., s.v. "Consuls des Marchands," 5:355. After making this observation, Denisart quoted extensively from *Mémoires et pieces au Conseil.* Ibid., 5:359–63.

126. [Louis Marie Prud'homme], *Résumé général, ou extrait des cahiers de pouvoirs, instructions, demandes, et doléances* (N.p., 1789), 3:395–400.

127. The following discussion does not distinguish between the petitions submitted separately and jointly by the Parisian Merchant Court and the *six corps.* Because the campaign was a joint undertaking—and in fact all three petitions were written by the same lawyer—any distinctions between the arguments of the Parisian Merchant Court and the *six corps* seem artificial.

128. In addition to these utilitarian, commerce-based arguments, the petitioners advanced a number of arguments for repeal that might have been penned centuries prior. These include arguments that the declaration was in derogation of merchant courts' longstanding rights, as recognized through various edicts and rulings, and that the petitioners were motivated by their devotion to "the general good" or "the public good," rather than by any "particular interest." See, for example, *Mémoires et pieces au Conseil,* part 1, 241, and part 2, 325. The petitioners, however, quickly moved beyond such traditional arguments.

129. *Mémoires et pieces au Conseil,* part 1, 248. This sentence is one of several that the petitioners appear to have borrowed wholesale from Burlamaqui, who expressed the same thought as follows: "Since the ultimate end of man is happiness; and, in fine, since he cannot attain to happiness but by the help of reason; does it not evidently follow, that right in general is whatever reason approves as a sure and concise means of attaining happiness?" Jean Jacques Burlamaqui, *The Principles of Natural and Politic Law,* trans. Nugent (Cambridge: [Harvard] University Press, 1807), 1:36.

130. *Mémoires et pieces au Conseil,* part 1, 248.

131. Ibid., part 1, 285.

132. Ibid., part 1, 239.

133. Ibid., part 1, 236.

134. Ibid., part 1, 253.

135. Ibid., part 1, 257.

136. Ibid.

137. Ibid., part 1, 255.

138. Ibid., part 1, 255–56 (emphasis in original).

139. Ibid., part 1, 257.

140. Ibid.

141. Ibid., part 1, 228.

142. Amalia D. Kessler, "A 'Question of Name': Merchant-Court Jurisdiction and the Origins of the *Noblesse Commerçante*," in *A Vast and Useful Art: The Gustave Gimon Collection on French Political Economy,* ed. Mary Jane Parrine (Stanford: Stanford University Libraries, 2004), 54–55 (also on-line at http://www-sul.stanford.edu/depts/hasrg/frnit/gimon_papers.html).

143. "Considérations sur les contraintes par corps pour dettes civiles," in *Journal de Commerce,* September 1760, 128–43. Szramkiewicz confirms that merchant courts sent noblemen to prison for failing to pay bills of exchange. Szramkiewicz, *Droit des affaires,* 180.

144. "Considérations sur les contraintes par corps," in *Journal de Commerce,* 142.

145. That a seemingly technical question of jurisdiction directly implicated noble status is suggested by the fact that Denisart's law dictionary includes a discussion of whether noblemen are subject to merchant court jurisdiction within its definition of "Nobles, Nobility." Jean-Baptiste Denisart, *Collection de décisions nouvelles et de notions relatives à la jurisprudence actuelle,* s.v. "Nobles, Noblesse" (Paris: Chez la veuve Desaint, 1771), 3:414.

146. For example, Guyot, a classically trained jurist, argued that language from the 1563 edict first establishing the Parisian Merchant Court proved that merchant courts had jurisdiction only over defendants with merchant status. Citing the edict's provision that merchant court jurisdiction extended to "suits and differences between merchants concerning merchandise only," he argued that the term "merchants" would be superfluous unless it was intended to limit jurisdiction to those parties having the formal, legal status of a merchant: "If the legislator had wanted judges and consuls to adjudicate every matter concerning trade, every stipulation concerning merchandise, it would have been easy for him to give them a general and indefinite competence: it is because he did not give them such an extensive authority that he restricted it to suits *between merchants and merchants* concerning merchandise. These words *between merchants* suppose that it is possible to have disputes concerning merchandise, without being a merchant." Pierre Jean Jacques Guillaume Guyot, *Répertoire universel et raisonné de jurisprudence civile, criminelle, canonique et bénéficiale,* s.v. "Consul" (Paris: Chez Panckoucke, 1777), 15:106 (emphases in original).

147. Jean Toubeau, *Les institutes du droit consulaire ou les elemens de la jurisprudence des marchands* (Bourges, 1700), 1:284–85.

148. Rogue, *Jurisprudence consulaire et instruction des négociants* (Angers: Chez A. J. Jahyer, 1773), 1:11.

149. Louis-Sébastien Mercier, *Tableau de Paris,* new ed. (Amsterdam, 1782; repr., Geneva: Slatkine Reprints, 1979), 12:164 (emphases in original).

150. Jean Egret, *The French Prerevolution, 1787–88,* trans. Wesley D. Camp (Chicago: University of Chicago Press, 1977), 180.

151. J. Tarrade, "Le groupe de pression du commerce à la fin de l'ancien régime et sous l'Assemblée Constituante," *Bulletin de la Société d'Histoire Moderne et Contemporaine, Revue d'Histoire Moderne et Contemporaine* 2 (supplément) (1970): 24; Jean-Pierre Hirsch, "Honneur et liberté du commerce," *Revue du Nord* 55 (1973): 336; Jean Hilaire, "La Révolution et les juridictions consulaires," in *Une Autre justice: Contributions à l'histoire de la justice sous la Révolution française,* ed. Robert Badinter (Paris: Fayard, 1989), 245.

152. Chamber of Commerce of Picardy, letter attached to petition requesting that *le commerce* be granted representatives at Estates General (n.d.), AP D^1B^6/1 (20).

153. Merchant Court of Beauvais, letter attached to petition requesting that *le commerce* be granted representatives at Estates General (9 December 1788), AP D^1B^6/1 (30).

154. Merchant Court of Auxerre, letter attached to petition requesting that *le commerce* be granted representatives at Estates General (around December 1788), AP D^1B^6/1 (29).

155. Merchant Court of Arles, letter attached to petition requesting that *le commerce* be granted representatives at Estates General (20 November 1788), AP D^1B^6/1 (25).

156. Merchant Court of Auxerre, letter attached to petition, AP D^1B^6/1 (29).

157. Chamber of Commerce of Picardy, petition requesting that *le commerce* be granted representatives at Estates General (30 September 1788), 3, AP D^1B^6/1 (22).

158. Merchant Court of Calais, petition requesting that *le commerce* be granted representatives at Estates General (n.d., fall 1788), 3, AP D^1B^6/1 (37).

159. Gabriel François Coyer, *Développement et défense du système de la noblesse commerçante* (Paris: Chez Duchesne, 1757).

160. Kessler, "'Question of Name,'" 56–59.

161. Toubeau, *Institutes du droit consulaire,* 1:306.

162. Ibid., 1:296.

163. Ibid.

164. Ibid.

165. Henry C. Clark, "Commerce, the Virtues, and the Public Sphere in Early Seventeenth-Century France," *French Historical Studies* 21, no. 3 (Summer 1998): 415–40.

166. Jean-Claude Perrot, *Une Histoire intellectuelle de l'économie politique* (Paris: Éditions de l'École des hautes études en sciences sociales, 1992), 98.

167. Savary, *Parfait négociant,* 1:27.

168. Ibid.

169. Ibid.

170. Toubeau, *Institutes du droit consulaire,* 1:297.

171. Ibid.

172. Ibid., 1:298.

173. Ibid.

174. John Shovlin, *The Political Economy of Virtue: Luxury, Patriotism, and the Origins of the French Revolution* (Ithaca, N.Y.: Cornell University Press, 2006), 49–65.

175. Montesquieu, *Spirit of the Laws.*

176. Coyer, *Développement et défense,* 136.

177. Ibid., 10.

178. Ibid., 64–65.

179. Ibid., 137.

180. Merchant Court of Arles, petition requesting that *le commerce* be granted representatives at Estates General (n.d., fall 1788), AP $D^1B^6/1$ (26).

181. Ibid.

182. Merchant Court of Beauvais, petition requesting that *le commerce* be granted representatives at Estates General (n.d., fall 1788), AP $D^1B^6/1$ (31).

183. Ibid.

184. Ibid.

185. Chamber of Commerce of Guienne, petition requesting that *le commerce* be granted representatives at Estates General (14 October 1788), AP $D^1B^6/1$ (33).

186. Ibid.

187. Merchant Court of Brioude, petition requesting that *le commerce* be granted representatives at Estates General (n.d., fall 1788), AP $D^1B^6/1$ (35).

188. Ibid.

189. Shovlin, *Political Economy,* 121–32.

190. Pierre Augustin Caron de Beaumarchais, "Les deux amis, ou le négociant de Lyon," in *Œuvres complètes de Beaumarchais,* new ed. (Paris: Laplace, Sanchez et compagnie, 1876), 45.

191. "Considérations sur le bonheur dans la profession du commerce," in *Journal de Commerce,* August 1761, 92.

192. Ibid., 86.

193. In thus arguing for representation on the grounds of both modern, functionalist and traditional, corporatist conceptions of commerce, the petitioners would seem to typify Paul Friedland's more general description of the pamphlet literature produced in response to the calling of the Estates General. As Friedland observes, "public opinion had convinced itself that the resurrection of the Estates General was somehow in keeping both with France's historical precedent and with the enlightened principles of universal reason." Paul Friedland, *Political Actors: Representative Bodies and Theatricality in the Age of the French Revolution* (Ithaca: Cornell University Press, 2002), 92.

194. Egret, *French Prerevolution,* 138–43.

195. Bossenga, *Politics of Privilege,* 47–69.

196. Ibid., 47–69; Michael Kwass, *Privilege and the Politics of Taxation in Eighteenth-Century France: Liberté, Égalité, Fiscalité* (Cambridge: Cambridge University Press, 2000).

197. Bossenga, *Politics of Privilege,* 47–69.

198. Jean Hilaire argues that the fact that the merchant courts survived the Revolution is not as surprising as it seems and can be explained by such mundane factors as the judges' success in ensuring continuity in personnel and practices throughout the revolutionary period and the Constituent Assembly's relative lack of interest in these institutions. Hilaire, "La Révolution." Hilaire is surely correct that the merchant courts' ability to maintain continuity in personnel and practices was important in helping to preserve

their substantive and procedural law largely intact. But the courts' ability to maintain such continuity was ultimately contingent on the Assembly's decision to authorize their continued existence as distinct, merchant-run institutions. And while Hilaire is no doubt right that the merchant courts were not at the top of the Assembly's list of concerns, it is clear—as Hilaire himself acknowledges—that the Assembly did consciously choose to preserve them. Significantly, as argued below, the arguments that proved successful in justifying the courts' continued existence were a reconfigured version of the discourse of merchant virtue that had long served to legitimate them. In short, Hilaire's exclusive focus on the revolutionary period obscures the deeper conceptual (and institutional) developments that contributed to the merchant courts' extraordinary longevity.

199. Egret, *French Prerevolution,* 198.

200. Tarrade, "Groupe de pression," 24; Hirsch, "Honneur," 337.

201. Session of 27 May 1790, *Archives Parlementaires,* 15:684–88.

202. Ibid., 15:684 (deputy Paul Nairac).

203. Ibid.

204. Ibid., 15:685.

205. Ibid.

206. Ibid., 15:687 (deputy Goupil de Préfeln).

207. Ibid..

208. Ibid., 15:685 (deputy Paul Nairac).

209. "Décret sur l'organisation judiciaire, du 16 août 1790, sanctionné par lettres patentes du 24 du même mois," tit. 12, art. 1, in *Archives Parlementaires,* 18:110; Leclerc, *Juridiction consulaire,* 258.

210. "Décret sur l'établissement d'un tribunal de commerce dans la ville de Paris," in *Archives Parlementaires,* 22:517–18; Leclerc, *Juridiction consulaire,* 260; Denière, *Juridiction consulaire,* 228.

211. "Décret sur l'établissement," art. 1, in *Archives Parlementaires,* 22:517; Leclerc, *Juridiction consulaire,* 258–59.

212. "Décret sur l'établissement," arts., 2–3, 6, in *Archives Parlementaires,* 22:518; Leclerc, *Juridiction consulaire,* 259–60.

213. "Décret sur l'établissement," art. 7, in *Archives Parlementaires,* 22:518. Because Paris was not a coastal city, the statute establishing the Parisian *tribunal de commerce*—unlike the August 1790 decree authorizing the creation of *tribunaux de commerce* across the country—did not specify that electors might be "shipowners and ship captains." "Décret sur l'organisation judiciaire," tit. 12, art. 7, in *Archives parlementaires,* 18:110.

214. Historians who have pondered why the Allarde Law appeared when it did (see, for example, Bossenga, *Politics of Privilege,* 168–69) ought to consider this revolutionary restructuring of the Parisian Merchant Court and its electoral procedures. Given that the court traditionally served as a power base for Paris's leading guilds, the elimination of the guilds' longstanding role in selecting the court's judges likely served to undermine the guilds' power. This, in turn, surely facilitated their abolition shortly thereafter.

215. Leopold Goirand, *The French Code of Commerce and Most Usual Commercial Laws* (London: Stevens and Sons, 1880), 4.

216. See, for example, the arbiters' reports from the years 1791–93 (AP D^{6}B^{6}/20, D^{6}B^{6}/21) and 1794–98 and 1801 (AP D^{6}B^{6}/21). For an indication of the many con-

tinuities between the prerevolutionary merchant courts and the *tribunaux de commerce* both during and after the Revolution, see Hilaire, "La Révolution," and Claire Lemercier, "The Judge, the Expert, and the Arbitrator: The Strange Case of the Paris Court of Commerce (ca. 1800–ca. 1880)," in *Fields of Expertise: Paris and London, 1600 to the Present Time,* ed. Christelle Rabier (Newcastle-upon-Tyne, Eng.: Cambridge Scholars, forthcoming).

217. Roger Houin and Michel Pedamon, *Droit commercial: Actes de commerce et commerçants, activité commerciale et concurrence,* 7th ed. (Paris: Dalloz, 1980), 6; René Roblot, *Traité élémentaire de droit commercial de Georges Ripert,* 12th ed. (Paris: Libraire générale de droit et de jurisprudence, 1986), 1:16.

218. Alexis de Tocqueville, *The Old Regime and the French Revolution,* trans. Stuart Gilbert (New York: Doubleday, 1955).

219. Session of 24 March 1791, *Archives Parlementaires,* 24:325–26 (deputy Le Chapelier).

220. Ibid., 24:325.

221. Denière, *Juridiction consulaire,* 230.

222. Noël et al., *Mémoire,* quoted in Denière, *Juridiction consulaire,* 233.

223. Ibid., quoted in Denière, *Juridiction consulaire,* 231.

224. *Réflexions donnés par Devarenne, Levé, Vieillard, Guiot, Juselin et Gillet sur le mémoire lu par le prévôt de marchands, M. Gillet en l'assemblée tenüe a l'hotel de ville* (17 May 1776), AP D^1B^6/25 (4969).

225. Denière, *Juridiction consulaire,* 236.

226. Session of 24 December 1793, untitled decree, art. 1, in *Archives Parlementaires,* 82:252 (deputy Villers); Leclerc, *Juridiction consulaire,* 294. Leclerc mistakenly identifies the decree as having been issued on December 23, 1793 (3 nivôse, an II).

227. Session of 24 December 1793, untitled decree, arts. 3, 7, in *Archives Parlementaires,* 82:252; Leclerc, *Juridiction consulaire,* 294.

Conclusion

1. Claire Lemercier, *Un si discret pouvoir: Aux origines de la Chambre de commerce de Paris, 1803–1853* (Paris: Découverte, 2003); William H. Sewell Jr., *Work and Revolution in France: The Language of Labor from the Old Regime to 1848* (Cambridge: Cambridge University Press, 1980), 162–93.

2. Claire Lemercier, "The Judge, the Expert, and the Arbitrator: The Strange Case of the Paris Court of Commerce (ca. 1800–ca. 1880)," in *Fields of Expertise: Paris and London, 1600 to the Present Time,* ed. Christelle Rabier (Newcastle-upon-Tyne, Eng.: Cambridge Scholars, forthcoming).

3. As a number of scholars have suggested, a continued preoccupation with the problem of moralizing economic behavior would seem to be a defining feature of French policy well into the twentieth century. John Shovlin, *The Political Economy of Virtue: Luxury, Patriotism, and the Origins of the French Revolution* (Ithaca, N.Y.: Cornell University Press, 2006), 218–20; Barry Nicholas, *The French Law of Contract,* 2d ed. (Oxford: Clarendon Press, 1992), 212.

4. Lynn Avery Hunt, *Politics, Culture, and Class in the French Revolution* (Berkeley:

University of California Press, 1986), 150–51; Edna-Hindie Lemay, "La composition de l'Assemblée nationale Constituante: Les hommes de la continuité?," *Révue d'histoire moderne et contemporaine* 24 (July–September 1977): 345.

5. See Suzanne Desan, *The Family on Trial in Revolutionary France* (Berkeley: University of California Press, 2004); Michael Kwass, *Privilege and the Politics of Taxation in Eighteenth-Century France: Liberté, Égalité, Fiscalité* (Cambridge: Cambridge University Press, 2000); David A. Bell, *Lawyers and Citizens: The Making of a Political Elite in Old Regime France* (Oxford: Oxford University Press, 1994).

6. Michael Kwass, "Consumption and the World of Ideas: Consumer Revolution and the Moral Economy of the Marquis de Mirabeau," *Eighteenth-Century Studies* 37 (2004): 187–213; John Shovlin, "The Cultural Politics of Luxury in Eighteenth-Century France," *French Historical Studies* 23 (2000): 577–606; Shovlin, *Political Economy;* Thomas E. Kaiser, "Money, Despotism, and Public Opinion in Early Eighteenth-Century France: John Law and the Debate on Royal Credit," *Journal of Modern History* 63, no. 1 (March 1991): 1–28.

7. Keith Michael Baker, *Inventing the French Revolution* (Cambridge: Cambridge University Press, 1990), 224–51. See also Sewell, *Work and Revolution,* 78–86; Henry C. Clark, *Compass of Society: Commerce and Absolutism in Old-Regime France* (Lanham, Md.: Lexington Books, 2007), 299–302.

8. See, for example, Alfred Cobban, *The Social Interpretation of the French Revolution* (Cambridge: Cambridge University Press, 1964); Gail Bossenga, "Protecting Merchants: Guilds and Commercial Capitalism in Eighteenth-Century France," *French Historical Studies* 15 (Autumn 1988): 693–703.

9. Philip T. Hoffman, Gilles Postel-Vinay, and Jean-Laurent Rosenthal, *Priceless Markets: The Political Economy of Credit in Paris, 1660–1870* (Chicago: University of Chicago Press, 2000), 157 (describing how the new, impersonal market in annuities brokered by Parisian notaries assisted men and women of the Old Regime in dealing with the problem of the life cycle).

10. See, for example, Daniel Roche, *The People of Paris: An Essay in Popular Culture in the Eighteenth Century,* trans. Marie Evans and Gwynne Lewis (Leamington Spa, U.K.: Berg, 1987), 160–94; Colin Jones, "The Great Chain of Buying: Medical Advertisement, the Bourgeois Public Sphere, and the Origins of the French Revolution," *American Historical Review* 101 (February 1996): 13–40; Sarah Maza, "Luxury, Morality and Social Change: Why There Was No Middle-Class Consciousness in Prerevolutionary France," *Journal of Modern History* 69 (June 1997): 199–229; Shovlin, *Political Economy.*

11. Another question that merits further exploration is the relationship between the (increasingly anonymous) markets for short- and long-term credit—and in particular the relationship between the negotiable instruments examined in this book and the annuities, or *rentes,* recently studied by Philip Hoffman, Giles Postel-Vinay, and Jean-Laurent Rosenthal. Hoffman, Postel-Vinay, and Rosenthal, *Priceless Markets.*

12. Claire Lemercier similarly concludes in her analysis of the nineteenth-century Parisian *tribunal de commerce* that "there never was a single 'Law Merchant.'" Lemercier, "The Judge, the Expert."

Index